✒ THE JEWISH
COMMUNITY of
INDIANAPOLIS

THE MODERN JEWISH EXPERIENCE

Paula Hyman and Deborah Dash Moore, editors

Contents

Key to caption credits:

IHS   Indiana Historical Society Library, Indianapolis
ISL   Indiana State Library, Indianapolis
JWF   Jewish Welfare Federation of Indianapolis
AJHS   American Jewish Historical Society, Waltham,
       Massachusetts

Copyright © 1984 by Judith E. Endelman

All rights reserved

No part of this book may be reproduced or utilized in any form
or by any means, electronic or mechanical, including photocopying
and recording, or by any information storage and retrieval system,
without permission in writing from the publisher. The Association
of American University Presses' Resolution on Permissions constitutes
the only excepttion to this prohibition.

Manufactured in the United States of America

Library of Congress Cataloging in Publication Data
Endelman, Judith E.
    The Jewish community of Indianapolis, 1849 to the
present.

    (The Modern Jewish experience)
    Includes index.
    1. Jews—Indiana—Indianapolis—History.   2. Indian-
apolis (Ind.)—Ethnic relations.   I. Title.   II. Series:
Modern Jewish experience (Indiana University Press)
F534.I39J54 1984   977.2°52   83–49513
ISBN 0–253–33150–1
1 2 3 4 5 88 87 86 85 84

THE JEWISH COMMUNITY of INDIANAPOLIS

1849 to the Present

Judith E. Endelman

INDIANA UNIVERSITY PRESS

Bloomington

PREFACE

The origins of this history of the Indianapolis Jewish community can be traced back to the time of the American Bicentennial celebrations of 1976. Stimulated by the occasion of America's two-hundredth anniversary, Americans, who are notoriously future-oriented, became more reflective about their past. Except for relatively small groups of antiquarians, the preservation of the past—in the written word, in the restoration of old buildings, in the preservation of old records and papers—had been rejected by most Americans as contradictory to American notions of progress. Suddenly, the ranks of preservations, genealogists, and historical society members swelled as Americans developed an interest in the past. Many groups whose history was separated, both in time and place, from the events leading up to the independence from Great Britain were inspired to attempt to record their own history. The eighteenth-century connection no longer seemed to matter. Perhaps it was a sign of America's increasing acceptance of the durability of ethnic group loyalty. One heard few defensive recitations of the names of the Greeks (or Italians or Jews) who were in America in 1776. Only the federal government seemed eager to prove that the War of Independence was not a "white man's war." The U.S. Postal Service issued a series of stamps showing "Contributors to the Cause," featuring a black (Salem Poor), a Jew (Haym Salomon), a Spanish-American (Peter Francisco), and a woman (Sybil Ludington), all of whom helped the revolutionary cause. The message of the stamps seemed to be that America had always provided equal opportunity and permitted equal participation in civic life for all its citizens. Whether or not most Americans agreed with this implicit claim, the endurance of ethnicity, which these stamps also reflected, was certainly an important element in the 1976 celebrations. The new positive attitude to group particularism was expressed in the new terminology which came into usage in the 1970s. Italians, Jews, and blacks had previously been known as "minority groups," implying that what was significant about them was their relative powerlessness in the presence of the majority. Now they became "ethnic groups" who had something, i.e., "ethnicity," that white Anglo-Saxon Protestants were lacking.

In the flush of excitement produced by the Bicentennial, many local Jewish communities set about collecting records and recording the history of their own communities. In Indianapolis Julian Freeman, a longtime leader of the community, became chairman of a committee whose task was to collect records, minute books, aniversary volumes, reports, photographs, and other relevant materials from the files of local Jewish agencies, organizations, and synagogues. The committee managed to collect a

wealth of material. Where there were scanty records, some of the committee members produced brief histories of various local organizations. Other
committee members conducted interviews which they recorded on tape to
add another dimension to the historical record. Julian Freeman assembled
much of the collected material into a narrative form, but an actual communal history was not completed.

In the fall of 1979 I was asked to take over the project and complete the
community history. I could do so only because I had the firm foundation of
Julian Freeman's work as well as the invaluable source materials collected
by the original committee.

What I have written is not so much a history of the Jews who have
lived in Indianapolis, but a history of the community they have created.
My interest has been in the institutions they developed and the purposes
they served. I have attempted to follow social change in the community as
it is reflected in the changing nature and function of communal institutions.

Certainly no Jewish community speaks with one voice, and Indianapolis is no exception. In my exploration of the varied experiences of
Indianapolis Jewry, I have relied on many individuals who shared their
particular perspective and life experience with me. Many individuals gra-
ciously loaned me materials and generously shared their thoughts with
me. I cannot mention all who did so by name, but I am indebted to all of
them. My greatest debt is to Frank H. Newman, former executive vice-
president of the Indianapolis Jewish Welfare Federation. His interest in
producing a communal history led to the formation of the original committee. Without his unflagging support and enthusiasm, this history would
never have been written. He always managed to find time in his busy
schedule to share his thoughts on the Indianapolis Jewish community with
me. In addition, he read portions of the manuscript and provided valuable
comments. Julian Freeman, who sadly did not live to see this history
completed, shared all of his research materials, his notes, and his own im-
pressive knowledge of the community with me. I am deeply grateful to
both men.

Lee Barnett spent many hours with me, sharing the results of her own
research into the community's history as well as her experiences as a
lifelong resident of Indianapolis and a onetime worker for the community's social service agency. Jonathan Sarna, a historian at Hebrew Union
College, read the manuscript and offered important recommendations and
analytical perspectives. L. C. Rudolph, a librarian at Lilly Library of Indiana University, and Jack Glazier, an anthropologist at Oberlin College,
read portions of the manuscript. I benefited from the suggestions both
made. In addition, Jack Glazier generously shared with me some of the
results of his own research into the Sephardic community. I would like to
thank Isaiah Kuperstein, who translated portions of a Workmen's Circle
minute book for me. Gordon Levi looked through hundreds of photo-
graphic negatives taken by photographer Zalman Cohen in order to find

photographs of Jewish events and organizations to use in this book. I am grateful for his help.

I am grateful to the following individuals who provided me with many of the photographs which appear in this book: Robert Baerncopf, Lee Barnett, Rebecca Glogas, Miriam Landman, Gordon Levi, Pearl Levi, Ann Ofengender, and Ruben Reiswerg.

The Indiana Historical Society generously supported this project. In addition, the Society's library has become a depository for all the photographs and archival and manuscript materials collected for the project. Under their careful supervision, this material will now be preserved for future generations. I am personally grateful to Gayle Thornbrough, executive secretary of the Indiana Historical Society, who has given me endless encouragement and assistance. Her enthusiasm for the project has been extremely gratifying. Paula Corpuz and Lana Ruegamer, editors at the Indiana Historical Society, gave the manuscript a close reading and offered much help and advice. The staff of the Indiana Historical Society Library gave me help in all phases of the project. In particular, Timothy Petersen, picture librarian, and Eric Pumroy, manuscripts curator, provided me with invaluable assistance. The Oxford Centre for Postgraduate Hebrew Studies in Yarnton, England, offered comfortable and stimulating surroundings in which to complete the writing of this history.

In the classic formula of the preface, the author's family is always thanked last, probably because phrasing this acknowledgment is the hardest to do. Faced with the task of putting one's gratitude into words, what can one say? It is barely adequate to say that I am deeply indebted to my husband, Todd Endelman, who read the entire manuscript and offered many valuable suggestions. He has also willingly acted as a sounding board as I struggled to formulate my impressions of Indianapolis Jewry. My children, Michael and Flora, have learned to live in surroundings that include piles of minute books and boxes of index cards. While they have been understanding of my commitment, they probably will not be sorry that I have finished. The gestation period of my daughter, who was in *in utero* when I began my research, was not only briefer but less painful than the process of creating this book. For five years I have carried this history. Due to the help and encouragement of many, the fruit of my labors is now completed. I share the joy of accomplishment with many, but not the errors, which, of course, are my own.

Judith E. Endelman
Bloomington, Indiana

✎§ THE JEWISH
COMMUNITY of
INDIANAPOLIS

Introduction

IN THE POPULAR IMAGINATION, New York City has always been strongly identified with the American Jewish experience. New York was the site of the first Jewish community in North America, and (except for a brief period in the eighteenth century) it has remained the country's largest Jewish community. At last count, more than 20 percent of all American Jews were living within the borders of the "largest Jewish city in the world." New York City has come both to symbolize American Jewry and to provide a central focus for its activities. If American Jewry is a country, then New York is its capital, with nearly all of the country's Jewish organizations headquartered there. Jewishness pervades the city in a way that delights its Jewish visitors from the provinces. Yiddish words appear regularly in its newspapers; knishes are street food; and parking regulations are written to accommodate the observance of Jewish holidays.[1]

The dominance of New York City and the experience of the Jews who live there has extended from the popular imagination into the realm of Jewish scholarship as well. Beginning with studies of the earliest New York Jewish community—David de Sola Pool, *Portraits Etched in Stone* (1953) and Hyman Grinstein,

1

Rise of the Jewish Community of New York 1654–1860 (1945)—
the New York Jewish experience has been heavily documented.
Studies of the eastern European immigrant community—Moses
Rischin, *The Promised City: New York's Jews 1870–1914* (1962)
and Irving Howe, *World of Our Fathers* (1976)—along with the
outpouring of novels, memoirs, and other literary works on the
subject—Abraham Cahan, *The Rise of David Levinsky* (1917),
Michael Gold, *Jews Without Money* (1930), and Alfred Kazin, *A
Walker in the City* (1951)—have helped to create an entire typol-
ogy of American Jewish history based solely on the New York experience. To delineate the established Jews who originally came
from the Germanic states and the more recently arrived Jews from
eastern Europe, one speaks of "uptown Jews" and "downtown
Jews," referring to the areas of New York in which these two
groups lived. Similarly, the Lower East Side, Manhattan's immigrant neighborhood, has become the archetypal American Jewish
immigrant neighborhood, a status which has only been enhanced
by the many published collections of photographs of the district,
such as Allan Schoener's *Portal to America: The Lower East Side
1879–1925* (1967).

Indeed, it is hard to consider American Jewry without reference
to New York Jewry. Yet, if one is to understand fully the American
Jewish experience, one must look beyond New York to the dozens
of medium-size cities, the regional centers of the West, the South,
and the Midwest, which have a history of Jewish settlement dating
back to the mid–nineteenth century. While the Jews who came to
America in the seventeenth and eighteenth centuries settled in the
port cities along the Atlantic, the German Jews who came in the
first half of the nineteenth century followed the path of westward
expansion. During this period dozens of new Jewish communities
emerged in the towns and cities along the Erie Canal, the
Mississippi and Ohio, and the Great Lakes, and in the Gold Rush
towns of the Far West. At the time that the first Jews were settling
in Indianapolis, other Jews were establishing communities in
places like Columbus, Ohio; Louisville, Kentucky; Atlanta, Georgia; and San Francisco, California.

An examination of the history of Jewish settlement in these and
other cities reveals striking similarities among them. Moreover,
while there are definite similarities and parallels with the New

York experience, there are important differences as well. In these other cities, the first Jewish residents were usually German Jewish peddlers who had become prosperous enough to give up peddling and open a retail store. As merchants and shopkeepers of a young and expanding city, they helped to further the city's economic growth. Moreover, because of the public nature of retail trade, these early German Jewish merchants became well known in their respective communities. In almost every photograph of the main street of an American city in the late nineteenth century, one can see the prominent sign board of a German Jewish retailer, whether it be Lazarus in Columbus, Ransohoff in Salt Lake City, or Strauss in Indianapolis.

The prominence of Jews in the early history of a city may very well have affected the later course of Jewish-Christian relations. Historian John Higham has argued this point convincingly in a perceptive essay on American anti-Semitism. According to Higham, the degree to which Jews were involved in the early growth of a city and had achieved a notable and respected place in public and private life before the era of mass immigration directly influenced how later generations of Jews were received. In cities where early German Jewish settlers achieved a respected place in the community and assimilation proceeded to the point of extensive intermarriage, the later arrival of eastern European immigrants did not appear as disruptive as in cities in which this had not occurred. Old-line, patrician leaders managed to maintain rapport with the non-Jewish elite, while at the same time developing institutions to acculturate the newcomers. If the proportion of Jews in the population remained relatively stable, so much the better. Then Jews did not stand out or appear to be a menacing and threatening group.[2]

Higham's description of the ideal situation for the development of minimal anti-Jewish discrimination describes Indianapolis to a rather remarkable degree. The first Jews to settle in Indianapolis came when the city was just beginning to develop. Many of them became successful clothing merchants and tailors, providing a basic and necessary service to the city's residents. From the records available, it appears that these early German Jewish residents felt a degree of security, comfort, and acceptance that they had never before experienced. In the free and open atmosphere of the growing

Hoosier capital, many Jews rose to positions of prominence. They mixed with non-Jews and intermarriages were not uncommon. An article in the *Indianapolis News* of December 6, 1894, identifying the "leaders in Indianapolis business and professional life" included two German Jewish merchants—Leopold Strauss and Herman Bamberger. An accompanying article, "Interesting Events of Twenty-five Years," described the growth of the city's "Hebrew churches." Moreover, throughout its history, the Jewish community of Indianapolis has never been large. Even with the addition of the eastern European immigrants, the Jewish population always remained between 1 and 2 percent of the population.[3]

Through the 1870s the Jewish communities of the Midwest remained small and relatively homogeneous. Diversity and growth, as well as conflict, came with the arrival of immigrants from eastern Europe. Most eastern European immigrants remained in New York. Many, however, moved on to settle in midwestern, western, and southern cities. In the late nineteenth century, nearly every American Jewish community saw a new and separate community of immigrant Jews develop within its own city. The clash between New York's uptown and downtown Jews is well known. This same battle was played out elsewhere as well, although with less force.

The intensity of the conflict between German and eastern European Jews reflected the degree to which the newcomers appeared to threaten the social position of the older German Jewish community. If the number of new arrivals was relatively small, and if the German Jewish elite felt secure, relations between them remained benign. In every city, however, no matter how secure the Jewish community, native Jews quickly established institutions to speed the acculturation of the Yiddish-speaking foreigners. The many institutions organized by New York's uptown Jews for this purpose have achieved prominence. Less familiar are the institutions that were organized in every other Jewish community to help Americanize the new arrivals. For example, while New York's uptown Jews organized the Educational Alliance, a settlement house on the Lower East Side, Indianapolis's north side Jews founded Nathan Morris House, a settlement house on the city's south side.

With the arrival of eastern European Jews in New York, Indianapolis, and elsewhere, Jewish life expanded and diversified. Local Jewish institutions multiplied, with new synagogues—

usually organized by nationality, since the eastern European Jews were by no means a homogeneous lot—lodges, benevolent associations, and cultural societies of all descriptions. In Indianapolis a community of Sephardic immigrants created another nexus of societies with a separate synagogue and other institutions. Not only did language, background, and affiliation separate newcomers from old-timers, but there was also the barrier of poverty. Before the arrival of the immigrants, cities such as Indianapolis probably had almost no Jewish poor. The new immigrants were impoverished, and they generally settled in the poorest districts of the city. In New York, while the resident German Jews lived in middle-class comfort uptown, the immigrants moved into the Lower East Side and similar poor neighborhoods. Similarly, while most of Indianapolis Jewry resided in the comfortable districts of the north side, the new immigrants settled in an industrial and residential area just south of the city center.

In the smaller inland cities, however, Jewish poverty was short-lived. Unlike New York, the smaller cities of the interior never had a true Jewish working class. Nearly all of the children of the pants pressers, tailors, and carpenters graduated from high school, and many attended college. Moreover, unlike the Lower East Side, the full-blown Jewish immigrant neighborhood that was the south side of Indianapolis in its heyday did not last much beyond one generation. As soon as they could, many Jews moved north to better neighborhoods. By the late 1920s contemporaries already believed that the south side Jewish community was dying. Its death was only delayed by the Great Depression, which slowed migration out of the neighborhood. It finally died in the post-war era.

By 1950 it was estimated that only about 10 percent of the Jewish community still lived on the south side, and those that remained were primarily elderly. Since the 1950s the "Jewish" neighborhood of Indianapolis—the site of all the communal institutions as well as the place of residence of most Indianapolis Jews—has been the far north side, a primarily upper middle-class district. Along with the demise of the south side as a Jewish neighborhood, distinctions between Germans, eastern Europeans, and Sephardim faded as all three groups became economically successful. While the eastern European and Sephardic immigrants may have had a harder time than the German Jews who arrived during a period of economic expansion, for the most part all three groups achieved economic success within one generation.[4]

While in many important ways the experience of Indianapolis Jewry has paralleled the history of the Jewish communities of New York and other Eastern cities, there are important differences as well. Indianapolis Jewry has managed to support a viable Jewish life in a city and state which has never been particularly receptive to ethnic and cultural diversity. Indiana has always had an exceptionally large number of white, native-born Protestants in its population. In 1920, 95 percent of Indiana's population was native-born, and 97 percent was white, giving it the largest proportion of white, native-born population in the nation. Moreover, in 1920 nearly three-fourths of all Indianans lived on farms, in rural areas, or in towns with less than 25,000 residents. Even the state's urban dwellers maintained an affection for the nostalgic imagery of the rural past.[5]

In such a setting, the maintenance of a distinctive way of life had to be vigorously pursued. Each group of Jewish immigrants to Indianapolis faced the same task—to accommodate the patterns of life they had known in Europe to the environment of midwestern America. Through the institutions they established, Hoosier Jews created a community that suited their particular time and place. This history will examine the results of the interaction between Jewish life and Hoosier culture, and the many institutions developed to adapt Jewish life to its new American setting.

While Indianapolis Jewry did not experience as much anti-Semitism as Jews in some other cities for reasons noted above, the weaving of Jewish life with Indiana culture has not always been a smooth process. Jews have suffered from discrimination and anti-Semitism, most notably during the era of the Ku Klux Klan in the 1920s. How the Jewish community responded to anti-Semitism and discrimination reflected the degree of self-confidence and sense of security Jews felt in Indianapolis.

Jewish accommodation and conflict has not been confined to encounters with the non-Jewish community. Various political and religious factions as well as loyalties to each "old country" divided the community into a series of discrete groups, each with its own allegiances. Eventually, seemingly unbridgeable divisions narrowed and then vanished. Intragroup accommodation is thus another important part of the community's history.

The process of accommodation, like change itself, is never-ending. One need only compare the programs of the city's Jewish institutions of today with their original objectives to realize that all of them have moved far from their founder's purposes. The Indianapolis Jewish community has not remained static, but has continued to grow and change as the city has changed. Only this seems inevitable—that the process of change and transformation will continue.

⅏ I

Point of Arrival

THE EARLY YEARS 1849—1880

ON OCTOBER 25, 1858, a small celebration took place at Pari-sette's, a popular Indianapolis saloon and restaurant. Some sixty Jewish residents of Indianapolis, several Jews from nearby small towns, the Indianapolis rabbi, Judah Wechsler, members of the press, and the guest of honor, Rabbi Isaac Mayer Wise of Cincin-nati, editor of the *American Israelite* and tireless promoter of Re-form Judaism, gathered to commemorate the consecration of the first synagogue in the Hoosier capital. Only two years earlier, in 1856, fourteen men had founded the Indianapolis Hebrew Congre-gation, the city's first synagogue. Now the congregation, with a mere twenty-six members (i.e., male heads of families), had rented a downtown hall in which to hold services. It was a humble be-ginning, but it meant that the Indianapolis Jewish community now had a home, and all assembled were confident that the Jewish community of Indianapolis was destined to grow and flourish. Ac-cording to the reporter from the Indianapolis *Daily Citizen*, who attended the "Hebrew Festival," as he called it, it was an evening of warmth and pride, in which the participants rejoiced in what they considered were the many recent Jewish accomplishments of the times.[1]

8

After a splendid dinner, which concluded with ice cream, cake, and "native wine," a series of toasts were proposed—to Alexander Franco, "the Pioneer Hebrew of Indiana"; to the intelligence and enterprise of the Jews of Indianapolis; to Lionel de Rothschild on taking his seat in the British Parliament; and to the dawning of a new era of tolerance, which this event was said to represent. Speakers praised the American system for allowing diversity and encouraging the free practice of religion. Reflecting on the celebration, the *Daily Citizen* concluded, "This is destined to become a large church, as our Hebrew population is increasing in proportion with the growth of the city."[2]

The *Daily Citizen*'s prediction proved to be correct. The increase in the Jewish population of Indianapolis closely paralleled the growth of the city, always remaining between 1 and 2 percent of the total population. The third largest city in Indiana in 1850 (the older Ohio River towns of New Albany and Madison were larger), Indianapolis was the state's largest city by 1860. Similarly, although Jews settled in other Indiana towns before any moved to the capital city, Indianapolis Jewry was the dominant Jewish community in the state within a few years of the celebration of Parisette's.[3]

The first Jews to move to the territory west of the Alleghenies came as independent fur traders and peddlers. Living in isolated trading posts, supplying the native Indians with goods in exchange for furs, roaming the heavily forested frontier, these men did not stay long in one place. When a peddler succeeded to the extent that he could do business from a primitive shack instead of peddling his goods from place to place, his trading post often became one of the first structures in a community which later became a major city. Thus, Jewish traders were among the first settlers in such communities as Louisville; Detroit; Green Bay, Wisconsin; Easton, Reading, and York, Pennsylvania; and Montgomery, Alabama.[4]

The lives of these Jewish frontiersmen were lonely, and men who chose such a life made a decision (whether consciously or not) to abandon most Jewish observance. The practice of Judaism requires a community, and there was no Jewish community anywhere in the Old Northwest before the early 1820s, when a small community developed in Cincinnati. Those traders who remained in their isolated posts often married women from the Indian tribes with whom they traded or the daughters of French-Canadian or

American pioneer families and adopted their ways over the course of time. The career of John Jacob Hays (1766/70–1836), the only Jew known to have lived in the Indiana Territory, is fairly typical. A son of Baruch Hays, a Tory, and his first wife, Prudence, Hays left his native New York City and settled somewhere in the Northwest Territory, in the late eighteenth century. His first western home may have been Vincennes, the capital of the Indiana Territory, where he married Marie-Louise Brouillet, the daughter of French-Canadian settlers, in October 1801. Beginning in 1809, Hays held a succession of government posts in the Indiana and Illinois territories. In 1820, President James Madison appointed him Indian agent for the Potawatomi and Miami Indians, and thus he was transferred to the old stockade of Fort Wayne, becoming the first known Jewish resident of that city. He remained in Fort Wayne for only three years and died in Cahokia, Illinois, in 1836[5]

After the conclusion of the War of 1812, which lessened the threat of Indian attack, and spurred by the prosperity of the years 1814–1819, which permitted many to purchase land and pay the costs of travel, a wave of settlers rolled over the North Central states. Between 1810 and 1820, a half million new pioneers came to settle in the five states of the Old Northwest Territory, 100,000 of them in Indiana. However, there were few Jews among these crowds of prospective farmers, and the federal census of 1820 revealed only four Jews besides John Jacob Hays who were living in the new state at that time.[6]

The most prominent of these was Samuel Judah (1798–1869). Born in New York City to Bernard S. and Catherine Hart Judah, Samuel Judah graduated from Rutgers College in 1816, studied law, and was admitted to the bar. Settling in Vincennes in 1818, he developed an extensive law practice and was considered one of the ablest attorneys in the state. A close friend of Henry Clay, Judah became active in politics and was a member of the Indiana House of Representatives from 1827 to 1829 and from 1837 to 1841, being elected speaker in 1840. In 1830 he was appointed United States district attorney for the state of Indiana, serving until 1833. Judah married Harriet Brandon in Piqua, Ohio, in 1825 and died in Vincennes in 1869. As far as is known, Judah did not formally convert to Christianity, although his children were not raised as Jews.[7]

The only other known Jewish residents of Indiana in 1820 were two brothers, Phineas and David Israel (dubbed "Johnson" by the Indians with whom they traded), who were trading along the Whitewater River in the southeastern portion of the state. The two brothers and David's wife, Eliza, lived in Brookville and Connersville, and a son, Edward Isaac, born to David and Eliza Israel Johnson in Connersville in 1819, was apparently the first Jewish child born west of the Alleghenies. In 1820 David Israel Johnson and his family left Connersville and settled in Cincinnati, thereby boosting the Jewish population of that community to six. This was the first Jewish community in the Old Northwest, and it would continue to develop, becoming one of the largest and most influential Jewish communities in the country prior to the massive influx of eastern European Jews at the end of the century.[8]

The Jewish population of the Old Northwest would have remained scattered and inconsequential had it not been for German Jewish immigration which, beginning in the 1830s, caused the American Jewish population to soar from 6,000 in 1830 to 150,000 in 1860. From the eastern seaboard these immigrants fanned out across the continent, dotting the landscape with hundreds of new Jewish communities in all parts of the country.[9]

The migration of German Jewry in the mid-nineteenth century was part of a larger German emigration that sent more than 1.2 million Germans to America between 1820 and 1855. Of these immigrants, about 2 to 3 percent were Jewish. However, while both Germans and Jews came to America seeking economic betterment, additional motives were at work in the Jewish case. As Napoleon's armies conquered Europe, the principles of the French Revolution were imposed on lands that fell under French control. Jewish emancipation, which had been granted by the National Assembly to the Jews of France in 1790 and 1791, was extended to Jews in many of the German states. However, this civic and economic freedom was short-lived. The final defeat of Napoleon in 1815 and the restoration of the old regime brought an end to Jewish civil equality. Governmental policy toward the Jews became even harsher in reaction to the Napoleonic innovations. The situation of Bavarian Jewry, whose legal position had not improved even during the Napoleonic period, was particularly acute. The number of Jewish families in a locality was not allowed to increase; hence, generally only an eldest son, who would receive his father's

Schutzbrief (protection letter), would be allowed to marry and settle in the community. A younger son had to wait for the death of a
childless *Matrikelbesitzer* (possessor of a registration certificate)
before he could even contemplate marriage. With such a gloomy
future it is no wonder that large numbers of young, unmarried
German Jews began emigrating. As one German Jewish newspaper
observed in 1839, "The Jewish emigration appears to be less due to
greed for gain than to consciousness of being unable in any other
way to achieve independence or to found a family."[10]

The German Jewish immigrant in the mid-nineteenth century
was, typically, either an unmarried second, third, or fourth son
from a Bavarian village or a single woman from such a village who
saw her marital prospects as extremely limited by the laws regulat-
ing Jewish settlement and marriage. Their single status permitted
these Jewish immigrants to be mobile in a rapidly expanding country. Not content to remain on the relatively crowded eastern seaboard, many a young immigrant set off for Albany or Easton, Cincinnati or Louisville, and from there, pack on his back, peddled his
wares among farmers in the surrounding countryside. He might return nightly or weekly to the city to replenish his stock, usually
bought from a Jewish merchant who had prospered sufficiently to
be able to abandon peddling for shopkeeping.

Peddling had many advantages for the newly arrived German
Jewish immigrant. With only a little capital—goods could often be
obtained on credit—and even less English, the young immigrant
could fill a pack and start knocking on doors. Like the Yankee
peddler, the German Jewish peddler filled a real need, supplying
goods to farms and villages far from urban distribution centers. It
was not an easy life: the peddler had to learn how to contend with
dogs, unfriendly farmers, bad weather, and the loneliness of the
open road. Bernard Baum, who later owned a successful dry goods
store in Evansville, Indiana, described his first, rather unsuccessful,
day as a peddler, when he set out from Louisville with a heavy
pack of calico, muslin, other dress goods, and a few pairs of ladies'
hose:

> The first day I went towards the Bardstown Road, applied to many
> houses trying to sell some of my load, but were shown the door, and in
> some houses were introduced to a big dog. So I tramped till I were out
> of the city and succeeded to sell a pair of hose for 30¢. Was so fatigued

could not proceed either way, so I sat by the roadside to rest. When about 5 p.m. a teamster hawling a load of cordwood into the city came by I applied for a lift, and paying him my 30¢ hawled me back to the city. . . .

After this inauspicious beginning, Baum changed the selection of goods he was carrying and did much better. In less than a year, he had graduated to peddling with a horse and wagon, an important sign of economic advancement.[11]

The goal of every peddler was to settle down and open a store. Many peddlers achieved this goal, and by 1850 hundreds of small towns in the Midwest, the West, and the South were home to German Jewish shopkeepers. At first there might not be more than one or two families in a town, but when a town grew, and with it the number of Jewish merchants and their families, a congregation might be established. Often a congregation grew out of a loosely organized *minyan* or burial society. The establishment of a congregation in a town, in turn, frequently induced families from other small towns in the area to move there.

By 1850 there were isolated Jewish families living in a number of Indiana towns. Samuel Kahn and Isaac Kahn, both originally from Alsace, were merchants in Bloomington. Edward and Louis Frohman opened a dry goods store in Rushville in 1847. Adam Gimbel, whose sons were the founders of Gimbel Brothers and Saks Fifth Avenue, arrived from Bavaria in 1835 and peddled along the Mississippi River before opening his first dry goods store in Vincennes in 1842. By the time Gimbel sold his firm forty years later, he owned four stores in Vincennes. The Beitman and Wolf clothing store opened in Wabash in 1846. Some of the more prosperous communities attracted more than just one or two Jewish families, so that by 1850 there were synagogues in Fort Wayne (1848) and Lafayette (1849); by 1853 Evansville and Madison also had congregations.[12]

No Jews settled in Indianapolis before the end of the 1840s because for its first twenty-five years the city held few attractions for merchants. Selected as the site for the state capital in 1820, the city was laid out in 1821 by the surveyor Alexander Ralston and was modeled after Washington, D.C. The location was selected because the legislature wanted to move the capital from Corydon in the south, the region of the state that was settled first, and put it at the center of the state. For the first ten years or so, Indianapolis was not much more than a sleepy frontier village. The 1830s brought the first substantial population increase, which included some Irish who came to work on the National Road, which went through the city, and on the canal system. The Irish were followed by the Germans, who settled in Indianapolis in larger numbers. However, the real transformation of Indianapolis from town to city did not begin until 1847 when the first railroad line, the Indianapolis and Madison, was completed, linking the capital with the outside world. The completion of the rail line stimulated the city's growth, and the population increased from some 6,000 in 1847 to 8,000 in 1850. Where previously the town's major business had been politics, now manufacturing and jobbing concerns began locating in the city. Seven more railroad lines were built, and by 1855 Indianapolis was linked by rail to Chicago, Detroit, Cleveland, Cincinnati, Louisville, and St. Louis. Throughout the decade of the 1850s the city grew at a rapid pace, and by 1860 its population surpassed that of the older Ohio River towns of Madison and New Albany and stood at 18,611, an increase of 131 percent over the 1850 figure.[13]

With the rapid expansion of Indianapolis, Jewish merchants were soon attracted to the capital city. In 1849, two years after the first rail line to Indianapolis was completed, the first Jews settled in the city. These early pioneers were Alexander and Sarah Franco and Moses Woolf. We know little about these three beyond the bare facts recorded by the census enumerators in the 1850 federal census. The census described Franco, then a man of forty-five and a native of Poland, as a merchant. Woolf, a twenty-seven-year-old clerk, and Sarah Franco, also forty-five years old, were both natives of England. The census listed the three as sharing one household along with Abraham Joseph, a twelve-year-old native of Ohio. Very likely Woolf was the Francos' boarder and clerked in their store. Sometime later in the year (they do not appear in the census), the Knefler family, described in later newspaper accounts as political refugees from the Hungarian uprising of 1848, also settled in Indianapolis.[14]

The commercial attractions of the growing city and the nucleus of a Jewish community gradually brought more Jews to Indianapolis, and the community grew slowly. In 1852 Isaac Leeser of

Philadelphia, editor of the Jewish monthly, the *Occident,* traveled to Louisville via Indianapolis and Madison. He reportedly found only one Jewish family in Indianapolis "but in [Madison], however, we became acquainted with several Israelites. . . ." Three years later, in July, 1855, Rabbi Isaac Mayer Wise of Cincinnati, editor of the *American Israelite,* passed through Indianapolis and Terre Haute enroute to St. Louis and "found a few honorable Jewish merchants in Indianapolis; viz, Franko [sic] Wolf [sic], Dessar, Glaser, Dernham, Herrmann, Altman and others who organized a congregation shortly thereafter."[15]

The organization of the synagogue took place the following year, on November 2, 1856, when fourteen Jews gathered at the home of Julius Glaser to approve the constitution and bylaws of Indianapolis's first congregation, the Indianapolis Hebrew Congregation (IHC). The constitution and bylaws were then read to another group of thirty-one men who signed their approval.[16]

The earliest members of Indianapolis's Jewish community were a remarkably homogeneous group. The names of thirty-two of the forty-five men who approved the constitution and bylaws of the synagogue can be located in the city directories of the period. Nineteen were in the clothing business: sixteen were proprietors of retail and wholesale clothing establishments, two were clerks in clothing stores, and one was a tailor. Of eighteen clothing stores listed in the 1859 Indianapolis city directory, ten, or 55.5 percent, were owned by Jews. In addition to the clothing merchants, there were three physicians (one of whom was also a druggist), two peddlers, one optician, one clothes cleaner (known as a "dyer and scourer"), one jeweler, one grocer, and a deputy clerk of Marion County (Frederick Knefler). One man, Henry Rosenthal, had no occupation listed. Within this small group there were at least six sets of brothers. Many of the brothers were in business together.[17]

The members of this group were primarily young men in their twenties and thirties. At least eight of them were bachelors who boarded in homes or boarding houses. Married or single, they lived above their shops or near them along the few unpaved, muddy streets extending a scant half-mile from the Circle. They were a mobile group. Whereas some of them had come to Indianapolis directly from Europe—like Herman Bamberger from Hesse-Darmstadt in 1855 and the Knefler family from Arad, Hungary, in

1850—most had moved to Indianapolis from other towns in the Old Northwest where they had originally settled. The Glaser brothers—Julius, Samuel, Lewis, and Max—clothing merchants, came to Indianapolis from Cincinnati in 1855. Isaac Rosenthal, a physician and druggist, also moved from Ohio in 1855. Unlike many congregations founded during the period of heavy German Jewish migration, the founders of IHC were not all recent emigrants from Germany. Some had lived in America (or England) for a substantial period and had become acclimated to American ways. They chose an English, rather than a Hebrew name for their congregation. Similarly, in contrast to many synagogues established at the time, the earliest minute books were kept not in German but in English, although German was used in sermons and taught in the congregational school throughout the 1860s.[18]

With the establishment of the congregation, the Jewish population of Indianapolis began to increase. As Herman Bamberger, a founding member of IHC, observed at the dedication of the congregation's first synagogue building in 1868:

> The Jewish population increased from that period more rapidly, as is always the case in towns where congregations are established, and thus induce Israelites living in smaller towns, where no opportunity of observing their religious rites exists, and where they live isolated from their kindred and friends, to join their brethren.

Bamberger had identified two important functions of the American synagogue. Not only did it enable Jews to organize themselves as a religious community and participate in Jewish worship, but it also served as a focal point for Jews to gather together to enjoy the company of other Jews. A third and equally important function of the early synagogue (which Bamberger did not mention) was to provide for Jewish burial of the dead. The need to bury the dead often provided the incentive for a Jewish community to organize, since even the most religiously lax Jew would not want to be buried anywhere but in a Jewish cemetery. Communities without cemeteries faced the difficult task of transporting the dead to the closest Jewish cemetery. At the first organizational meeting of IHC, $125 was pledged for the purchase of cemetery land. Two years later, in 1858, the congregation purchased three-and-one-half acres of ground south of the city from W. Y. Wiley. (The cemetery, located at South Meridian and Kelly streets, is still in use by the congregation.)[19]

In addition to the purchase of cemetery land, another early concern was finding and furnishing suitable rooms for meetings and worship services. By August 1857, the congregation had hired its first religious functionary, S. Berman, who was employed as _hazzan_ (cantor), _shammash_ (sexton), and _shohet_ (ritual slaughterer), at an annual salary of $120. The same September, in anticipation of the group's first High Holy Day services, a committee was appointed to "procure Machsorim [prayer books], Talisim [prayer shawls], Sefer [Torah scroll], and Shofer [ram's horn]." Although the group was nominally Orthodox, as is evidenced by the continuing concern over the supply of kosher meat and the butchering skill of the _hazzan_, by 1857 some members were expressing interest in a more liberal form of service. While the congregation adopted the traditional Ashkenazi liturgy in October 1857, it also agreed at the same meeting to send to Cincinnati for a copy of _Minhag America_, Isaac Mayer Wise's recently published Reform prayer book, which abridged and modified the traditional Hebrew ritual.[20]

Hired initially for only the High Holy Days, Berman stayed a year, resigning when his request for a raise was denied. His salary having been raised to $300, he now wanted $400 for the year. (S. Berman went on to serve Congregation Keneseth Israel, a newly organized synagogue in Richmond, Virginia.) The congregation then hired Judah Wechsler of Evansville as _hazzan_ and _shohet_ for $350 a year. In order to meet this advance in salary, the small congregation of twenty-six was forced to raise its dues and institute a series of new charges. Married men would pay higher dues than bachelors, nonmembers who wanted to purchase kosher meat would have to pay a surcharge, and nonmembers would be given the opportunity of purchasing reserved seats in the sanctuary.[21]

The Bavarian-born Judah Wechsler (1833–1905) was educated at the University of Würzburg and the Würzburg _yeshivah_, then under the direction of Seligman Baer Bamberger, a leader of German Orthodoxy known as the "Würzburger Rav." Although Wechsler received rabbinical ordination from this traditional institution, he left his Orthodoxy behind in Germany. In each American congregation that Wechsler served, he gently steered the community to adopt more Reform practices. Although by 1858 the members of IHC had already begun to modify Jewish tradition, certain traditional practices, such as the maintenance of the dietary laws, were still important to them. Wechsler's duties as a *shoḥet* probably took up a great deal of his time, as he was required to call at every married member's house twice a week to kill poultry for the household. Shortly after Wechsler arrived in Indianapolis, his skill as a *shoḥet* was questioned, and the board asked Wechsler to "provide Testimonials from Rabbi Wise [Isaac Mayer Wise] or other rabbis certifying to his ability as a *shoḥet*." A testimonial was received from Wise, the members were satisfied, and Wechsler continued as *shoḥet* and *ḥazzan* until 1861, when membership declined so precipitously that the congregation could no longer afford him.[22]

When Wechsler arrived in Indianapolis in 1858, the group was still meeting in temporary quarters, having moved from a room donated by a member, Dr. Isaac M. Rosenthal, to a room on the third floor of Blake's Block, opposite Bates House at the corner of Washington and Illinois streets (later site of the Claypool Hotel). Shortly after Wechsler came, the congregation dedicated its first permanent home, a room in Judah's Block* on East Washington Street opposite the Courthouse, on October 24, 1858.[23]

The Indianapolis Hebrew Congregation was only one of many religious institutions founded in Indianapolis in the 1850s. Just as the synagogue was the center of social life for the Jewish community, the church served a similar purpose for many. While the small Jewish community struggled to raise funds to rent a hall, Christian Hoosiers erected about a dozen new churches, filling the skyline with church spires. Although some of the churchmen, in particular the Presbyterians, had a certain strictness and intolerant spirit, they never singled out the Jewish community for any special campaign of assault. The churchmen were more concerned with attempting to eliminate certain forms of behavior, such as drinking, dancing, and card playing, than in attempting either to convert the Jews or deny them the right to worship. The establishment of the "Hebrew church," as it was often called, was pointed out with pride, and, in fact, when the congregation decided to build their

---

*Owner of the building was John M. Judah, son of Samuel Judah, attorney of Vincennes and one of the first Jewish residents of the state. Rabbi Morris Feuerlicht, rabbi of IHC and student of Indiana Jewish history, claimed that although John Judah was raised as a Christian, he was proud of his Jewish heritage and rented the room to the young congregation at a discount.

first synagogue in the mid-1860s, they received donations from non-Jewish residents.[24]

During these years the population of Indianapolis was probably more cosmopolitan than at any time since, with large settlements of Germans, Irish, and blacks, and smaller numbers of French, English, and Jews. Although native-born Protestants locked horns with the large and influential German population over the drinking issue (in 1855 a state prohibition law, later found to be unconstitutional, briefly closed the beer gardens, the center of German social life), generally interethnic conflict was slight, and there was little tension among groups. The Jews who settled in Indianapolis in the 1850s and 1860s felt welcome, comfortable, and at home. They were proud to add a synagogue to the capital city's growing list of institutions, a "lasting Ornament to our City," as the congregation's secretary, Adolph Dessar, called it, a visible symbol of the Jewish community's dedication to the American principle of religious liberty. As Dessar wrote in the secretary's annual report for 1858:

> Gentlemen, it behooves us now to show to our good Neighbors, our fellow-Citizens that the Jew is a Man of as fine Sensibilities, that he can appreciate the kindness of his fellow-Citizens, and that at last, but not least, he can hold dear that freedom of Religion which he is enjoying equally as well as his Christian Brethren.[25]

A year later, the congregational secretary's report was less sanguine. Membership had declined from twenty-six to nineteen, and the congregation was plagued with financial difficulties. The synagogue had been forced to suspend members for nonpayment of dues (annual dues were now five dollars for married members and one dollar for single members) and institute further surcharges for nonmembers (a three dollar annual fee for the privilege of receiving kosher meat, and a charge for the use of a seat in the sanctuary). Two more years of decline followed: congregational membership dwindled from sixteen in 1860 to a low of thirteen in 1861.[26]

Out of a Jewish population that was estimated at over 180 by 1860, it was clearly a minority who affiliated with the synagogue. A larger number continued to purchase kosher meat and probably attended services on occasion. For the most part, however, Judaism, which had circumscribed and regulated every aspect of life in Europe, was governing a smaller and smaller part of the immigrants' lives. Many immigrants simply failed to maintain traditional Jewish practices, not because they were attracted to Christianity, but because it was often difficult to maintain Jewish observances in America and easy to give them up.

However, while many Jews readily abandoned most traditional religious observances or grew increasingly lax in their practices, socializing and gathering with other Jews remained important. Given the relatively small size of the community, a surprising number of secular and social institutions were established in the 1860s. While some of the members of these secular organizations were also members of IHC, many others were not. Organizations established in the 1860s and early 1870s included the Indianapolis Hebrew Benevolent Society (founded January 1861); the Young Men's Literary and Social Union (founded December 1862); a B'nai B'rith lodge, Abraham Lodge No. 58 (founded 1864); a lodge of the Independent Order of B'rith Abraham (founded 1865); the Harmonia Club (founded 1867); the Young Men's Bachelor's Association; the Tree of Life Mutual Benefit Association (founded October 1870); and, later in the 1870s, a chapter of the Order of Kesher Shel Barzel. The only women's group of the period, the Hebrew Ladies Benevolent Society, established in 1859, was both a charity society and a kind of women's auxiliary of the synagogue, and was organized at the suggestion of Judah Wechsler, then rabbi of the congregation. The first officers were all wives of congregational members.[27]

Most of these organizations left few traces, and little is known of them. (Only the B'nai B'rith lodge remains active.) However, the extant minute book of the Tree of Life Mutual Benefit Association reveals the activities and concerns of what was probably a fairly typical Jewish organization of the period. The Tree of Life Mutual Benefit Association provided its members with sick benefits, loans, burial benefits, as well as death benefits for their descendants. The group raised funds principally by sponsoring an annual ball, a popular method of fund raising at the time. The organization also engaged in relief work on occasion. For example, in October 1873, the members sent $100 to their "suffering coreligionists" in Memphis and Shreveport, where yellow fever had recently struck. Beyond the benefits and the chance to engage in charity work, an important attraction for the members was undoubtedly the regular meetings, which provided them with an opportunity to socialize and be with other Jews.[28]

However, while maintaining contact with other Jews remained important to the members of this relatively isolated Jewish community, social interaction with non-Jews was frequent enough that marriages between Jews and non-Jews were not uncommon. Any small Jewish community always faces the problem of providing an adequate number of potential marriage partners. The high number of unmarried Jews, particularly women, in eighteenth- and early nineteenth-century America has been explained as the result of an inadequate number of potential marriage partners in the small Jewish communities of the period. This problem was intensified in small midwestern communities by the large number of single men who often formed the nucleus of the community. While they continued to maintain organized social contact with other Jews, marriages between Jewish men and non-Jewish women were probably fairly numerous in Indianapolis. The number of intermarriages was substantial enough that the original constitution of IHC specifically denied membership to men with non-Jewish wives. That this exclusion had to be spelled out is rather interesting. Obviously, it assumes that these men would have wanted to join the synagogue. In the traditional communities of their birth, the marriage of a Jew to a non-Jew signaled the departure of the former from the Jewish community. A Jew who married a non-Jew was symbolically dead, and prayers of mourning were said for him. In mid-nineteenth-century America, however, it was already understood that one could take the radical step of marrying a non-Jew, yet still wish to remain part of the Jewish community. In fact, within a few years after the constitution was written, the complete denial of synagogue membership to Jews with non-Jewish wives was softened to allow intermarried Jews to become members as long as they professed allegiance to Judaism and agreed to raise their children as Jews.[29]

It is not known how many new members, if any, were gained by this strategy. Membership in IHC continued to decline for another year and a half after its adoption in 1860. As Secretary Herman Bamberger sadly reported in his annual report of September 1861, "From a scarcity of members and the effects of the War Times, we were compelled to dispense with the service of a *chasan* [Judah Wechsler had left that summer for a pulpit in Portsmouth, Ohio] and engage the service of a *shochet*, Mr. Hart. Our beautiful Synagogue stands now desolated."[30]

Not only a lack of members and financial woes threatened to close the young synagogue. Attendance was poor at Saturday morning services, presumably because this was a busy day for the retail merchants who made up most of the membership. In April 1858 the board passed a resolution urging that "members of I.H.C. when in their power to do so, attend the worship every Sabbath morning, according to our faith." Such admonitions had little effect, however; and the congregation sometimes lacked a *minyan*. Internal division over whether the congregation should join the Reform movement further weakened the congregation and nearly caused it to dissolve, according to one of the synagogue's founders. In a history of the congregation written in 1899, Herman Bamberger commented:

> internal dissensions caused by differences of opinion as to the mode of worship, mainly due to the fact that the membership was composed of men born and raised in different portions of Europe and tenaciously clinging to old habits, brought the Congregation nearly to disruption.

Every early American synagogue faced the problem of attempting to satisfy the varied and often conflicting needs of congregants with different backgrounds and religious habits. It was not unusual for these conflicts to split a congregation into factions, with the like-minded resigning to form their own synagogue.[31]

By 1862 the adherents of liberalism were gaining the upper hand in Indianapolis. Although no faction ever publicly resigned in anger, the synagogue began to adopt more and more of the trappings of the Reform movement. After a public plea raised $457 and increased the membership to twenty-five, the board once again began a search for a new religious functionary. This time the advertisement, which appeared in the *American Israelite*, requested a candidate with "modern Reform principles." The man who took the post in March 1862 was Max Moses. Under his guidance, the congregation adopted *Minhag America*, Isaac Mayer Wise's Reform prayer book, in place of the traditional prayer book and introduced a choir. However, a number of the congregants were not ready

either for these changes or for a leader of "modern Reform principles," and Moses resigned within six months, blaming the continuing dissension in the congregation for his early departure. A major
complaint of the traditionalists was that Moses's butchering knife
was not sharp. After Moses resigned, however, further changes
were introduced: a collection for a melodeon, a small reed organ,
was taken up among "all resident Israelites," and mixed seating of
men and women in the sanctuary was introduced. Yet other traditional practices were maintained, such as the dietary laws and the
prohibition against making a fire on Sabbath and Holy Days. (The
board, horrified when their *shoḥet*, Mr. Hart, lit the gas in the
synagogue on Yom Kippur, promptly fired him.)[32]

Although the reforms introduced by Moses disturbed some
members of the congregation, IHC's next religious leader, Isidor
Kalisch (1816–1886), was strongly identified with the Reform
movement. A native of Krotoschin in Prussian Poland, Kalisch had
studied at *yeshivah* and then at the universities of Berlin, Breslau,
and Prague. He became a journalist, wrote poems and articles that
were considered dangerously radical for the time, and in 1849 had
to leave Germany. In America, he turned to the rabbinate and in
1850 became Cleveland's first rabbi. An active participant in the
Conference of Moderate Reform elements held in Cleveland in October 1855, Kalisch helped to edit Isaac Mayer Wise's prayer book,
Minhag America.[33]

Kalisch agreed to a salary of $600 as long as he was not required
to act as *shoḥet*. He remained with the congregation only a year,
abruptly resigning in August 1864 to accept a pulpit in Detroit
even though IHC agreed to increase his salary to $800. Dur-
ing Kalisch's brief term of office the congregation succeeded in
establishing a school, an important accomplishment for the young
community. It was not until the years following the Civil War
that the Indiana public schools were firmly established with regular financial support. Because the public school system was so
weak, many children attended private schools, were tutored at
home, or were simply uneducated. With the IHC school now
established, Jewish children could receive instruction in a Jewish
setting. The school's curriculum included Hebrew, English, and
German.[34]

After Kalisch's abrupt departure, Judah Wechsler, who had

served the congregation as *ḥazzan* and *shoḥet* from 1858 to 1861, reapplied for his old job. Although ultimately Wechsler was rehired at the salary that he requested ($1,200 plus moving expenses), Wechsler's anti-abolitionist views invoked a certain hesitation on the part of the board. Wechsler, like Isaac Mayer Wise, believed that the fiery sermons of abolitionist preachers had led the nation into war. The IHC board saw this attitude as disloyal and hired Wechsler with the understanding that he remain silent on the subject. With the nation now plunged into a bloody war, Indianapolis Jewry did not want to be perceived as having a leader who was less than vigilant in his support of the Union cause.[35]

The congregation Wechsler returned to serve in 1864 was much stronger and more prosperous than the one he had left in 1861. By 1865 there were sixty-three members, and a committee had been appointed to raise funds for a new synagogue. A second committee had been formed to find a suitable place for a schoolhouse. With funds raised at a successful Temple Fair held on Thanksgiving Day, 1864, and donations from congregants, a lot was purchased on East Market Street, between New Jersey and East streets, formerly the site of the log cabin home of the antislavery campaigner, Henry Ward Beecher.[36]

Late in 1865 the dedication of the cornerstone for the Market Street Temple took place. The elaborate ceremony was attended by Governor Conard Baker, Mayor John Caven, members of the Indianapolis Common Council, other civic notables, and Rabbi Max Lilienthal of Cincinnati, one of the leading Reform rabbis in America. Conscious of the historic importance of the occasion, the congregation placed a metal box under the cornerstone containing copies of the records, constitution, and bylaws of the congregation, the constitutions of a number of other Jewish organizations of Indianapolis, copies of the American Jewish newspapers and Indianapolis newspapers of the day, American coins, and other items. For the small group who had founded the congregation a mere nine years earlier and at times despaired of its survival, it was a day for proud rejoicing.[37]

The sixty-three members of the Indianapolis Hebrew Congregation in 1865 were far more prosperous than the fourteen founding members of the congregation had been in 1856. The Jewish community had shared in the increasing wealth and rapid growth of the city during the Civil War. Indianapolis was the main recruiting station for the state and a bivouacing area for troops going to the front. Six military installations as well as a state arsenal were located in or near the city. Most of the time ten to twelve thousand soldiers were stationed within the city, and this had greatly increased the business of local establishments, attracting more artisans and businessmen to the city. Large new industries were attracted to the city. Among the largest was Kingan and Company, a pork-packing concern with interests in Ireland, England, and Australia, which began operations in Indianapolis in 1864.[38]

Indianapolis Jewry, concentrated as it was in the clothing trade, benefited not only from the general expansion of business, but specifically from lucrative government clothing contracts. For example, the clothing firm of Glaser Mitchel and Company, owned by the brothers Julius, Samuel, Lewis, and Max Glaser and Jacob Mitchel, made uniforms during the war for the Union Army. Similarly, Herman Bamberger, who began manufacturing hats and caps in 1860, prospered during the war years by supplying headgear to small regiments of volunteers. Many clothing firms, such as H. Rosenthal and Company and Joseph Kohn, advertised that they had "military goods constantly on hand." The increasing business opportunities attracted more Jewish clothing firms to Indianapolis; one was the firm of Katzenstein and Wachtel, a wholesale clothing house started by the youthful Julius Katzenstein and Moses Wachtel, who had come from Winona County, Minnesota, in 1863.[39]

There were many new faces in the IHC sanctuary in Judah's Block and in the shops and streets of the growing city. By 1865 over half of the residents of Indianapolis were newcomers, a statistic reflected in the growth of the Jewish community as well as of the general populace. As the population rose from 18,611 in 1860 to 40,000 in 1866, the Jewish population, remaining at a steady 1 percent, grew from 180 in 1860 to 400 in 1866.[40]

The Jewish community had more than doubled in these six years, and it would nearly double again in the next seven years, but occupationally there was little change in the Jewish community during the 1860s. The Jews of Indianapolis remained firmly established in the clothing trade and about 70 percent of the clothing establishments in Indianapolis during the 1860s were Jewish-owned.* Some of them, such as Glaser, Mitchel and Company, Moritz Brothers, and Myers and Strauss, were branches of Cincinnati firms managed locally by younger sons or brothers of the Cincinnati owners. The successful Cincinnati firm of Moritz Brothers and Company sent "young Solomon" to Indianapolis, and he succeeded in establishing a profitable branch of the firm in the city. Other firms relied heavily on Cincinnati for their buying. However, most were independently owned, often by Jews who had succeeded first as peddlers or shopkeepers in the small towns surrounding Indianapolis. The firm of Glick and Schwartz, manufacturers of hoopskirts, was started about 1866 by two German Jews who were former peddlers. They sold their hoopskirts, as well as needles, thread, hooks, and other notions, to peddlers. Other Jewish firms were on the periphery of the clothing business—auction houses which bought clothing (and other goods) to sell at auction, and dyers and scourers. A number of Jews were liquor dealers, tobacconists, grocers, and, of course, peddlers.[41]

Those Jews who arrived in Indianapolis during the prosperous 1860s came originally from western and central Europe—Prussia, Bavaria, Alsace, and England. Many of them had lived in the United States for some years before settling in Indianapolis in small towns such as Bloomington, Evansville, and Peru, Indiana, where they had achieved some financial success, so that by the time they settled in Indianapolis they were no longer raw immigrants but were comfortable and familiar with American cultural and political life. It was not long before they were participating fully in the civic and political life of the city. Acculturation for these early Jewish residents, then, was a relatively rapid and smooth process, as numerous examples demonstrate. This is not to say that among midwestern cities Indianapolis was unique. Since nearly everyone in the young cities of the Midwest was a migrant—if not from Germany, France, Ireland, or Great Britain, then from the older cities of the Atlantic coast—there was no

*The concentration of German Jews in retail trade was common throughout America at the time. In Columbus, Ohio, for example, the proportion of Jews in the clothing trade was even greater. In antebellum Columbus, every Jewish family but one entered the clothing business, and by 1872 every retail clothing store listed in the Columbus city directory was owned by Jews. For Columbus see Marc L. Raphael, *Jews and Judaism in a Midwestern Community: Columbus, Ohio, 1840–1975* (Columbus, 1979), pp. 40–41.

large, ensconced native elite capable of excluding all newcomers. Jews naturally took part in civic and political life, as did the French, the Germans, and the Irish. During the Civil War some Jews, of course, served in the Union army. Those who enlisted from Indianapolis included Herman Bamberger, David Dessar, C. B. Feibleman, and Frederick Knefler. When Abraham Lincoln's funeral train passed through Indianapolis in 1865 members of "One of the Hebrew Associations [probably B'nai B'rith] . . . turned out and went down with the Odd Fellows" to the Statehouse to view the body of the dead president. Like many of the city's public buildings, the synagogue was draped in mourning and remained so for thirty days. At the end of each service, the congregants recited a prayer for the beloved leader.[42]

In the postwar era, Jews began to take an active part in local politics. While some Jews had run for political office before him, the first successful Jewish candidate in Indianapolis was Leon Kahn, who was elected to the Indianapolis Common Council in 1869. An immigrant from Franenberg in Lorraine, Kahn lived in Bloomington from 1851 to 1864 before settling in Indianapolis. An active member of IHC, Kahn served on the Indianapolis Common Council for eight years between 1869 and 1881. Another Jew with political ambitions was Joseph Harris, an immigrant from London and owner of the United States Dye-House, who offered himself in 1865 as an "independent union candidate" for councilman from the fifth ward. In his political advertisements Harris described himself as "an old citizen of the ward." In the best American tradition of authentic ward politics, Harris promised that, if elected, he would "pledge himself to aid in securing cheap gas, light taxes and to look after the interests of the ward in the Council and see that it has its fair share of all public improvements." Despite his promises, Harris was not elected.[43]

Five years earlier, the marriage of Joseph Harris's youngest daughter, Sarah, to Joseph Solomon on January 25, 1860, had been a social event worthy of note, as it was the first Jewish wedding to be performed in the Hoosier capital. Both Jews and non-Jews "of all denominations" attended the wedding, another demonstration of the degree of social integration that existed. And while the event was considered sufficiently exotic to receive an extensive description in the *Indiana Daily State Sentinel*, the interest in the festivities was one of friendly curiosity rather than hostile conde-scension.[44]

A sense of security which, as American Jewry realized, was confirmed by the guarantees of the bill of rights, gave the Indianapolis Jewish community the confidence to oppose publicly a move that would have infringed on their religious freedom. At the close of the Civil War in February 1865, a group of 453 persons led by Calvin Fletcher, Indianapolis banker, devout Methodist, and active Republican, presented a memorial to both houses of the Indiana General Assembly recommending the adoption of a constitutional amendment acknowledging "Almighty God as the source of all authority and power in civil government, the Lord Jesus Christ as the ruler among nations, and his revealed will as of supreme authority." The Jewish community openly campaigned against the adoption of this amendment, and after some consideration both houses rejected the proposal. It is not known what effect the Jewish campaign against the bill had on the legislators. Quite probably the legislators realized the unconstitutionality of the bill without the reminder from the Jewish community. However, the fact that members of the Jewish community could openly oppose Fletcher, one of the city's most influential men, reveals a great deal about their place in the community.[45]

The presence of a substantial and active German community also contributed to Indianapolis Jewry's feelings of security. Although not all of Indianapolis's Jews were originally from the German states, a majority were, and they shared with the large and influential German community a pride in German culture and its intellectual accomplishments, as well as a desire to retain the German language. Indianapolis's Jews supported and participated in the many German associations established in the city, such as the Männerchor, the German singing society founded in 1854, and the German-English School. When the German-English School commemorated the opening of its new building on July 4, 1866, with a parade, the B'nai B'rith Abraham Lodge No. 58 sponsored one of the decorated wagons in the parade. Moreover, the congregation's own school offered instruction in German as well as in Hebrew and English.[46]

While the Germans formed the largest immigrant community in Indianapolis in the 1860s and 1870s, none of the immigrant communities was particularly large. Throughout the nineteenth and twentieth centuries, Indianapolis, and Indiana in general, never attracted a large number of foreign-born immigrants. During the great influx of the 1850s, for example, Indiana received a smaller proportion of immigrants than any other state in the old Northwest. Moreover, during the "Long Depression" of the 1870s and 1880s, a period coinciding with the beginnings of mass migration from Europe, the percentage of foreign-born residents in Indianapolis actually began to drop (although in absolute numbers there was a modest increase), declining from 22 percent of the population in 1870 to only 5 percent in 1920. Indianapolis had a smaller percentage of foreign-born residents than any of its nearby urban rivals. (Columbus, Ohio, another landlocked capital, also had a small proportion of immigrants.) Similarly, the proportion of immigrants in the state population always remained small. In 1900 Indiana's neighbors had the following percentages of foreign-born residents: Wisconsin, 24.9; Michigan 22.4; Illinois, 20.1; Ohio, 11. Indiana's foreign-born population was only 5.6 percent of the total. Perhaps the relatively small number of Jewish immigrants and of immigrants in general also contributed to smooth the process of acculturation for those who did settle in Indianapolis.[47]

Finally, in 1868, the increasingly prosperous community had a synagogue of which it could be proud. The rabbi of IHC was now Mayer Messing (1843–1930), who remained with the congregation for forty years. Born in Genivkowa, East Prussia, Messing came from a rabbinic family and served as rabbi for a number of German communities before emigrating to America in 1867. Messing was the first Jewish religious leader in Indianapolis to participate in civic life and he earned a reputation as an active charity worker and civic leader. He was a founder and first president of the Indianapolis Humane Society and served on the boards of the Industrial Home for the Blind, the Fresh Air Mission, and the Indiana Red Cross. Secretary of the Hebrew Ladies Benevolent Society for twenty-five years, at times he assumed almost full responsibility for the relief of Jewish transients in the city. Messing was not only the leading rabbi in the state, he was also one of the few *mohelim* in the region. Between 1871 and 1910, Messing traveled to communities throughout Indiana and in neighboring states to perform circumcisions.[48]

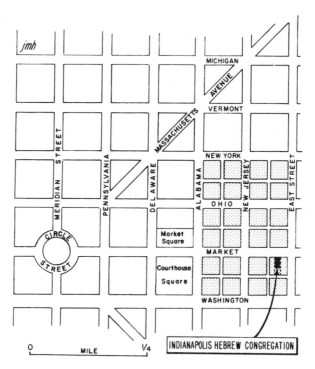

Map 1:   1860s

Messing arrived in Indianapolis in time for the High Holy Days in October 1867, replacing Judah Wechsler who had abruptly resigned in September. A year later, on October 30, 1868, the congregation dedicated its new synagogue building. Isaac Mayer Wise once again came from Cincinnati to preside over the celebration. A joyous procession paraded the few blocks from the old synagogue on East Washington Street to the new one on East Market Street, a handsome, two-story, brick building with stone façade, built in the then-popular Renaissance style.[49]

The fifty-eight members of IHC formed a small and close-knit community. They lived with their families on the streets surrounding the synagogue north and east of the Circle, mainly on East, Ohio, New York, and Alabama streets (see Map 1). By 1870 there were about five hundred Jews in Indianapolis in a total population of 48,211. The city was still enjoying the effects of a long postwar economic boom, and the capital was astir with new industries—pork-packing plants, cotton and woolen mills, foundries, and factories. Boosters called it "the greatest inland city of America" and predicted that its population would double within the next five years. However, the prosperity of the sixties did not continue through the seventies. The Panic of 1873 hit Indianapolis particularly hard, and during the "Long Depression" from 1873 until about 1887 the city wrestled with strikes, money shortages, high unemployment, bank closings (ten in thirteen years), and a slackening of population growth. During the boom years of the preceding decade the city's population had increased 156 percent, but during the hard times of the seventies the increase was only 55.6 percent.[50]

Indianapolis Jews, for the most part, were able to weather the years of depression. As merchants and shopkeepers they suffered less than workers or manufacturers. Having settled in Indianapolis when the city was still young and growing, they had found a niche in the city's economy. By 1882 half the employed Jews in the city were shopkeepers, retailers, or wholesalers. Most of the remaining 50 percent worked in related occupations, such as tailoring and peddling.[51]

In 1887 the discovery of large subterranean pools of natural gas just north of the city brought prosperity and ushered in an era that had been called the "golden age of Indianapolis." In many ways this period was a golden age for the early German Jewish community as well. Having grown up with their adopted city, they had attained the respectability that comes with being both middle-aged and middle-class. Having worked hard all their lives, they could now afford to sit back and relax a bit. They could undertake charitable and civic work and send their children off to college. They could move away from the increasingly commercial area around the Circle to one of the big houses on North Meridian or North Pennsylvania. Their wives could leave the management of the household to one or two servants and devote themselves to charity work, perhaps with the newly organized Council of Jewish Women or Temple Sisterhood. The organized Jewish community had matured as well with a full range of organizations. In the years that followed, the German Jewish community, settled and established, would savor the respectability and status their hard work had earned them.

❧ II

Achievement and Acceptance

THE GERMAN JEWISH COMMUNITY

1881—1920

IN THE LATE NINETEENTH CENTURY, Indianapolis resembled a large country town. Cows roamed the streets; gentlemen walked to their businesses; small mule-drawn streetcars quietly hauled passengers along a few central arteries. Life was comfortable, quiet, and cozy. As Charlotte Cathcart wrote in a reminiscence of her Indianapolis childhood, it was a town in which "almost everyone knew everyone else. . . ." "A comfortable, homey community," wrote Claude Bowers, "with no pushing or shoving, where the people lived normal lives and . . . businessmen went home for lunch." In 1880 the population of Indianapolis was only 75,056. Forty years later it was 314,194. If, as Hoosier writer Meredith Nicholson claimed in 1904, Indianapolis was a town that became a city "against its will," by 1920 it could no longer be described as an overgrown country town. It was unquestionably a city.[1]

The proportion of foreign-born residents in the city was small by comparison with many other cities—about 10 percent in 1900. The newer immigrants lived far from the genteel neighborhoods of Charlotte Cathcart, in their own districts on the city's south and west sides near the stockyards, railroads, and most of Indianapolis's major industries.[2]

32

In the 1880s the foreign composition of Indianapolis began to change. Although Germans retained their numerical superiority and cultural independence, Hoosiers of Irish and French ancestry were no longer distinguishable from the "native" citizenry. The newest immigrants to Indianapolis, as in other cities across the country, came from southern and eastern Europe. Italian, Russian, Polish, and Hungarian communities began to form on the city's south and west sides. The Jewish community of Indianapolis underwent similar changes. Those mid-nineteenth-century immigrants who had come primarily from Germany but also from Poland, Lithuania, England, and France were now "Americans"; they had become "native" Jews. Perhaps they still spoke English with an accent, but that did not prevent them from sitting on the board of the influential Commercial Club or from holding membership in the Republican Columbia Club along with other leading citizens.[3]

The rapid success of many German Jewish immigrants was striking. Many of them achieved not only great material prosperity but social respectability as well, trading the grime, dirt, foul air, and overcrowding of the south side for the bucolic calm, stately houses, and treelined avenues of the north side. The story of Jennie Efroymson Wolf (1873–1965), who lived her entire life in houses on Meridian Street, demonstrates what could be achieved in a lifetime. Born in Indianapolis in 1873 to Jacob and Minna Efroymson, immigrants from Lithuania and Prussia respectively, her early years were spent on the south side, living above her parents' dry goods store on South Meridian Street. In 1891 she married her first cousin Louis Wolf, an immigrant from the Prussian town of Strasburg who had been living in Indianapolis since 1882, and they set up housekeeping one block north of her parents' home.[4]

By 1900 the Star Store, a small department store Wolf and his brother-in-law G. A. Efroymson had opened in 1888, was prospering, and the Wolfs moved out of the south side to 1901 North Meridian. As the family prospered—they bought H. P. Wasson and Company in 1912—their address "improved." They moved eleven blocks north, then another seven blocks north, and finally leaped fourteen blocks north to their last home, an ample mansion at 5130 North Meridian, in one of the city's finest neighborhoods.[5]

If the achievement of the Wolf family was extraordinary, it was only so by a matter of degree. Though only a few reached the summit, hundreds of immigrants trod the same path, first exchanging their peddlers' packs for a horse and wagon, then moving on to a small store and, for the fortunate and clever, to larger and larger stores. As their standing rose, so did their street addresses, since the city's finest residential areas were on the north side. Of the small group of Jews who constituted the city's Jewish elite in the late nineteenth and early twentieth centuries, most had started as tailors, peddlers, or retail clerks. Those who were not themselves immigrants were the children of immigrants. The careers of only a few will be recalled here, but they represent dozens of others whose lives followed a similar pattern.

The Jewish community of mid-nineteenth-century Indianapolis was a community of hardworking shopkeepers, clerks, tailors, and peddlers. While there was no widespread poverty, there was no great wealth either. By the end of the nineteenth century, the early Jewish settlers had become more prosperous as a whole. A smaller number of them had become very successful. As wealth became more stratified, occupational diversity increased as well. By 1900 there were Jewish lawyers, doctors, and bankers, although as in other cities Jews remained concentrated in retail trade.

An early Jewish resident of Indianapolis who became a successful retail clothing merchant was Leopold Strauss (1844–1914). At twenty-one, Strauss emigrated from his native town of Chronberg (near Frankfurt-am-Main) and settled in Indianapolis in 1865. A tailor by trade, Strauss took a job as a clerk in the Eagle Clothing Store, then owned by two German Jewish brothers, Morris and Louis Greisheimer. In 1871 Strauss became a partner and in 1879 he bought out the Greisheimers. That same year he married Lina Rothschild (1855–1939), a native of Esslingen, Germany.[6]

Under Strauss's management, the Eagle Clothing Store prospered, and Strauss became one of the city's leading retailers. At a time when customers normally bargained with shopkeepers in Indianapolis, Strauss locally pioneered the concept of fixed prices for all customers. In 1899 he brought in Abram L. Block (1864–1936), a progressive merchandiser from Brooklyn, New York, to become his partner, and a few years later the name of the firm was changed to L. Strauss and Company. Block, who had a flair for advertising, coined the phrase "Strauss Says," which was featured in the company's advertising. Block became president of L. Strauss in 1910. Strauss's son, Arthur, was secretary.[7]

Strauss, a founder of the Indianapolis Merchants' Association, became active in the movement for civic improvement. His links to his past were more tenuous. Although he belonged to Das Deutsche Haus and the Indianapolis Männerchor—a reflection of his German origins—he, like many other German Jews in the period, maintained no synagogue affiliation. He did, however, belong to the Americus Club, a Jewish men's social club that was founded in 1892 and maintained a clubhouse on North Alabama Street.[8]

Another of the city's leading retailers was William H. Block (1855–1928), an Austrian-born teacher who emigrated to America in 1874. Shortly thereafter, Block went to Cleveland and began peddling goods through the mining districts of Ohio, but he disliked the rough and unsettled life of a peddler and quit. Over the next few years he tried his hand at farm work, telegraphy, and school teaching, only to take up the pack again, this time in southwestern Ohio and eastern Indiana. His second attempt at peddling was more successful than the first. After several years of retracing the same route he came to know his customers. He then began carrying only samples, keeping his stock in his hotel room, taking orders, and then shipping the goods out by truck. A few years later he was able to give up peddling completely and opened a small store, the Block and Thalman Wholesale and Retail Department Store, in Kokomo, Indiana, with his partner, Abe Thalman. In 1894 Block severed his partnership with Thalman, and two years later moved to Indianapolis and opened a small department store on Washington Street between Illinois and Meridian. With fixed prices, a small markup, and a rapid turnover, the store did well and was incorporated in 1907 as the William H. Block Company. Three years later Block built an eight-story building at Illinois and Market streets, directly across the street from the large interurban (electric railroad) station where scores of trains daily deposited Hoosiers in from the country for a day's shopping.[9]

For the first quarter of this century, Block was a major force in the city's commercial development. Under his close personal supervision, the company came to do business worth $15 million annually. He invested heavily in commercial real estate, forming the Mercantile Realty Company to manage his holdings. Although he was a onetime president of the Merchants' Association, a founder of the Merchants Heat and Light Company, an active member of the Chamber of Commerce, and a generous contributor to Riley Hospital, the Community Fund, and other charities both Jewish and non-Jewish, Block did not assume a leadership role in either the Jewish community or in civic life. While Block, unlike Leopold Strauss, was a member of the Indianapolis Hebrew Congregation (IHC), both men represented a common pattern among the German immigrants. Having left the intensely Jewish world of their youth behind them, many German immigrants maintained only a weak interest in Judaism and Jewish life. For many, the only affiliations they maintained were with Jewish social organizations. Like Strauss, Block belonged to the German Jewish men's social clubs, the Indianapolis Club, and, later, Broadmoor Country Club.[10]

William H. Block married Amelia Miller of Bellaire, Ohio, in 1883, and the couple had five sons. After Block's death, three of his sons, Meier, Rudolph, and Edward, took over the management of Block's. The downtown store was expanded several times, and branches were opened first in the suburbs and later in other cities. In 1962 the department store became part of the Allied Stores Corporation of New York.[11]

While men like Strauss and Block took no leadership role in the Jewish community and moved increasingly in non-Jewish circles, the third major retailing family, Efroymson-Wolf, represented a very different form of accommodation to American life. Soon after Louis Wolf (1866–1955) and his brother-in-law Gustave A. Efroymson (1870–1946) began in business in 1888 with the Star Store, a small department store at 360 West Washington Street, the firm prospered, and other members of the large family were brought in to the business. A wholesale jobbing business, Efroymson and Wolf, was also added to the operation and installed above the Star Store. In 1912 Louis Wolf, his nephew Frank Wolf, G. A. Efroymson, and his brother Meyer Efroymson (1871–1946) purchased H. P. Wasson and Company, a leading department store. Under the management of Efroymson and Wolf—G. A. Efroymson was the firm's president—Wasson's maintained its reputation as a store for high-quality, fashionable goods and custom dressmaking. In 1930 Efroymson sold his interest in Wasson's to Louis Wolf, who passed the presidency to his son Walter E. Wolf (1899–1977) in 1953.[12]

Both G. A. Efroymson and Louis Wolf served as presidents of IHC (Efroymson from 1902–1905 and Wolf from 1911–1913), and both men have descendants who still maintain positions of leadership within the Indianapolis Jewish community. G. A. Efroymson maintained a strong commitment to Jewish causes throughout his life and was probably the most significant lay leader of Indianapolis Jewry for the first decades of the twentieth century. A native Hoosier (born in Evansville), Efroymson assumed the presidency of the newly organized Jewish Federation in 1905 and held the position for a total of twenty-three years. When Efroymson took the presidency of the new organization, the Jewish Federation was primarily a charitable society, dispensing coal, groceries, and money for rent; locating husbands who had abandoned their wives; feeding and housing transients; and making small loans to immigrants who wanted to purchase a stand in the city market or a horse for peddling. By the end of Efroymson's presidency, the Jewish Federation had become the central organization of Indianapolis Jewry, overseeing the work of its constituent agencies in education, social services, and cultural and recreational activities. (The work of the Jewish Federation will be discussed in the following chapter.)[13]

The garment trade in America has always attracted large numbers of Jews. Although the garment industry in Indianapolis was not well developed, the city's largest garment manufacturer was Jewish and, like G. A. Efroymson, a native Hoosier. Henry Kahn (1860–1934), founder of the Kahn Tailoring Company, was born in Bloomington, the son of Isaac Kahn (1829–1887), an Alsatian immigrant, and Belle Hirsch Kahn (died 1886), a Parisian. Isaac Kahn came to this country in 1844 and settled in Bloomington, where he was one of the pioneer merchants of that city. In 1866 the family moved to Indianapolis and Henry attended the public schools as well as Butler University.[14]

In the summer of 1886 Henry Kahn opened a small tailoring shop on East Washington Street near Meridian. His business prospered, but rather than continue in custom tailoring Kahn shifted to mass production. In 1903 he founded the Kahn Tailoring Company, which became one of the country's largest manufacturers of men's suits and military uniforms. In addition, Kahn Tailoring also operated a dozen retail outlets, although most of the firm's suits were sold in general clothing stores. In Indianapolis the company had sales rooms in the Kahn Building at Meridian and Washington streets; the factory was at 800 North Capitol Avenue.[15]

Henry Kahn did not take a particularly active role in organized

Jewish life, but through his company he provided employment for hundreds of newly arrived Jewish immigrants in Indianapolis. During the years that there was a local Industrial Removal Office (IRO) in Indianapolis to help Jewish immigrants find employment outside of New York City (1904–1918), Kahn Tailoring actively cooperated with the local IRO agent, offering immigrants jobs. While Ashkenazi Jews also worked there, the firm hired a particularly large number of Sephardic Jews, many of whom came to Indianapolis specifically to work at Kahn Tailoring. In an era when industries did not normally provide social services for their employees, Henry Kahn ran Kahn Tailoring with a kind of enlightened paternalism. The company extended itself far into the lives of its workers to provide for many of their needs. It maintained a social welfare department whose welfare workers periodically visited the homes of employees. It also provided its employees with a house physician, sick benefits, a savings department, and a night school. Because so many of the workers did not know English, all work in the factory utilized a system of color-coding. Social gatherings were often held at the factory in the evening, and while factory workers ate their lunch the factory orchestra played music in the company lunch room.[16]

Henry Kahn married Sara Lang of Indianapolis in 1884. Active in the Council of Jewish Women and a member of the board of directors of the Indianapolis Orchestra, she was a member of the board of governors of the Jewish Federation from its inception in 1905 until 1907. The couple had one daughter, Claribel, whose husband, Mortimer C. Furscott, became president of the firm after the death of Henry Kahn in 1934. During the First and Second World Wars Kahn Tailoring was a major supplier of officers' uniforms, but in the post–World War II period the firm experienced a decline. In 1954 Kahn Tailoring merged with Globe Tailoring of Cincinnati, and the Indianapolis plant was closed.[17]

While many German Jews remained in retail trade and operated successful jewelry, furniture, grocery, or clothing stores, Sol S. Kiser (1858–1935) and Sol Meyer (1866–1939), co-founders of the Meyer-Kiser Bank, were clothiers who became bankers. These first cousins came to Indianapolis from Fort Recovery, Ohio. Sol Kiser was the son of Gottlieb Kiser (born 1831) and Fannie Steinfeld Kiser (born 1833), both natives of Hesse-Kassel in southwestern

Germany. Sol Kiser left Fort Recovery at the age of twenty and moved to Union City, Indiana, a town just south of Fort Recovery on the Ohio border, where he clerked in a store for three years.[18]

Sol Kiser remained in Union City until 1881, when he moved to Indianapolis. He clerked in a clothing store for five years and then in 1886 opened his own clothing store on West Washington Street. In 1888 his first cousin Sol Meyer came to Indianapolis to work as an accountant in the engineering department of the Pennsylvania Railroad. Meyer had left school at fourteen and become a telegrapher with the Lake Erie and Western Railroad to help support his widowed mother. Meyer rose through the ranks, and when he resigned from the Pennsylvania Railroad in 1895 to open a real estate, loan, and insurance business with his cousin he was chief acountant in the superintendent's office. In April 1906, the two men founded the Meyer-Kiser Bank with Meyer as president and Kiser as vice-president. The bank, which became one of the largest lending institutions in the state, financed many of Indianapolis's important commercial buildings and hotels, including the Hotel Lincoln, the Spink-Arms Hotel, the Electric Building, and the Roosevelt Building. In addition to the bank, the two men also maintained interests in real estate, insurance, and brokerage. In 1926 Sol Kiser retired from the firm because of ill health. Five years later in May 1931, an inability to liquidate its loans along with heavy withdrawals by depositors forced the Meyer-Kiser Bank to close its doors, another victim of the Great Depression.[19]

Sol Kiser was one of the group of American-born Jews who moved to Indianapolis in the late 1880s and 1890s, prospered, and then assumed leadership positions both within the developing Jewish community and the general community. Jewishly, he was concerned not only with the synagogue and the social clubs of the north side but also with the newly arrived eastern European Jews of the south side. Kiser was chairman of the committee that organized the Jewish Federation in 1905 and briefly served as its first president.[20]

Prior to the founding of the Federation, which was organized in part to consolidate fund-raising efforts within the city, local representatives collected funds for the benefit of a small group of national Jewish charities. Sol Kiser represented the Cleveland Jewish Orphans' Home and the National Jewish Hospital in Denver and also served as a trustee of both organizations. He was an active member of B'nai B'rith, holding the presidency of District Grand Lodge No. 2 from 1896 to 1897. He was the only person to serve as chairman of the local committee of the Industrial Removal Office (1904–1918). Sol Kiser was treasurer for the Indiana committee of the American Jewish Relief Committee during the First World War and also assisted in the Liberty Loan drives. He also served as vice-president (1895) of the Americus Club. He was president of IHC from 1895 to 1898 and chairman of the building committee that oversaw the construction of the congregation's new building at 10th and Delaware streets in 1899.[21]

Outside the Jewish community, Kiser participated in several organizations concerned with the civic improvement of the city and state. From 1901 to 1910 he was a director of the influential Indianapolis Commercial Club (later the Chamber of Commerce) and was its vice-president for two years. He was the first treasurer of the State Park Commission and directed the campaign to raise funds for the establishment of Turkey Run and McCormick Creek parks.[22]

Sol Kiser was married to Dina Salzenstein (1862–1917), a native of Pleasant Plains, Illinois, in 1889. She was active in the local Council of Jewish Women and the Temple Sisterhood. After Dina Kiser's death, Sol Kiser married Kate Weis of Cleveland in 1922.[23]

Sol Meyer, Sol Kiser's partner and cousin, maintained memberships in IHC, B'nai B'rith, the Chamber of Commerce, and other organizations but did not take an active leadership role. Aside from his reputation as one of the city's leading bankers, Meyer is perhaps best known as the owner of Indianapolis's professional baseball club from 1907 to 1914. He married Florence Strauss in Washington, D.C., in 1897, and they had three sons.[24]

Samuel E. Rauh (1854–1935), like the cousins Sol Meyer and Sol Kiser, was a German Jew who moved from Ohio to Indianapolis in the late nineteenth century. He became one of the city's wealthiest men. Born in Germersheim in the Rhenish Palatinate in western Germany to Elias and Hanna Abrahams Rauh, his family left Germany in 1866, when he was thirteen, and settled in Dayton, Ohio, where his father engaged in the fur and hide business. In 1874, at the age of twenty, Samuel Rauh came to Indianapolis and established a branch of E. Rauh and Sons, hide and fur dealers. Two years later, Samuel Rauh's elder brother, Henry (1852–1922), joined him in Indianapolis, and the two became prominently identified with the industrial interests of the city.[25]

For the next sixty years the activities of the Rauh family had a profound impact on the economic life of the city, as Samuel Rauh established one business after another. In 1880 he established the first fertilizer factory in the Midwest, E. Rauh and Sons Fertilizer Company. His brother Henry served as president of the company. In 1884 Samuel Rauh erected a small slaughterhouse and then a second slaughterhouse, known as the Indianapolis Slaughtering Company, of which he was president. The company consolidated with the Indianapolis Abbatoir Company, and he became a director. His brother was vice-president.[26]

In 1890 Samuel Rauh organized and built the Moore Packing Company, a meat-packing concern, and became its president. That same year, he became vice-president and a director of the Indianapolis Dessicating Company, one of the first plants organized in the country for the disposal of city garbage. Four years later he founded and became president of the Indianapolis Hauling Company, which collected garbage, ashes, and waste materials from city residences. Rauh was an organizer and director of the Union Trust Company; a director of the Kokomo Steel and Wire Company, which later merged with the Continental Steel Corporation; helped organize and was first vice-president of the Federal Union Surety Company; and was an organizer of the Home Heating and Lighting Company and of the Indianapolis and Noblesville Traction Company. He became president of the latter organization and later vice-president when it was reorganized as the Central Indiana Traction Company. In 1895 Samuel Rauh was elected to the board of directors of the Belt Railroad and Union Stock Yards Company, and in 1897 he became president both of the Belt Railroad and of the Peoples Light and Heat Company, which later became a part of the Indianapolis Power and Light Company.[27]

During Rauh's thirty-two-year presidency the Belt Railroad and Stock Yards developed into a major industry in Indianapolis and became one of the largest stockyards in the country. To promote the stockyards Rauh made trips through the East, urging buyers to travel to the Indianapolis market. He modernized equipment, introducing telephones, trucks, and modern loading machinery.[28]

For six years, Rauh was president of the city Board of Park Commissioners under mayors Joseph E. Bell and Charles W. Jewett. He was also a director of the Athenaeum, a member of the Chamber of Commerce, and served on the board of governors of the Indianapolis Board of Trade. Although an immigrant himself, Rauh remained a member of the governing board when the Board of Trade endorsed the program of the Immigration Restriction League of Boston, which called for the use of a literacy test as a means of excluding undesirables from southern and eastern Europe. During the years that Rauh was active in Democratic party politics, he was suggested as a possible mayoral and, later, gubernatorial candidate. His brother Henry was a member of the Indianapolis Common Council from 1893 to 1895.[29]

The magnitude of Samuel Rauh's influence in the city's economic life is perhaps best symbolized by the special three-page section in the *Indianapolis Star* in honor of his seventy-fifth birthday. Surrounding a large photograph of Rauh and a laudatory biography are congratulatory advertisements from the many companies in which he had an interest and dozens of other firms which did business with his many enterprises.[30]

Although Samuel Rauh's importance in the city's economic history is unquestionable, he was less prominent in the leadership of the Jewish community. An organizer and at one time president of the Indianapolis Club, the Jewish men's social club at 2312 North Meridian, he was also a member of the building committee for IHC's new synagogue at 10th and Delaware, and served as chairman of the Indianapolis Association for the Relief of Jewish War Sufferers during World War I. His wife, Emma (1861–1934), a Hoosier native, daughter of Charles Falk Sterne and Eugenia Fries Sterne of Peru, Indiana, was also more dedicated to civic than sectarian causes. She did, however, sit on the first board of the Jewish Federation as the representative of the Nathan Morris House, the south side Jewish settlement house established in 1904. But it was to their adopted city that they were most devoted, and in 1928 the Rauhs donated their family home at 3023 North Meridian to the city, "an offering . . . as part payment of [our] debt for the opportunities Indianapolis has given us." The home became the site of a branch of the public library known as the Rauh Memorial Library until it was torn down in the mid-seventies to make room for the expansion of the Children's Museum. Samuel and Emma Rauh had three children. Their son, Charles Sterne Rauh] (1883–1956), was president of the Belt Railroad and Stock Yards from 1929 to 1956.[31]

Flora Mayer Rauh (1870–1959), the wife of Henry Rauh, remained active in Jewish causes longer than her sister-in-law. She was president of the Nathan Morris House from 1907 to 1909 and served on the board of the Jewish Federation from 1905 to 1911. By 1914, however, she had embraced Christian Science—one of a small group of Indianapolis Jews to do so—and no longer worked for Jewish charities and settlements but for such organizations as the Indianapolis Civic League, the Boys' Club, Fairview Settlement, and the Children's Aid Society. Henry Rauh, however, maintained a lifelong commitment to Jewish causes. Before the Jewish Federation was established, he solicited funds for the Montefiore Home for the Aged in Cleveland; from 1905 until his death in 1922, he was a member of the board of governors of the Jewish Federation serving as treasurer for many years.[32]

By the late nineteenth century most German Jews were small businessmen. The movement of Jews into the professions—a phenomenon of later years—was barely perceptible. Yet, as early as the 1870s, a small number of the native-born sons of German Jewish immigrants were entering the professions, several achieving local prominence in their fields.

Louis Newberger (1852–1916) and Nathan Morris (1857–1903) were well-known attorneys in Indianapolis, founders of one of the pioneer commercial law firms of the city. Newberger, a native of Grant County, Indiana, attended North Western Christian University, later Butler University, graduating in 1872. After reading law in the office of William Wallace, Newberger opened his own law office and shortly afterward joined Nathan Morris in establishing the firm of Morris and Newberger. The firm, which represented some of the state's largest business concerns, later became Morris, Newberger and Curtis with the addition of James B. Curtis as a third partner.[33]

Nathan Morris was born in the gold-mining district of California. His father was from Prussia, his mother from England. The couple had married in London in 1845 and shortly afterward emigrated to America. After two years in New York City they pressed on to California, arriving there in 1849, the year gold was discovered in the Sierra foothills. In 1871 the family moved to Indianapolis, and Morris entered the service of McKeen and Company, wood engravers. In 1875 he took up the study of law in the office of Chapman, Hammond and Hawes. Morris graduated from Central Law School and was admitted to the bar in 1877. He remained in the firm until the death of General George H. Chapman, one of the partners, at which time he formed a partnership with Louis Newberger.[34]

Both partners were active in civic and Jewish affairs. Newberger was president of B'nai B'rith District Grand Lodge No. 2. He served on the board of the Jewish Federation from its founding in 1905 until 1912, and before that he collected funds for the Jewish Chautauqua Society and the National Farm School. In addition to memberships in the Columbia Club, the Chamber of Commerce, and IHC, Newberger helped organize and was first president of the Indianapolis professional baseball club. In 1914, two years before his death at the age of sixty-four, Newberger married Parthenia Nicholson. (One detects a certain ambivalence in Newberger's choosing to marry a non-Jew but waiting until he was well into his sixties to do so. His partner Nathan Morris never married.)[35]

Although Nathan Morris was well known in legal circles, it was the tragic circumstances of his death that brought him a kind of posthumous fame. In the early morning hours of Easter Sunday, April 12, 1903, a fire broke out in the two-story brick house on North Alabama Street which Morris, a bachelor, shared with his sister, Rebecca, her husband, Dr. Joseph Haas, and their children. Before the fire department could reach the home, it was engulfed in flames. All of the family members managed to survive the conflagration, except for the Haases' twelve-year-old son, Frank, and Nathan Morris. It was believed Morris died trying to rescue his young nephew.[36]

The touching story of a bachelor uncle giving his life to save his nephew appealed to the Victorian sentiments of many of the citizens of Indianapolis. The crowd at the joint funeral of uncle and nephew was so large that it overflowed the IHC sanctuary, spilling out onto the streets. Numerous civic associations composed memorials to Nathan Morris. The memorial prepared by the Indianapolis Bar Association to its deceased president illustrates the impression Morris's death left on his contemporaries. "It was his generous consideration for others . . . which, on a dreadful Easter morning, excluded from his mind all base consideration for himself and moved him to give his life . . . for . . . his sister and her children. . . ."[37]

In addition to the verbal acknowledgements of Morris's selfless act, two more lasting memorials to Nathan Morris were established. Morris had been eulogized as a man charitable to the poor and concerned with their welfare. In 1904, a year after his death, a group of Jewish women established Nathan Morris House, a settlement house on the south side for the Jewish poor of Indianapolis. (The activities of Nathan Morris House will be discussed in the next chapter.) A second memorial to Nathan Morris was an elaborate fountain constructed at the intersection of Massachusetts Avenue, Park Avenue, and Walnut Street, a gift to the city from Morris's legal colleagues across the country. Henry Wollman, a New York City attorney, organized the fountain memorial, which was completed in 1909. Although the city agreed to maintain the fountain in perpetuity, the increasing volume of motor traffic at this busy intersection forced the city to raze the fountain in later years.[38]

Other early Jewish lawyers in Indianapolis included Ralph Bamberger (1871–1947), son of Herman and Caroline Bamberger, and Isidore Feibleman (1873–1954), son of Charles and Rachel Feibleman. These two Indianapolis-born sons of German immigrants were graduates of Indianapolis High School No. 1 (later Shortridge High School), Indiana University, and Indiana Law School. Their firm, Bamberger and Feibleman, founded in 1898, is one of the oldest in the state.[39]

By the late nineteenth century Jews were also represented in the profession of medicine. Alfred Jaeger (1876 or 1877–1965), a native New Yorker, was a surgeon and obstetrician-gynecologist. He was active in professional medical organizations, holding such offices as president of the Indianapolis Medical Association, chairman of the Indiana Medical Association's surgical section, and director of the Department of Women's Diseases of the Public Health Center. Active in Jewish causes as well, Jaeger was at one time president of the local B'nai B'rith chapter, vice-president of the Jewish Welfare Fund, and served for nineteen years on the board of the Jewish Family Services Society.[40]

Edgar F. Kiser (1880 or 1881–1958), younger brother of banker Sol S. Kiser, was a graduate of the Indiana University Medical

School, where he later taught as clinical professor of medicine and lecturer on the history of medicine. Kiser was at one time superintendent of the City Hospital Dispensary, which was located in the ground floor of police headquarters. Before the First World War it was the city's first-aid station for accident victims and emergency cases in the downtown area, predating the establishment of the ambulance and emergency room system.[41]

In the profession of journalism there was one well-known Jewish practitioner during the period. Max R. Hyman (1859–1927), a native of Edinburg, Indiana, was a reporter for the *Indianapolis Herald*, editor of *Hyman's Handbook*, publisher of *The Centennial History of Indiana*, and at the time of his death an editor for the *Indianapolis Star*.[42]

The careers of the more prominent members of the German Jewish community reviewed here indicate the extent of the achievements of the early Jewish community. Though Indianapolis Jews constituted a small minority in a growing city, many moved easily into the economic life of the city without appearing to threaten the economic or social well-being of the larger community. Before 1920 Indianapolis citizens saw no need for restricted neighborhoods, restricted clubs, or professional school quotas. These obstacles to advancement appeared primarily in the years after World War I and hindered a later generation of south side, eastern European Jews. However, while wealthy Jews lived where other wealthy citizens lived and belonged to some of the same clubs and associations—the Columbia Club, the Commercial Club, Das Deutsche Haus (later called German House, and, after 1917, the Athenaeum)—the process of self-selection kept Jews out of most country clubs and some social clubs. Even the most highly assimilated Jews (as we noted in the previous chapter, even those Jews who had married non-Jews) retained a strong social tie to the Jewish community. This accounts for the numerous Jewish social clubs established in the 1860s and 1870s. For the highly acculturated Jews—the William Blocks, the Leopold Strausses, the Samuel Rauhs—these Jewish social clubs represented their most important link to the Jewish community. First at the Americus Club (founded 1892), and later at the Indianapolis Club (founded 1908),* which

---

*Note, in both instances, the absence of any Jewish identification in the names given to what were both specifically Jewish clubs.

became Broadmoor Country Club in 1925, these men could relax and share their leisure hours with others just like themselves. Few if any Jews sought to join non-Jewish clubs; they believed they would not feel comfortable there, preferring to socialize with other highly acculturated Jews like themselves. Instead, they organized their own clubs, patterned after those of the Protestant elite. As long as Jews maintained their own clubs and the invisible fences around certain non-Jewish social clubs were not breached, no real fences needed to be erected. The *Red Book of Indianapolis*, Indianapolis's closest equivalent to the *Social Register*, listed the city's Jewish social clubs along with non-Jewish clubs and included Jews in its list of leading families. The days on which Jewish dowagers were "at home" to receive visitors were listed along with the "at home" days of non-Jewish women.[43]

In the leading cities of the eastern seaboard—New York, Philadelphia, and Boston—this was not the case. As immigration from southern and eastern Europe began to rise in the 1880s, members of the wealthy Protestant establishment began to mark themselves off into closed groups, excluding even the most successful Catholics and Jews, along with recent immigrants. They formed patriotic societies such as the Daughters of the American Revolution and anti-immigration organizations such as the Immigration Restriction League; established select country clubs (The Country Club in Brookline, Massachusetts, in 1882 was the first American country club); and eagerly subscribed to the *Social Register*, which first appeared in New York City in 1888. This list of fewer than two thousand families, "comprising an accurate and careful list of [society's] members," conspicuously failed to include a single Jewish name. It was as if the Schiffs, the Guggenheims, and the Warburgs simply had not existed. Indianapolis society, however, did not feel threatened by the likes of the Rauhs, the Blocks, and the Kahns. The Jewish community was small and, if not native-born, at least "westernized." Moreover, there was no ominous, growing community of impoverished "foreign" Jews to raise concern.* While Indianapolis Jewry may have been excluded from in-

---

*During the years of mass migration, while the Jewish population of Indianapolis remained a fairly steady 1 percent of the city's population, the proportion of Jews in New York City increased dramatically. Between 1880 and 1890 the Jewish proportion of the population more than doubled from 4 to 9 percent and nearly doubled again between 1900 and 1910 from 11 to 23 percent. *Encyclopaedia Judaica*, s.v. "New York City."

timate social gatherings, the success and influence of many of its members were not ignored but were acknowledged and recognized by the general community.[44]

Although their social worlds may have been different, the German Jewish merchant community shared with the Protestant elite a concern in the development of civic order for their city. Moreover, German Jewish merchants felt they had a responsibility to help maintain social stability which could only advance economic growth. By the first part of the twentieth century, German Jews began appearing on the boards of a variety of civic and charitable enterprises designed to promote social order. Mayer Messing (1843–1930), rabbi of IHC from 1867 to 1907, served on the board of the Fresh Air Mission, the Indiana Red Cross, and was first president of the Indianapolis Humane Society. His assistant and successor, Morris M. Feuerlicht (1879–1959), who served IHC from 1904 to 1946, pursued similar interests. He was president of the Children's Aid Society for twenty-one years. He was later the first Jew appointed to the State Board of Charities and Corrections, serving on that board from 1920 to 1931. Edward A. Kahn (1875–1943) was active in the first War Chest drive in 1918 and headed the local Liberty Loan drive. A founder of the Community Fund in 1920, the successor to the War Chest, Kahn was president of the Fund in 1931 and campaign chairman in 1932. Charles B. Sommers (1873–1941), another Indianapolis businessman and Cincinnati native, was the chairman of the first War Chest drive.[45]

Other Jews, although limited in number, served in the political sphere. As was mentioned previously, Leon Kahn served on the Indianapolis Common Council for eight years between 1869 and 1881. He was followed by Henry Rauh, who served from 1893 to 1895. Ralph Bamberger in 1903 and Aaron Wolfson in 1917 and 1919 won election to the Indiana General Assembly. Although never elected to office himself, Leopold G. Rothschild (1871–1924), nicknamed the "Baron," became the political confidant of Senator Albert J. Beveridge and his most trusted advisor. In return for his loyalty, Beveridge secured for Rothschild the post of collector of customs at Indianapolis in 1906. Earlier, in 1903, Rothschild had been appointed assistant United States attorney general by attorney general Charles W. Miller. In the same period Leopold Levy (1838–1905), a German Jewish immigrant who began his career as a peddler in Peru, Indiana, was elected state treasurer on the Republican ticket and held office from 1899 to 1903.[46]

The question of whether German Jewry suffered from a more personal kind of social discrimination, whether they felt excluded from the socially and politically elite non-Jewish circles in the city is difficult to answer because writers rarely address themselves to this question. One contemporary source seems to indicate that anti-Semitism in Indianapolis was perceived as a barrier to success. John Judah, the son of a Jewish father—Samuel Judah—and a non-Jewish mother—Harriet Brandon Judah—did not consider himself a Jew but had a Jewish surname. Apparently fearing that this surname might act as a barrier to his own sons' success, he solicited his friends' advice on the matter. In 1887 Judah wrote to a friend in New York, J. B. Cleaver, asking if Cleaver thought his sons should change their name. After extolling the virtues of "the name of the mighty tribe" of Judah, Cleaver concluded:

> There is but one thing stronger—more relentless, fuller of purpose than your Kingly blood; and that is, *Christian* Prejudice. Who would contend with that, enters life's race too heavily handicapped, ever to pass the wire a winner. . . . Much as I despise and hate this Christian prejudice, I confess its power. . . .

Cleaver suggested that Judah's sons exchange their Jewish surname for the maiden name of their (non-Jewish) mother. John Judah seems to have been convinced of the argument. By 1895 his sons were going by the name of Brandon, the surname of their paternal grandmother.[47]

Another more benign description of the world of Jewish-Christian relations appears in the high school diaries of Claude G. Bowers (1878–1958), a well-known journalist who served as ambassador to Spain and then Chile during the presidency of Franklin D. Roosevelt. Bowers kept a diary during his years at Indianapolis High School No. 1 that reveals a high degree of unrestricted social intercourse between Jewish and non-Jewish students. In 1898 Bowers's high school classmates elected Sara Messing, the daughter of Rabbi Messing, and Abraham Cronbach, who later became a well-known Reform rabbi, as their commencement speakers. Jewish students participated in school clubs and worked on the school's prestigious newspaper, *The Echo*. Apparently the admittance of

Jews into social clubs continued at university. When one of Bowers's Jewish friends, Lawrence Davis, later an Indianapolis attorney, began at Butler University in 1897, he joined Phi Delta Theta fraternity, declaring proudly to Bowers that it was "the same that [William Henry] Harrison, Joe Blackburn of Ky, Ex-Vice-President [Adlai E.] Stevenson and other celebrated men belong to." Bowers himself had a number of close Jewish friends. He "called on" Sara Messing and held long philosophical discussions with Cronbach. Yet he apparently considered that these Jews were not typical of most Jews and that is why he could befriend them. He described Cronbach, the brilliant son of impoverished immigrants from Posen, as "a Jew but one of an exalted type," a rather backhanded compliment. Cronbach, reported Bowers, was infatuated with a classmate, Eunice Curtis. However, after he presented Miss Curtis with a poem he composed in her honor, Mrs. Cronbach informed her son that "she objected to his having any intercourse with an [sic] Gentile." According to Bowers, Cronbach then stopped calling on Eunice Curtis, an action which Bowers found "strangely sentimental for one like Abbie." Apparently Bowers could not understand this allegiance to particularism in someone who was as liberal and open-minded as his friend Cronbach. However, while there is no record of the Curtis family objecting to a Jewish boy calling on their daughter, the bar that Mrs. Cronbach put up to the continuation of the relationship was probably welcomed by both families. The barriers—both real and psychological—that prevented completely unencumbered social integration served two different sets of needs, Jewish and non-Jewish.[48]

The question of exclusion, as we have noted, is partially one of perception. North side Jewry may not have felt excluded from certain clubs and circles because they had no desire to participate in them, preferring the activities of their own clubs and societies. By the turn of the century the German Jewish organizational network included not only the synagogue, IHC, but also clubs for women, men, and young people.

By the 1880s the slow transition to Reform which had begun in IHC twenty years earlier was completed. Now the issue facing the congregation was the problem of the synagogue's location. The neighborhood around Market and East streets was changing. Distressed by the proximity of brothels and bawdy houses to the

synagogue, the board appointed Henry Rauh and two others to investigate ways of "suppressing" the houses and other "nuisances."
There were other problems as well. Due to the growth of the congregation, seating in the sanctuary was now inadequate, and,
perhaps more importantly, many of the congregants had moved
north to more prosperous neighborhoods a considerable distance
from the synagogue, a problem that would eventually face every
Jewish institution in the city.[49]

Although the board appointed several committees to look into
the matter of a new home for the congregation, no action was
taken. In 1897 the Hungarian Hebrew Ohev Zedeck Congregation
offered IHC $10,000 for the Market Street temple, "including Pews,
Chandelliers, carpets, furnaces and all fixtures in basement." An
Orthodox synagogue founded in 1884 by a group of Hungarian
immigrants, the *hungarische shul* (as it was known) was the third
synagogue established in the city. (Sharah Tefilla, the *polische shul*,
was the second.) The board decided to accept the offer of the Hungarian congregation, and in 1899 IHC purchased a lot at 10th and
Delaware streets, where they dedicated their new synagogue on
November 2, 1899.[50]

Isaac Mayer Wise traveled from Cincinnati for a third time to
participate in the dedication ceremonies of a new Indianapolis
synagogue, this one a building in the "classic-renaissance" style, a
popular choice for late nineteenth-century synagogue design. Constructed of Indiana limestone and designed by the architectural
firm of Vonnegut and Bohn, the building was described as having
an "imposing [front] arch . . . of large dimensions . . . [which gave]
the Temple a dignified, refined, and monumental appearance,"
characteristics which appealed to the middle-class sensibilities of
the congregants. But even the members of this Reform congregation were unsure about the desirability of installing a stained-glass
window depicting the descent of Moses from Mount Sinai on the
east side of the sanctuary above the entrance. A donation from
Emma Eckhouse, in memory of her husband, Moses, the stained-
glass window too strongly evoked church architecture for some
members; others were disturbed by the depiction of Moses, believing that it violated the prohibition against the making of images.
To resolve the matter a committee wrote to Isaac Mayer Wise for a
ruling, and he gave the disputed window his blessing. Rabbi Morris

M. Feuerlicht later claimed that it was the first window depicting a human figure to be installed in an American synagogue.[51]

Mayer Messing, who had been appointed rabbi of IHC in 1867, continued ministering to his growing congregation, but by 1901 the burden of work was becoming too much for one man. For the next few years the board discussed hiring an assistant rabbi to help with the High Holy Days. Finally, in 1904, the post of associate rabbi was offered to a man who would have a profound influence on the Indianapolis Jewish community: Morris M. Feuerlicht, then serving a congregation in Lafayette, Indiana.[52]

Morris Feuerlicht was born in Tokay, Hungary, and came to the United States as an infant. Son of Rabbi Jacob Feuerlicht (1856–1920), who was ordained at the *yeshivah* in Pressburg, Hungary, Morris Feuerlicht spent his childhood in Boston, Massachusetts. He was graduated from the University of Cincinnati and then in 1901 from the Hebrew Union College. His first rabbinic post was in Lafayette, Indiana, where he served until he took the position of associate rabbi at IHC in 1904. Four years later after forty years as rabbi of IHC, Mayer Messing resigned, and Morris Feuerlicht became the senior rabbi, a position which he too would hold for forty years.[53]

Feuerlicht exemplified the kind of rabbi many Reform congregations were seeking—an American-trained rabbi who could be their spokesman to the city's gentile elite. Feuerlicht undertook this assignment with zeal. He became a prominent local figure who was often in the public eye. A popular lecturer, Feuerlicht was in constant demand as a speaker for high schools, service clubs, women's clubs, professional societies, and churches throughout the state. When visiting dignitaries, Jewish or non-Jewish, came to town, he frequently helped to host them. When Feuerlicht debated Clarence Darrow in 1928 on the topic "Is Man a Machine?" before an audience of 8,500, the press unanimously declared Feuerlicht the winner. Feuerlicht's services came into play not only as the representative of the Jews, but in other capacities as well. Because of his gentle humor and reputation for even-handedness, Feuerlicht was several times called on to mediate deadlocked labor disputes. In his half century of service to IHC, Feuerlicht became a force to be reckoned with in the Jewish community. If a project had his blessing, it would very likely succeed.[54]

In 1860 Joseph Solomon, an English cigarmaker, and Sarah Harris were married in what was reported as the "first public Jewish ceremony in this city." Governor Ashbell Willard and the Rev. August Bessonies of St. John's Catholic Church were among the guests. In this picture taken some years later, Joseph Solomon is seated on his wife's right. (IHS).

Eleventh Annual **Purim** Masquerade Ball.

OF THE

Indianapolis Hebrew Congregation

MONDAY EVENING, MARCH 22d, 1875,

At **Mozart Hall.**

Yourself and Lady are respectfully invited to attend.

COMMITTEE OF ARRANGEMENTS.

Jos. Schwabacher.   Henry Rosenthal.
Sol. Mossler.   D. Loewer.   Louis Dessar.

COMMITTEE OF INVITATION.

J. Mitchell.   Jos. Mayer.   Jos. Solomon.
J. B. Dessar.   M. Griesheimer.

RECEPTION COMMITTEE.

Leon Kahn.   Jos. Schwabacher.   Sol. Mossler.

FLOOR COMMITTEE.

John Lyon.   A. Selig.   Sam Kauh.
L. Manheimer.   Leopold Strauss.

MUSIC BY PROF. VOST'S FULL ORCHESTRA.

TICKETS, $2.00.

Baker, Schmidlap & Co., Printers.

Invitation to a Purim masquerade ball sponsored by the Indianapolis Hebrew Congregation in 1875. (IHS)

In 1899 Isaac Mayer Wise dedicated this building at 10th and Delaware for the Indianapolis Hebrew Congregation. (IHS)

The Eagle Clothing Company opened on Washington Street near Meridian in 1853. It was purchased in 1871 by Leopold Strauss, who had begun there as a clerk in 1866. He changed the name to L. Strauss and Co. In this picture from the 1880s, note a competitor, Famous Eagle Clothing, two doors away. (ISL)

William H. Block's first Indianapolis store opened in 1896 at 7–9 East Washington Street. The store remained at this location until 1911 when it moved to Market and Illinois. (ISL)

Congregation Sharah Tefilla, the *polische shul*, constructed this synagogue with its classic front and ionic columns at South Meridian and Merrill streets in 1910. (IHS)

The founders of Sharah Tefilla were among the first eastern European immigrants to settle in Indianapolis. (IHS)

FOUNDERS OF SHARAH TEFILLA

לזוכר עולם

ANSEL WOLF

MOSE GOLDSTEIN

HENRY MARKS, Sec'y. and Treas.

SOLOMON SAGALOWSKY

BENNETT GOLDBERG, Vice-Pres.

JACOB EFROYMSON

ISAAC SAGALOWSKY

JACOB GROSSMAN, Vice-Pres.

ADOLPH EBNER

Kahn Tailoring Company employees at their annual picnic at Broad
Ripple about 1906 or 1907. Most of the workers were Jewish immigrants. In this picture many of them are waving small American
flags. (ISL)

Members of the local chapter of the Order of Brith Abraham, col-
loquially known as the "hungarische group," at the Monument Circle in 1911. (IHS)

Isaac Elhanan Neustadt, Lithuanian immigrant, rabbi of Sharah Tefilla, Knesses Israel, and Ohev Zedeck, and founder in 1911 of a city-wide Talmud Torah, United Hebrew Schools. The school is known today as the Bureau of Jewish Education. (IHS)

Samuel A. Katz, rabbi of Congregation Sharah Tefilla from 1923 to 1949, was the first Orthodox rabbi to remain in the community for more than a few years. In 1926 he helped organize the Vaad Hakehillos. (IHS)

Knesses Israel, the *russische shul*, constructed this building at 1023 South Meridian Street in 1923. (IHS)

חנוכת הבית פון
כנסת ישראל קאנגרעגיישאן

א הערליכע איינלאדונג פאר אינדיאנאפאליסער אידען
אויף א היילינע שמחה, די איינוויייהונג פון אונזער נייע שוהל !

ווילקאמען אין נאמען פון נאם ווינשען מיר אלע ברכות צו אייך פון נאמעס הוי,
איהר ווערט היערדורך איינגעלאדען צו זיין ביי דעם

חנוך פון אונזער נייער שול

וועלכע האט זיך געענדיגט בויען

וואס וועט שטאטפינדען זונטאג, 26, טען אגוסט, 2 אזר
אין 1023 סאום מערידיען

אלע מיטגליעדער און פריינדע ווערען הערצליך איינגעלאדען צו זיין ביי דער
שמחה.   די פיינסטע מוזיק.   די בעסטע רעדנערס וועלען אדרעסירען.

דער טאג וועט בליבען ביי יעדען איינעם אן אייביגע היילינע אנדיינקונג.

אכטוגספאל, די קאמיטע.

The Congregation Keneses Israel
WILL DEDICATE
Its New Synagogue, which has been recently completed.

The Ceremonies will take place
Sunday, August 26,th, 2 P. M.
at 1023 S. Meridian

1923.
Rifkind Chicago
M.M. Feuerlicht—Speaker
dedicating

Prominent Speakers will address.   Good Music is promised.

All friends as well as members of the Congregation are urged to attend.

Hirschfeld Printing Co., 410-412 W. Court St., Cincinnati, O.   THE COMMITTEE.

Poster in English and Yiddish announcing the dedication of Knesses
Israel's new building in 1923. (IHS)

An early Boys Club basketball team. The coach, manager, and several of the players were Jewish. (IHS)

Jewish servicemen and Jewish Federation workers and friends pose outside the Communal Building in 1918. Samuel B. Kaufman, superintendent of the Jewish Federation from 1908 to 1921, is seated to the left of the flag. (IHS)

Children at the Communal Building listen as Mrs. Andrews of the Indianapolis Public Library tells them a story, ca. 1920. (IHS)

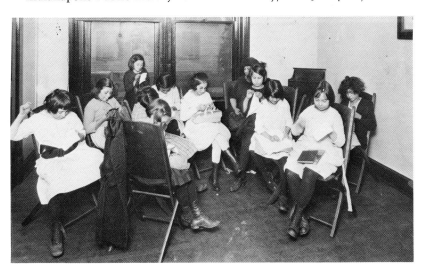

A sewing class at the Communal Building, ca. 1920. (IHS)

Children enjoying a milk break at Camp Ida Wineman, the Jewish Federation's fresh air camp, in the early 1920s. The camp was located on the White River at Broad Ripple. (IHS)

This picture of two north side couples departing for an afternoon party dates from the 1920s. (IHS)

This picture of north side couples enjoying an afternoon party also dates from the 1920s. (IHS)

As soon as they were able, most Jewish immigrants left the crowded, narrow streets of the south side for the bucolic, tree-lined avenues of the north side. Members of the younger generation of north side Jews at a Pals Club dance at the Indianapolis Club in the 1920s. (IHS)

G. A. Efroymson, business and civic leader, president of Real Silk
Hosiery Mills, was president of the Jewish Federation for almost
twenty-five years. He also served as president of IHC from 1902 to
1905. (IHS)

Like many liberal ministers and rabbis of the Progressive era, Morris Feuerlicht used his ministry as a platform for social action. Reform Judaism in general stressed the importance of the teachings of prophetic Judaism over rabbinic Judaism, and the directive to "seek justice" struck a sympathetic chord in the age of the social gospel. Feuerlicht actively encouraged his congregants to devote themselves to social service as he did. He influenced almost every organization established by the native Jewish community to aid the impoverished arrivals from eastern Europe. Feuerlicht drafted the bylaws and constitution of the Jewish Federation, helped organize the local committee of the Industrial Removal Office, and helped the Sephardim purchase their own cemetery and synagogue. In 1896 a group of women, all members of IHC, organized the Indianapolis section of the National Council of Jewish Women (NCJW). Primarily a religious study group, the organization also attempted some social service projects. In their first year, for example, they organized "an industrial school for [forty] poor girls . . . teaching darning, patching and making over clothes." After a few years, however, the group began to founder. In December 1904 the local branch reorganized, and with Feuerlicht's help and encouragement, the women developed a strong social orientation to the group.[55]

While German Jewish women helpd the immigrant poor and worried about the white slave trade at Council meetings, their husbands and brothers pursued charitable, social, and cultural interests at B'nai B'rith lodge meetings. The oldest local B'nai B'rith lodge, Abraham Lodge No. 58, was founded in 1864. In the 1880s Esther Lodge No. 323 was established and the two groups coexisted until they merged in 1907–1908 to form the Indianapolis Lodge. The Indianapolis members of B'nai B'rith raised funds and participated in the organization's national projects. Before the era of mass migration from eastern Europe, these were primarily orphanages such as the Cleveland Jewish Orphan Home, old age homes, and hospitals, such as the National Jewish Hospital in Denver for tuberculosis patients. After 1881, in response to the increasing numbers of arriving Jewish immigrants, B'nai B'rith sponsored English and Americanization classes, trade schools, and relief programs.[56]

All was not earnest and serious charitable work, however.

Elaborate entertainments were an important part of the B'nai B'rith program, and the Jewish lodge members were apparently as fond of the minstrel show as their non-Jewish counterparts. Esther Lodge, the younger and livelier of the two lodges, put on at least two minstrel shows at German House. For the second one, in December 1906, they published a four-page "newspaper," the *Schmooz Gazette,* combining Jewish vaudeville jokes, minstrel jokes, a spoof of F. P. Dunne's famous "Mr. Dooley"—"Mr. Dooley on the B'nai B'rith Minstrels"—and articles on the activities of B'nai B'rith.[57]

A homegrown version of B'nai B'rith—the Montefiore Society—which attracted a slightly younger group of men, also developed at this time. In 1885 a group of about ten boys ages eleven to fifteen who were native-born sons of German Jewish immigrants met after Sunday School (they all attended IHC) at William Emden's house and organized the Youths' Social Society. The club was to be devoted to educational and charitable activities, and its first program was a charity benefit on January 10, 1886, featuring poetic recitations by Ralph Bamberger, Jacob Kaufman, and others, and closing with a magic lantern show. The society established a small library, regularly debated current issues (capital punishment and women's suffrage) and religious issues (confirmation and Sunday services), sponsored musical and literary programs, and published a journal, the *Youths' Social Journal.* Through charity balls and public picnics, the Youths' Social Society raised funds which they regularly contributed to the Cleveland Jewish Orphan Asylum, the Montefiore Home, and IHC.[58]

As the members of the Youths' Social Society matured, their plans for the club became more ambitious. In 1893 the members attempted to organize a YMHA (Young Men's Hebrew Association), renting rooms in the When Block. Within six months the experiment had failed, but the Youths' Social Society lived on, transforming itself into the Montefiore Society in September 1893.[59]

A major undertaking of the Montefiore Society was the sponsorship of an annual public subscription lecture series at Tomlinson Hall. The series, which began in 1894, featured speakers on Jewish and non-Jewish topics, dramatic readings, and musical programs. The first year, for example, the series included a lecture by Rabbi Joseph Krauskopf of Philadelphia entitled "Only a Jew," a reading from David Copperfield by Leland T. Powers, and a concert by the New York Philharmonic Club. In 1895 the proceeds from the series were given to the city's free kindergarten movement. The society published a literary magazine, the *Montefiore Magazine*, which lasted for a year (1893–1894), and they seem to have been as fond of producing minstrel shows as were the B'nai B'rith men. Several of the participants in the Montefiore Society's "Show of Minstrelsy" at Männerchor Hall in October, 1896 (a benefit for the Hebrew Ladies Benevolent Society), appeared in the B'nai B'rith minstrel show ten years later.[60]

A few months after the Youths' Social Society became the Montefiore Society, Samuel J. Steinberg (d. 1903), one of the group's founders, launched an ambitious publishing effort. The *Jewish Youth* was to be a monthly magazine devoted to "Judaism and Jewish youth." The first issue appeared in February 1894, and it and subsequent issues contained articles about Israel, great figures in Jewish history, stories and poems with Jewish themes, news about YMHAs in other cities, and social news of Indianapolis Jewish youth. The *Jewish Youth* did not survive for more than a few issues, but it documented the activities of a confident, native-born generation, forging a new Jewish identity and new Jewish institutions in the American Midwest. The Montefiore Society lasted only a few years longer, until about 1898. The first organization to sponsor serious discussions of Jewish topics for the general community, the Montefiore Society pioneered in its lecture series, which combined lectures on both Jewish and non-Jewish themes. The society's proceeds were dispensed in an equally even-handed manner—to both Jewish and non-Jewish charities. After the demise of the Montefiore Society, lectures such as these did not once again become a regular feature of Jewish life until the establishment of the Open Forum series sponsored by the Kirshbaum Center in the late 1920s.[61]

In many ways the Montefiore Society symbolized the values and accomplishments of a generation. Its members, the first American-born generation of Indianapolis Jews, moved in a thoroughly American world. From their rabbi and synagogue the society's members learned to channel their Jewishness into the support of social and charitable causes. As the children of the second generation, they inherited from their parents a commitment to civic responsibility. To an observer, the Montefiore Society and other

German Jewish organizations of the late nineteenth century may not have seemed more concerned about the Jewish poor than any other needy group in the city. This, however, was soon to change. As the immigrant Jewish community began to expand rapidly after 1900, native and immigrant Jews found themselves drawn closer and closer to one another until each group was irrevocably changed by the other.

 III

Immigrants and Natives

THE SOUTH SIDE JEWISH COMMUNITY

1881—1920

"THE JEWISH POPULATION of Indianapolis numbers 250," reported the Russian Jewish newspaper *Ha-Meliz* in 1884, yet "even though the Jewish community is so small, it is divided into two camps—the Orthodox and the Reform. The Orthodox are Russian and Polish Jews who are strictly Orthodox [and] live, crowded and impoverished, in a small street in the southern part of the city." The German Reform Jews, on the other hand, lived "in ivory towers, in the northern part of the city, in the wealthy section inhabited by the aristocracy." They were among the city's major retailers, were active in civic life, and included lawyers, doctors, and judges. Rather than spend their money on their children's Jewish education, however, they spent it on their secular education. *Ha-Meliz*'s correspondent commented that in Indianapolis he "saw for the first time people of twenty and twenty-five who did not know how to pray in Hebrew." Reflecting on his visit to Indianapolis, with its highly Americanized community of middle-class Reform Jews and its small struggling community of impoverished Orthodox immigrants, the correspondent could only conclude that there was "no hope for Judaism in the next generation in this city."[1]

This reaction was not unique. In the early 1880s the dominance in America of the German Jewish community and Reform Judaism seemed complete. In 1883 when the first class of the Hebrew Union College was graduated nearly every synagogue of importance in the United States belonged to the Union of American Hebrew Congregations, the federation of Reform synagogues. No one could foresee that within ten years the eastern European immigrant communities that were taking root in cities across America would outnumber those of their German brethren and bring new life and ideas to the American Jewish community.

In 1880 there were approximately 250,000 Jews in America, most of them immigrants or children of immigrants from central Europe who identified with Reform Judaism. By 1900 approximately 500,000 immigrants from eastern Europe had entered the country, and by the First World War there were about 2 million Jewish newcomers. In all by 1924 when restrictive legislation put an end to mass immigration 2.25 million Jewish immigrants from eastern Europe had settled in America. The new arrivals completely engulfed the older German Jewish community, leaving the latter a tiny minority in the American Jewish population, although a highly successful and socially prestigious one.[2]

There had been some Jewish immigration from eastern Europe to America before this period, and in the 1870s it was fairly substantial. But in 1881 it became a mass movement that continued unabated until interrupted by the First World War and then halted by the immigration restriction laws of the 1920s. In 1881 a wave of pogroms and a set of harsh new anti-Jewish decrees in Russia made economic survival, always precarious, now even more difficult for the great mass of Jews in the Pale of Settlement. Hundreds of thousands of them concluded that a decent life for themselves and their families was impossible in Russia and their only alternative was to start a new life in America, the *goldene medinah* (the golden land).

Because the German Jewish immigration had coincided with the period of westward expansion, German Jewish communities had grown up all across the face of America, including the South, the Midwest, and the Far West. By the late nineteenth century, however, this geographic expansion was coming to an end. The new centers of growth in America were the industrial cities, especially those in the East. And it was in the cities that eastern European Jews settled, many of them finding jobs in the rapidly developing garment industry. Within a short time they became a highly visible minority, characterized by habits and customs that were quite different from those of the established Jewish community.

Between middle-class German Jews and newly arrived immigrants there were bound to be profound disagreements and tensions. Even the languages they used were different. While German and native Jews spoke English and, in some cases, German, the immigrants spoke Yiddish. In the eyes of the Americanized native community the immigrants appeared obsessively pious, with their Old World beards, dozens of religious prohibitions and noisy *shuls*. To the immigrants who had been raised in the universe of traditional Judaism, the Reform Jews appeared not much different from Gentiles, with their churchlike temples with organs and choirs, clean-shaven ministers, and ignorance of many Jewish customs and practices. Native Jews regarded the nonreligious immigrants with even more hostility, considering them a motley mixture of socialists, communists, anarchists, Zionists, and trade unionists. These secularized immigrants in turn often saw the native Jews as capitalist exploiters and, in many instances, "bosses," since many immigrants found employment in the needle trades, initially dominated by German Jews.

Given these differences, it was not going to be easy to integrate the newcomers into the existing communal institutions. They would not have felt comfortable joining Reform temples, B'nai B'rith lodges or the Council of Jewish Women, nor were they welcome. In Indianapolis, as in other cities, they settled in their own neighborhood and quickly established their own synagogues, charities, benevolent societies, and social organizations.

Of the hundreds of thousands of eastern European Jews who emigrated to America, most remained in New York City and other east coast centers. Relatively few ventured west; those who did probably went to join relatives who had previously settled in midwestern or western communities. The number who settled in Indianapolis was relatively small in comparison to those who made their homes in New York, Boston, Baltimore, and Philadelphia. Nevertheless, their presence changed the face of the Indianapolis Jewish community and of the city as well. While no immigrant group in Indianapolis was particularly large in the early twentieth century, the Jews formed the largest foreign-born community. However, its exact size at various times is difficult to ascertain. In W. R. Holloway's history of Indianapolis written in 1870, he estimated the Jewish community at five hundred. In the 1890s the first large influx of eastern European Jews arrived, and by 1894 the *Indianapolis News* estimated that there were 2,125 synagogue members in the city. The *Jewish Encyclopedia*, published in 1905, gave contradictory figures for the Jewish population of Indianapolis, reporting it in the article on Indianapolis as 4,000, and in the article on the United States as 2,300. By 1907 a new survey estimated it at 5,500. Two estimates from the Industrial Removal Office, based on information from local correspondents, gave the Jewish population of Indianapolis as 7,000 in 1910 and 6,000 in 1912. The less than scientific basis for the population statistics accounts for the wide fluctuation and inconsistency of the figures. The first estimate with any reliability came from a 1948 population survey conducted by the Jewish Welfare Federation that found fewer than 7,000 Jews in the city; the previous population estimate of 10,000 was revised accordingly. Since 1978 the Jewish Welfare Federation has estimated the city's Jewish population at between 10,000 and 11,000. For most of its history the Jewish population has made up 1 percent of the city's population. However, in the period immediately following World War I, the proportion of Jews in the city rose to a high of about 2.5 percent. It later declined.[3]

While the total Jewish population of the city is difficult to estimate, with different sources giving conflicting figures, the proportion that was eastern European in origin is even harder to determine. The federal census of 1910 recorded 2,177 individuals in Indianapolis whose native language was Yiddish. That same year Samuel B. Kaufman, superintendent of the Jewish Federation, estimated that there were about one thousand immigrant Jewish families in the city. In an unpublished master's thesis, C. B. Fall calculated that there were 5,000 Jewish immigrants in Indianapolis in 1916. (She arrived at that figure by determining that there were 1,000 individuals who regularly bought kosher meat and extrapolated from there.) From these figures, one could conclude that the immigrant Jewish population in 1910 (including native-born children) was between 4,000 and 5,000, or between 67 and 83 percent of the total Jewish population of the city. Immigrants probably formed the majority of the Jewish population by 1900 when the total Jewish community was probably less than 4,000.[4]

South Side Synagogues and Cultural Organizations

Although the early immigrant Jewish community was small and its resources limited, that did not prevent the newcomers from establishing a variety of religious and communal institutions. The earliest eastern European immigrants in Indianapolis settled on the south side, an old, inexpensive, industrial and residential district inhabited by groups of Irish, Germans, and blacks. Sharah Tefilla, first of the south side *shuls,* began as a small prayer group or *minyan* about 1870. Known as the *polische shul* because of its members' Polish origins, for several years the congregation met in a series of rented rooms in the developing Jewish neighborhood of the south side, an area bounded by Morris Street on the south, Capitol Avenue on the west, Union Street on the east, and Washington Street on the north (see Map 2, p. 115). In its early years, the synagogue moved frequently and changed rabbis equally often. In 1873 they were meeting at 145 South Meridian, and their rabbi was Moses Helfinbein. In 1874 the group's location was the west side of Delaware, south of South Street. In 1876 they were meeting at the corner of South and Pennsylvania, and their rabbi was Aaron Benson, who was also employed by the Indianapolis Hebrew Congregation as a janitor. Around this time, the congregation took the name Chevro Bene Jacob. In 1877 their rabbi was Isaac Silverman, who also ran a butcher shop at 220 South Meridian. From 1878 through 1881 the rabbi of Chevro Bene Jacob was C. Fagalsong (spelled variously in the city directory as Feigisohn or Ferguson), who also served as *shohet* not only for his own congregation but also for the members of IHC.[5]

Although eventually it became one of the more prosperous of the Orthodox congregations, in its early years Sharah Tefilla faced a constant struggle to survive. In the early 1880s some of the members thought that the cost of maintaining the synagogue was too great and that the congregation should disband. The congregation was then meeting in a rented hall above a junk shop at Pennsylvania and South streets. Kitchen chairs were the furnishings, and a cupboard draped with a prayer shawl served as an ark for the Torah. To keep the little congregation alive, Samuel Steinberg, one of the members, stopped work at noon every Friday and visited the members to collect a few cents from each until there was enough to pay the rent and hire a rabbi for the High Holy Days. By the time the holidays arrived a little canvas bag had been filled with contributions, and Sharah Tefilla survived. In 1882 Chevro Bene Jacob took the name Sharah Tefilla and purchased a building at 352 South Meridian. The last rabbi to serve the congregation in the 1880s was Simon Glassman.[6]

Sharah Tefilla remained in their building at 352 South Meridian for twenty-eight years and in 1910 moved to a new structure at South Meridian and Merrill streets. A handsome building with a classic front and ionic columns, it is believed to have been designed by George V. Bedell (1861–1948), the Indianapolis architect who also designed Holy Trinity Catholic Church in Haughville, a Slavic neighborhood on the west side of Indianapolis.[7]

To outsiders the eastern European community may have appeared to be a cohesive and homogeneous group. In fact, it was a composite of many smaller communities marked off from each other by their region or country of origin. Litvaks, Galitzianers, Russians, and Hungarians did not feel comfortable *davening* together, as each group had its own particular customs and traditions and looked askance at the others' ways of doing things. Louis Hurwich (1886–1967), first principal of the United Hebrew Schools (1911–1916), recalled in his memoirs that the Hungarians in particular had a reputation for being snobs; it was said, perhaps maliciously, that if a Litvak was the tenth man to arrive at the Hungarian *shul*, thereby completing the *minyan* necessary for communal worship, they waited until they found another man to begin. In a similar vein, Samuel B. Kaufman (d. 1934), superintendent of the Jewish Federation from 1908 to 1921, commented that the Hungarian congregation would not engage "a Rabbi even if he were Moses himself as long as he were not a Hungarian." Although non-Hungarians could attend services at Ohev Zedeck, they were required to sit in the back while the best seats at the front were reserved for the Hungarian members and their families.[8]

The Hungarian Hebrew Ohev Zedeck Congregation was established in 1884. Like Sharah Tefilla, in the early years the members of Ohev Zedeck worshiped in a series of rented storefronts—at Market and Delaware, at 43 North Tennessee (Capitol Avenue), and at Louisiana and Virginia. Unlike the other synagogues established by the eastern European immigrants, Ohev Zedeck was never located on the south side, nor were the Hungarians ever really a part of the south side community. A close community, with many families related through marriage, the Hungarians all lived in proximity to one another in a small area east of the Monument Circle on East New York and Ohio streets and on College Avenue. In 1899 Ohev Zedeck purchased IHC's building at Market and East streets, which was close to many of the members' homes.[9]

In addition to their synagogue, the Hungarian Jews established several other institutions. In 1880 they organized the First Hungarian Society. (This may have been a benevolent society or an early *minyan*.) In the mid-1880s Samuel Federman, who later served as rabbi of the Hungarian synagogue (1889–1894), headed a Hungarian Jewish School at 350 South Meridian. In the same period a group of Hungarian Jews organized a benevolent society, the Indianapolis Jüdische Bruder Verein. The Bruder Verein provided its members with sick benefits and medical care and also sponsored social and charitable activities.[10]

The third of the Orthodox immigrant synagogues, Knesses Israel, was founded in 1889 by Russian immigrants. Known as the *russische shul*, it was first located in a house at the northwest corner of Eddy and Merrill streets. By 1893 the congregation had outgrown its first home, and a new building was constructed across the street, at the northeast corner of Eddy and Merrill streets. However, this building too proved inadequate, and in 1919 a lot was purchased at 1023 South Meridian upon which a new synagogue was erected in 1923.[11]

Over the years a steady stream of men served the Orthodox congregations as rabbis and cantors. The position rarely paid more than a small salary, and turnover was frequent. For many years Sharah Tefilla and Knesses Israel shared rabbis. Abba Chaim Levinson, Moses Rivkind, Isaac E. Neustadt, Solomon Levin, and Samuel A. Katz served both congregations jointly. Many of these rabbis also served as *shoḥetim*. Some may have held other positions as well. In the early years these men fulfilled the traditional function of the rabbi, which was much more narrowly defined than either the Reform rabbi of the period or the Orthodox rabbi of later decades. In eastern Europe the rabbi's major responsibility was to study Talmud, interpret questions of Jewish law *(halakhah),* and give two sermons a year, which were homiletical discourses in Yiddish on the Torah portion. Members of immigrant congregations did not look to their rabbis for leadership, for pastoral counseling, or as their representative to the larger community. The status and role of the Orthodox rabbi changed and eventually came to resemble the position of the rabbi in American Reform Judaism. But in the early years, while the Reform community looked to rabbis Messing and Feuerlicht for leadership and direction, there was no similar figure in the Orthodox community. Without strong leadership the Orthodox community remained divided and fractious. Each congregation remained relatively small—in 1905 each had between 45 and 60 families—while the Reform temple had a membership of about 200 families. Organizations which were developed to benefit the entire Orthodox community—a communal Talmud Torah, a mutual burial society, and an organization to supervise *kashrut*—were continually undermined by the petty jealousies and antagonisms that lingered among groups of Polish, Russian, Hungarian, and Sephardic Jews.[12]

The first eastern European immigrants to settle in Indianapolis felt most comfortable worshipping in a synagogue with their own *landsleit*. With time, however, ties to the "old country" weakened, and eventually some of the more prosperous south side Jews began to view the attachment to the "old country" as divisive. In 1903 seven successful businessmen who were south side residents— Charles Medias, Emil Mantel, B. Jacobson, Benjamin Fishbein, M. Sablosky, Henry Bloom, and Sol Trotcky—organized the United Hebrew Congregation, so named "in order to put away with the prejudice of nationality which is in existence here." (Ironically, the founders of UHC were all Galician immigrants.) Beyond their desire to found a synagogue that would not be identified as Russian, Hungarian, or Polish, the founders were also trying to establish a middle ground between the radical Reform of IHC, which they believed was "too far from Judaism," and the Orthodoxy of the immigrant *shuls*, which was unresponsive to the American milieu and did nothing to encourage the younger generation to remain faithful to Judaism.[13]

In the summer of 1904, when the congregation numbered about forty families, its first president, Benjamin Fishbein (d. 1927), contacted Charles I. Hoffman (1861–1945), who had just been ordained at the newly reorganized Jewish Theological Seminary in New York. The American-born Hoffman, an attorney and editor of the Philadelphia *Jewish Exponent* before entering the Seminary, was a disciple and close friend of Solomon Schechter, chancellor of the Seminary. As Schechter's protégé, Hoffman represented the liberal wing of modern American Orthodoxy, the forerunner of today's Conservative Judaism. Although he had been offered a position as assistant to the well-known Henry Pereira Mendes at Shearith Israel in New York, Hoffman decided to accept the offer of the young midwestern congregation, and his mentor, Schechter, came to Indianapolis for the dedication and induction ceremonies in August 1904. The synagogue's building was a renovated church at Union Street and Madison Avenue, and because of its location it became known as the "Union *shul.*" It was also jokingly called the *frantzische* [French] *shul* because of the relative decorum at its services.[14]

The members of this upwardly mobile congregation wanted a synagogue service that was sedate and "respectable" to match their new economic status. Even so, some of the members apparently had trouble putting the old habits to rest. Hoffman privately complained that some members wandered about the sanctuary and talked during services. While this behavior was perfectly acceptable in an Orthodox *shul*, it was out of place in Reform and Conservative services, which looked to the decorous and quiet Protestant church service as the model of appropriate behavior.[15]

Hoffman's position as rabbi was also more closely akin to the Reform than to the Orthodox model. He gave a sermon in English every Saturday and introduced some English prayers into the service. He established a congregational religious school with an enrollment of about seventy children. However, his ambitious plans were constantly thwarted by the frequent lack of a *minyan* at Saturday services and a chronic lack of funds. During his brief stay in Indianapolis (1904–1906), Hoffman also managed to organize a Jewish Culture Society (January 1905) which met regularly for discussions and lectures on Jewish subjects; helped to found a Zionist organization; and was a member of the committee which organized the Jewish Federation. He had many more ambitious plans for his congregation, but the Union *shul* was not large enough or prosperous enough to support them. Eager to accomplish more and in a larger setting, Hoffman resigned in 1906 to take the pulpit of Ohev Shalom in Newark, New Jersey, where he remained for over forty years.[16]

Although the future of the Union *shul* may have seemed in doubt at the time of Hoffman's departure, the congregation survived and prospered. It became the south side's largest and most influential synagogue, with active women's, men's, and youth groups.[17]

Not only were the south side synagogues differentiated by the national origins of their members, but there were economic differences between the congregations as well. While the Union *shul* membership was probably the most broadly middle class, it was followed by Sharah Tefilla and Knesses Israel in that order. The poorest of the Ashkenazi synagogues was Ezras Achim, called the "peddlers' *shul*" because of the many peddlers in the congregation. Founded in 1910, it was the last congregation established by eastern European immigrants. Ezras Achim met in a barnlike, unpainted buildng at 708 South Meridian Street.[18]

The national groups within the eastern European immigrant community may have had their differences, but underneath lay shared experience, a common history, and similar customs. Although there were slight dialect differences, Russian, Polish, and Hungarian Jews all spoke Yiddish and prayed and celebrated holidays and life cycle events in a similar manner. The great bulk of Jewish immigrants to America came from this eastern European milieu. A much smaller number came from the lands of the Ottoman Empire. While 750,000 eastern European Jews settled in America between 1910 and 1924, 20,000 to 25,000 Sephardic Jews arrived, primarily from Turkey, Greece, and Syria. These Sephardic Jews settled in only a few American cities. The largest number settled in New York, smaller numbers in Seattle, San Francisco, and Atlanta, in that order. In 1913 Seattle had 600 Sephardim, San Francisco and Atlanta each had 100. The Indianapolis Sephardic community was estimated to number 50. The establishment of the Indianapolis Sephardic community dates from 1906 when Jacob and Rachel Toledano, Sephardic Jews from Monastir (now Bitola), then a part of Turkish Macedonia, chose to settle in Indianapolis. Why they came to Indianapolis is not known. Once they were settled, however, a number of Monastir Jews followed them to Indianapolis.[19]

Sephardim, descendants of Jews who had lived in the Iberian peninsula before the expulsions of 1492 and 1497, were among the first settlers of the New World. Coming either directly from Spain or Portugal or by way of western Europe, many were merchants of substantial means. With their knowledge of several languages and their family connections in the West Indies, Holland, and England, they prospered in the mercantile centers of the American colonies. For several decades Sephardic Jews formed the majority of the few hundred Jews in America, although by 1730 they were already outnumbered by the Ashkenazim.

The Sephardim who arrived in America at the end of the nineteenth century and the beginning of the twentieth bore little resemblance to their eighteenth-century cousins. The newcomers came from the lands of the Ottoman Empire, where the precarious economic situation of Jews had been further weakened by Turkey's wars with Russia, Italy, and the Balkan states. In 1908, when Turkish military conscription was extended to include non-Moslems, and the Young Turk movement had created an atmosphere of constant political turmoil, the rate of Jewish emigration increased. These immigrants brought with them customs, foods, and music which had taken on an oriental flavor. To the great majority of American Jews, who were Ashkenazim, the Sephardim with their dark complexions and "eastern" habits appeared uncomfortably exotic and foreign. Perhaps the greatest gap between the two groups was linguistic. While the Ashkenazim spoke Yiddish, a Judeo-German dialect, most of the Sephardim spoke Ladino, a Judeo-Spanish dialect.

The initial reception of the Sephardim by the Ashkenazim created wounds that did not heal quickly. Sephardim were deeply hurt by the claim of some Ashkenazi immigrants that they were not Jewish because they could not speak Yiddish. Moreover, they resented the designation "Turk" which was used to single out all Sephardim. Isolated from the eastern European immigrant community by barriers of language and custom, Sephardic immigrants shunned the institutions of the Ashkenazim and created their own community. Sephardic families who were already more or less established took in new arrivals as boarders. In 1907 the Jewish Federation superintendent reported that a group of six single "Turkish" Jews had arrived in Indianapolis and, with the Federation's help, moved into a house at 1024 South Illinois Street. Several of these men, among them Isaac Cohen and Ike Aroesti (who later changed his family name to Morris), had initially been enticed on their arrival at Ellis Island to sign up for jobs in a West Virginia coal mine. Speaking no English and with no other prospects, they had no idea that the work would be so arduous and exploitative. After working in the mines for about two months, they found themselves falling deeper in debt to the company store. They escaped one night by hopping onto a freight car and eventually stopped off in Indianapolis where they had heard there were jobs. Almost immediately several of them found work with the railroads. The initial group of six attracted more Sephardim, and by August 1907, there were twelve "Turkish" Jews living together at 822 South Meridian Street.[20]

Slowly the Sephardic community grew and became more secure as the more established families helped newcomers get settled and find jobs and men who had come alone were able to send for their wives and families. In 1913 the Sephardim organized their own synagogue, Congregation Sepharad of Monastir. Initially the congregation held services in the Jewish Federation's Communal Building at 17 West Morris Street.

While the eastern European immigrants turned their backs on the Sephardim, the Reform community reached out to help the new arrivals whose resources were so limited. In 1919 with the help of Rabbi Feuerlicht, IHC, and other Jewish Federation officers, the Sephardic group purchased a former Lutheran church at the corner of Morris and Church streets and converted it to a synagogue. Three years earlier, in 1916, the group had purchased land for their own cemetery on Kelly Street, again with the help of Feuerlicht and his congregation. By 1919, when the congregation purchased its own building, the Sephardic community probably numbered over two hundred, and it was no longer composed of only Monastirlise. After David Eskenazi, who was from Salonica, settled in Indianapolis in 1914, more Saloniklise Jews emigrated to Indianapolis. Other families came from Aleppo in Syria and Canakkale in Turkey, as well as a few other Levantine cities. In acknowledgment of this broadening of its geographical base, the congregation's name was changed from Congregation Sepharad of Monastir to Etz Chaim Congregation. Early rabbis or cantors for the synagogue included Samuel Lehias, a Rabbi Jahon (1916–1919), and Shabatai Israeli (1920–1924). Isaac B. Cohen, one of the first Sephardic settlers, often served as the group's cantor. Most of these men were not ordained rabbis, and they served the congregation on a part-time basis.[21]

While the synagogue is often considered the center of Jewish religious life, the survival of Orthodox Judaism depends on a number of other institutions of almost equal importance. At the very heart of traditional family life is the *mikveh* (ritual bath), which the married woman is required to use every month at the end of her menstrual period. The first *mikveh* in Indianapolis was built in the early part of this century next to the Hungarian synagogue, Ohev Zedeck, on East Market Street. It was later moved to a site adjacent to the Ezras Achim synagogue on South Meridian Street.[22]

Equally important to Orthodox Jews is the maintenance of the traditional rituals of death and burial. While each synagogue had its own cemetery plot and various fraternal societies provided members with free burial rights, many south side Jews wanted a Jewish burial society that would wash and prepare the body for burial, sew shrouds, and provide a hearse. Since each synagogue was too small to support its own burial society, in 1910 a group of south side Jews, led by L. R. Bryan, Isadore Kroot, and a Mr. Nickbarg, organized Linath Hazedeck, a community-supported free burial society. (*Linat ha'zedek,* pronounced linas ha'tsedek by Ashkenazim, is Hebrew for resting of the righteous. It was also used to mean a hospice or hospital for the poor.) For a number of years, the society was broadly supported by members who paid two dollars annual dues. Slowly, however, the petty jealousies among the synagogues spread to Linath Hazedeck. Sharah Tefilla, claiming that Linath Hazedeck had shown favoritism in its assessment of burial costs and that it was controlled by a small clique, organized its own burial society. The Hungarians never joined in supporting Linath Hazedeck but organized their own burial society, as did the Sephardim. Their men's and women's burial societies, the Rochessim and Rochessot (*rohetzim, rohetzot,* the washers), were organized in 1921.[23]

Not only the stricter observance of Jewish law and custom set south side Jewry apart from north side Jewry. Reform Judaism rejected the traditional belief in the return of the Jews to the land of Israel, and the Reform movement was firmly opposed to political Zionism. The Reform view held that Judaism was a religion; Jews were not a nation but were members of the nation in which they lived. Reform Jews in America were Americans of the Jewish faith; thus they had no allegiance to any other land. There were individual Reform Jews who disagreed with this position and Reform rabbis who became Zionist leaders, notably Stephen Wise and Abba Hillel Silver. For the most part, however, the Reform movement and most Reform rabbis were anti-Zionist. The eastern European immigrants held different attitudes. They felt the sense of Jewish peoplehood which Reform Jewry had rejected. They had lived in tightly knit communities in eastern Europe where they had been a nation apart. They had a pride in being Jewish, and their traditional form of Judaism, which encompassed all areas of their lives, separated them even further from their non-Jewish neighbors and heightened their sense of being a people. While most Orthodox rabbis repudiated political Zionism because of the belief that all Jews would be returned to Zion with the coming of the Messiah, there was a seldom-articulated folk belief that supported the idea of the return of the Jews to Zion with the help of man's intervention. Like most Reform rabbis of their day, Messing and Feuerlicht rejected political Zionism, and most of their congregants supported this position. While the Jews of the south side did not themselves contemplate *aliyah* (after all, they could have emigrated to Palestine from Europe, as some Jews did, but chose America instead), they supported the idea of the return to Zion and the creation of a Jewish state.

Zionist organizations in Indianapolis were not particularly durable in the early decades of the twentieth century. The first was probably the Mebaashereth Zion Society (*mevasseret tzion*, herald of Zion), founded in 1898, a year after the first Zionist Congress in Basel, Switzerland. Because of its geographic isolation from other Zionist groups, the young organization corresponded with Stephen S. Wise, then honorary secretary of the Federation of American Zionists, to determine "what . . . is required of the Zionists and the ways and means the Eastern organizations are promoting the Idea."

By 1899 the Mebaashereth Zion Society had 28 members. It is not known how long Mebaashereth Zion was active. By 1905 a second Zionist organization, Banner of Zion, was holding weekly meetings at Nathan Morris House, the Jewish settlement house. The organization had a membership of 40 to 50 men, "mostly of foreign birth," and emphasized "self-culture [and the] study [of] the conditions of their people with a view ... to their improvement." By 1912, however, the Banner of Zion had been abandoned, and there was no Zionist organization in the city. In 1916 Louis Hurwich, principal of the United Hebrew Schools, and a group of like-minded persons decided to establish a Zionist society in Indianapolis. They invited two well-known Chicago Zionists, Judge Hugo Pam (1870–1930) of the Cook County Superior Court and Max Schulman, to speak at the founding meeting of the association, which was successfully established in the spring of 1916.[24]

For the Orthodox Jew, the synagogue not only filled a religious need but also served as a kind of social center where he could go to socialize with his *landsman* (countryman). For the nonreligious immigrant, a variety of benevolent societies and other organizations came into existence to fill this need. Benevolent societies also served another important function, providing death and sick benefits for their members at a time when health and life insurance plans were not widespread. Larger communities usually supported benevolent societies, known as *landsmanshaftn*, that were organized by immigrants from the same town or region in Europe. Although the Hungarians organized a *landsmanshaft*, the Indianapolis Jüdische Bruder Verein, sometime in the early 1890s, for the most part, the Indianapolis Jewish community was not large enough to support a network of *landsmanshaftn*. As frequently happened in many smaller Jewish communities, the Workmen's Circle, a Jewish socialist organization, stepped in to fill the void left by the absence of *landsmanshaftn*. Like the *landsmanshaftn*, the Workmen's Circle, which was founded in New York City in 1892, provided its members with the all-important insurance and death benefits and also organized educational, social, and cultural affairs. In addition, it offered the working-class, nonreligious Jew an opportunity to maintain his identity as a Jew outside the framework of synagogal life. In Indianapolis, as in other medium-sized Jewish communities, the Workmen's Circle "became for the 'comrades,' " as sociologist Arthur Leibman has pointed out, "the institutional source of their Jewish identity," a means of maintaining the tie to the "old country" and to organized Jewish life without the synagogue.[25]

In Indianapolis there was an active Workmen's Circle branch by 1908. It held its meetings at Nathan Morris House. By 1913 there were two branches of the organization, both of which met at the Federation's newly opened Communal Building. (Obviously, the members of the Indianapolis branches were not militantly socialist or they would never have met in a building that was supported by the money of capitalists.) In the 1920s Branch 175 purchased its own building at 1218 South Meridian Street and continued to use the Communal Building only for occasional mass meetings.[26]

Because Jews in smaller communities were attracted to the Workmen's Circle for a variety of reasons—not primarily left-wing political ones—the programs in cities like Indianapolis reflected the members' mixed motives for joining. The support of socialism was important to many of the members, and some of the branches' socialist programs included holding a May Day banquet, sponsoring a debate on the role of the socialist movement in America, and collecting funds to send to the Socialist Party and to political prisoner defense funds. The desire to maintain their Jewish identity, to participate in Jewish culture, and to support world Jewry motivated other programs. Workmen's Circle members raised money for Jewish war relief, for the purchase of Liberty Bonds, and for the Hebrew Immigrant Aid Society and helped to promote the Jewish Federation's Americanization classes. The Workmen's Circle program supported the study and use of Yiddish, the language of the Jewish worker, rather than Hebrew, the language of prayer, and many branches established Workmen's Circle Schools. To further the cause of Yiddish culture and transmit it to their children, the Indianapolis chapter supported both a local Yiddish library and a Yiddish school (an afternoon school).[27]

By 1918 the number of eastern European immigrants who were coming to Indianapolis was declining, while many of those who had arrived before the war had moved out of the working class to become shopkeepers and small merchants. The Workmen's Circle had drawn its support from Yiddish-speaking working-class immigrants and therefore began to experience difficulties in enlisting new members. As a consequence, the organization relaxed its membership standards. While in many cities the Workmen's Circle included many middle-class Jews, by the 1920s Indianapolis Branch 175 began to admit non-Jewish members who presumably qualified by virtue of their socialist leanings as well as their desire to use the Circle's attractive benefits scheme. Among the Jewish members, on the other hand, there were many who did not champion socialist ideals, a phenomenon that was not restricted to the Indianapolis Workmen's Circle. At a meeting of Branch 175 in July 1921, Comrade Berman was publicly denounced for holding membership in the Republican Club (party?), apparently in response to Berman's accusation that the picnic committee had committed financial irregularities. Rather than expel Comrade Berman on the spot, however, the chapter appointed a committee to meet with Berman and ascertain where his true political sympathies lay— with the Republicans or the Workmen's Circle![28]

The Workmen's Circle remained an important south side institution through the early 1920s. The movement was weakened, however, by a fight between the right (social democrats) and left (Communists) wings for control of the organization, which raged throughout the 1920s. The Bolshevik Revolution of 1917 had led to factional disputes within the socialist movement. Some Jews sided with the Bolsheviks; others remained with the socialists; and power struggles for control of left-wing groups splintered many organizations. Ultimately, the socialists maintained control of the Workmen's Circle, and the Communist members gradually left and joined the new Jewish Communist groups that sprang up in the 1920s and 1930s.[29]

The Sephardim did not join the Workmen's Circle for the obvious reason that they did not speak Yiddish; nor did they have great sympathy, with a few exceptions, with the socialist movement. They did, however, have the same needs as their Ashkenazi brethren—a desire to socialize and spend time with other Sephardim. In 1915 twenty Sephardic men organized the Young Men's Sephardic Club. At first the men met in the Communal Building; they then moved to rented quarters at 854 South Meridian, their clubhouse becoming a kind of social center for the Sephardic community. Like the Workmen's Circle and the more traditional *landsmanshaftn*, the weekly meetings of the Young Men's Sephardic Club provided an opportunity for Sephardic immigrants to meet together in friendly surroundings in which they might speak their own language, and offer help and support to one another in coping with the exigencies of American life. (It is not known if the club ever provided insurance benefits.) In 1927 the group purchased a two-story building at 1002 South Capitol Avenue and remodeled it with help from the Jewish Welfare Fund. The second floor became a clubroom where members met each Sunday to play cards or pool, or discuss current affairs. At other times the clubrooms were used for bar mitzvah parties, receptions, meetings, dinners, and so forth; the ground floor was rented out to Sephardic shopkeepers. The building was sold in 1948.[30]

South Side Women's Organizations

Although the benevolent societies and the Workmen's Circle organized a range of social and cultural activities, their major appeal was the death and sick benefits which they provided. The societies organized by immigrant women had a different focus: not the provision of benefits for their immediate families, but the temporary relief of the needy and the sick. In the mid-nineteenth century, every American community large enough to support a synagogue also had a Hebrew Ladies Benevolent Society ministering to the poor and sick. The earliest Jewish women in Indianapolis had organized the Hebrew Ladies Benevolent Society in 1859, which functioned as a kind of charitable society and women's auxiliary of the synagogue. In 1896 the next generation organized a branch of the National Council of Jewish Women, which emphasized social service. As the eastern European immigrants became established and some of them began to prosper, their women also turned to charitable endeavors. In 1902 eastern European women organized two charitable societies. In April 1902, twenty-six women formed the Hungarian Hebrew Ladies Benevolent Society. The Hungarian Ladies, who admitted male members until 1920, visited the sick and, after investigation, provided the needy with clothing, food, or money. They also functioned as a burial society for Hungarian women, sewing shrouds and washing the bodies of the deceased. The name was later changed to the Hebrew Ladies Benevolent Society.[31]

A few months later, on August 7, 1902, a second group of women organized the South Side Hebrew Ladies Charity Organization, founded for the purpose of "operating a temporary shelter for the homeless poor." As the rate of immigration from Europe increased, so had the problem of Jewish transients, men (and some women) who wandered or, more commonly, rode the trains from city to city. In each city they would throw themselves on the mercy of the Jewish community and receive one or two nights' food and lodging, then go on to the next town. The organization's shelter house, located at 907 Maple Street, provided temporary board and lodging for Jewish transients. After the Industrial Removal Office started sending men to Indianapolis for work, these men also stayed at the Shelter House if they arrived when the Jewish Federation office was closed. When the Jewish Federation began dispensing relief in 1905, the Federation agreed to pay for one night of board and lodging for Jewish transients at the Shelter House but usually only on the condition that the wanderers agree to look for work. After only a few months of dealing with transients and their requests for board and lodging or for money for transportation to another city, the Federation's superintendent and board of governors began to suspect many of the transients of abusing the kindliness of their coreligionists. For a few months in 1908, the Jewish transients were sent to the Friendly Inn and Wood Yard, a shelter established by the Indianapolis Benevolent Society in 1880 as a place for transients to work in exchange for room and board. Here they could earn their keep, but several of the wanderers refused to eat the Inn's nonkosher food. The Federation then experimented with the procedure of having the men work at the Friendly Inn's work yard and receive credit at a kosher boarding house based on the amount of work performed, an offer very few of them took up. This mechanism apparently proved too unwieldy, and within a short time the Federation was utilizing the Shelter House once again.[32]

The South Side Hebrew Ladies were repeatedly criticized by the Federation for their naive willingness to believe every poor wanderer's sad tale of misfortune. Because they did not conduct a "scientific" investigation of each case and instead eagerly provided a hot meal and a warm bed to every down-and-out *shnorrer* (beggar), they were accused of promoting indigence. For their part, the South Side Ladies, who operated their shelter for three years before the

Federation was established, saw their own influence rapidly eroded by the Federation and its combination of money and power. The Federation officers, while not all male, included some of the Jewish community's wealthiest and most prominent men. The women who served on the board were generally wives of successful businessmen. In his first annual message as president, G. A. Efroymson declared that "if all will contribute to the Federation, and refer all applicants to us, we will have ample funds to assist the worthy and you will be relieved of the continual requests for assistance that are now being made." Clearly, the South Side Hebrew Ladies, whose fund-raising events never earned enough money, could not compete with the Federation. However, they obviously derived a personal satisfaction from running the shelter, and for many years they remained independent and refused to become a constituent agency of the Federation.[33]

Because of the large numbers of Jewish transients in the early years of the twentieth century, the Shelter House quickly outgrew its first quarters and moved to a larger home at 808 South Illinois in 1906. In 1920 the Shelter House sold its building to Linath Hazedeck and moved to 835 Union Street, where they undertook care for the elderly as well. There had been little need for elderly care in Indianapolis up to this time, as most aged parents lived with their children, and the occasional few who were childless and needed care were sent to the Montefiore Home for the Aged in Cleveland. However, with the increasing Americanization of their children, many elderly immigrants did not feel comfortable in their children's homes, where *kashrut* and other religious practices were frequently not observed, and so the Shelter House took on this new function. For six years the Jewish Shelter House and Old Home (the name was changed in 1922) cared for the elderly and the transient under one roof, but this arrangement finally became unmanageable. In 1926 the care of transients was moved first to the home of Mr. and Mrs. Louis Glogos at 820 South Capitol and in 1928 to Mr. and Mrs. Sam Siegel's home at 818 South Maple.[34]

The twin tasks which the women had assumed—care of homeless transients and of the elderly—became increasingly difficult for them because of the increasing numbers demanding care and the rising costs of providing board and lodging. In January 1921, Mathilda (Mrs. Henry) Newman, the Shelter House president from

1910 to 1923, and Hannah (Mrs. William) Frankfort approached the Federation for financial assistance. G. A. Efroymson, the president, refused the request, questioning the need for a Jewish old folks' home in Indianapolis, but offered to make the Shelter House an affiliate of the Federation. Although affiliation would have brought an end to their financial difficulties, the women were still unwilling to give up their independence, so they applied to the Community Chest for an appropriation. When the Community Chest asked the Federation's opinion in the matter, the Federation replied that "the Federation has not found a need for a Jewish Old Folks' Home here." The request to the Community Chest was, of course, turned down, and, although the women were wary of losing their autonomy, they had little choice and in 1921 voted to affiliate the Shelter House with the Federation. After four long years of negotiations, it became a constituent agency in 1925.[35]

Just as the Sephardic men had felt a need to establish their own self-help and social club, so too had the Sephardic women. They did not join the Ashkenazi women's groups but organized their own group in 1925, a sisterhood of Etz Chaim, known as the Society. One of the projects for which they raised money was the Fundo Secreto, or secret fund. Two or three Sephardim supervised the fund and dispensed it to needy Sephardic families for the purchase of food, clothing, or coal.[36]

If women's realm encompassed the nurturing and caring for their own families as well as for the homeless, the indigent, and the helpless, it also included providing their husbands and children with the sustenance to complete their daily tasks. The Jewish housewife wanted her family to be well-fed and well-nourished for long days behind the counter, the sewing machine, or the school desk. Because many families' budgets were slim while their appetites remained hearty, Jewish housewives often marched off to their daily shopping as if into battle, ever on guard against short measure or short change. When prices rose, the shopkeepers, butchers, and bakers were often met with cries of outrage from their customers. In many cities immigrant Jewish women responded to price increases with more than mere grumbling; they organized consumer boycotts.

The first kosher meat boycott in Indianapolis was part of a national boycott of the nation's leading (nonkosher) meat-packers. In

January 1910, in reaction to rising meat prices, a boycott began in Cleveland, Ohio, with some 11,000 families agreeing that they would not eat any meat for sixty days. The boycott had broad popular support, and it quickly spread to other cities. Organized labor supported the movement, and the federal government tacitly supported it as well, as the Department of Justice immediately announced plans to prosecute the nation's leading meat-packers—Swift, Morris, and Armour—known as the "beef trust." In Indianapolis, however, the boycott movement had little support. Although consumers objected to the high prices they were forced to pay, they continued to buy and eat meat. The only boycott activity in the city was on the Jewish south side. In protest against price increases of two to five cents per pound for kosher meat, approximately two hundred families refused to purchase meat, alleging that the price increases were the result of a secret agreement among the district's four kosher butchers. At a meeting at the Workmen's Circle Hall at 921 South Meridian on Sunday, January 24, 1910, the boycotting families organized the Hebrew Cooperative Society with the intention of establishing a cooperatively run butcher shop to sell kosher meat at cost to the Jewish residents of the south side. The society planned to finance the shop by selling one thousand shares at two dollars per share. If the butcher shop proved successful, the Hebrew Co-operative Society hoped to establish a cooperative grocery and bakery as well. Apparently none of these plans ever materialized.[37]

If the plans of the meat boycotters in 1910 were ambitious, two food boycotts in the immediate postwar period had a simpler objective: to force retailers to lower prices. Organized by south side women, these boycotts followed the pattern of the 1902 New York kosher meat boycott, drawing on the strength of the neighborhood network and the power of the pocketbook to persuade women, who were the family shoppers, to join. One of the chief organizers of these two apparently successful boycotts was an immigrant seamstress, Paula Zukerman Brodsky (ca. 1890–1966). Zukerman had met her husband, Charles Brodsky, an immigrant tailor, on a picket line in New York. Unable to find work there, the family, which by then included an infant son, Louis, was sent to Indianapolis by the Industrial Removal Office in 1912. Charles received work at New York Tailors and later was employed at Kahn

Tailoring. A nonreligious family, the Brodskys were active supporters of the Workmen's Circle.[38]

Paula Brodsky's first boycott was directed at the south side bakers. With wheat prices falling, consumers felt that the price of
bread should fall as well. Housewives became increasingly angered
by the bakers' continuing high prices. Paula Brodsky decided to organize a boycott of the bakers. She went from house to house and
held meetings in her living room, encouraging women to boycott
the neighborhood bakers until they lowered their prices. When
enough women had agreed to join, they organized picket lines outside the bakeries. One bakery, Schmidt's, agreed to settle with the
boycotters and lowered their prices, but the other bakeries continued for some time to ignore the boycott. However, they eventually
lowered their prices as well. After the success of the bakery boycott
another was organized against the kosher butchers to protest their
price increases. Utilizing the same techniques that had defeated
the bakers, it, too, was successful. Similar kosher meat boycotts
organized by immigrant women were staged in New York City in
1902 and 1917, in Boston in 1902, and in Paterson, New Jersey, and
Philadelphia in 1907.[39]

South Side Hebrew Schools

The synagogues, the lodges, and the charitable societies were all
established by the immigrants to serve their own needs. When the
immigrants looked to the future, however, they realized that if
their children were going to maintain these institutions and continue Jewish traditions, they had to prepare them by providing
them with a proper Jewish education. The immigrants from eastern
Europe left behind them a well-established system of Jewish
schools, beginning at the primary level with the one-room *heder*,
where young boys were first taught to read Hebrew and elementary
religious texts, through the *yeshivot* where adolescents and young
men studied the Talmud and other legal texts. In addition, almost
all boys regularly attended synagogue and as a matter of course
acquired the ability to *daven* in Hebrew and a knowledge of Jewish
rituals and customs. Generally, girls in eastern Europe were not
given any formal education.

The situation in America was entirely different. Jews no longer lived in an entirely Jewish milieu; their work patterns often made it impossible for them to attend *shul* regularly. Slowly and inexorably American customs and habits began to replace Jewish ones. Much of Jewish ritual and custom, which in Europe had formed a part of daily life, fell into disuse, so that what had been common knowledge to most European Jews now had to be formally taught to their American children. Many of the immigrants feared that if their children grew up ignorant of Hebrew, Torah, and Jewish customs and ceremonies, Judaism would not survive in America beyond the first generation.

The first Jewish school in Indianapolis had been established in 1863 by the German Jewish immigrants. Organized before public schools were well established in Indianapolis and at a time when many schools were denominational, at first it had provided both secular and religious education. However, by 1867 most members of the Indianapolis Hebrew Congregation were sending their children to public school. The IHC school became an afternoon school teaching only Hebrew and Jewish subjects. Succeeding waves of Jewish immigrants established their own schools where their children would be taught not only Hebrew but customs and ceremonies as they had practiced them in Europe. In the 1890s the Hungarians had their school on South Meridian Street. In 1896 a Chevrah Talmud Torah was organized. In 1904 the United Hebrew Congregation instituted a religious school with Rabbi Charles Hoffman serving as principal. By 1907 Sharah Tefilla had a school with an enrollment of sixty pupils. Unlike eastern European schools, these were all afternoon schools and educated both boys and girls.[40]

However, while each national group may have been able to support its own synagogue, the greater financial needs of a school made it difficult for each congregation to maintain its own separate school as well. It was not merely a question of money. American Jewry lacked the personnel to run and staff such schools. In general, the most learned and pious Jews in eastern Europe did not emigrate to America, a *treife* (nonkosher) land which they eyed with suspicion. And while many of the men who did emigrate probably had enough of a Jewish education to enable them to teach their children the rudiments of Hebrew and Jewish law, most found the prospect uninviting. To be a poorly paid *melammed* (elementary teacher), teaching the rudiments of Hebrew to a mass of restless young boys crowded into a dark, overheated basement room every afternoon was not the path to success in America. The thankless task of teaching Hebrew was generally left to a man either too old or too incompetent to make a living in any other fashion. In his unqualified hands was laid the responsibility of passing Jewish knowledge on to the next generation.

One solution to the difficulties of maintaining a series of separate and struggling congregational schools was for each synagogue to close its own school and cooperate in the sponsorship of one community Hebrew school or Talmud Torah. One large school drawing on a wider pool of students and supporters would not only be more efficient, but with a larger income base it would also be able to attract more competent teachers and purchase better teaching materials. While this might appear to be a logical and rational solution to the problem, the emotional bias which prevented cooperation among the national groups first had to be overcome. Moreover, while parents might grumble about their children's poor Jewish education, apathy as well as a tendency to cling to the old ways of doing things hindered any change.

The eventual development of a community-supported Hebrew school in Indianapolis was due to the vision, foresight, and perseverance of Rabbi Isaac Elhanan Neustadt (ca. 1871–1913). Born in Lithuania and educated at a *yeshivah* in Vilna, Neustadt was sent to America as a *meshuloh* (messenger) to raise funds for his *yeshivah*. While visiting Indianapolis to collect funds for the school, he was invited to stay and become rabbi of three of the Orthodox congregations—Sharah Tefilla, Knesses Israel, and Ohev Zedeck. Not long after he settled in Indianapolis, Neustadt became disturbed by the sorry state of Jewish education in the city, resolved to do something about it, and began campaigning for the establishment of a single, community-wide afternoon Hebrew school. By 1905 Neustadt had cultivated a small group of supporters and was raising funds. Five years later, the first election of officers and directors of the United Hebrew Schools took place. Classes began the next year, in November 1911. The school's governing board was composed of representatives from the four synagogues—Sharah Tefilla, Ohev Zedeck, Knesses Israel, and United Hebrew Congregation—which had cooperated in establishing the school.[41]

Before the establishment of the United Hebrew Schools, many

Jewish children, excluding those from the Reform synagogue, were educated in four small *hadarim* run by elderly *melammdim*. Many families did not want to see these men out of a job and felt that they should become teachers in the new school. Neustadt, however, had different ideas, and this is what made his plan unusual. He wanted a Jewish school founded on "scientific principles" staffed by the best teachers available. Rather than rely on the rather poor local pool of talent, he traveled to New York to recruit the best-qualified man to serve as the school's first principal and offered him an attractive salary to entice him to the Midwest. This man turned out to be Louis Hurwich, who stayed with the school for five years, from 1911 to 1916. Although Hurwich initially took the job in order to save enough money to attend engineering school, he remained in Jewish education and became well known in the field. After he left Indianapolis, Hurwich went to Boston, where he founded the city's Bureau of Jewish Education (1917) and Hebrew College (1932). He was also the founder of Camp Yavneh, one of the first Hebrew-speaking camps in America. Hurwich agreed with Neustadt that if the school was to succeed, its teaching staff had to be first rate and the teachers should be well paid for their efforts. Hurwich thus returned to New York to find teachers for the school and hired Aaron David Markson, Elimelech Gordon, and Pinchas Masie. Several of the school's early teachers went on to successful careers in Jewish education.[42]

The school opened on November 12, 1911. Classes met in the Sharah Tefilla synagogue on the south side and in the Ohev Zedeck synagogue on the north side (Market Street). The school was in session every day after public school and on Sunday. Support for the school came from fees—two dollars per month for the first child in a family and one dollar per month for each additional child, although many families who could not afford tuition paid nothing. Additional funds came from an annual Purim ball, occasional raffles, collections taken at circumcision ceremonies and other happy occasions, and donations collected by members of the board and the hard-working Ladies' Auxiliary, which was organized in 1913.[43]

The school was a great success, a pioneer program that began to be noticed and envied by other communities. The staff utilized the latest teaching techniques with instruction given in Hebrew (ivrit-be-ivrit). Communities elsewhere tried to set up similar schools; but they were not as successful, for it was the personality and drive of Neustadt that made the Indianapolis school work so well. When the forty-two-year-old rabbi died suddenly in 1913, the name of the school was changed to the Rabbi Neustadt United Hebrew Schools.[44]

Although honored in death, during his lifetime Neustadt was treated as poorly as any other Orthodox rabbi in the city. His combined congregational salaries came to only $450 a year, one-fourth what he had offered Hurwich as school principal. Some community members began to sense that Neustadt deserved more, and the community finally purchased a large house for him and his wife and eight children. However, the russische shul did not approve of this act of generosity. They terminated his contract, thus reducing his already meager salary, and hired Rabbi Solomon Levin to replace him. At the time of Neustadt's death, his wife was pregnant with their ninth child. After his death the community permitted the family to remain in the Union Street house and raised funds to support the family until the two eldest children were old enough to work.[45]

Rabbi Neustadt's vision was that the United Hebrew Schools would provide Hebrew education for all Jewish children in the city, including Reform (and unaffiliated) children. A third branch of the school opened in April 1912 at the Reform synagogue, but problems quickly surfaced. A controversy arose over the absence of a yarmulke or other appropriate headgear on some of the boys' heads. (The Reform movement does not required a headcovering, while to the Orthodox, it would be unthinkable to study Hebrew, the language of prayer, without it.) Greatly disturbed by this transgression, the board reaffirmed its policy by stating that "our Schools are strictly Orthodox, therefore [we] could not permit the students in any of our branches to sit bearheaded [sic] during school hours." Not surprisingly, the IHC branch did not last long. For a time, a north side branch met at Public School No. 1. The south side branch also met at Public School No. 6 from 1913 to 1916, until the United Hebrew Schools purchased their own building, a former church, at Union and McCarty streets. The school enrolled about two hundred children annually in its early years. For example, in February 1915 there were 224 children enrolled; in December 1918,

195 (160 on the south side, 35 on the north side). Perhaps 25 percent of all school-age Jewish children attended the school. Another two hundred children attended IHC's religious school. Between 150 and 200 children attended the Council of Jewish Women's Sunday School. Probably between 60 and 75 percent of all Jewish school-age children in the city received some Jewish education during the period.[46]

Neustadt's strong leadership, his careful nurturing of communal unity, and his dedicated fund-raising had brought the school to life. After his death, disharmony and a chronic shortage of funds began to plague the endeavor. In July 1915, Knesses Israel severed its ties with the school and attempted to establish its own school in the Jewish Federation's Communal Building. The effort failed, and the congregation returned to the school in May 1916. Then, in July of that year, Hurwich, noting the school's grave financial difficulties, offered his resignation, which was accepted. Teachers' salaries were lowered, and Bernard Isaacs, one of the teachers, was appointed principal and teacher. He held that position until 1919.[47]

The financial situation of the school improved over the next few years, as additional groups began to support the school and were invited to share in its management. In June 1917 the Ladies' Auxiliary gained representation on the board. Two years later, Ezras Achim, the peddlers' *shul*, was invited to join the board, and finally, in February 1920, the "Turkish" Jews were invited to send their children to the school and representatives to the board. An earlier request in July 1917 by the Sephardic congregation for a room for their teacher and class had been refused, but, with the school's enrollment down to 150 in 1920, the 25 additional Sephardic children were welcome.[48]

Making a Living on the South Side

The synagogues, the lodges, and the Talmud Torah represented the communal structure the immigrants created. The activities surrounding these institutions, however, filled only a small part of their daily lives. Unlike the German Jewish immigrant who was typically a peddler or small shopkeeper, the typical eastern or southern European immigrant was a garment worker or artisan. Even in a city such as Indianapolis without a well-developed garment industry, the greatest percentage of Jewish immigrants worked in the garment trade. Kahn Tailoring, one of the country's largest manufacturers of men's suits, was probably the single largest employer of Jewish immigrants in Indianapolis. Kahn Tailoring employed most of the Sephardim, including many unmarried women, and many Ashkenazim as well. Other immigrants worked for smaller firms, such as New York Tailors, English Woolen Company, or Shapiro and Levy Cap Company. Twenty-five percent of the immigrants sent to Indianapolis by the Industrial Removal Office (IRO) between 1911 and 1914, for example, had worked in New York's garment industry. This is where they found work in Indianapolis.[49]

The second largest group of skilled workers were carpenters and cabinetmakers. They worked for the city's automobile manufacturers—Nordyke and Marmon or American Car and Foundry Company—and for furniture manufacturers, such as Thomas J. Madden and Company, the city's largest. In 1907 a group of Jewish cabinetmakers settled in Shelbyville, twenty-five miles southeast of Indianapolis, and found work in that community's numerous furniture shops. Fourteen percent of the immigrants sent to Indianapolis by the IRO between 1911 and 1914 were carpenters and cabinetmakers. In some earlier years (1906–1907, 1907–1908, and 1909–1910) carpenters and cabinetmakers had outnumbered garment workers.[50]

Other immigrants were skilled tinsmiths, shoemakers, butchers, bakers, and painters. However, certain trades such as plumbing and plastering were closed to Jews. In 1910 there was reported to be only one Jewish plumber in the entire city of Indianapolis. Jewish plumbers and plasterers were thus forced to find other trades, or do what the many Jews did who had no trade—take up a pack to peddle. Many, known as "hucksters," also sold goods from a horse and wagon, but their route, unlike that of the earlier German Jews, was not through the rural countryside selling to farmers but through the city streets of their own south side, their cries mingling with those of the junk dealers and ragmen. Other immigrants sold goods from pushcarts or from stands at the city market. Their stock might consist of "sox, collar buttons and suspenders," or cigars and chewing gum.[51]

In addition to the peddlers, the pushcart owners, and the market vendors, immigrant Jews owned small shops—groceries, kosher meat markets, bakeries, small dry goods stores, and shoe repair shops—in the south side's Jewish shopping area, the 800 to 1200 block of South Meridian Street. Shapiro's Restaurant, one of the few Jewish businesses still located in the neighborhood, has been at its location at 808 South Meridian Street for over seventy years. This well-known enterprise was founded by Louis and Rose Shapiro, immigrants from Odessa, who came to America in 1905. On arriving in Indianapolis, they began peddling coffee, tea, sugar, and flour from a wagon, using their living quarters as a storage area for these bulky commodities. When the floor collapsed in one building where they were living, they quickly moved out and set up their home storeroom at 808 South Meridian, formerly the site of a fish shop. Not long after, they opened a retail grocery business, the American Grocery Store, at the same address. The addition of a few tables to serve prepared food was an innovation of the 1930s. The restaurant was an immediate success, and it soon replaced the retail grocery part of the operation.[52]

Although most of the Sephardim worked at Kahn Tailoring, the Saloniklise Jews generally did not. One exception to this pattern was the Salonikli Naphtali Eskenazi, who worked at Kahn Tailoring before entering the wholesale produce business with his brother David Eskenazi and Mallah Mordoh. This was a popular occupation among the Saloniklise, who entered the produce business at all levels—as fruit peddlers, operators of fruit stands at the city market, or wholesale fruit brokers—and many of them became quite successful. Edward Dayan, an immigrant from Aleppo, Syria, entered business as a peddler of linens from door to door. By 1923 he had prospered enough to open the Circle Linen Shop on Monument Circle.[53]

Immigrant women also worked in the needle trades at Kahn Tailoring and other shops. Married women looked after their homes and families and often took in boarders or worked behind the counter of the family's grocery store, market stand, or small dry goods store. Influenced by Levantine attitudes toward women which discouraged them from appearing in public unescorted and reinforced the woman's traditional role within the home, most married women in the Sephardic community did not hold jobs outside the home but devoted themselves to cooking, cleaning, sewing, bread baking, and child rearing. A small minority worked at the market stands—the market was not open daily—or at Kahn Tailoring. The women were usually married by the age of twenty (the men by twenty-three) and their families tended to be larger than those of the Ashkenazim.[54]

Children often helped to supplement the family income, particularly by selling newspapers, sheet music, gum, and other small articles on the street. Saul Rabb (1904–1976), who became a well-known and respected criminal court judge, and his brother Harry helped their family by doing odd jobs and delivering newspapers. Saul Rabb recalled a time when his parents could not afford to buy warm boots for their six children, and "on cold mornings before I passed my Star route, I would wrap my feet and legs with old newspapers and then put on my stockings and shoes." During several periods, Rabb also carried an afternoon route for the *Indianapolis Times*.[55]

Like many south side families, however, the Rabinowitz (later Rabb) family did not remain poor. As historian Frederick Kershner has noted, "For the foreign-born, life in Indianapolis was a difficult but relatively brief journey with a happy ending—absorption to the American native stock on equal terms with other Americans of his own economic status." In the free and open environment of the Midwest, many eastern European immigrants were able to relive the classic American folk myth of "rags to riches," which in the case of several successful scrap dealers might be more accurately retitled the "riches from rags myth." Moses A. Rabb (1876–1957), a skilled watchmaker for many years, became an insurance agent in 1920. The son of Fishel Aaron Rabinowitz, a *hazzan* of Congregation Knesses Israel, Moses and his wife, Pauline Levensin Rabb (1876–1957), a Lithuanian immigrant, were able to send both their sons to college. Saul became an attorney and then a judge, his brother Harry a physician.[56]

By the early twentieth century, there were a number of south side Jews, particularly those who assumed positions of communal leadership, who were already prosperous merchants and businessmen. Charles Medias (ca. 1867–1938), a founder and former president of both the United Hebrew Schools and the United Hebrew Congregation, was a Galician immigrant who came to America in 1885 as a young man of eighteen. He began his business career in Indianapolis in a typically modest manner—peddling linoleum, oilcloth, and table coverings. After only two years, however, he had amassed enough capital to open a jewelry store on Washington Street with his *landsman* Emil Mantel (ca. 1863–1940). Mantel remained in the jewelry business for twenty-two years, but Medias left it in 1890 and opened a retail clothing store on Indiana Avenue, which was eventually taken over by two of his sons.[57]

Other members of the "Union *shul* crowd" prospered as jobbers, dry goods store owners, or manufacturer's agents, and by 1910 many of these Galician Jews had abandoned the south side as a place of residence and moved to an area seven to ten blocks north of Washington Street. They continued to return to the south side to attend their *shul* and sent their children to the Neustadt Talmud Torah at Union and McCarty streets, but their social lives and contacts were now on the north side. About 1910 they organized the Merchants Pleasure Club, which met in a house near the White River between Guilford and Winthrop streets. Here the memers played cards, socialized, and held weekly dinners with the members' wives taking turns preparing the meals. By the end of the First World War, most of the members of the Merchants Pleasure Club had moved again, this time to an area north of 38th Street, an indication of their increasing prosperity, and the Merchants Pleasure Club disbanded.[58]

It was not only among the membership of the "Union *shul*" that one could find prosperous businessmen. Among every national group there were similar success stories. Henry Glick (ca. 1857–1928), a wholesale produce dealer, was one of the wealthiest of the Hungarian immigrants. Tall and imposing, always impeccably turned out in hat, cane, and gloves, he helped bring many of his relatives over from Europe and then started them in a small grocery store, market stand, or pushcart selling fruits and vegetables which, of course, they bought from him. Martin Schwartz, another Hungarian, was one of a number of Jews in the liquor business. Some, like Schwartz, were wholesalers; others operated retail liquor stores; and still others, such as Samuel Grenwald, a Hungarian immigrant and president of the United Hebrew Schools from 1915 to 1917, were saloonkeepers. Jacob Solotken (ca. 1889–1959), a Russian immigrant, was one of the many scrap dealers who were able to turn "rags to riches." His firm, J. Solotken and Company, is still in business today, as is the Katz Bag Company, established by Russian immigrant Max Katz (ca. 1886–1959) in 1907.[59]

The movement of eastern European Jews into the professions has been primarily a phenomenon of the second and third generations, but even among the immigrant generation there were a small number who entered the professions. One of the first eastern European lawyers in Indianapolis was Leo Lefkovits (ca. 1877–1955), who came to Indianapolis from his native Hungary as a young child. He graduated in 1899 from the American Central Law School and for thirty-two years was credit manager of the Pettis Dry Goods Company. Henry Abrams (1892–1922), a south side resident and member of the United Hebrew Congregation, graduated from the Indiana Law School in 1916. He was elected to the Indiana General Assembly on the Republican ticket in 1919, served two terms, and was a candidate for a third term at the time of his death. In the assembly he was known as a supporter of Progressive causes, such as the child labor bill, the Indianapolis school lunch bill, a bill to compel children to provide for their needy parents, and similar proposals.[60]

Hard-working and ambitious as the immigrants might have been, to the native Jews they seemed at first to present a picture of unredeemed poverty. Exotic and strange in manner, custom, and language, the immigrants provoked in native Jews a variety of conflicting emotions. While they felt a sense of pity as well as empathy for the harsh conditions under which the newcomers had lived in Europe, native Jews also knew how strange and perhaps distasteful the immigrants must appear to the larger community. Moreover, native Jews feared that they might be linked with these very foreign newcomers, whose presence could potentially stir up a wave of anti-Jewish feelings from which native Jews would also suffer. However, while some members of the Protestant elite campaigned to restrict immigration from southern and eastern Europe, American Jewry felt too keen a sense of unity with their Jewish brethren to support this movement. Rather than shut the door, native Jews held out both hands to welcome the immigrants and to help them to rapidly adjust to their new surroundings.

Natives Help the Newcomers: The National Council of Jewish Women, Industrial Removal Office, and Jewish Federation

The women's organizations were the first to become aware of the needs of the eastern European immigrants. By the 1890s, when the first large group of eastern European families settled in the city, the German Jewish community was well established, with little poverty among its members. Members of the Hebrew Ladies Benevolent Society energetically applied themselves to helping the many indigent families among the new arrivals. The women dispensed an old-fashioned, comfortable kind of charity in money, groceries, or coal given personally to each needy family by a weekly visitor who was to acquaint herself with the family's "moral and physical [needs which were] necessary for their proper uplifting." But the conditions of the twentieth-century poor could not be alleviated by nineteenth-century methods, and the Hebrew Ladies Benevolent Society did not endure. Its natural successor was the Indianapolis section of the National Council of Jewish Women (NCJW), founded in 1896 and reorganized in 1904. An organization very much in the Progressive social settlement mold, with a greater appreciation for the new scientific principles of social welfare, when the HLBS disbanded in 1908, the NCJW took over many of its functions.[61]

The NCJW was concerned not only with relieving immigrant poverty but also with eradicating criminal and deviant behavior among the immigrants. The NCJW developed a close working relationship with the Jewish Federation, established in 1905, to provide social services to the immigrant community as well as help those who had strayed from the straight and narrow path of model behavior. In 1903 Indiana became the first state to enact a juvenile court law, and the Marion County Juvenile Court with its use of volunteer probation officers became a national model. In 1906 the women of the Council, along with the Federation's superintendent, agreed to act as juvenile court probation officers and oversee all of the Jewish as well as some of the non-Jewish cases. In 1906–1907 they handled fourteen cases, of whom six were Jewish children. The Federation's superintendent, Samuel J. Levinson, supervised two additional Jewish cases. In 1907–1908 three Council members followed fifteen children, six of whom were Jewish. Other Council members assisted the Federation superintendent in making weekly "friendly visits to the homes of the poor," that is, to families who were on the Federation relief rolls, as well as visits to hospital patients on a regular basis. In 1909 the Council built a cottage to house two Jewish tuberculosis patients in the City Hospital's tuberculosis colony located on the hospital's grounds. The women also visited south side schools to provide counseling for "problem children."[62]

A national concern of the NCJW was to keep single immigrant girls from falling prey to the lures of the white slave trade. In Indianapolis Council women kept track of every immigrant girl who came to the city alone, visited them regularly, and helped them to become established. At one time, the Council planned to open a hostel for single immigrant women, but this never materialized. The Council also organized English classes for immigrants at the Nathan Morris House. For several years, Sara Kahn, wife of Henry Kahn, was in charge of the Council's Immigrant Aid Committee.[63]

While many of the Council's programs aided Jews who were either in distress or had fallen afoul of the law, the NCJW also engaged in "preventative work," that is, projects whose purpose was to reduce the number of potential Jewish juvenile delinquents, truants, and prostitutes.* Social reformers had seized on the idea of the playground as one means of keeping slum children off the streets and providing a diversion from the attractions of petty crime. In 1907 the Council established a playground at south side School No. 6, which had a heavily Jewish population. With Council members acting as playground supervisors, the women claimed that the playground was used daily by over 200 children, 140 of whom, they estimated, were Jewish.[64]

Another early Council program, which continued for many years, was a "School in Jewish History," later called the Council Religious School, established at the Nathan Morris House in 1908. Providing courses in Jewish history and Judaism to childen who were receiving no other religious education, the school used Council members as volunteer teachers and attracted an annual enrollment of between 150 and 200 children. Anna Mantel, daugh-

*From the small number of juvenile offenders, one could conclude that the number of Jewish juvenile delinquents in Indianapolis was quite small. During this period, we know of one Jewish-run brothel in the city. It had a Jewish madam and at least one Jewish prostitute.

ter of Galician immigrant Emil Mantel, was the first principal of the school, which met on Sunday mornings. (She later married Morris Fishbein, son of Benjamin Fishbein and well-known editor of the *Journal of the American Medical Association.*)[65]

For the most part, the members of the NCJW were among the city's wealthiest women. North side residents, members of IHC who were freed from the rigors of housekeeping by a staff of servants, they were able to devote their days to charitable work.* Many of the Council's most active members also participated in a variety of non-Jewish charities as well. A typical member of the group was Emma Eckhouse (1857–1941), the Council's energetic president from 1904 to 1914. A native of Kokomo, she married Moses Eckhouse, who died when she was still a young woman. Like many young, well-to-do widows, she then devoted the rest of her life to Jewish and non-Jewish charitable causes. In addition to her leadership of the Council, she was a member of the Jewish Federation board of governors from 1905 to 1910, treasurer of Nathan Morris House, secretary and treasurer of the Jewish Foster Home, and vice-president of the Hebrew Ladies Benevolent Society. She was also active in the Children's Aid Society and a member of the boards of the Flower Mission, which provided hospital care for the chronically ill, and the Elenore Hospital for children.[66]

Another active member of the NCJW was Jennie Efroymson Wolf, wife of department store owner Louis Wolf. Jennie Wolf was the first treasurer of the group after it was reorganized in 1904 and later served as president. She was active in non-Jewish causes as well. Wolf was instrumental in the development of several health and nutrition programs for school children. She helped to organize the Nutrition Food Program for Undernourished Children in Public Schools, which had its origin at School No. 6 on the south side. The program later became the National Food Program for children in public schools. Wolf also aided in originating the Sight Testing and Hearing Testing Program in the public schools, a project which began at School No. 7 on Bates Street. During the Second World War, she was director of the Indiana Victory Gardens Program and in 1940 she was active in the federal government's Youth Eco-

---

*Not all members of the NCJW fit this precise description. The group included middle-class members as well. Fanny Hoffman, for example, wife of Rabbi Hoffman of UHC and a south side resident, was a Council member.

nomic Council. A member of the board of governors of the Jewish Federation, Jennie Wolf served as its financial secretary for many years.[67]

The same year that the NCJW reorganized as an organization devoted to the social welfare of the immigrant poor, a similar group of Reform women established a social settlement for the south side Jewish community. Named Nathan Morris House in memory of the Jewish attorney who had perished in a fire the previous year, the aim of its founders was to provide a social and educational center for the south side Jewish community. Located initially on Russell Avenue, it later moved to the Jewish Federation's new quarters at 821 South Meridian. When the Jewish Federation was organized in 1905, Nathan Morris House became one of the first constituent agencies.[68]

The programs of Nathan Morris House were designed to provide immigrants with vocational training as well as help them acculturate to American life. The settlement house sponsored courses in dressmaking, typing, cooking, and dancing, as well as English and American citizenship classes. A branch of the Indianapolis Free Kindergarten Society met at Nathan Morris House, and the settlement also sponsored a reading room, neighborhood entertainments, and lecture series in both Yiddish and English. Meeting rooms were also provided for neighborhood organizations such as "The Banner of Zion," a Zionist society that met there regularly. To help immigrant mothers learn American child-rearing methods, kindergarten teachers held monthly mothers' meetings and led earnest discussions on "the problem of training children." The message underlying all these programs was that the immigrants should abandon Old World habits and patterns for new American ones.[69]

While charity-minded Reform women focused their energies in organizations like the National Council of Jewish Women and Nathan Morris House, the B'nai B'rith lodge* provided its members with the opportunity to support a variety of social service programs for the benefit of the south side community. With the NCJW, B'nai B'rith cosponsored English and naturalization classes for Jewish immigrants. For several years (around 1910), the lodge supported a

---

*Abraham Lodge No. 58 and Esther Lodge No. 323 had merged about 1907 to form Indianapolis Lodge No. 323.

weekly free milk station at the Nathan Morris House, a kind of well-baby clinic where mothers brought their babies for examination by an attending physician and nurse. The clinic nurse also made periodic home visits to suggest to the mothers the proper methods of hygiene and health care and the correct diet for their infants. While Council members acted as juvenile court probation officers, B'nai B'rith brothers visited Jewish inmates in Indiana penal institutions — Pendleton Reformatory, Greencastle Penal Farm, and Plainfield Boys' School. During some years the lodge's social service committee conducted religious services and held Passover seders for Jewish prisoners. Lodge meetings often featured speakers on contemporary Jewish problems. Beginning in 1910 for several years the Indianapolis lodge published a monthly magazine, the *Menorah*. [70]

In 1901 the national leadership of B'nai B'rith agreed to participate in a scheme to distribute immigrants to the inland cities of America. The Indianapolis lodges' participation in this project ultimately led to the organization of the Indianapolis Jewish Federation. The inspiration for the Industrial Removal Office, whose purpose was to disperse eastern European Jewish immigrants across the country, came from some of New York City's leading philanthropists: Cyrus Sulzberger, Nathan Bijur, Isaac Isaacs, and others. These men, leaders and board members of New York's United Hebrew Charities, were worried about the financial strain of caring for the many destitute immigrants landing in New York. They felt that Jewish communities throughout the country should help to shoulder the burden the newcomers had placed on New York's Jewish charities. They also felt that the concentration of immigrants in New York City was creating the potential for tremendous social upheaval, both in nativist reactions to the Jewish immigrants and in mass unemployment of these immigrants should New York's garment industry falter. By distributing Jewish immigrants throughout the country and finding them occupations outside the Jewish-dominated needle trades, the IRO's promoters hoped to "normalize" the Jewish immigrant community. The geographical distribution of immigrants along with their occupational diversification, it was believed, would also help to combat anti-Semitism, as the IRO's supporters feared that the continued growth of the Lower East Side ghetto could only lead to further restrictions

against immigration. The restrictionists, whose ranks were growing in proportion to the increasing numbers of immigrants, must
not be given the chance to point to a crime-ridden, unhealthy, and
overcrowded New York Jewish ghetto as an argument for further
restriction.[71]

In 1901 the Baron de Hirsch Fund, whose activities to this point
had been focused on encouraging immigration from eastern Europe,
became convinced of the need to relieve the congestion of the New
York ghetto and established the Industrial Removal Office. B'nai
B'rith, which by now had lodges in every American city, agreed to
participate in the resettlement plan. The national leadership asked
their membership to organize local committees in cities in the
Midwest, the West, and the South to help resettle Jews sent there
by the IRO. The Indianapolis lodges began the task of resettling
immigrants in 1904, along with rabbis Feuerlicht and Messing who
handled removal cases through the Relief Society established by
IHC. However, it quickly became apparent to the IRO leadership
that if they had any hope of resettling substantial numbers of immigrants in the city they could not rely solely on volunteer workers. This approach had already failed in other cities.[72]

Because of the failure of the volunteer system, in 1902 the IRO
instituted the policy of paying the salary of a local agent and, to
encourage communities to take a larger number of removal cases,
paying a fee to the community for each immigrant they absorbed.
By 1903 there were local IRO agents in nine cities, including Detroit, Cincinnati, and Omaha. The IRO paid part of the local
agent's salary plus $10 for each single man and $25 for each family
settled in the city. The payments were to cover the costs of one
month's rent and two weeks of groceries. The local community
would have to pay the rest of the agent's salary and any additional
relief and resettlement costs, as well as office and administrative
expenses.[73]

This offer was presented to the local Industrial Removal
Committee formed to coordinate the immigrant resettlement
work. The committee's formation itself represented a milestone for
the community, as it was the first cooperative undertaking between the north side and south side communities. The members of
the committee included all of the city's rabbis—Isaac Neustadt of
Knesses Israel, Albert Kantrowitz of Sharah Tefilla, Jacob Hartman

of Ohev Zedeck, Charles Hoffman of UHC, and Mayer Messing and Morris Feuerlicht, the committee's secretary, of IHC. The remaining officers were Sol S. Kiser, the banker (chairman) and Joseph Borinstein, the successful scrap metal dealer (treasurer). While the bulk of the committee belonged to the Reform Indianapolis Hebrew Congregation (the industrialist Samuel Rauh, retailers Louis Wolf, Elias Segar, and Joseph Wineman) other congregations were represented as well (Benjamin Fishbein from UHC, Adolph Marer from Ohev Zedeck, and others).[74]

Early in 1905 the committee began meeting to consider whether to use the offer from the IRO as a base to establish a Jewish federation for the city. The federation movement had begun in 1895 with the establishment of Boston's Federation of Jewish Charities, and by 1917 there were twenty-three federations located in every region of the country, including such cities as Cincinnati (1896), St. Louis (1901), Buffalo (1903), and San Francisco (1910). These institutions had all been created for a common purpose—to coordinate local social service and philanthropic institutions and to unify fund raising for all Jewish institutions, both local and national. In each city German Jews controlled the federation, although many of the services it provided were for the eastern European community.[75]

Morris Feuerlicht was assigned the task of drafting a constitution and bylaws for the Indianapolis Jewish Federation, and it took many meetings for the committee members to agree on the name, the organizational structure, and the objectives of the federation. The committee persevered, however, and on July 1, 1905, the Jewish Federation opened its doors in temporary quarters in the Nathan Morris House on Russell Avenue. A few months later, in November 1905, both institutions moved to a rented building at 821 South Meridian Street.[76]

The relatively wide communal representation of the local Industrial Removal Committee was not repeated in the Jewish Federation's board of governors. The officers and board members were drawn from the wealthiest and most prominent Jewish citizens of the city, such as Abram L. Block of L. Strauss and Company; Louis Newberger, a prominent attorney; and G. A. Efroymson, one of the city's leading merchants. The only rabbinical members of the Federation's first board of governors were the Reform rabbis Mayer

Messing and Morris Feuerlicht, the latter of whom was the board's recording secretary. Although an Orthodox rabbi was usually represented on the board, the Jewish Federation of Indianapolis remained under the control of the Reform community, as it did in other cities.[77]

The objectives of the Jewish Federation were twofold: to establish a unified method of fund raising and to utilize the collected funds to support local and national Jewish organizations dedicated to the relief of the "deserving poor," the prevention of want and distress, the discouragement of pauperism, and the provision of educational facilities for "deserving Jews." The first objective, the consolidation of fund raising, was probably the most significant. Organizations which became constituents of the Federation or applied for an allocation surrendered their right to conduct any fund-raising activities beyond the collection of dues. They were prohibited from sponsoring "any ball, bazaar, fair, excursion, picnic, theatrical benefit, or other form of entertainment for which tickets are offered for sale in Indianapolis to members of the Federation." Similarly, national organizations which attempted to conduct fund-raising campaigns in Indianapolis risked losing their Federation allocation. The Federation claimed no role in the management of its constituent societies beyond ascertaining their financial needs and determining that Federation funds were used appropriately. Obviously, however, financial control gave the Federation a great deal of authority, and within a rather short period of time, the Federation became the major front of power within the Jewish community.[78]

From the beginning, the funds raised by the Federation were to serve a dual purpose—to aid the local community and to extend aid to world Jewry. Of the eight organizations that comprised the first constituent societies of the Federation, four served the local community (the Hebrew Ladies Benevolent Society, the Nathan Morris House, the Indianapolis committee of the Industrial Removal Office, and the Indianapolis section of the National Council of Jewish Women) and four served the national community (the Cleveland Jewish Orphan Asylum, the National Jewish Hospital in Denver, the Montefiore Home for the Aged in Cleveland, and the National Farm School).[79]

The purpose of the Hebrew Ladies Benevolent Society was to

dispense relief, a major objective of the Jewish Federation as well. The Society affiliated with the newly organized Jewish Federation, and the two attempted to work out a better method of handling the relief cases, since the ladies' methods were considered neither scientific nor efficient. To avoid duplication, no case was taken by either the Society or the Federation's superintendent without a consultation between them. To ensure that no unworthy cases were handled, each case was investigated by the superintendent and visited by a committee from the Society. In the Federation's second annual report (March 31, 1907), the report of the Benevolent society was enthusiastic. The following year, however, the Society had no message in the year-end report, and the task of visiting the homes of poor had been taken on by the Council of Jewish Women. In May 1908 the Hebrew Ladies Benevolent Society disbanded. The Federation with its paid professional staff was now the major source of relief for impoverished Jews.[80]

The Federation's method of dispensing relief, more than anything else, exacerbated the tensions between the south side community and the north side Reform community. The conflict over relief reflected profound cultural differences between immigrant and native. In the closed small world of the European *shtetl*, the *shnorrer* was as much a part of the community as the baker or butcher. Going on his appointed rounds, knocking on each door, he was a part of everyday life. The few coins his neighbors gave him made them feel they were helping someone less fortunate than themselves. Jews felt *rahmanot* (a mixture of pity, sympathy, and mercy) for the unfortunate beggar. There was no question of mistrust or of determining if the beggar was really impoverished. Nor was any thought given to whether these endless small collections were serving to perpetuate the beggar's poverty. This was the traditional form of charity, it was comfortable, familiar, and it was not questioned. The Federation leadership, however, were not only urban dwellers who had learned to distrust the begging stranger at the door, but they were also influenced by new American attitudes toward charity and social work. These theories suggested that certain forms of charity were degrading, tended to make the receivers dependent, and served to perpetuate their poverty. Rather than encourage the poor to become lifelong beggars by handing them a few coins at each door, the new social-work theorists argued that the poor should be given real help to become self-supporting. This could be accomplished by making lump-sum payments to them and, more importantly, by providing them with help to secure full employment and thus get off the dole.

Neither side, however, could see any merit in the other's charity methods. South side Jews saw the Federation as hard-hearted and cruel, while the Federation viewed south side Jews as naive, their charitable efforts as "pauperizing" and demoralizing to the charity recipient. The Federation declared itself as the central agency for relief and promised to eradicate traditional house-to-house *shnorring*, which many immigrants treasured as the traditional form of *zedakah* (charity). The Federation actively campaigned against this kind of charity, insisting that all relief cases be referred to its office. Here applicants for relief would be subjected to a thorough investigation by the Federation's superintendent, who checked the veracity of the applicant's story. The first of the Federation's superintendents was Samuel D. Wolf, a multilingual sixty-year-old widower who served from July 1905 until August 1906. He was replaced by Samuel J. Levinson, a young man who held the post from August 1906 until November 1908. Levinson was followed by Samuel B. Kaufman, who remained from December 1908 until his resignation in 1921. Prior to his appointment as superintendent, Kaufman was an attorney and the rabbi of the United Hebrew Congregation but resigned both positions to assume the superintendency of the Federation.[81]

It was not only the veracity of an applicant's story that concerned the Federation but whether applicants would accept Federation rules. Just as organizations that received donations from other sources were denied Federation funds, so too, applicants who were found to have already collected funds either door-to-door or from federations in other cities would be refused relief. Requests for money for transportation to another city, especially if the superintendent felt the applicant could find work in Indianapolis, were almost always refused. The Federation was especially eager to expose men who traveled from city to city, living off the largesse of the Jewish community. It was deeply critical of south side Jews for believing these transients' stories and helping them to lead a life of indolence. One typical story involved a man who had lost a leg in a railroad accident in Chicago in 1904. According to superintendent

Levinson, since his accident W "had visited almost every large city in the Union," taking up a collection in each to send him to his next destination. Hoping to put an end to W's wandering, Levinson offered him a job, but "he demanded a foot. This was refused and so again the people were up in arms and made a collection of $15 to purchase a foot for the unfortunate." Levinson noted, "The women who made the collection, in hunting about for a limb found one belonging to W and left it for repairs. Of course W got the $15 and hurried out of town." In Levinson's view, "To encourage such transients seems to be the delight of those who will not listen to the reasons advanced by the Federation for non-assistance of the applicants."[82]

Not only did the Federation usually deny relief to transients, but it also denied aid to families deserted by the male breadwinner. This policy probably angered south side Jewry even more than the policy on transients, because to refuse aid to a deserted family meant that a mother and her children would go hungry. The Federation, however, claimed that upon investigation many cases of desertion were actually found to be the result of collusion between husband and wife. The wife would agree to be deserted, often by a husband who was unemployed or barely making a living, on the understanding that she would then apply to the Federation for support. As the deserted family, like the transient, was a national problem, local federations cooperated with one another in locating these husbands and returning them to their families or in having them arrested for non-support. Many south side families, however, found it hard to see a mother and children refused assistance, even though the unemployed husband might have left the city to find work elsewhere with his wife's full knowledge.[83]

The Federation preferred requests for assistance that would help an immigrant family become self-supporting or improve their standard of living. It almost always approved requests for help, particularly in the form of small loans, to purchase a stand in the city market, open a small shop, or purchase a horse and wagon for peddling. It also usually approved requests for temporary aid arising out of a serious illness, an inability to pay a hospital bill, or to support a family during illness. The Federation sent many tubercular patients to convalesce at the National Jewish Hospital in Denver. A medical committee, composed of a number of Jewish physicians, volunteered their time to examine and treat impoverished Jews at no charge.

The Federation also funded a Jewish Foster Home (founded in 1907) for families struck by tragedy or struggling with illness or unemployment. Located at 714 Union Street and under the supervision of Mrs. Lena M. Jackson, the Foster Home cared for orphans who were too young to be sent to the B'nai B'rith-sponsored Cleveland Jewish Orphan Home and provided a day nursery for families with no adult in the home to watch young children during working hours. The home also served as a detention center for Jewish cases that came through the Juvenile Court, and the Federation hoped that it would eventually become the Jewish orphanage for the state. The apparent need for such an institution, however, was not long lasting. As immigrant families became economically secure, family life stabilized, juvenile delinquency declined, and the number of potential clients for the home rapidly diminished. By 1910 the number of dependent children had dwindled; the few remaining children were boarded out to families; and the Foster Home was "temporarily disbanded." (It never reopened.)[84]

The free medical care, the day nursery and orphanage, the settlement work, and other services of the Federation still did not assuage the anger of many south side residents. They saw the Federation's treatment of charity applicants as impersonal and demeaning and disliked its restrictive relief policy. Though he served on the organizing committee and on the board of governors from 1906 to 1913, Rabbi Neustadt was deeply critical of the Federation's attitude toward charity applicants and privately conducted his own relief work. The difference between Neustadt's approach and the Federation's, noted Louis Hurwich, was the difference between the "machine and the heart." The Federation viewed each request for relief as a case, whereas Neustadt saw each applicant as a human being with feelings and emotions. A number of south side residents shared Neustadt's outlook and dispensed their own private charity. Moses A. Rabb, for example, made secret deliveries of coal and groceries to needy families. He also taught English to immigrants and helped them obtain their citizenship papers.[85]

Sephardim in Indianapolis rarely approached the Federation for relief, although many Sephardic families could have used some help, especially in their early years in town. Too proud to ask the

Ashkenazi-controlled Federation for aid and then submit to the humiliating procedure of an investigation, they were aided instead by the Fundo Secreto of the Sephardic women's group, which provided relief in a discreet manner. Many a needy family would find coal or groceries or clothing placed on their doorstep. The fund was not really regarded as charity since the recipients were expected to return the money when they were able. However, if a donation came from the Federation, needed as it might be, it was often returned. One member of a particularly large Sephardic family recalls that one time they received a box of clothing from the Federation. The children were excitedly trying on the new clothes when their father walked in the door. Learning that the clothes had come from the Federation, he ordered the children to take them off and return them.[86]

Both Sephardim and Ashkenazim were more willing to accept the Federation's free medical care and legal aid. A group of Jewish doctors provided free medical treatment and consultation. They also examined tubercular patients to determine if they should be sent to the National Jewish Hospital in Denver (at Federation expense). The Federation offered legal aid to immigrants who were often subjected to harrassment and hauled into court on spurious charges or peddlers who were arrested for peddling in restricted districts or for peddling without a license. Women applied for Federation help in locating deserting husbands and having them arrested for non-support or in obtaining a divorce. Young children were brought into juvenile court for truancy or for selling gum or newspapers on the downtown streets. However, while the Federation's superintendent and members of the Council of Jewish Women frequently acted as probation officers for these children, the Federation had in fact helped to write the city ordinance that these children violated. Here was another instance in which the middle-class standards of the Federation leaders clashed with the working-class values and standards of the immigrant community. While poor families depended on the money their children earned selling newspapers or other articles on the downtown streets, the Federation viewed young children in the congested downtown area as a public nuisance. In 1919 the Federation proposed banning children under eleven from selling on downtown streets, an ordinance that was passed by the city council in 1920.[87]

Nathan Morris House, the social settlement established by a group of women in 1904, was easily incorporated into the Jewish Federation, and it became the center for its social and educational facilities: a library of Yiddish books, meeting rooms for south side Jewish organizations, a kindergarten, the Council of Jewish Women's Sunday school, classes in sewing, typing, English, American citizenship, lectures, and dances. Almost from the beginning, there was a feeling that the work was hampered by the lack of space. In December 1912 the Federation purchased the building of the Hoereth Athletic Club at 17 West Morris Street to serve as its new Jewish community center.

Remodeled and dedicated on October 19, 1913, the building was named the Communal Building. Rabbi Morris Feuerlicht suggested this name in order to convey the principle that this was a building to serve the whole community. The building included an auditorium-gymnasium, game rooms, meeting rooms, a library, and showers. Outside was a large playground. In 1922 the Caroline M. Kahn Memorial Log Cabin was erected on the Communal Building grounds, and Boy Scout Troop No. 50, which was organized by the Federation in 1915, as well as other troops, used the cabin for their meetings. A small house adjacent to the Communal Building was also purchased as a meeting room for the kindergarten.[88]

Public health was another field in which the Federation became more active. The B'nai B'rith lodge organized a free milk station or well-baby clinic at the Nathan Morris House that was later transferred to the Communal Building. It was eventually taken over by the City Board of Health. In June 1919 the Federation board voted to sponsor monthly public meetings to furnish south side residents with information on tuberculosis. The following September, a committee was appointed to investigate the advisability of opening a dental clinic at the building. The committee recommended the establishment of a dental clinic that would service the entire south side, primarily the children, and would offer basic dental care as well as education in dental hygiene. A small fee would be charged. The clinic, which opened on January 21, 1920, was extremely successful. Open two afternoons a week, it was staffed on a partially volunteer basis by a Jewish dentist, the first of whom was Phillip Falender (1899–1960). Although the Federation also considered opening a medical dispensary at the Communal Building, it never did, and a tuberculosis clinic was finally opened by the City Board of Health in the building next to the Communal Building. The Federation paid only for the heat and light for the clinic, which was opened in July 1920.[89]

Although medical and dental clinics were seen as ways to improve the general health of slum dwellers, reformers and social workers in the Progressive era viewed the crowded urban environment as basically unhealthy. As an extension of their city health programs, many social settlements operated fresh air camps for city children so that they could enjoy the salutary benefits of country air. The Federation wanted to establish a "summer fresh air mission for sickly and undernourished mothers and children" and for "pre-tuberculosis" and convalescing tuberculosis patients. For a few years before it opened its own camp, the Federation sent those in greatest need of fresh country air to the Summer Mission of the Fairview Settlement, which was sponsored by the *Indianapolis Star*, or to the *Indianapolis News* Fresh Air Camp. Then, in 1918, Joseph Wineman, Federation president at the time, deeded to the Federation for one dollar land and buildings on the White River at Broad Ripple for a summer camp to be known as Camp Ida Wineman, in memory of his deceased wife.[90]

The camp opened in the summer of 1918 for six weeks with forty-eight children in attendance, each staying for one to two weeks. Initially there was no charge for the camp, but eventually a fee scale based on ability to pay was instituted. Although the camp was considered a success, the water source for the camp was found to be polluted after only two summers of operation. The camp continued at the same site for several more seasons, but because of the pollution bathing in the White River was forbidden and distilled water had to be used for drinking. In addition, the periodic overflow of the White River made improvements to the site impossible. Eventually, conditions at the camp became so difficult that the site was abandoned, and from 1927 to 1929 the camp was held at the Laurel Halls Stock Farm Company, until Big Eagle Camp was purchased in 1930.[91]

The establishment of a local Industrial Removal Committee and the offer of the New York office to pay part of a local agent's salary had stimulated the communal leadership to organize a local federation in 1905. The relationship between the Indianapolis Jewish Federation and the IRO continued from 1905 to the end of the First World War. For the first ten years, the removal work occupied a substantial part of the superintendent/agent's time. The IRO wanted to be kept constantly informed of local industrial conditions and the types of skilled workers they could send to Indianapolis. The agent and his labor committee visited local employers to interest them in hiring the removal men and then reported to New York on the number and type of worker each firm would hire. Most of the removal men were taken in by Jewish firms, such as Kahn Tailoring (the major employer of immigrants), the People's Outfitting Company, the Star Store, and Unger's Bakery, but others went to work for Nordyke and Marmon, Stout's Factory Shoe Store, and the American Car and Foundry Company. Some firms, such as the Parry Buggy Manufacturing Company, which offered to hire removal men, were assiduously avoided by the office because of the notoriously low wages they paid their workers.[92]

David Bressler,* the IRO's general manager, often complained that he was not running an employment bureau, but in many ways he was, since the inland cities would usually refuse to accept an applicant unless they had a job for him at hand or were reasonably sure that they could find him one immediately. Just as New York was trying to rid itself of the burden of the Jewish unemployed, Indianapolis did not want to add to its own relief rolls, and the Federation was chary of creating "a New York problem" of its own. A smooth arrangement for matching removal applicants with available jobs was never satisfactorily worked out, and it led to much grumbling on both sides. The New York office complained that Indianapolis was too demanding, particularly in the kind of applicants they would accept. Indianapolis, in turn, complained that their requests for shoemakers, carpenters, or tailors either went unfilled or were filled by men who were incompetent. In

---

*David M. Bressler (1879–1942) was a young attorney in 1900 when he became manager of the Roumanian Relief Committee. When the Industrial Removal Office absorbed the work of the Committee, Bressler became general manager of the IRO. He headed the organization during its most active years and resigned in 1916 after the First World War had already greatly reduced its work. Bressler later joined the American Jewish Joint Distribution Committee and was active in a variety of Jewish relief organizations.

1910 the local agent, Samuel B. Kaufman, complained to Bressler about two such cases: Kive Stensky, who claimed he was a shoemaker, had actually "spent all his years as a merchant"; and, as for "Jacob Reiss, whom you sent here as a carpenter," Kaufman continued:

> ... the truth of the matter is that he never worked as a carpenter for one single minute of his life. He was employed in New York City as a conductor. When he was discharged, he wanted to leave New York, so he got a friend of his, who is a carpenter, to tell your investigator that they were both working as partners in the trade.[93]

A greater problem than the shoemaker who could not work fast enough to suit his Indianapolis employer or the tailor who wanted to open his own shop was the number of unskilled workers who applied to the IRO for removal to an inland city. Bressler estimated that at least half of his applicants had no trade at all and argued that Indianapolis, like all of the American Jewish communities, had a responsibility to take its fair share of these more troublesome cases. In a letter in October 1908 to Edward A. Kahn, then president of the Jewish Federation, Bressler restated the basic philosophy underpinning the removal movement:

> It is the [unskilled worker] to a very large extent ... that has created the social problems of the community, and while we must make every legitimate effort to send out skilled people it is no less incumbent upon us to bring home to the other communities in the United States that the problem of the unskilled ... is in some degree theirs as well as that of New York. We do not ask Russia to send any people to the United States nor can we express a preference for the particular kind that should come to New York. ... Simply because New York is the gateway is no sufficient reason that New York should be expected to shoulder the entire burden. ... A thousand such families must in time, because of their bulk become a serious problem, while ... this thousand divided into very small groups and scattered, will work out their own salvation.

Bressler acknowledged that most of these families would probably require some assistance at first but insisted that this was "only a temporary condition."[94]

The New York strategy was to send a dozen or so unskilled workers to each community, with the community expected somehow to take care of them. But the specter of a dozen or so new families on relief and wage earners who would be difficult to place in jobs was frightening to a small community like Indianapolis. Indianapolis only took unskilled applicants after much pressure from the New York office. When problems developed, the local agent was quick to suggest returning them to New York. Levinson and, later, Kaufman, the local agents, took a rather dim view of many of the removal cases and of the immigrant community in general, finding them too high-handed and demanding for their station. Kaufman's remarks to Bressler in a letter of February 1910 are unusual only in that they are slightly more vehement than his usual comments about the removal cases: "The immigrant Jew, as a rule, belongs to the stiff-necked people more than any other Jew. He is hard to please and often, the more you try to do for him, the less he will appreciate."[95]

Kaufman complained of the many gamblers, socialists, and deserters among the removal men. He felt that they were infecting the Indianapolis community with urban vices. But most disturbing to the Federation were the "loafers," the men who did not seem to want to work, who quit perfectly good jobs because the work was too hard or the wages too low, and then demanded relief or a return ticket to New York. Yet, as much as Kaufman might have wanted to refuse these people help, he was afraid of them in one sense because of the trouble they might stir up against his office in the immigrant Jewish community. In a flurry of anger over one large and particularly troublesome family which he desperately wanted to be rid of, Kaufman wrote to Bressler in August 1910:

> what would you do if Mrs. Meyer and her seven little children would stand either on a Hester Street corner or on Fifth Avenue . . . and cry that they were starving and there would be a large crowd around them trying to find out the cause of their distress, and the woman would say she was sent here with her husband by the I.R.O. of Indianapolis; that they were promised work and assistance; that her husband cannot find suitable employment; that they have no means of livelihood—would you say "Let them severely alone if they fail to make good?"[96]

However, the Federation leadership's greatest fear was not so much that a troublesome family would incite the immigrant community against the Federation but that the growth of a foreign enclave of destitute Jews with many families on relief would make the non-Jewish community more anti-Semitic and more eager to restrict immigration. The fear that one bad family would spoil it for everyone made the Federation leadership particularly nervous when any Jew was less than a model citizen. As Kaufman commented, "If a person raps on a door, the whole community can hear it and what will the Christians say when they hear of such a case? One family like this is liable to cause a lot of prejudice. . . ."[97]

Despite the many difficulties that the local IRO committee encountered in receiving and settling immigrants, it did bring a substantial number of families to Indianapolis, and many of them made a successful adjustment to their new life in the Hoosier capital. After three weeks in Indianapolis, Charles Brodsky wrote to the New York office, "Of course we cannot judge yet about the prospects in this place, but at all events we expect to do better than in New York." The Brodsky family adjusted well to life in their new home, and their children still live in Indianapolis. After a month in Shelbyville, Joe Kausser claimed that he would not return to New York for $1,000. Even the misanthropic Kaufman crowed, in a note enclosing a pawn ticket to redeem goods that Mayer Reisberg left in New York, "This shows how prosperous your I.R.O. men are becoming in our city . . . as you now have to send the belongings they left with the New York loan offices. How much more prosperous Indianapolis is than New York!"[98]

However, to examine only the families who were settled in Indianapolis, whether satisfactorily or with some difficulty, does not give a full picture of the IRO experience in the city. At least one-third of all the immigrants sent to Indianapolis remained in the city only briefly before returning to New York or moving on to other cities, such as St. Louis, Chicago, or Cincinnati. In some years the number who stayed in the city was barely more than half of those sent. From 1905 to 1907 only 59 percent of the IRO immigrants (79 out of 134) still remained in the city a year after they had been sent there. An underlying cause for the relatively large number who did not stay was undoubtedly the capital's shaky economic condition, which often made securing decent jobs for the newcomers a difficult task. Beginning with the failure of the natural gas supply in 1901, Indianapolis suffered a long period of economic decline, which was only abated by the increased industrial activity at the outbreak of World War I. During this long period of economic sluggishness, certain years were more difficult than others. The panic of 1907, for example, struck more sharply in Indianapolis than in other cities, and the effects lingered for a longer period of time than elsewhere. "Conditions are extremely bad here," IRO agent Samuel Levinson wrote to New York in November 1907, "many mechanics and laborers are crowding the streets . . . [and] men drift in daily from Cincinnati, Columbus, and other cities looking for work." Because of the futility of seeking employment for prospective removal cases, the Indianapolis IRO office finally closed down in January 1908, and did not reopen until six months later. Even then, employment prospects remained poor, and the Indianapolis office had difficulty finding jobs for removal men.[99]

Between 1905 and 1914, approximately 425 removals (counting each single man or each family as one case) were sent to Indianapolis, and about 285 of these remained in the city for at least one year. The Jewish Federation estimated that, including families who were drawn to Indianapolis because of IRO families that had already been sent there (the "magnet effect"), between 400 and 500 families were settled in Indianapolis directly or indirectly through the IRO. However, the outbreak of hostilities in Europe in August 1914 dramatically altered IRO operations. The number of applicants fell sharply, placements became difficult, and the office's financial resources dried up as Jewish philanthropic organizations began sending large amounts to Europe for war relief. No longer could the New York office pay the local agent's salary or more than one week of board and lodging for a removal case. Bressler asked Kaufman to take whatever cases he could and "keep the machinery of distribution intact so that an efficient and speedy distribution may be effected when immigration is resumed—a circumstance confidently to be expected when the war ends." The greatly reduced number of cases he was asked to accept, coupled with the city's revived economy, made it easy for Kaufman to comply with Bressler's request. Kaufman cheerfully accepted whatever removal cases he was sent, but the IRO never again resumed full-scale operations, and it was dissolved in 1922.[100]

The conclusion of the war, followed by the final imposition of restrictive immigration laws, made an organization like the Industrial Removal Office almost an anachronism. Not only were there only small numbers of new immigrants, but the immigrants of the prewar period were prospering and had no need of the kind of help the IRO offered. Nor was the Jewish Federation as dependent on the IRO as it once was. By 1920 it no longer relied on regular payments from New York for survival. For forty years the organized American Jewish community had looked to Europe as the seemingly endless source of immigrant Jews who would need their help and support. The native community had put prodigious energy into organizations whose purpose was to acculturate and Americanize the Jewish immigrant. Now these organizations were forced to begin a search for a new purpose. Moreover, as the immigrant community became more established and more prosperous, the sharp division between immigrant and native began to soften, and the differences between them became less clear. Immigrant Jews began leaving the old neighborhood and moving north, where many joined existing north side Jewish institutions. Others established new institutions geared to the needs of an Americanized and increasingly middle-class eastern European community. Cut from its European moorings, in the next decade American Jewry began not only a search for a new purpose, but it also began to develop its own independent and distinctive identity.

৺৳ IV

On Native Ground

THE TWENTIES

FEW PERIODS IN HISTORY have ended so decisively as the era of mass immigration. During the four years of World War I, immigration was cut off completely. It resumed in an even greater intensity after the war as Jews fled Bolshevik Russia and the ravaged states of eastern Europe. But there was a new hysteria growing in America. After 140 years of an open-door policy that had let in a flood tide of immigrants, a reaction began to set in. The restrictionist movement, led by members of the eastern Protestant elite and with roots in the nineteenth century, began to gain more supporters and more strength. Prominent scholars led serious discussions on the supposed genetic inferiority of southern and eastern European peoples. The fear that these peoples were diluting the allegedly superior northern and western European gene pool only helped to further the restrictionist cause. After twenty years of campaigning, the movement had its first victory in 1917 when Congress passed a literacy test law excluding any immigrant unable to read forty words in any language. The restrictionists ultimately hoped to enact a stiffer exclusion act. The events of the next few years helped them to reach their goal.

111

Nativism and the Jewish Response

While there had always been a nativist undercurrent in American life, the anti-German campaign which surfaced after America's entry into the First World War was a wholly different phenomenon. It was a national hysterical reaction against Germans, German-Americans, and all of German culture. School boards banned the teaching of the German language in public schools. Symphony orchestras removed German music from their musical programs. German House in Indianapolis changed its name to the Athenaeum. On a more ludicrous level, sauerkraut became known as "liberty cabbage," hamburger as "Salisbury steak." All German-Americans, no matter how long they had lived in America, were distrusted and suspecting of harboring a secret allegiance to Germany. With the loyalty of so large a group as the German-Americans in doubt, all other Americans also became suspect. Flag-waving, patriotic rallies, and Americanization days, organized for the purpose of demonstrating the depth and sincerity of one's patriotism, began to appear regularly on the civic calendar.

At the conclusion of the war the feverish anti-Germanism was transformed into a more generalized xenophobia, a distrust of all foreigners. The suspicion that many immigrants were political radicals or anarchists heightened fears. The bombings and other activities of the anarchists coupled with the events of the Russian Revolution of 1917 helped to further fuel the flames of what became a hysterical anti-foreign and anti-radical campaign. It culminated in the Red Scare and the Palmer raids of 1919–1920, which seized thousands of alien radicals and deported hundreds of them. The cries for 100 percent Americanism coupled with the great disillusionment evoked by the scenes of European destruction brought more followers to the restrictionist camp. Many Americans wanted to shut the gate to Europe, the seeming source of both political radicalism and the senseless tragedy of the war. Amid growing agitation for immigration restriction, the Johnson Act, imposing quotas on immigration, became law in 1921. In 1924 a more stringent system of quotas was enacted, bring mass immigration to an end. The effect was dramatic. In 1924 50,000 Jews entered the country; in 1925, only 10,000.[1]

In the four decades between the pogroms of 1881 and the close of World War I, American Jewish leaders were caught up in the problems associated with the new arrivals. They had created organizations to settle them, relieve their poverty, find them jobs, disperse them, and Americanize them. In return, American Jewish religious and educational institutions benefited from a steady infusion of Jews who, despite their poverty, were the bearers of a traditional way of life which America had as yet been unable to nurture. Not only did existing institutions benefit from the new immigrants, but the newcomers also established institutions of their own, which added to the cultural and religious diversity of American Jewish life.

The end of mass immigration brought dramatic changes to the American Jewish community. No longer could a community such as Indianapolis expect to expand, aside from small annual increases due to the natural birthrate. After the early 1920s, the growth rate of the Indianapolis Jewish community slowed considerably. In 1922 the Jewish population of Indianapolis was estimated at 10,000, the same figure that was given in 1934. This figure, as noted previously, was inflated. After the first population study of 1948, the estimate was lowered to 7,200. The Jewish population during the twenties and thirties was probably closer to 6,000. Since 1978 the Jewish Welfare Federation has estimated the city's Jewish population at between 10,000 and 11,000. (For an extended discussion of population figures, see chapter 3.)[2]

In the years immediately following World War I, the proportion of Jews in Indianapolis, which had previously remained steady at 1 percent of the population, reached a high of 2.5 percent. As a result of the end of mass immigration as well as the declining birthrate (a reflection of rising social status), the growth of the Jewish community could no longer keep pace with the growth of the city. The proportion of Jews in the city declined once again to 1 percent of the population, where it has remained. Similarly, the percentage of Jews in the American population climbed to a high of 3.6 in 1927 and then began slowly to decrease for the same reasons.[3]

During the immigration era, each few years had brought new groups of Poles, Hungarians, Russians, and Sephardim. After 1920, with the exception of the relatively small number of Nazi-era refugees and the Soviet immigrants the 1970s, no new immigrant groups came to Indianapolis, and relatively few new organizations were established. The only new synagogue to be founded after 1920—Central Hewbrew Congregation (1923)—was established not by newcomers but by Orthodox eastern European Jews who had left the south side and moved to the middle-class north side.

The northward thrust of the Jewish community was not a new phenomenon, but in the 1920s the pace of movement accelerated to the point that contemporary observers began to predict the demise of the south side Jewish community. Not only was the "old neighborhood" breaking up; without the constant influx of new arrivals from Europe, the Jewish community began to lose its distinctively eastern European flavor. As a higher proportion of the community became American-born, the use of Yiddish declined along with the observance of traditional rituals. Synagogues that had been founded on a "strictly Orthodox" basis began to modify their practices—introducing mixed seating into their sanctuaries, for example. Rancor among national groups within the larger Jewish community—Hungarians, Litvaks, Galitzianers—began to subside, to be forgotten almost entirely by American-born generations, who often viewed the old antagonisms as somewhat comical. The rift between the Ashkenazim and the Sephardim, however, which reflected a wider divergence of cultural experience, lasted longer.

As the Jewish community of Indianapolis moved into the twenties, it became increasingly middle class. In fact, while the movement of Jewish immigrants into the middle class could be said to characterize the decade of the 1920s throughout the country, in smaller cities such as Indianapolis, the transformation was more rapid and widespread than in larger cities. As sociologist Nathan Glazer has observed, the proportion of manual workers in Jewish communities tended to drop as one went from large to small cities, a reflection in part of the simple facts of opportunity. In smaller cities such as Indianapolis Jews faced fewer barriers to success, partly because there were fewer Jews in competition. Without having experienced a great struggle, the immigrant garment worker or peddler was now often the proprietor of his own retail business—the pants presser had his clothing shop; the peddler his dry goods store; the shoemaker his shoe store—and his American-born children often attended a university or perhaps even a professional school.[4]

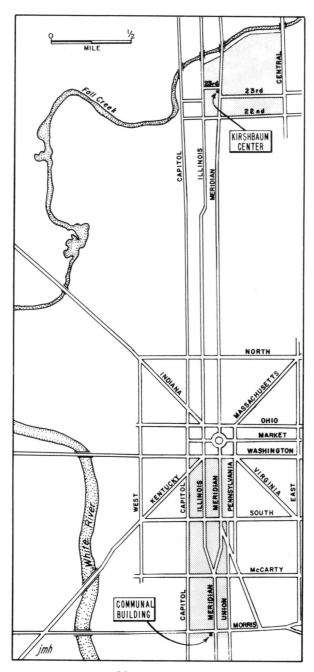

Map 2: 1920s

As families moved upward economically, they changed their residences to match their rising fortunes. The first move was often to Union Street in the more prosperous eastern section of the south side. After that, many families moved out of the south side altogether to addresses farther and farther north. With these moves out of the south side, the community lost some of its cohesiveness. In the south side the Jewish community had been concentrated on only a few streets—Maple, Eddy, and South Illinois. Now it was more scattered, although still concentrated in one area of the city. Only a few families lived in the western part of the city; fewer still lived to the east. Most lived in the north in an area whose center in 1925 was described as being just below Fall Creek and west of Central Avenue (see Map 2). By 1932 it was estimated that 65 percent of Indianapolis's Jews lived on the north side, 25 percent on the south side, and 10 percent in other parts of the city. The major new Jewish institutions of the twenties—the Kirshbaum Center, Central Hebrew Congregation, and Congregation Beth-El Zedeck— were all located in this new Jewish population center of the north side.[5]

The same forces that brought sweeping changes to the Indianapolis Jewish community in the twenties were at work in all American Jewish communities throughout the decade. As the prosperity of the war years and then the twenties made Jews more economically secure they abandoned the areas of first settlement for middle-class districts. Even New York City's Lower East Side emptied dramatically, declining from 353,000 in 1916 to 121,000 in 1930. However, this still left a large number of Jews in the neighborhood. Moreover, since those who remained tended to be not only the poorer Jews but also the more religious ones, traditional Jewish life continued to flourish in the New York ghetto. A smaller community like Indianapolis could not sustain a comparable exodus from the area of first settlement without suffering serious permanent damage. The reduction of the Indianapolis south side to 25 percent of the Jewish population in 1932 meant that only 1,600 to 1,700 Jews remained there. Without a certain degree of population density, traditional Judaism faces a constant struggle to survive. In the 1920s five Orthodox synagogues, along with the Talmud Torah, Linath Hazedeck, the *mikveh*, and various kosher meat markets and bakeries remained on the south side. Together

Louis and Masha Glogos boarded Jewish transients in their south side home from 1926 to 1928. A native of Russia, Louis Glogos was *shammash* of Congregation Sharah Tefilla for many years. (IHS)

Most south side Jewish children attended Public School No. 6. In this 1925 picture of an eighth grade class, at least eighteen of the thirty children pictured are Jewish. Although most of the city's residential neighborhoods and schools were segregated at this time, note the three black children in the class. (IHS)

In 1933 approximately 25 percent of the Jewish community still
lived on the south side. Meridian was the district's main street.
These snapshots of young south side residents from the 1930s are
now displayed at Reiswerg's butcher shop in Broad Ripple. (IHS)

A Dobrowitz family seder on the south side in the 1930s. The long
seder table extends through several rooms. Standing in the back
holding a baby is Daniel Firsch, who served as president of the
Zionist Organization of America in 1949. (IHS)

Members of the Sephardic community gather at their clubhouse on South Meridian Street to honor a visiting rabbi, about 1921 or 1922. Note Israeli and American flags hanging in the background. (IHS)

A Girl Scout troop sponsored by the Jewish Community Center, photographed in the late 1920s. (IHS)

Morris M. Feuerlicht was rabbi of
Indianapolis Hebrew Congregation
from 1904 to 1946. (IHS)

George Rabinoff, executive director of the Jewish Federation from
1921 to 1928. (AJHS)

Allan Bloom, first executive secretary of the Jewish Community Center Association, served from 1929 to 1949. He was first hired as educational director of the Communal Building in 1925. (IHS)

Basketball, the "Indiana madness," was an important part of the Communal Building and Kirshbaum Center athletic programs and their teams played in the city's amateur leagues. Here a Kirshbaum Center team poses with their coach. (IHS)

Congregation Beth-El Zedeck built and occupied this building at 34th and Ruckle Streets from 1925 until 1958 when they sold it to Congregation B'nai Torah and moved to the far north side. (IHS)

As a new graduate of the Jewish Theological Seminary, Milton Steinberg's first pulpit was Congregation Beth-El Zedeck, which he served from 1928 to 1933. (AJHS)

Sara Weinberg (on left), the Jewish Federation's first professional case worker, and Edith Steinberg, wife of Rabbi Milton Steinberg and chairman of the Federation's unemployment committee, outside the Communal Building in 1932. (IHS)

Sarah Goodman, the only woman to serve as president of the Jewish Welfare Federation, was a leader in many Jewish and civic causes, including the Indianapolis Symphony. (IHS)

Jacob A. (Jack) Goodman, a founder of Real Silk Hosiery Mills in 1920, was president of Congregation Beth-El Zedeck and of the Jewish Welfare Federation and was active in many other Jewish organizations. (IHS)

they faced an uphill battle to maintain a viable south side Jewish community.[6]

While the smaller number of Jews who remained in the area of first settlement faced a future of diminishing resources, those who moved out found themselves growing closer to the German Jewish Reform community. The division between "uptown" and "downtown" Jews softened as the two groups became neighbors. This tended to occur more rapidly in smaller communities, such as Indianapolis. In the largest cities, such as New York City, many of the wealthier German Jews moved out to an area of third settlement, perhaps an elite suburb, and thus continued to maintain some distance from the eastern Europeans. In medium-sized cities, where this occurred less frequently (although some of the wealthiest German Jews in Indianapolis did move out to the far north side during the 1920s), the two communities tended to come together faster. The first marriages between German and eastern European Jews—evidence that the two groups were growing closer—occurred during the twenties.

The immigrant generation had made the transition from working class to middle class with relative ease, not having had to surmount discriminatory barriers to Jewish advancement. After all, if a garment worker's ambition was to open a dry goods store on South Meridian Street, who was to block his way (aside from the forces of the market place)? While Jewish business ambitions were rarely thwarted, the native-born, college-bound children of these merchants and small manufacturers faced serious obstacles—the first in American Jewish history—to their social and professional advancement. In the 1920s as they began to enter universities and professional schools, which had long been Protestant-dominated, they faced newly erected discriminatory quotas. Xenophobic Protestants, who felt threatened by the changes transforming America, responded to Jewish attempts to enter elite institutions with alarm. Having succeeded in restricting immigration from eastern and southern Europe, these narrow-minded Protestants now erected barriers to Jewish entry into the professions, desirable residential neighborhoods, private clubs, and business and industrial corporations. In Indianapolis, for example, there were no Jewish members of any country club (except for Highland Country Club), and Jews were not admitted to the University Club, Propylaeum, and most other clubs. The exceptions to this rule were the Athenaeum and the Columbia Club. Certain residential neighborhoods were also restricted. Some firms, notably Eli Lilly and Company and L. S. Ayres Department Store, were believed to maintain a policy of not hiring Jews.[7]

The introduction of quotas and the restriction of employment opportunities were only part of a larger wave of anti-Semitism that plagued America until the mid-1940s. For most of the 1920s Henry Ford's *Dearborn Independent* churned out a steady flow of virulent anti-Semitism. Beginning in May 1920 Ford began publishing, in serialized form, *The Protocols of the Elders of Zion*, a scurrilous forgery whose theme was a Jewish conspiracy to rule the world. While the *Dearborn Independent* could be dismissed as the work of a demented eccentric, albeit an influential one, the rapid growth of the Ku Klux Klan in the twenties, reflecting the wide appeal of its message of intolerance for all but white Anglo-Saxon Protestants, was more unsettling. In the case of Indianapolis, the problem was also closer to home. The Ku Klux Klan was founded in Georgia in 1915 by Colonel William J. Simmons. Initially a small, local group, it grew rapidly, aided by the efforts of two professional publicity agents, Edward Y. Clarke and Mrs. Elizabeth Tyler, who were hired in 1920 to conduct a nationwide membership campaign. The organization, with its message of hatred toward Catholics, blacks, Jews, immigrants, "wets," and radicals, grew rapidly in the fertile ground of the xenophobic twenties. By 1925 between 4 and 5 million Americans were Klan members.

The Klan was first introduced into Indiana in 1920, and it proved to have a particularly strong appeal to Hoosiers. By 1923 the Klan claimed 400,000 members in Indiana, about 10 percent of the state's population. Opponents put the figure at less than 300,000, which is probably more accurate. Using a variety of contemporary sources, historian Kenneth T. Jackson estimated that between 1915 and 1944 the Indiana Klan had a total of 240,000 members. This was the highest membership of any state Klan. The Ohio, Texas, and Pennsylvania Klans followed in that order. Moreover, a much higher proportion of the state's population belonged to the Klan than in any other state of the Old Northwest. This reflected in part the distinctive composition of Indiana's population. Indiana stood out from surrounding states as having retained a relatively homogeneous population of old-stock Americans. Relatively few immigrants settled in Indiana at any period, and thus the state had only small numbers of Catholics, Jews, and immigrants. There were also no cities in the state to compete with neighboring Chicago, Cleveland, or Detroit. Indianapolis, the state's largest city, was quite small compared to these metropolitan giants. The state not only had a higher proportion of rural dwellers than neighboring states, but Hoosiers retained a stronger attachment to the rural ideal. Many were alarmed at the growth of the state's urban centers in the postwar era, associating them with moral decay, irreligiosity, crime, and foreign culture.[8]

Moreover, many rural dwellers were fundamentalist Protestants, many of whom harbored a fierce anti-Catholicism. Catholic immigrants were doubly hated, not only for their "bandanna handkerchief standard of living" but because of anti-Catholic fears of the power of Rome. Often rural Protestants also held traditional anti-Semitic views as well, although their anti-Catholicism appears to have been more intense. The migration of southern blacks to northern cities which began during the First World War increased the population of Indiana's cities and heightened existing anti-black feeling. Between 1910 and 1930 the nonwhite population of Indianapolis doubled from 22,000 to 44,000, constituting more than 12 percent of the city's population by 1930. The southern part of the state, with its strong ties to the south and border states, had always held a large reservoir of anti-black prejudice. The northward migration of blacks to the state only increased it.[9]

The fears and hatreds directed toward these three groups— Catholics, blacks, and Jews, in decreasing order of intensity— became the platform on which the Klan built its Indiana program. However, while these were the Klan's articulated enemies, the real, unspoken enemy was change. The Klan represented for many a last, desperate attempt to return to an idealized world which was no more (and probably had never actually existed). They wanted to recapture the pioneer America of myth and legend, when all American faces were white and even the immigrants spoke English. Indiana, according to the myth, had been inhabited by hardy pioneers hewing out an existence in the wilderness, building their log cabins at the edge of the forest, and farming the land. This world had vanished long before most Klan members were born, and, ironically, the state actually had a lower proportion of Catholics and immigrants in its population in 1920 than it had had in 1900. In 1900 18 percent of the state was Catholic; in 1920 only 10 percent was Catholic. During the same period, the black population of Indiana increased by 34 percent, yet Catholics were the Klan's most hated enemies. The reality of a situation, however, is not usually a persuasive argument for hatemongers and their followers.[10]

The Klan in Indiana fought its enemies verbally and symbolically. Its weekly newspaper, *The Fiery Cross,* conducted a war of words, its columns filled with hate material. Parades of masked marchers through the center of a town, cross burnings, threatened boycotts of supposedly Jewish-dominated businesses, and above all, the secrecy of the movement created an atmosphere of fear and terror without the use of physical violence.[11]

Above all else, however, the history of the Indiana Klan in the twenties is the story of the development of an effective political machine under the leadership of David C. Stephenson, who became Grand Dragon of the Indiana Realm in 1923. Stephenson's abilities, as much as anything else, probably contributed to the Klan's extraordinary success in Indiana. The high point of Klan political influence was the election of 1924. The Klan candidate, Ed Jackson, was elected governor, and the Klan was believed to control the Republican party. The 1925 state legislature was overwhelmingly Republican. While the number of Klan legislators is not known, it was assumed that the majority either were Klan members or sympathetic to the Klan. Internal struggles within the Klan, however, led to the defeat of all Klan-sponsored legislation. A few months after the 1925 legislature adjourned, Stephenson, who had once boasted "I am the law in Indiana," was in jail for the rape and murder of Madge Oberholtzer. Dissension within the ranks and Stephenson's arrest and conviction caused many to abandon the Klan and opened the way for a series of investigations of Klan affairs. Slowly, its power began to wane. The 1929 landslide election of Democrat Reginald H. Sullivan as mayor of Indianapolis signalled the end of Klan influence in local politics.[12]

The Klan did not constitute a direct threat to the security of the Jewish community. However, there was concern over the Klan's anti-Semitism and a fear over the potential danger it represented. Disagreements arose over the appropriate method with which to respond. Most appear to have agreed with Rabbi Jacob Bienenfeld, editor of the *Indiana Jewish Chronicle* from 1922 to 1923, that the best tactic was to remain silent in the face of Klan propaganda. Bienenfeld advocated "silent contempt" and defended the constitutional right of the Klan to sell its newspaper, *The Fiery Cross*, on the streets of Indianapolis, adding a hopeful note that "we can not imagine that mud-slinging articles will gain for the dispensers thereof, adherents." Others, clearly a minority, advocated offensive action. Jacob H. Hahn, an Indianapolis attorney and candidate for state senator in the Republican primary of 1924, believed "that the Jews should ... retaliate in the same manner as they are dealt with." It is not known exactly what he had in mind. Bess Robbins (ca. 1905–1961), a young attorney, called for a concerted public campaign against the Klan, advocating a ban on street sales of *The Fiery Cross:*

> It is up to the *Indiana Jewish Chronicle,* "the voice of the Jewish people of Indiana," ... and ... the prominent and influential Jewish citizens of Indianapolis to immediately stop the sale of [*The Fiery Cross*] upon the streets of Indianapolis. Every Jewish club, sorority, fraternity and every influential group of Jewish citizens should let their sentiments be known to the mayor ... to the final end that the voices of the newsboys shouting *"The Fiery Cross* — Tells you all about the Ku Klux Klan" may be silenced.[13]

One Jewish organization which did adopt an anti-Klan program was the local B'nai B'rith lodge, which in May 1925 urged its members to organize sentiment among businessmen and professional men to deal with exposed Klansmen, spread publicity through lodge bulletins, advise the Jewish community of any Klan violations of the law, and maintain contacts with other local groups.[14]

While the B'nai B'rith's tactics were to work behind the scenes, the approach of the American Unity League, the chief anti-Klan organization on the national scene, which attracted many Jewish members, was more public and vocal. In June 1923, Jacob Morgan, an Indianapolis attorney then president of the Indianapolis B'nai B'rith, was elected president, and Ralph Bamberger, an attorney and son of IHC charter member Herman Bamberger, was elected treasurer of the Indianapolis chapter of the league. In June 1923, in view of reports that the Klan was planning a statewide meeting with public demonstrations in Indianapolis early in July, the American Unity League sent a large delegation to a city council meeting to press for an ordinance banning the wearing of masks in public. Such an ordinance had already been proposed twice by councilman Otto Ray but had not been passed. The league brought a reported one thousand sympathizers to the council meeting, but the anti-mask ordinance was defeated six to two.[15]

Direct action against the Klan was rare, however. The Klan's virulent verbal attacks and its apparent political power created an atmosphere of fear. In this setting, Jewish leaders felt that the best response was to demonstrate that Jewish behavior in no way justified anti-Semitic allegatons. Community leaders reminded their followers that every Jew must be a model citizen beyond reproach. The Federation sponsored a strong Americanization program, whose goal was to ensure that every immigrant Jew in the city became a naturalized citizen. Federation leaders kept a careful check on Jewish donations to the Community Fund and encouraged Jews to give generously, lest they be accused of receiving more in Fund appropriations than they put in. Community leaders sponsored the creation of a board to reduce supposed irregularities in the distribution of sacramental wine. (The Klan was allied with the "bone-dry" forces of the Anti-Saloon League.) The board stipulated that only Jews with synagogue membership could receive wine. Membership lists were carefully cross-checked to make sure that those who held multiple synagogue memberships did not receive an extra supply of wine. The B'nai B'rith lodge introduced the singing of the "Star Spangled Banner" to close lodge meetings. In these and other ways, Jewish leaders obviously hoped that they could somehow convince the Klan that American Jews were patriotic, loyal, good citizens. Indianapolis Jewry had fallen into the trap of blaming themselves for the occurrence of anti-Semitism.[16]

Jews were also urged to close ranks and forget their differences so as to show a united front against the Klan. In an editorial in the *Indiana Jewish Chronicle* in March 1923, Morris Strauss commented:

> we certainly feel safe in venturing to assert that a careful analysis of the disease—anti-semitism—would conclusively prove it to be due, to a very appreciable extent, to the curse of discord among various Jewish

elements ... we can, should, and must break down those barriers that we have erected to separate us.

It is obviously absurd to think that anti-Jewish prejudice results from any kind of intracommunal controversies or divisions. However, the tendency to close ranks, to stick together, has been a common reaction of Jews to an anti-Semitic campaign.[17]

A year later, Strauss summarized a speech given by Rabbi Markowitz at the state meeting of B'nai B'rith at Lafayette, in which the rabbi declared that "the greatest enemy of the Jew is himself." Strauss agreed, adding, "Many will flay the enemies without as being most dangerous, ... but they pale into insignificance when compared to the greatest destroyer, the Jew himself, ... by his lack of harmony and ignorance of the traditions of his faith." This last argument, that Jews needed to increase their Jewish knowledge in the face of attack, was one of the themes of Rabbi Feuerlicht's *Rosh Hashanah* sermon at IHC in 1923. Said Feuerlicht, "these white-robed men ... should not be allowed to take the Bible away from us," adding that "if we give it more study the Klansmen will have greater reverence toward us."[18]

All of these arguments assume not only that Jews are responsible for anti-Semitism but that anti-Semitic arguments have a rational basis. In actuality, the prejudices and hatreds of Klan followers were based on irrational fears and emotions. The actions and activities of real Jews have had very little to do with the growth of anti-Semitic movements anywhere. There is no doubt, however, that Indianapolis Jews were frightened by the Klan. Afraid to take direct action against their enemies, Jews retreated instead to self-criticism. In recalling the turbulent decade Feuerlicht wrote in his memoirs that "Klan terrorism made any kind of active resistance short of rioting and shooting seem futile." During the period Feuerlicht became the single most important spokesman for the Jewish community against the Klan, "publicly representing the case for harmony and brotherhood as opposed to the Klan's call for disunity and discord." His charming personality, sense of humor, genuine tolerance for others, and public-speaking abilities catapulted him into the public eye during the twenties as a defender of minority interests. Feuerlicht became a popular speaker for service, business, church, and women's organizations throughout the state that, as he put it, "wanted to hear some kind of pronouncements from the minority or unpopular side of the subject." Rather than attack head on, Feuerlicht preferred to satirize and ridicule the Klan's exaggerated kind of Americanism and then "appeal to the better judgment and higher patriotism of [his] audience." Since few individuals were willing even to poke fun at the hooded order publicly, Feuerlicht's fame spread, and he earned a reputation as an "outspoken foe of the Ku Klux Klan."[19]

He was often called upon to "represent" the Jewish community at interfaith gatherings or important civic events. He helped organize two interfaith meetings during the 1920s to show the Klan that Indianapolis was not completely in its grip. On December 15, 1925, a huge crowd filled the Cadle Tabernacle, a supposed Klan stronghold, to hear Rev. S. Parkes Cadman, president of the Federal Council of Churches of America, decry group strife and plead for brotherhood. Feuerlicht gave the opening prayer at the meeting; Bishop Frederick D. Leete of the Indianapolis Methodist District and Msgr. Francis F. Gavisk, chancellor of the Indianapolis Catholic diocese, also participated.[20]

While Feuerlicht was perhaps the only Jew to take to the lecture circuit to fight the Klan, others quietly organized efforts to defeat them at the ballot box. Since membership in the Klan was secret and anti-Klan voters might unknowingly vote for a Klan candidate, public identification of candidates who were unsympathetic to the Klan was essential. Thus, for example, in October 1924 the Ladies Auxiliary of the Hebrew Free Loan Society endorsed the candidacy of Captain William E. English for state senator because of "Capt. English's friendliness to the Jewish people and the fact that he is not a Klansman or in sympathy." That same month the normally nonpartisan *Indiana Jewish Chronicle* published a list of Republican and Democratic candidates who either did not belong to the Klan or were unalterably opposed to it. Two prominent Jewish businessmen—Charles Sommers, owner of D. Sommers Furniture Company and Gibson Automotive Supply Company, and Albert Goldstein of Goldstein Brothers department store—waged a private campaign to expose politicians who were secretly Klansmen. They approached the *Indianapolis Times*, the first city newspaper to oppose the Klan openly, and together they hired private detectives to trail local politicians in order to detect those who were Klan members.[21]

The Klan effectively exercised power under Stephenson because it became a political machine. Even though they must have realized the futility of it, Jewish candidates ran for state office in each election throughout the decade, even in Republican primaries, although that party was the center of Klan strength. In the 1924 Republican state primary, Jessie Levy, a young woman lawyer, Jacob H. Hahn, a lawyer, and Louis Markun (ca. 1900–1973), a theater owner, were all candidates for the state legislature. Hahn promised, if elected, to "introduce laws for the protection of all against those who wear masks" and for the registration of all secret societies with the secretary of state. Of the three candidates only Markun survived the primaries, but he was ultimately defeated. He was finally elected to the General Assembly in 1929 after the Klan's power had declined. In 1926 Jessie Levy and Henry Winkler, a Democratic attorney, ran for the legislature. Winkler alone made it to the general election before going down to defeat. In 1928 Markun and Bess Robbins (Kaufman), a Democratic attorney, both made it to the general election for the legislature. She eventually served in the House in the 1933 and 1935 sessions.[22]

Although there were no Jews elected to either state or municipal office during the era of Klan control, Jews did hold appointed political offices, serving on a variety of city and state commissions and boards. Sol Schloss of Schloss Brothers clothing merchants was appointed president of the Indianapolis Board of Health in 1923 (and reappointed in 1925) by Mayor Samuel Lewis Shank, an outspoken Klan opponent. Schloss, who was praised for his leadership of the board of health, was the first businessman to serve on the board. William B. Miller, one of two Jewish graduates in the Indiana Law School class of 1924, was appointed deputy prosecuting attorney for Marion County in 1926. Lawrence B. Davis was elected president of the Indianapolis Bar Association in 1924, the third Jew to hold the office. (The others were Nathan Morris and Louis Newberger.) Albert S. Goldstein was elected president of the Merchants Association twice in the twenties.[23]

In the final analysis, although the Klan may have stirred up latent anti-Semitic feelings and exacerbated social discrimination which the Jewish community always experienced to some degree, its activities probably had little direct effect on the Jewish community. There was a Klan attempt to boycott movie theaters owned by Jews. Movie theaters, rather than some other group of

Jewish businesses, were probably singled out because of the connection in anti-Semitic thought between Jews and the corruption of morals, an association Protestant fundamentalists often made with the movies as well. However, as far as is known, no Jewish theater owner was forced to close his theater. Klan attempts to force the dismissal of Jewish employees from Methodist Hospital by threatening a boycott of the hospital were also unsuccessful because the hospital superintendent refused to be intimidated. An attempt to block the construction of Congregation Beth El's synagogue at 34th and Ruckle, which some saw as a Klan-inspired action, was defeated by a ruling of the Board of Zoning Appeals, and construction proceeded. Many Jews refused to be intimidated. When the Klan launched their "buy American" campaign, Louis and Rose Shapiro promptly changed the name of their store, the American Grocery Store, to Shapiro's and decorated the façade with Jewish stars. When a burning cross appeared on the shoreline during a Beth El steamboat cruise from Broad Ripple to Pleasure Island, the *Indiana Jewish Chronicle* remarked that "this did not dampen the enjoyment of the evening, but reflected how foolish some men will act to display their ignorance and deviltry in such manner."[24]

The Klan, of course, was eventually discredited. By 1928, the year the *Indianapolis Times* won a Pulitzer Prize for its "savage campaign" against the Ku Klux Klan, there were less than 7,000 paid-up members in the entire state.[25]

One should not assume that while the Klan's power lasted the Jewish community was paralyzed into inaction against other perceived threats to its integrity. The Indianapolis Jewish community in the 1920s was a self-confident community, and it had earned the respect of the larger community. In 1925 George Rabinoff reported to the Jewish Federation board that he had recently learned that the Wheeler City Rescue Mission, a Protestant missionary enterprise, had been conducting sewing classes and religious services for a group of young Jewish girls. A committee appointed to investigate the matter approached the mission and expressed their displeasure with these direct attempts to convert Jews to Christianity. Although the mission admitted that they had carried on the Jewish work for four years, they agreed to discontinue it after being told that the Jewish community disapproved.[26]

The Changing Role of the Jewish Federation

Disturbing as the Klan or other external threats might have been, for most of the decade Jewish energies were focused on internal community affairs. With the abrupt end of mass immigration, many of the community's institutions, which had been developed to aid the immigrants' adjustment to American life, became unnecessary. The Nathan Morris House and later the Communal Building had provided social and educational programs for immigrant Jews and their children. By the mid-1920s their clientele was rapidly disappearing, due to the increasing prosperity of the community and the absence of further immigration from Europe. The number of potential students for the Federation's English and naturalization classes declined. In 1926 Leo Kaminsky (1887–1953), a lawyer and himself the son of Polish immigrants who headed the Federation's Naturalization Committee, noted with some regret that the number of unnaturalized persons was decreasing with each passing year. Similarly, when enrollment in the Federation-sponsored evening English class dropped below ten pupils, the minimum required by the city board of education, the board refused to continue paying for the teacher. However, the Federation's English Instructon Committee wanted to continue to offer the class for the six students who were enrolled, and the Federation agreed to pay the teacher's salary of six dollars per week.[27]

Other Federation-sponsored neighborhood projects also felt the effects of the restriction of European immigration and the exodus of Jews from the south side. By 1922–1923 the children's dental clinic and the baby clinic, both operated by the Indianapolis Board of Health at the Communal Building, were serving almost as many non-Jews as Jews. Thirty-nine percent of the children treated at the dental clinic and 50 percent of the babies seen at the baby clinic were not Jewish. The decline in the number of Jews utilizing these subsidized health services may have also reflected the increasing prosperity of south side Jews, who were now able to seek private health care.[28]

In its first sixteen years, the Jewish Federation focused its energies on the relief of poverty in the immigrant community. At each weekly meeting of the Federation's officers, the superintendent presented the cases which had been dealt with in the previous week. In some instances, he merely reported how they had been handled: M. L. was given a gross of matches to peddle; B. W. was given a job at the stockyards. In other cases, he requested the officers' advice or authorization to proceed. Should baby M., who was now in an orphanage, be sent to join his father in Boulder, Colorado, as his father requested? Should he hire a private detective to investigate a white slave trade case or find a husband who had deserted his wife and prosecute him? In the years before the First World War the executive committee reviewed twenty-five to thirty such cases a week. Many of those requesting aid were transients who stayed in the city briefly but just as many were permanent residents.[29]

Not only did relief cases consume the largest part of the officers' and superintendent's time during the era of immigration, but expenditures for relief accounted for a substantial share of the Federation's budget. From 1906 to 1914, expenditures for relief (e.g., for groceries, rent, furniture, coal, clothing, tools, transportation, board and lodging, Passover supplies, and medical expenses) averaged 25.5 percent of the yearly budget. Much of the non-relief part of the budget was also directly related to immigrant adjustment: expenditures for the health clinics, Americanization classes, south side social and educational facilities, etc. In the 1920s direct relief began to take a diminishing share of the budget. In his presidential report for 1922–1923, G. A. Efroymson reported that "due to better industrial conditions and to few immigrants locating here" the Federation had spent less on relief work and noted that "if there is no great increase in immigration, our relief work will likely continue to decrease." Direct relief had constituted 34.2 percent of total expenditures in 1909–1910, and 32.5 percent in 1914–1915; it was 17.8 percent in 1924–1925. As Efroymson predicted, the proportion spent on relief continued to decline throughout the decade.[30]

Instead of reducing the scope of its activities, the Federation sought to compensate for the loss of its poor immigrant clientele by expanding into new areas. During the early 1920s, the board of governors debated the new direction the Federation was to take. In 1916 Raphael Kirshbaum, a wealthy German Jewish immigrant, had left $60,000 to the Federation, $50,000 of which was to establish an old-age home and orphanage as a memorial to his deceased wife Flora. The Federation leadership was not sure, however, that the community needed such an institution. For the next nine years the Federation board, the Kirshbaum Bequest Committee, and the Kirshbaum heirs wrestled with the question of how to use the legacy. Their first step was to hire a consultant to survey the Jewish community and assess its needs; in March 1919 Maurice Hexter, superintendent of the United Jewish Charities of Cincinnati, was engaged to do the survey.[31]

Several of Hexter's recommendations, such as the establishment of a free medical dispensary on the south side and an increase in recreational and group work among young people, were incorporated into three alternative plans presented by the Bequest Committee in October 1921: (1) to construct a building next to the Communal Building to house medical and social gatherings; (2) to erect a centrally located community center to house the activities of such organizations as B'nai B'rith, a Young Men's Hebrew Association, the Jewish Federation, the Council of Jewish Women, Boy and Girl Scouts, and so forth; and (3) to build an old-age home, which, although not needed at present, would be needed in the future. None of the proposals proved completely satisfactory, however, and none was acted on. In July 1922, the Bequest Committee offered a new proposal. It recommended the construction of an institution to provide proper care for old people, adult convalescents, mothers, and infants requiring health-building and for summer camp work. The Kirshbaum heirs were satisfied with the proposal and were willing to appeal to the probate court to approve the necessary changes, but George Rabinoff (1893–1970), who had become superintendent of the Federation in 1921, was not satisfied. In February 1925 he made a new suggestion.[32]

Rabinoff suggested that the Jewish Shelter House and Old Home become a constituent agency of the Federation, in which case there would be no need for another old-age home. The south side Jewish community was breaking up, and there was a growing Jewish community on the north side without social and educational facilities. The large mansion at 23rd and Meridian that had housed the Indianapolis Club was for sale. The club, founded in 1907 with Albert M. Rosenthal (ca. 1876–1935) of the Standard Paper Company as its first president, was disbanding and transferring its activities to the newly completed Broadmoor Country Club on Kessler Boulevard, of which Rosenthal again was the first president. A son-in-law of Raphael Kirshbaum and a trustee of the Kirschbaum estate, Rosenthal helped to negotiate the reinterpretation of the Kirshbaum bequest. Rabinoff suggested that the Federation use the Kirshbaum money to purchase the Indianapolis Club for use as a Jewish community center. The board approved the plan, and none too soon, as the Kirshbaum heirs had threatened that if the Federation did not reach a decision by July 15, 1925, the bequest would be given to another charity. The trustees of the estate approved the plan, and although the club was about to be sold to another party, Rosenthal, in his dual role as a Kirshbaum trustee and a director of the Indianapolis Club, agreed to sell the clubhouse to the Federation for use as a Jewish center. The Indianapolis Club was purchased, and the architectural firm of Vonnegut, Bohn and Mueller was hired to draw up plans for the remodelling of the club.[33]

Forced into a reexamination of their purpose by the receipt of the large Kirshbaum bequest, under the firm and persuasive guidance of George Rabinoff the Federation had found a new role. By all accounts, it was obvious that the Jewish community was prospering; there were few new immigrants coming to the city; and there was a growing Jewish middle class. The clientele the Federation had been organized to serve was rapidly disappearing. Institutions, however, tend to be self-perpetuating. Rather than declare its work done and merely close up or reduce its services, the Federation had begun to search for new goals. Rabinoff seized on the idea of providing social, educational, and recreational activities for the Jewish middle class, an idea the board eagerly adopted. This represented a dramatic shift from the original purposes of the Federation. No longer was it an organization run by the elite for the benefit of the misfortunate; rather, the leaders and directors of the Federation now became their own potential clientele.

The Jewish Federation was well served during these years of transition. Through the seven years (1921–1928) that George Rabinoff served as its superintendent and executive director (the title was changed in 1927), he guided the Federation through a series of sweeping changes in its structure and orientation. Under his leadership, the Federation was transformed from a highly centralized organization run by a small board of governors and one professional to an administrative body overseeing the work of constituent agencies that were functioning with a great deal of autonomy and were led by their own professionals and boards. Rabinoff, a native of New York City and a graduate of the New York School of Social Work, was one of the first trained Jewish social workers in the country and a pioneer in the field of Jewish communal service. Before coming to Indianapolis, he was superintendent of the Hartford (Connecticut) United Jewish Charities, 1914–1918; an official of the national Jewish Welfare Board, 1918-1919; and director of case work for Cincinnati's United Jewish Social Agencies, 1920–1921. Rabinoff left Indianapolis in 1928 to become the associate executive director of the Bureau of Jewish Social Research (1928–1932) and was instrumental in establishing the Council of Jewish Federations and Welfare Funds, the national umbrella organization of local federations, serving as its first executive (1932–1935).[34]

The organization which represented the Federation's new middle-class orientation, the Jewish Community Center Association, was created in June 1926. The JCCA was to function as an autonomous affiliate of the Federation to operate the Kirshbaum Community Center, the Communal Building, and any other recreational or educational efforts of the Federation. However, to retain some control of the organization, the Federation board would appoint one-fourth of the Association board. Allan Bloom (ca. 1899–1972), who had been hired as educational director by the Federation in September 1925, became general secretary of the JCCA, overseeing the work of the Communal Building and the Kirshbaum Center. Leonard A. Strauss (ca. 1898–1954) of the Kahn Tailoring Company was elected the first president of the Association.[35]

The Kirshbaum Center was dedicated in November 1926, and it was an immediate success. It became the center of Jewish life for the north side, offering a "diversified program and a common meeting ground without the touch of philanthropy" that characterized the Communal Building. While the two centers offered some programs that were similar—boys and girls clubs, game rooms, dances, minstrel shows (always very popular), athletics (especially basketball; both centers had teams which played in the city's amateur leagues)—each also organized specific programs geared to its own constituency. The Communal Building sponsored English and naturalization classes and housed dental and medical clinics. Until 1929 the Federation's administrative offices, as well as all of its facilities for relief work, were housed under its roof. The Federation leadership did not have condescending attitudes toward the Kirshbaum Center as it did to the Communal Building with its whiff of poverty, its poor Jews and *shnorrers.* While the aim of Communal Building programs was to uplift as well as to Americanize its clientele, Kirshbaum Center programs were designed to help the middle-class participants fill their leisure time constructively.[36]

The Kirshbaum Center housed more adult education programs than did the Communal Building. In its first year of operation, Professor Jacob R. Marcus of the Hebrew Union College in Cincinnati delivered six lectures on Jewish history, and the Center organized an adult literary group, opened a library, and inaugurated one of its best-known programs, the Open Forum. The Open Forum, a subscription lecture series featuring nationally famous speakers, was a popular institution in many American cities in the twenties, but it had not yet been introduced in Indianapolis. As its organizers hoped, the Open Forum became a part of Indianapolis civic life, and the series, "dedicated to the public discussion of . . . interesting subjects, free from sectarian influence and open to all," attracted many non-Jewish subscribers. Jewish topics were discussed only rarely. These were primarily reserved for the "Jewish study courses," another lecture series. The program of speakers for the Open Forum's maiden season set the pattern for ensuing years. It included Rabbi Solomon B. Freehof, actress Louise Closser Hale, anthropologist George A. Dorsey, Reverend John Haynes Holmes, and historian Will Durant.[37]

Programs such as the Open Forum clearly set the Kirshbaum Center apart from the Communal Building. For, while many of their programs were similar, interest in Communal Building programs did not extend beyond the south side. It remained a settlement house serving the needs of residents of a poor neighborhood. In contrast, the Kirshbaum Center offered cultural programming to appeal to the more educated residents of the entire city. The development of the Kirshbaum Orchestra in 1927, like the Open Forum, is another example of a Kirshbaum Center program filling a previous void in the city's cultural life. The first Kirshbaum Orchestra consisted of about thirty amateur musicians who played under a series of professional leaders. By 1928 Ferdinand Schaefer (ca. 1861–1953) took over the orchestra. Schaefer, a German-born violinist and conductor, came to Indianapolis in 1903 and had been associated with earlier attempts to establish a symphony orchestra in the city.

For a city that claimed to love music, Indianapolis was in the curious position of having been unable to support a symphony orchestra for more than a season or two. Several attempts at establishing a regular orchestra had failed. Using the Kirshbaum Orchestra as a nucleus, Schaefer decided to expand it into a regular orchestra of sixty chairs and to present a series of public concerts. His project met with the enthusiastic encouragement of Leonard A. Strauss, president of the Jewish Community Center Association and a respected amateur musician himself. The musicians gave a few preliminary concerts in 1929–1930 and their first official concert on November 3, 1930, in Caleb Mills Hall. It was a great success and was followed by three more concerts. Thus, the Indianapolis Symphony was born. Leonard Strauss became chairman of the Indiana State Symphony Society, which was organized in the spring of 1931 to support the symphony. He was also a founder of the Ensemble Music Society and the National Association of Chamber Music Musicians.[38]

With the establishment of the JCCA, group work and recreational programs no longer fell directly under Federation supervision. New staff members with expertise in the field as well as lay people with interests in the area were brought in to administer and organize this aspect of the Federation program. George Rabinoff, the Federation executive director, hoped to establish a similar agency to supervise the Federation's relief and social work programs, but the process was more difficult.

In October 1921, the Jewish Federation board approved Rabinoff's suggestion that it establish a standing case committee to meet regularly and advise with him on family problems and relief expenditures. In suggesting the formation of such a committee, Rabinoff had a secret agenda. He was not only looking for an interested group to advise him in relief matters, but he hoped to coopt onto the committee many neighborhood "troublemakers," people who were critical of the Federation's relief methods and conducted their own charity work, often at cross-purposes with the Federation.[39]

The Family Service and Relief Committee, with Julius Falender (1877–1951) as its first chairman, included members of many small south side charity societies. Rabinoff hoped that by bringing these people into the decision-making process they would come to see the value of the professional case work method and abandon their old-fashioned methods, which he and other professionals believed encouraged house-to-house beggars and transients. The plan, however, did not succeed because the neighborhood committee members mistrusted the Federation too much and could not be convinced of the merits of the "impersonal" case work method over their own style of charity work. Since the experiment had failed, Rabinoff reorganized the committee in 1928 and filled it with a group of business and professional men and women who understood the doctrines of scientific case work and who would help, he hoped, influence others to see its value.[40]

Rabinoff's next step in the slow process of professionalizing relief work was to hire an additional staff member to handle social service work. Rose Bogen, a Yiddish-speaking visiting nurse, began in 1921 to take on some of the case work and also direct the Federation's summer health camp, Camp Ida Wineman. After Bogen left, there was for a time only a half-time family visitor. Then in July 1926, Sara Weinberg, a young social worker from Cleveland, became the full-time case worker, and the Federation's social services were transferred entirely from volunteer to professional hands. Weinberg's area of responsibility was broad. She cooperated actively with many other social agencies, such as the schools, courts, and employment bureaus. With the help of the Family Service and Relief Committee, she organized the city's Jewish doctors to provide a consultation service on medical problems for indigent Jewish patients. Weinberg also provided vocational guidance, arranged for child boarding, handled the registration for Camp Ida Wineman, and stayed in close contact with the administration and clientele of the Jewish Shelter House and Old Folks Home where she sent transients. Thorough records were kept on every case she handled. When Rabinoff resigned as executive director in 1928 he suggested that the Family Service and Relief Committee be made into a constituent agency. The Federation president, G. A. Efroymson, concurred, as did H. Joseph Hyman, Rabinoff's successor. Finally, late in 1928, the Federation approved the creation of the Jewish Family Service Society under terms similar to those of the Jewish Community Center Association.[41]

The board of directors of the Jewish Family Service Society represented the Jewish organizations already active in social service in the city. Eight of the twenty-one board directors were selected by the following organizations: the Jewish Federation, the Jewish Welfare Fund, the Council of Jewish Women, the Jewish Shelter House and Old Folks Home, the Medical Advisory Board of the Jewish Federation, the Bikur Cholim Society, the Linath Hazedeck Society, and the Hebrew Free Loan Association. The remaining thirteen directors of the Society were elected at-large. Attorney Jackiel W. Joseph (b. 1887) was the Society's first president.[42]

The elaborate charitable and educational network developed by the Indianapolis Jewish community by the 1920s was remarkable, but it was not unique. For a variety of reasons, American Jews did not make use of municipal relief programs or nonsectarian charities but preferred to create their own charity and self-help programs. No matter how secure they felt in America, Jewish pride, as well as a strong reluctance to let non-Jews know about Jewish problems, made them reluctant to turn to outsiders for help. This in turn led to the development of a sophisticated network of Jewish communal agencies. Certainly no other American group developed such an elaborate system.

As group work and social services fell increasingly under the province of specialized agencies, the Jewish Federation board concerned itself primarily with fund raising and the allocation of funds. The Federation jealously guarded its fund-raising monopoly, dealing harshly with organizations that attempted to violate it. Groups receiving funds from the Federation who attempted to conduct separate campaigns of any kind in the city (including bazaars, raffles, etc.) lost their right to receive Federation funds. Then, in 1918, overwhelmed by the spirit of civic unity that followed America's entry into the war, the Jewish Federation surrendered its campaign monopoly* and became part of the War Chest, whose

*Although the Federation may have abandoned its fund-raising campaigns, through the Indianapolis Association for the Relief of Jewish War Sufferers—the

first drive was conducted in the city in May of that year. The War Chest was conceived as a means of consolidating the collection and administration of the various war funds in the city as well as local charities. The creation of one mechanism to collect all funds would, it was hoped, be more efficient as a lower proportion of the money raised would then have to be used for the administration of the campaign itself. Similar campaigns had already been successfully conducted in many other American cities. Charles B. Sommers (1873–1941), a wealthy Jewish businessman, was chairman of the first War Chest campaign in Indianapolis.[43]

The Federation entered into the relationship with the War Chest* enthusiastically and became an active member of the Council of Social Agencies, an organization of approximately eighty social welfare agencies created by the Community Fund in 1923. Upon joining the War Chest the Federation agreed to conduct no separate fund-raising. Money which had previously been given to the Federation would now be donated to the Community Chest. Federation board members were not only expected to make substantial donations to the Community Chest but also to work in the campaign by soliciting donations from members of the Jewish community and providing Jewish campaign workers. (In 1923, for example, the Federation was asked to provide one hundred Jewish workers for the campaign.)[44]

The mechanism created by the Community Chest required the Federation to submit its budget, including the donations it made to non-Indianapolis institutions, to the Chest board for approval. It then received a monthly payment from the Chest. However, the relationship was still young when serious problems began to surface due to the inability of the Community Chest to meet its campaign goals. After the Community Chest informed the Federation in June 1921 that the Federation would receive only 75 percent of

local branch of the American Jewish Relief Committee—money was raised throughout the war years for the devastated Jewish communities of Europe. The Indianapolis Association was organized in 1915 with Samuel E. Rauh, chairman; G. A. Efroymson, vice-chairman; Joseph Wineman, treasurer; and Michael Bamberger, secretary. Because of the pressing needs of European Jewry, their quota of $25,000 was tripled to $75,000 in 1918. Indianapolis Association for the Relief of Jewish War Sufferers, *Report*, 1917, 1918; idem, flyer, Feb. 1, 1918, JWF Records.

*The War Chest became the Community Chest in 1920. In 1923 it became the Community Fund. It is currently known as the United Way.

the amount it had requested ($27,000 instead of $36,000), the Federation board appointed a committee to solicit funds from Jews who had not yet contributed to the Community Chest. Presumably, the Federation leadership hoped that if they produced more for the campaign their stipend would be increased.[45]

However, as the Community Fund's inability to meet its campaign goal became a chronic problem, some Jews began to argue against putting ever-increasing pressure on Jewish participation in the Community Fund campaign. In 1924, when the Community Fund campaign again did not reach its quota, the Federation board was divided as to how much further effort should be made among the Jewish community. They finally decided that the Jewish community should not be singled out for a further fund-raising effort. Fearful lest they be accused of taking more from the Fund than they put in, however, the Federation began keeping careful records of how much money Jews were contributing to the Fund. In May 1925, it was reported that 458 Jewish contributors had donated $55,476. A year later, the Federation annual report included a detailed analysis of Jewish contributors to the 1926 Community Fund campaign. Jewish contributors numbering 442 had given $60,152, of which over half, $37,170, had come from only twenty-two donors. The Jewish contribution made up 9.2 percent of the total collection of $651,077. Not only were Jews giving in a much higher proportion than their numbers in the city, but the "Jewish" contribution of $60,152 was actually twice that of the Community Fund's allocation to the Federation of $30,651.[46]

When the Jewish Federation initially joined the War Chest, the War Chest board agreed to honor all of the Federation's budgetary commitments, including its appropriations to national Jewish organizations. When Community Chest campaigns began to fall short the allocations to national institutions were the first to be questioned. In 1921 the Community Chest eliminated $7,500 from the Federation budget, the amount allocated to national Jewish institutions. When the Federation board explained to the Community Chest that these institutions—for example, the Cleveland Orphan Asylum, the National Jewish Hospital in Denver, and the National Desertion Bureau—were actually used for local relief, the Community Chest board was satisfied and agreed to reinstate these items in the Federation budget. This explanation, however, was really only half the story. The Federation's commitment to these and other national organizations went beyond the mere fact that they may have extended services to a member of the Indianapolis Jewish community. The strength of the relationship of Indianapolis Jewry to world Jewry created a basic incompatibility between the objectives of the Federation and those of the Community Chest. The Community Chest was solely concerned with local needs, while the Federation was equally committed to local and world Jewish needs. By relinquishing the right to raise and allocate funds, the Federation jeopardized its ability to send funds for the relief of Jews in need throughout the world.[47]

Faced with decreased support from the Community Chest, the Federation began to borrow money to pay off its commitments to outside organizations. In 1927, for example, the board borrowed $4,000 from the Meyer-Kiser Bank for this purpose. As deficits and interest payments began to mount, the Federation board began to consider organizing an independent fund-raising campaign. The board first discussed the idea in May 1925, but decided instead to make a concerted effort to raise additional pledges to the Community Fund. Eight months later, George Rabinoff proposed that the Federation organize a campaign for those local causes, in particular religious and educational institutions, which did not fall under the purview of the Community Fund. (The Fund did not support sectarian activities.) Rabinoff was especially concerned that the Jewish Educational Association (JEA), the new name of the United Hebrew Schools, needed a stronger financial base. The JEA, which received no support from the Federation, depended upon tuition and the proceeds from an annual Purim Ball.[48]

A committee was appointed to study the situation, and in April 1926 chairman Ralph Bamberger (1871–1947) presented its report. The committee recommended the creation of a broad and thoroughly representative "Jewish Council" to consider requests for funds from Jewish agencies not presently supported by either the Jewish Federation or the Community Fund and to raise the funds necessary to meet its appropriations. Eight more months of discussion followed, and in January 1927 the structure and scope of the "Jewish Council," whose name was changed to the Jewish Welfare Fund, were defined. It would be an autonomous constituent of the Federation. Its purpose would be to study, pass upon, and raise funds for the following purposes: to supply local Jewish capital fund needs; to support local Jewish movements for which support could not be claimed from the Community Fund; to meet Federation deficits due to the insufficiency of the Community Fund; to fulfill requirements of national institutions not being adequately supported; and to aid other national institutions that might be entitled to support from Indianapolis (see Table 1).[49]

By design, the board of the Jewish Welfare Fund represented a much greater cross section of Indianapolis Jewry than did the board of the Jewish Federation. The first chairman was Jacob A. (Jack) Goodman (1885–1949), hosiery manufacturer, Zionist, and leader of Congregation Beth-El Zedeck. Other members of the first board

Table 1.

First Jewish Welfare Fund Campaign, Recommended Major Appropriations (1927)[a]

Jewish Federation	$10,500	to cover deficits of 1926–1927
Hadassah	1,000	capital fund for building hospital in Palestine
Jewish Educational Association	19,182	includes $1,000 in deficits to May 1927
B'nai B'rith	17,500	for Cleveland Orphan Asylum campaign
United Palestine Appeal	17,500	1927 appropriation
Young Men's Sephardim Club	1,700	capital fund for remodelling Sephardim Community Center
Hebrew Immigrant Aid Society	500	for immigrant diversion program to South America
Miscellaneous institutions	5,500	
Subtotal	73,382	
Reserve fund	7,000	
Total	80,382	

[a]Jewish Federation Minute Book, Jewish Welfare Fund, Board of Directors, May 4, 1927.

included Daniel Frisch (1897–1950), a militant Zionist active in the Zionist Organization of America; David Calderon of the Sephardic community; Rabbi Samuel A. Katz (ca. 1872–1949), the leading south side Orthodox rabbi; Mrs. Rachael Domont (b. 1886) and Charles Medias (ca. 1867–1938), two of the strongest supporters of the Jewish Educational Association; Philip Grenwald of the Hungarian community; and Samuel E. Rauh (1854–1935), an old-line German immigrant and one of the wealthiest Jews in the city.[50]

It is the focus on the "big giver" that has always distinguished Jewish fund raising, and it set the tone of the very first Jewish Welfare Fund campaign in Indianapolis. Setting the pattern of solicitation for all future campaigns, the Fund solicited contributions from big givers first. However, the first campaign was not a success, raising only 62 percent of its goal. The following year, 1928, the Fund introduced a pre-campaign formal banquet dinner for big givers, a strategy that has become a mainstay of most community welfare fund and federation campaigns since then but was something of an innovation at the time. The 1928 dinner was at the home of Charles Sommers. The second Jewish Welfare Fund campaign in 1928 was more successful than the first; having learned from the errors of the first campaign, the Fund lowered its campaign goal and was able to exceed its quota (see Table 2).[51]

The Rise of Conservative Judaism

In the 1920s the Jewish Federation through the Kirshbaum Center began to provide for the secular needs of the growing Jewish middle class of the north side. As Jews prospered and left the south side, their rising social status was often reflected in a desire for a different kind of Jewish worship experience than the old style south side *shul* provided. While many north side Jews continued to return to the south side to attend synagogue—even though this meant transgressing the religious prohibition against riding on the Sabbath or Festivals—others wanted to be able to attend services in their own neighborhood. Moreover, they wanted a synagogue that was less "old world" than the typical south side *shul*. While some eastern European Jews did join the Indianapolis Hebrew Congregation, the only true north side synagogue (Ohev Zedeck was actually

Table 2.
Proceeds Raised by Jewish Welfare Fund
Campaigns from 1927 through the
Depression[a]

Year	Amount Raised	Number of Subscribers
1927	49,695	824
1928	68,606	954
1929	88,305	1078
1930	88,305	1078
1931	59,229	849
1932	36,100	860
1933	39,000	700
1934	51,167	1024
1935	49,685	1395
1936	65,005	1465
1937	62,671	1815
1938	73,600	2052
1939	131,400	2421

[a]Source: H. Joseph Hyman, "Your Jewish Welfare Fund," *Jewish Post*, Feb. 9, 1940.

located in the central business district), the great majority did not feel comfortable there. Generally, their social status and their background did not match that of the typical IHC member. In addition, they found the ultra-Reform IHC service too stripped of familiar traditions, too formal—in short, not *heimish* enough for their tastes. During this period, for example, IHC had eliminated the *bar mitzvah* ceremony and banned the wearing of the *tallit* and the *yarmulke*. These middle-class Jews were searching for something between the extremes of Reform and Orthodoxy. They found it in Conservative Judaism.[52]

Many of the founders of Congregation Beth El, the second north side synagogue, were former leaders of Sharah Tefilla. By 1915 Alexander Cohen, himself a former president of Sharah Tefilla but now a north side resident, organized a small group of Jews who were then living near 16th and Illinois streets to worship together for the High Holy Days. The following year the enlarged group of fifteen to twenty worshippers rented a room at 21st and Talbot streets and hired a rabbi to deliver a sermon in Yiddish and act as a cantor. In 1917 services were held at the Oriental Masonic Lodge at

21st and Central Avenue, but still no services were conducted beyond those for Rosh Hashanah and Yom Kippur. In the fall of 1918 Mrs. Henry Marks died and her sons attempted to gather a daily *minyan* so that they could say *kaddish* for her. Although they were eventually forced to hire men to make up the *minyan,* the *minyan* provided the impetus to expand the High Holy Day worship services into a full-fledged synagogue.[53]

In 1920 the growing congregation rented a larger hall at 30th and Talbot streets and hired a rabbinical student from the Jewish Theological Seminary to lead the fall services. The following summer, Joseph A. Borinsten, a successful scrap dealer and former president of Sharah Tefilla who was then president of the group, convinced a small group of men to join him in the purchase of a lot at 30th and Talbot streets for a permanent synagogue. In 1922 the group hired its first rabbi, Jacob Bienenfeld, who also became the editor and publisher of the *Indiana Jewish Chronicle.* Bienenfeld remained at Beth El until 1925. He later served as rabbi of the Downtown Synagogue in New York City.[54]

The campaign for a building now begun in earnest, the congregation purchased a new lot at 34th and Ruckle as a site for their synagogue. (Note how in each succeeding year the group moved farther north.) After delays in construction due to neighborhood protests, which many Jews believed had an anti-Semitic base, construction on the building, designed by the firm of Vonnegut, Bohn and Mueller, began in the spring of 1924.[55]

At the time of the completion of its building in 1925, Beth El was still nominally Orthodox, but the congregation was strongly veering to the greater liberalization of certain traditional practices. The large, 1,100-seat sanctuary was designed with both family pews in which men and women could sit together and special sections where men and women could sit separately.[56]

The dedication of the synagogue and the installation of its new rabbi, Isadore Goodman (ca. 1896–1962), were marked by elaborate ceremonies held during Hanukkah, the festival of dedication, in December 1925. The ceremonies began with a violin solo by Ferdinand Schaefer. All of the city's rabbis were on the program, including Samuel A. Katz, who delivered a speech in Yiddish. The program's two featured speakers were Rabbi Herbert S. Goldstein of New York City, president of the Union of Orthodox Jewish Congregations of America, and, incongruously, the governor of Indiana,

Ed Jackson. Jackson had been elected governor in 1924 with generous backing from the Ku Klux Klan, but at the time of the Beth El dedication D. C. Stephenson, the leader of the Indiana Klan, was behind bars for rape and murder, and the Indiana Klan was coming apart. Did the assembled audience appreciate the heavy irony in the theme Jackson chose for his address, freedom and tolerance of religion in America?[57]

Isadore Goodman, the congregation's new rabbi, remained at Beth El for only two years before leaving to become rabbi of Congregation Talmud Torah of Flatbush in Brooklyn. A highly educated man with degrees from New York University and Columbia University, he taught semitics at Butler University during his stay in Indianapolis. Goodman later became rabbi of Congregation Baron Hirsch of Memphis, the largest Orthodox congregation in the country.[58]

In the fall of 1927 the congregation was once again without a rabbi, so it brought a young rabbinical student from the Jewish Theological Seminary to serve for the High Holy Days. The congregation was so impressed by Milton Steinberg (1903–1950) that they offered him the rabbinical post after he completed his studies the following summer. Although Steinberg remained with the congregation only five years, he had an enormous impact on Beth El.[59]

By the time Steinberg assumed the pulpit of Beth El, the congregation had merged with the Hungarian Congregation Ohev Zedeck (in March, 1927) and changed its name to Congregation Beth-El Zedeck. Many Hungarians had moved to the north side; their old neighborhood near their East Market Street synagogue was breaking up. At a meeting held early in 1927 to discuss the future of the Hungarian congregation, George Rabinoff suggested a merger between the two units. The response was favorable; the East Market Street building was sold; and the proceeds were applied to the mortgage of Beth El's new building. Although the feelings of the Hungarian Jews about their fellow Jews had softened after many years in America, they still maintained a strong group identity. Accordingly, they refused to include in the merger agreement the merger of their cemetery, which remained reserved for Hungarians only. To this day, the Ohev Zedeck Cemetery Association oversees the cemetery and serves as a vehicle for the maintenance of group identity.[60]

Congregation Beth-El Zedeck was Milton Steinberg's first pulpit. He came to it enthusiastically with many new ideas he was eager to try, and he found a congregation that was extremely receptive to the changes he wanted to make. The result of the modifications was that Beth-El Zedeck shifted rather rapidly from being identified with modern Orthodoxy to left-wing Conservative Judaism. Some of the changes brought its worship services closer to the Reform model, while in other respects the congregation remained quite distinct (such as its strong support for the Zionist movement). Greater emphasis was placed on the decorum and dignity of worship services than was common in Orthodox custom, and the traditional *kabbalat shabbat* service at sundown on Friday was replaced by an after-dinner evening service, which included a sermon on provocative and serious topics. Under the direction of Cantor Myro Glass (ca. 1895–1971), who came at the same time as Steinberg, music became an integral part of the services, with a mixed choir for Friday night services, an all-male choir for the High Holy Days, and a children's choir for children's services.[61]

Steinberg also placed great importance on the congregational Sunday school, which supplemented the program of the Jewish Educational Association. He succeeded in raising the school enrollment to 275 and introduced a confirmation class and a high school study group, both of which he taught. He also helped to establish the Beth-El Zedeck's Men's Club, which was open to all Jewish men in the city. Membership grew to 200, about half of whom were members of the Indianapolis Hebrew Congregation, and Steinberg was able to bring in several out-of-town speakers to address its meetings.[62]

While a student at the Jewish Theological Seminary, Steinberg had been profoundly influenced by Mordecai M. Kaplan, founder of Reconstructionism and the most liberal member of the seminary faculty at the time. Kaplan's philosophy of Reconstructionism rejected the notion of the divine authority of Jewish law and emphasized Jewish peoplehood. His teachings appealed to rabbinical students like Steinberg, who came from Orthodox homes but were unable to accept the faith of their parents. Yet these students, like many second-generation American Jews, retained a strong attachment to Judaism, its customs, languages, culture, and nationalism. Steinberg carried Kaplan's ideas with him to Indianapolis, and his congregants at Beth-El Zedeck eagerly adopted them. Beth-El

Zedeck became a center for Jewish nationalist activity and the nexus of the Zionist movement in the city. Many of the city's Zionist leaders were also leaders of Beth-El Zedeck.

In May 1925, for example, a city-wide celebration of the opening of the Hebrew University in Jerusalem was held at Beth El with the famous man of letters Maurice Samuel as the guest speaker. In February 1926, a statewide Zionist convention held at Beth El elected Jacob A. (Jack) Goodman, then president of the congregation, the first chairman of a permanent state Zionist organization formed at the meeting. Later presidents of the Indianapolis Zionist District included Milton Steinberg (1930) and Myro Glass (1933 and 1934). Daniel Frisch, president of Beth-El Zedeck in 1940, later served as national president of the Zionist Organization of America.[63]

While Steinberg brought ideas and creativity that helped shape the identity of Beth-El Zedeck, the congregation had been kept alive for many years before his arrival by Jack and Sarah Goodman (ca. 1886–1975). Jack Goodman, cofounder of Real Silk Hosiery Mills and later of National Associated Mills, married Sarah Wolf, the daughter of Viennese immigrants, when both were in their late thirties. Before her marriage Sarah Wolf had worked as a kindergarten teacher and as the executive secretary of the Municipal Theatre Association of St. Louis. She had also busied herself in a variety of volunteer causes related either to children or music and theater. From her brother Dr. Alexander S. Wolf, who had once served as Theodore Herzl's private secretary, she developed an early attachment to Zionist ideals and hopes. After her marriage and move from St. Louis to Indianapolis, Goodman became active in Matinee Musicale and the Little Theater (later Booth Tarkington Civic Theater). She was instrumental in helping to organize the Kirshbaum Orchestra, which eventually became the Indianapolis Symphony. She remained particularly devoted to the symphony and served on the Indiana State Symphony Society board for many years. She was active in many Jewish organizations in the city (she was president of the Jewish Welfare Federation in 1953–1954, the only woman president to date) and served on many national Jewish boards — United Jewish Appeal, Hadassah, and others.[64]

Although both Goodmans were active in a variety of civic causes in the 1920s and 1930s in particular, they devoted nearly all their spare time to Beth-El Zedeck and contributed a great deal of money to its upkeep as well. As presidents of the congregation and of the sisterhood, respectively, they ran the synagogue as a one-family affair. (He was congregational president from 1925 to 1935; she was sisterhood president from 1928 to 1937.) The bookkeeping and mimeographing, for example, were done at Real Silk Hosiery, the Goodmans' company. When Steinberg, a young bachelor, arrived in Indianapolis he soon became very close with the Goodmans who showered him with attention and practically adopted him as a son.[65]

Trouble began to develop when Steinberg returned from New York in the fall of 1929 with his nineteen-year-old bride, Edith Alpert. Edith Steinberg was a reluctant *rebbitzin*. She had no religious interests and resented the role into which her marriage had forced her—especially the intrusions into her personal life, the lack of privacy, and the congregants' expectations that she would attend services regularly, participate actively in the sisterhood, and so forth. Eventually a rift developed between the two women. Edith Steinberg disliked Sarah Goodman's dominant personality and inclination to interfere in their personal affairs, a pattern which had developed before the Steinbergs' marriage. After the inevitable break between the two women two factions arose within the congregation, based on the personalities involved as well as on long-standing rivalries within the membership. An offer Milton Steinberg received from the Park Avenue Synagogue in New York City provided a way out of a difficult situation, particularly since Edith Steinberg missed the arts and culture of New York City and found Indianapolis too provincial for her tastes. However, Steinberg left Indianapolis with some regret. While he felt a certain restlessness that many rabbis in smaller communities experience, missed having colleagues to turn to in matters of Jewish law, and was disturbed by his congregants' utter lack of Jewish knowledge, he liked the people very much and had made many close personal friends. His congregants were deeply disappointed by his departure, and the regret over his leaving lingered for a long time. Many kept in touch with him for years, and fifty years later congregants still speak of the influence Steinberg had on them as young adults and recall him in warm and loving terms. Steinberg's influence and ideals remained with Beth-El Zedeck long after he left. The rabbis who followed him all came from the left wing of the Conservative movement. The congregation has continued to make modifications in its practices very much in keeping with Steinberg's beliefs. The congregation currently affiliates with both the Conservative and Reconstructionist movements. Kaplan's teachings still form an important underpinning for the synagogue's activities and direction.[66]

Elias Charry, who followed Steinberg in the pulpit in 1933, continued to lead the congregation in the same direction. A forceful leader who became well known in the city, Charry, like Steinberg, was a graduate of the Jewish Theological Seminary and active in the Zionist movement. While he was at Beth-El Zedeck he served as president of the Indianapolis Zionist District and the Ohio Valley Zionist Region. Charry left Indianapolis in 1942 to assume the pulpit of the Germantown (Pa.) Jewish Center, one of the largest Conservative congregations in the country, where he remained until his retirement.[67]

New Efforts at Cooperation among Synagogues

At about the time that Congregation Beth El was preparing to break ground for its synagogue building, a third north side congregation was in formation. The Central Hebrew Congregation was established in March 1923 with the purchase of a church at 21st and Central Avenue. There was a double meaning in the choice of name: not only was the synagogue located on Central Avenue, but the organizers, pointing to the new Jewish neighborhood developing in the area between 15th Street and Fall Creek and Capitol Avenue and College Avenue, believed that their synagogue would be "centrally located" to the many Orthodox Jews who now lived on the north side.[68]

The Central Hebrew Congregation was a more modest enterprise than Beth-El Zedeck, and, while the latter quickly took the path from Orthodox to Conservative Judaism, Central Hebrew Congregation remained firmly in the Orthodox camp, declaring proudly that it was "the only strictly Orthodox Jewish congregation on the north side." In 1929 the congregation had about 125 families as members and an active women's auxiliary of 100. Max Sacks, a member, served as cantor during the year while the congregation hired a rabbi for the High Holy Days. Rabbi Feuerlicht of the Indianapolis Hebrew Congregation often helped with services on the second day of festivals, which were not observed at his own congregation. A Reform rabbi helping an Orthodox congregation in this manner would never have occurred in larger communities where the lines between Orthodox and Reform were more sharply drawn. The first full-time rabbi hired by the congregation was Nandor Fruchter (ca. 1908–1971), a refugee from Nazi Germany. He came to Indianapolis in 1942 from Congregation Beth Abraham in Zanesville, Ohio, and remained in Indianapolis until his death in 1971.[69]

The Orthodox community, organized initially along national lines, had been characterized by infighting and rivalry, but in the twenties a number of attempts at inter-synagogue cooperation were initiated as a means of bringing some order to matters of special concern to Orthodox Jews such as supervision of the city's kosher butchers, maintenance of the *mikveh,* and regulation of the *meshulaḥim* (collectors of donations for religious institutions in Palestine). In February 1924 an organization known as Machzieka Hadas (*maḥzikei ha-dat,* strengtheners of the faith) was established at the home of Moses Rivkind, rabbi of Knesses Israel. The committee's first actions were to attempt to regulate and supervise two areas of Orthodox life in which there have traditionally been many suspicions of irregularities—the city's kosher meat trade (to ensure that all the laws of *sheḥitah* were closely followed) and the *meshulaḥim* (to verify that these traveling charity collectors were not merely pocketing their donations). They formed two subcommittees, one to supervise the kosher butchers and one to investigate the visits of collectors for Holy Land charities and to issue a written document of approval to all legitimate *meshulaḥim.* However, the Machzieka Hadas did not endure, possibly because it did not have broad enough community support. In January 1926 a new organization, the Council of Jewish Congregations, or Vaad Hakehillos, was formed at the instigation of Samuel A. Katz, rabbi of Sharah Tefilla, and Isadore Goodman, rabbi of Beth El. Katz (ca. 1872–1949), a native of Russia, was rabbi of Sharah Tefilla for twenty-six years (1923–1949), the first Orthodox rabbi to remain in the city for more than a few years. This continuity of leadership probably helped the new organization to survive longer than Machzieka Hadas.[70]

The relative success of Vaad Hakehillos reflected both its broader communal support and the active participation of George Rabinoff, the Jewish Federation executive director, who welcomed any movement that encouraged community harmony. However, while Orthodox Jews shared common concerns and most Sephardim were still Orthodox, Sephardim did not participate in Vaad Hakehillos, which remained strictly an Ashkenazi affair. The greater harmony among the Jewish community did not yet extend to the Sephardim, who were still perceived by the Ashkenazim as different.[71]

The first act of Vaad Hakehillos was an attempt to improve the conditions of the *mikveh*, located on the south side of West Norwood Street, which was badly in need of repair. Although the bathhouse was not widely used, the Orthodox community considered its maintenance essential. The Vaad authorized all the kosher butchers to add three cents to the cost of all kosher chickens they sold, with the stipulation that the extra three cents would go into a fund to support the *mikveh*. Although there was some suspicion that not all the funds raised through the chicken surcharge were applied to the correct purpose, the *mikveh* was eventually repaired and remodeled. Under Rabbi Katz's direction, a group of women took over its supervision.[72]

Vaad Hakehillos also took responsibility for the collection of the Moas Chitim fund (*Ma'ot hitim*, pronounced mo'es khitim by Ashkenazim, is Hebrew for money for wheat), which supplied special Passover foods to poor families. This task was eventually taken over by the Jewish Federation, which received an annual allocation of two hundred dollars for Moas Chitim from the Jewish Welfare Fund.[73]

Another attempt at inter-synagogal cooperation came in response to the Indiana federal prohibition office's attempts to check abuses of the sacramental wine privilege. Under the prohibition laws, wine could be purchased for sacramental purposes only. Certain rabbis, particularly in big cities, were suspected of abusing the privilege by making large purchases of wine which they then sold to "congregants." In order to protect themselves from Klan disapproval, many Jewish leaders wanted to introduce a system to police sacramental wine distribution that would prevent both the abuse and the appearance of abuse. The Joint Board of Control for Sacramental Wine, set up under Federation auspices, was composed of representatives from each of the city's ten congregations. Wine was distributed from the congregations for members only. Membership lists were carefully cross-checked, so that Jews with a membership in more than one synagogue did not receive extra wine. Supporters of the Joint Board believed it effectively eliminated the opportunities for illegal traffic in sacramental wine. However, when the prohibition administrator was changed, the Joint Board was disbanded and wine distribution was no longer supervised by the community.[74]

The first successful cooperative venture of the Orthodox community had been the Talmud Torah of 1911. Although in its early years the school had maintained a north side branch (even one, for a time, at the Indianapolis Hebrew Congregation), by the twenties the institution was operating only one school in its building at Union and McCarty streets on the south side. By 1924 it was apparent to the school's leaders that they were losing large numbers of potential pupils because Jews were migrating to the north side and attending the Hebrew schools of the north side synagogues. In an attempt to regain its status as the community's Hebrew school, the Talmud Torah was reorganized in 1924 as the Jewish Educational Association (JEA). The school's board planned to open branches in the north side synagogues as well as maintain the south side school, which would be known as the Rabbi Neustadt United Hebrew School. The curriculum for the schools would be Hebrew, the Bible, Jewish history, ethics, and the customs of traditional Judaism.[75]

In October 1924 a north side branch known as the Ezra School was opened in the basement of the Central Hebrew Congregation, but these quarters proved inadequate. In April 1925 the school moved to 24th and Pennsylvania, and in March 1926 to the Kirshbaum Center, where it remained until October 1942. During the terms of Hyman Perez (1924–1926) and S. Kasdan (1926–1928) as JEA superintendent, the school's enrollment remained at about two hundred students. With the appointment of Meyer Gallin as superintendent and the institution of free tuition in 1928, enrollment rose to a high of 337 in January 1930. Funding from the newly organized Jewish Welfare Fund made free tuition possible, an innovation which succeeded in its goal of raising enrollment. However, the Jewish Welfare Fund was unable to continue this level of support. When tuition was reinstated in the early thirties, enrollments began to decline and remained at around two hundred throughout the thirties.[76]

The original founders of the United Hebrew Schools would never have considered affiliating with the Jewish Federation because they would not have wanted interference from what they considered to be a German-Jewish, Reform organization. However, funding had become a chronic problem for the Talmud Torah in 1922 when Rabbi Jacob Bienenfeld of Congregation Beth El appeared before the Federation's board of governors to request that the Federation consider affiliation with the United Hebrew Schools. To study the question, the Federation appointed a committee to conduct an informal survey of Jewish education in the city. According to the committee, only six hundred children in the city out of an estimated 2,500 school-age children—that is, 24 percent—were receiving any formal Jewish education. Actually, this conclusion was incorrect. The committee based its estimate on an erroneous Jewish population figure of 10,000. The Jewish population of Indianapolis in 1922 was probably closer to 6,000 than 10,000. There were probably only approximately 1,500 school-age Jewish children (or perhaps fewer) in 1922, and therefore about 40 percent of them were enrolled in Jewish schools. Ten years earlier, the number of Jewish children enrolled in Jewish schools had been about 60 percent of the total. The committee concluded that, because the six hundred pupils were enrolled in a total of six different, independent schools, the educational system was inefficient. They recommended that the four traditional schools consolidate and form a new board to oversee the unified schools. The IHC and Council of Jewish Women Sunday schools were not included in the plan because of the problems of jointly supervising Orthodox and Reform schools. Not only was this plan never implemented, but its underlying objective—i.e., to strengthen the JEA by providing it with an adequate source of income—was undermined by it since the plan created a backlash. A group of JEA supporters, distrustful of the Federation's motives and not wanting Jewish education to fall under Federation control, left the JEA late in 1927 and organized a rival school, the Indianapolis Talmud Torah. Because they viewed the Federation (and the Jewish Welfare Fund) as a Reform organization, the group feared that once the school was under the Federation's financial control attempts would be made to liberalize the school's traditional curriculum. The group ran a school at 923 South Illinois Street for about seventy students for two years, but in 1929 they were persuaded to disband and return to the JEA. After 1929 the Jewish Welfare Fund became the JEA's major source of funds.[77]

Secular Jewish Institutions

The concerns of the immigrant generation had been focused, for the most part, on the mechanics of survival and adjustment to American life, and the institutions that they established were primarily religious, relief, or benevolent societies. The cultivation of Jewish culture was not a high priority for these harrassed newcomers, and they did not establish organizations for this purpose. Their children, however, did not face the same difficulties as their parents, and many of them were eager to acquire and promote a knowledge of Jewish culture. As their ties to Orthodox Judaism weakened, the second generation was more likely to express its sense of Jewishness in secular ways. Unlike the older German-Jewish Reform community, which clung to the idea of Judaism as a religion and rejected the concept of Jewish peoplehood, the children of the eastern European immigrants embraced Jewish nationalism, particularly as they shed their Orthodoxy. A variety of Jewish cultural societies sprang up in the 1920s emphasizing a nonreligious Jewish identity, many of them with a strong Zionist flavor. Two Hebrew-speaking clubs were established, the Ivriah in October 1924, organized by a group of Ashkenazim, and the Yahudi Halevi Club (Yehudah HaLevi was a Hebrew poet in medieval Spain), established by a group of Sephardim, in March 1929. The Jewish Cultural Association, founded in January 1925, had similar purposes: "to spread Jewish thought, Jewish ideals, and Jewish culture among the Jewish masses; to develop Jewish national consciousness, . . . and prepare for Jewish national activity and restoration work in the Diaspora and Israel." Each meeting of the Jewish Cultural Association included a literary program, music, and a debate. The Sinai Club was organized in 1921 by younger members of the Hungarian congregation, but as the second generation did not retain the intense Hungarian identity of their parents membership in the club was not limited to Hungarians only. The Sinai Club became a popular organization, combining discussions of Jewish topics with social programs such as dances and picnics, providing a meeting ground for young Jews from different national backgrounds to meet and eventually marry. Intermarriages between individuals from the different Ashkenazi national groups occurred with increasing frequency in the twenties, breaking down the barriers between those groups.[78]

Among the young adult clubs organized during the 1920s were three clubs for university students, all established in 1927, reflecting the growing numbers of Jewish students attending university and professional schools: the Cosmo, a discussion club for Jewish women attending Butler University; Alpha Omega, organized by Jewish students at the Indiana University School of Dentistry; and the Jewish Student Union at Indiana University in Bloomington, which became the nucleus for the establishment of a Hillel house on the campus in 1935.[79]

The Jewish population of Indianapolis was never large enough to support a commercial Yiddish theater, but there were enough Jews interested in Yiddish drama to organize an amateur Yiddish theater group and to attend the performances of traveling Yiddish theater companies. The ambitious undertaking of the Indianapolis Yiddish Dramatic Club, organized in 1927, was to dramatize and produce the "better class" of Yiddish plays. Their first production, *A Mother's Burden*, was presented in May 1927 in the Manual High School auditorium. Yiddishists, who continued to support the local branch of the Workmen's Circle, could also enjoy the productions of traveling Yiddish theater troupes. In November 1925, the Workmen's Circle brought a production of *A Wedding in Siberia* to the Manual High School auditorium as a benefit for the Workmen's Circle old-age home. Other productions were purely commercial. In February 1926 the famous Vilna Troupe put on Sholem Aleichem's play *It's Hard to Be a Jew* in the Manual High School auditorium, the New York Yiddish Players performed at the South Side Turner Hall in February 1927, and the Detroit Yiddish Players presented *Shlomele Chochem* at Manual High School in October 1928. With the advent of Yiddish films, they too were given brief runs in the city.[80]

The earliest Jewish newspapers, established in the mid-nineteenth century, helped isolated American Jewish communities keep in touch with one another. _Occident_ and _American Israelite_ were newspapers with a national readership. In communities too small to support any local Jewish institution a subscription to a Jewish newspaper often provided the only means of maintaining a Jewish identity. As American Jewish communities began to grow, however, local or regional newspapers sprang up. These papers usually had a dual focus. They provided information on local Jewish activities—club meetings, synagogue developments, federation activities, social announcements, including notices of weddings, births, and deaths—and they also kept Jews informed of national and international events of Jewish interest. The _Indiana Jewish Chronicle_, established in July 1922, was a typical Jewish newspaper of this period. The first editor and publisher of the weekly statewide paper was Nathan J. Gould. Rabbi Morris Feuerlicht of IHC was editor-in-chief, and the editorial board included six rabbis from the major Jewish communities in the state. A year later the editor and publisher of the newspaper was Rabbi Bienenfeld of Congregation Beth El, and the business manager was Jennie Strauss Barnett (ca. 1885–1959). Bienenfeld remained only a year. In June 1923 Morris Strauss (ca. 1897–1973), a free-lance writer from Cincinnati and younger brother of Jennie Barnett, replaced Bienefeld as editor and publisher of the _Indiana Jewish Chronicle_ and remained until his retirement of 1969.[81]

The _Indiana Jewish Chronicle_ presented its readers with a weekly mixture of reprints of articles from other American Jewish newspapers, news of local Jewish organizations, and social notes and notices of upcoming events of Jewish interest. Focusing on the activities of the Indianapolis Jewish community, which was by far the largest Jewish community in the state, the _Chronicle_ also reported on the activities of the other Jewish communities of Indiana—Evansville, Lafayette, Fort Wayne, etc. A fairly large proportion of space in nearly every issue of the _Chronicle_ was devoted to reporting on all activities, both local and national, that were anti-Jewish as well as any instance in which a national or local political leader publicly denounced such activities. Throughout the twenties the _Chronicle_ reported extensively on the proposed institution of the quota system, most notably at Harvard University but also at other Ivy League schools, on the anti-Semitic charges published by the *Dearborn Independent,* and on the activities of the Ku Klux Klan, both nationally and locally. The *Indiana Jewish Chronicle* published lists of political candidates who were not Klansmen, printed Klan "jokes,"* reassured its readers that the Klan would be toppled by its own internal dissension, and generally provided a vehicle of expression for the fears and anger provoked by the Klan's anti-Semitic campaign.

The *Indiana Jewish Chronicle* was just one of many developments that signified the Jewish community's increasing security in America, of being at home in Indiana, and yet of maintaining identity as a Jewish community as well. The Jewish organizations established in the 1920s reflected the growing maturity of the Indianapolis Jewish community. No longer a predominantly immigrant community, the new Jewish institutions of the twenties represented the second-generation's identification both with America and their Jewish heritage and reflected their attempts to integrate these two identities. Older institutions were transformed as the needs of their members changed. Even the Orthodox synagogue, often perceived as a bastion of conservatism, underwent change. It came less and less to resemble the old world *shul* that had been so comforting to its immigrant founders. Instead it became not just a place to *daven* and socialize but also a community center with clubs and activities for men, women, and children. Even the Orthodox rabbi began to adopt some of the functions of the Reform rabbi (whose role was in turn modeled on the Protestant minister) as a leader and spokeman for his congregation. Samuel A. Katz, rabbi of Sharah Tefilla from 1923 to 1949, was the first Orthodox rabbi to assume this new role. Katz became a leader and spokesman for Indianapolis Orthodoxy, an Orthodox counterpart to the Reform leader Feuerlicht. While the Orthodox synagogue was becoming less "old world," Jewish religious attitudes were changing as well. Judaism diminished from an all-encompassing way of life to just one facet of one's life. Religious apathy increased, as demonstrated by the decline in the percentage of children receiving a Jewish education—from between 60 and 75 percent in 1915 to about 40 percent in 1922. However, while religious apathy in-

*An example: Why shouldn't Jews eat eggs? Because there are so many "Klux" in them. *Indiana Jewish Chronicle,* June 15, 1923.

creased, Jews began to express their Jewish identity in a variety of secular modes. Social clubs, cultural clubs, Zionist clubs, even fund-raising for Jewish causes—all provided an opportunity for Indianapolis Jewry not only to socialize together but to identify as Jews.

 V

Years of Crisis

DEPRESSION AND WAR

INDIANAPOLIS JEWRY IN 1929 was a relatively comfortable and increasingly middle-class community. Growing numbers of Jews were moving from the south side, the point of arrival for immigrant families, to the middle-class neighborhoods of the north side. Accompanying the economic success and acculturation of the Jewish community was the secularization of Jewish life. The new Jewish institutions enabled their participants to enjoy Jewish life without Judaism. Second-generation Jews flocked to the many new Jewish centers that were built in the twenties, eagerly participated in the activities of B'nai B'rith and other fraternal lodges, devoted a great deal of time to philanthropy, and supported Jewish hospitals, orphanages, settlement houses, and social agencies.

While the *shul* had been the center of Jewish life for many south side Jews, the Kirshbaum Center was the center of Jewish life for large numbers of north side Jews. It bore few similarities to its predecessor, the Communal Building. While the Communal Building was really a settlement house the major purpose of which was to Americanize its immigrant clientele the Kirshbaum Center was a middle-class recreational center, providing swimming pools and health clubs in place of English and sewing classes. For the

157

most part, the city's Jewish institutions were well supported. In 1929 the Jewish Welfare Fund had its first successful campaign, topping its goal of $141,160 and raising $176,610. IHC, eager to expand its building into a synagogue-center with educational and recreational facilities, had raised $187,000 in pledges at the time of the 1929 stock market crash. (The pledges were later cancelled.)[1]

No longer was the Jewish community composed primarily of garment workers, peddlers, and small shopkeepers. As Jewish students were attending all of the state's universities and professional schools, a Jewish professional class was emerging. Although vestiges of social discrimination remained, barring Jews from certain corporations, clubs, and neighborhoods, the era of Klan influence was over. In mid-October 1929 the middle-class American Jew, like his gentile neighbor, probably believed that he could look forward to "an illimitable vista of prosperity," in the words of the historian Dixon Wecter. After all, had not President Hoover predicted that "we shall soon . . . be within sight of the day when poverty will be banished from the nation."[2]

By November 1929, of course, the world looked quite different. While some politicians confidently predicted that prosperity was just around the corner, when prosperity finally came some ten years later the Jewish community found itself faced with a tragedy more terrible than the depression: the persecution and, ultimately, destruction of European Jewry.

The thirties and forties were unprecedented years of crisis for American Jewry. The community faced one tragedy after another: the economic displacement of the depression years; the persecution of German Jewry after Hitler's rise to power; American hostility to the admission of central European Jewish refugees; and British perfidy in Palestine. And, as a counterpoint to these international problems, there lurked the fear that American anti-Semitism, which reached a disturbing level in the 1930s and early 1940s, would be infected by the German example. Certainly many would have agreed with G. A. Efroymson, president of the Jewish Federation, who remarked in his presidential address in 1934 that never in his recollection had Jews faced such a serious crisis.[3]

The Great Depression

The depression halted the steadily rising fortunes of the Jewish community. In 1925 George Rabinoff had predicted the end of the south side Jewish community, but the depression dramatically slowed the northward migration of Indianapolis Jewry. By 1940 only 14 percent or 350 out of 2,500 families lived on the south side. Many remained only because depressed real estate values on the south side made it unprofitable for them to move. (In 1943, 56 percent of the Jewish families on the south side owned their own homes.)[4]

While the Jewish community faced unemployment, reduced income, and increased numbers of families on relief, the depression did not strike Indianapolis Jewry as harshly as it affected some other groups. In part, this was because of the community's essentially middle-class character. H. Joseph Hyman, Jewish Federation executive director from 1928 to 1945, believed that Indianapolis Jews suffered less from the depression than the general community because they were primarily middle class and possessed greater resources for earning a living. In addition, the kinds of occupations and industries in which Jews were employed were not as badly affected as some other parts of the economy. The depression did not strike all areas of the economy with equal force. The most severely affected industries were durable goods production—iron, steel, machine and auto parts, etc.—and the entire field of building and construction, fields in which Indianapolis Jews were conspicuously absent. While the depression hurt retail sales, a common area of Jewish occupation, the decline was not as devastating. For example, between 1929 and 1933 the value of new construction contracts fell by 90 percent and the value of building permits by 94 percent. In contrast, department store sales fell by less than 50 percent in the same period. Similarly, those employed in durable goods industries (e.g., building, roads, metals, iron and steel, lumber, railroads, etc.) were far more likely to lose their jobs than employees in consumer goods industries (e.g., food, farming, textiles, electricity, fuel, etc.). It has been estimated that employment in durable goods industries declined from 10 million in 1929 to 4 million in 1932–1933, while employment in consumer goods industries only fell from 15 million to 13 million in the same period.

A study of 2,097 households in New Haven, Connecticut, conducted in the spring of 1931, confirmed the vulnerability of those employed in building and construction and manufacturing. Of those men who normally worked in building and construction, 31.5 percent were unemployed, while of those who normally worked in trade, only 9.5 percent were unemployed. The rates of unemployment were highest for building and construction, followed by manufacturing, transportation, domestic and personal service, trade, and professional service. With Jews concentrated in consumer goods industries (especially the garment trade), retail sales, and increasingly in the professions, they were less vulnerable than auto industry workers, building contractors and steelworkers.[5]

The small proportion of Jews who worked as laborers or unskilled workers also increased the Jewish community's relative economic security. Unemployment in the 1930s tended to decrease as the skill required in the occupation increased. In the New Haven study, unemployment for men ran from 25 percent for unskilled (except domestic) workers, 20 percent for semiskilled, 19 percent for skilled workers, 11 percent for clerks and kindred workers, 1.5 percent for proprietors, officials, and managers, to 6 percent for professionals. For entrepreneurs (self-employed), 5.5 percent were without work, while 8.5 percent had had no earnings for at least one week before the study was conducted.[6]

In the Jewish community, as in the general community, there were some occupational groups that fared worse than others. The rising Jewish professional class probably suffered the least, since professionals in general were the least affected by the depression. By 1934 the *Jewish Post* estimated that the Jewish community included 55 attorneys, 18 doctors, 16 dentists, and 12 pharmacists. In 1948 the population survey found that 11.2 percent of employed Jews could be classified as professionals; 19.4 percent were "sales and kindred workers"; and 43.1 percent were proprietors of businesses. These three categories alone accounted for 73.2 percent of all employed Jews, and owners of businesses comprised nearly half of those surveyed.[7]

Jews in retail trade suffered declines in sales which often paralleled the slide in local industry. But again, all facets of retail trade were not equally affected. Then, too, enterprising store owners could always take the initiative to try to attract customers away from the competition. In Muncie, Indiana, for example, some of the Jewish retailers reacted to the decrease in sales by lengthening their hours; other shopkeepers were then forced to follow suit. Generally, it was sales of luxuries (jewelry, candy, restaurant meals) and durable goods which registered the greatest sales declines while purchases of essentials or nondurable items were less affected. Variety stores, grocery stores, women's clothing stores, and gasoline stations (the car was already considered a necessity by the early thirties) suffered far less than jewelry stores, restaurants, men's clothing stores, and furniture stores.[8]

By following the path of what consumers considered "essentials" in the 1930s, one can begin to see the pattern of who survived the depression and why. In the field of furniture sales, for example, declining family size along with the reduction in house sizes in the 1920s had put pressure on furniture sales even before the depression. After 1929 the only furniture being sold in any volume were necessities such as beds and bedding. Dining room or living room furniture sold poorly, since people "made do" with their old tables and chairs. These declining sales forced some furniture stores out of business. In Indianapolis, for example, the Great Western Furniture Store, owned by brothers Samuel and Jacob L. Mueller, closed its doors. Department stores and variety stores selling a diversity of products generally stayed afloat. Goldstein Brothers Department Store, for example, closed in March 1933, but it reopened a new store, known as the New Goldstein Brothers Department Store in August 1933, at Washington and Delaware streets. In addition to the traditional departments, the new store included a grocery store. Since food sales were less affected than some other retail fields, this addition may have helped the store survive.[9]

By the 1930s the automobile was already an essential part of American life. Those who owned cars kept and maintained them, although sales of new cars declined dramatically. In 1931 the number of cars on the road that were at least two years old increased by 11.9 percent over the number in 1929, while the number of cars under two years decreased by 36.3 percent. Sales of gasoline and automotive accessories for these aging cars—tires, batteries, parts—remained relatively stable. In Muncie, for example, sales of motor vehicles declined by 78.3 percent, while garage and repair work declined by 54.2 percent and gasoline sales by only 3.6 percent. In Indianapolis there were a number of Jews in the automobile business. Morris Maurer was an auto parts dealer. The brothers Julius and Max Elkin owned Elkin's Auto Parts and Tire Company. Charles Sommers was president of the Gibson Automotive Company and the Empire Automobile Company. Emil Mantel helped to organize Weissman Motor Sales. Sol Trotcky and his son Samuel operated a car wash and gas station, the Indianapolis Automobile Service Company.[10]

Closely linked to retail commerce were the Jewish financial institutions. Building on the great demand for consumer loans to buy durable goods in the 1920s, Robert Stolkin (ca. 1893-1960) founded the Indiana Finance Corporation, one of the nation's first automobile finance companies, in the 1920s. He later organized the Used Car Loan Company and the Used Car Finance Company. All of Stolkin's firms continued to operate throughout the depression. Another Jewish-owned consumer finance company, Schloss Brothers, also prospered in the thirties. The firm merged with the Indianapolis Morris Plan in 1936, and twenty-seven-year-old William L. Schloss became the president. However, the city's one Jewish-owned commercial bank, the Meyer-Kiser Bank, failed in May 1931. Organized in 1906 by first cousins Sol Meyer and Sol Kiser, the bank was still owned by the two families when it was closed for liquidation.[11]

While some north side Jewish businesses did go bankrupt, it was the less prosperous south side community that endured greater hardships during the depression. In January 1933 all but one of the forty-eight families receiving major assistance from the Jewish Family Service Society lived on the south side. With few luxuries in the family budget, there was often little that could be cut without severe consequences. The Sephardic community, the least well-to-do group within Indianapolis Jewry, suffered not only because they were already the most impoverished, but sales of men's suits, a major source of their livelihood, slid drastically. Men's clothing sales dropped far more than sales of women's clothing during the depression, a reflection of the different social values placed on male and female clothing. The national output of men's suits dropped by 25 percent from 1925 to 1930, while the production of dresses had fallen by only 13 percent in 1930. Since the great bulk of the Sephardim were employed by the Kahn Tailoring Company, a manufacturer of men's suits (in 1933 nearly 50 percent of the community worked there), many endured layoffs as men's suit sales declined. In addition to garment workers, Sephardic occupations included two market stand owners, eleven fruit peddlers (seven wholesale and four retail), two secondhand clothes dealers, six clothing store owners, three shoemakers, one baker, one grocer, and one candy store owner.[12]

Even on the south side, of course, there were Jews employed in areas which were relatively immune to depression. Jewish occupations included grocers, dry goods dealers, shoe store owners, bakers, peddlers, and a number of scrap and waste dealers. As in most cities, Jews dominated the scrap and waste materials business in Indianapolis, a natural outgrowth of the traditional Jewish trade in rags, old clothes and all used goods. By the 1930s many of these firms were quite large.[13]

Faced with the loss of the weekly paycheck, some families discovered other sources of income. With only a small investment a family could set up a small stand outside the city market (rents were lower than inside the market) selling fruits and vegetables or small items such as shoelaces, pins, and socks. The market was not even open every day, but some families' entire livelihood came from the sales made at their small market stand. When a group of women's clubs agitated to abolish the outside market stands in January 1932, the Federation board decided to fight the proposed ban. So precarious was the standholders' existence that if the stands were abolished, the board feared the standholders would be forced onto the relief rolls.[14]

Job scarcity is usually felt initially by young first-time job seekers. The problems of this group attracted the Federation's attention to the employment problem. A number of unemployed young men and women had applied to the Federation for assistance in finding employment. The board responded in a traditional manner. They decided to encourage Jews to hire other Jews. The board sent a letter to all Jewish businessmen in the city with a list of job applicants and their qualifications. This approach was not entirely successful, although a few temporary jobs were obtained. In cooperation with the Jewish Family Service Society, an unemployment committee was appointed, and committee members made personal visits to Jewish employers to try to encourage them to hire the Jewish unemployed. In 1931 Edith Steinberg, wife of Rabbi Milton Steinberg of Congregation Beth-El Zedeck, took over the supervision of the unemployment committee. Through personal contacts, she was able to place one third of the job applicants.[15]

Continuing in the same pattern of encouraging Jews to take care of fellow Jews, the unemployment committee recommended that the Federation's constituent agencies hire "needy Jewish persons" instead of non-Jews whenever possible. Drawing on the assumption that Jews had a special affinity for retail business and sales, the committee set up a course in salesmanship to help unemployed Jews improve their skills in this field. The high unemployment of the Sephardic community was a special concern of the committee. Because the Sephardim were poor even before the depression, Hyman, the Federation executive, feared that the continuation of their high rate of unemployment would cause "grave social problems" for the community. A special committee conducted a census of the group and found that nine out of forty young men age seventeen and older and five out of nineteen young women had no employment. Beyond special pleadings to Jewish firms to hire them, however, little more could be done.[16]

The rising number of unemployed Jews forced many families to turn to the Jewish Family Service Society for help, straining the agency's relief budget. The demand for direct relief, which had stabilized at a relatively low level by the mid-1920s, began to increase. During the period of mass immigration direct relief expenditures constituted about one third of the Federation budget. By 1924–1925 the amount spent on direct relief had declined to 17.8 percent. The case load of the Jewish Family Service Society had similarly fallen to a low of twenty-four major active cases in 1929. Four years later, in February 1933, the number of major active cases had risen to fifty-five. Although the allocation for direct relief had increased, it was not proportionate to the increase in applicants. The number of applicants more than doubled from 1929 to 1933, while the amount spent on relief increased by less than one third. Relief expenditures increased from $5,354 in 1926 to about $6,500 in 1928, $6,975 in 1929–1930, $7,767 in 1930–1931, and $9,154 in 1931–1932. Moreover, given the extreme distress of the period, the needs of each family were probably greater than in earlier years.[17]

Until the depression Jewish welfare agencies had taken sole responsibility for the needs of the Jewish poor. Poor Jews had naturally turned to Jewish agencies, rather than municipal or nonsectarian relief agencies, because of the commonly held feeling that Jews should take care of their own. Moreover, Jewish agencies provided a much higher level of care for their clients than other agencies. A study conducted in the 1920s comparing Jewish and non-Jewish agencies in twenty cities showed that the average relief expenditures per family by the Jewish agencies was twice that of the entire group and 72 percent higher than the average of the leading nonsectarian agencies. Jewish welfare workers regarded the lower relief payments of other agencies critically because they believed this tended to keep poor families impoverished. However, when faced with the greatly increased need for relief and greatly decreased funds, the Federation, with some misgivings, decided to participate in the federal relief and work programs instituted by the Roosevelt administration in the spring of 1933. In November 1933, H. Joseph Hyman reported that the names of twenty heads of families who had been receiving regular or intermittent relief had been submitted to the Civil Works Administration, thereby reducing the relief rolls of the Jewish Family Service Society. The Jewish Family Service Society was opposed to using public relief because of the inadequacy of the relief and the effect this would have on the families. However, the Federation insisted that they had no alternative but to seek public relief for their clients. Arrangements were made with the township trustees to give aid to the families which would be supplemented by the Jewish Family Service Society to bring it up to the agency's standard.[18]

Along with an increase in the number of unemployed persons, a rising number of transients sought aid as well. The number of transients assisted was 387 in 1928–1929, 545 in 1929–1930, 693 in 1930–1931, and 939 in the first ten months of 1931–1932. Whereas the transient in the past had frequently been a shrewd and impudent *shnorrer*, the transient of the 1930s was more typically an unemployed young man, genuinely in search of work. Many had hitchhiked west, having heard that there were employment opportunities in the Midwest. The disappointed ones made their way home, spending each night in a Jewish shelter house in a different city. With the rapid increase in the number of Jewish transients, expenses of the Jewish Shelter House in Indianapolis rose dramatically. Faced with these mounting costs, the Jewish Family Service Society decided to turn over the expense of lodging and feeding transients to the Federal Transient Bureau, organized in 1935. (With the severe unemployment, there was a general increase in transients.) Only those transients who required kosher food would be sent to the Jewish Shelter House with the Bureau paying the Shelter House a per diem rate. The Orthodox Jews were disturbed by the Jewish community's almost total abandonment of the traditional task of caring for the stranger. As it developed, the arrangement was short-lived. The Federal Transient Bureau was discontinued in September 1935, and the Jewish Family Service Society once again took over responsibility for Jewish transients.[19]

While their expenditures were reduced because of county relief and New Deal work relief programs, Jewish agencies eagerly seized the opportunities afforded by these programs to staff community agencies. Both the Kirshbaum Center and the Communal Building benefited from the federal work programs, which also, of course, helped to provide work for unemployed Jews. In 1933–1934, twenty-one Jews were placed in federal work relief programs under the Civil Works Administration (CWA) and Civilian Conservation Corps. In 1933 teachers from the CWA (later known as the Works Progress Administration or WPA) were brought in to conduct adult education classes for the JCCA. At the height of the WPA program—1936 to 1939—the project provided English and Americanization teachers, music, dancing, and arts and crafts instructors, game room attendants, and program assistants. Although most of the federal workers were not trained for their positions and some were clearly incompetent, others became valuable staff members. When the program was eliminated in January 1943, the JCCA was unable to hire staff to replace the free services of the WPA workers.[20]

For those families who were struggling to keep small businesses alive, the Jewish Community Credit Union provided small loans at low interest. The Credit Union had been organized in October 1929, just before the stock market crash, to help stimulate thrift and provide low interest loans. In 1930 the Credit Union, whose

office was at 119 South Meridian Street, made 123 loans totalling
$20,573, at 6 percent interest, and the Credit Union's officers re-
ported a great demand for loans. Membership in the Credit Union
was open to any Indianapolis Jew with an entrance fee of twenty-
five cents and the purchase of one or more shares of stock (par
value $5).[21]

While many unemployed Jews, like other idle Americans,
turned to the public library, "the poor man's club," as a place to
read or doze in a warm, quiet atmosphere, or sought occasional
release from their troubles in escapist movies like *Golddiggers of
1933*, increasing numbers also filled their time by participating in
the programs of the Kirshbaum Center and the Communal Building. Not only did membership increase (the result of a large
number of scholarships and deferred payment plans), but attendance rose dramatically. In 1928 total attendance at the Kirshbaum Center was 25,190; in 1932, 112,479. The greatest attendance increases were in the game room, the library, the lounge,
and at social affairs. Even attendance at the Communal Building
began to increase after years of decline, from 32,042 in 1928–1930
to 35,711 in 1931–1932. Because communal leaders believed the
south side community was dispersing, they had decided in 1925 to
establish the Kirshbaum Center and invest no further funds in
either the expansion or basic upkeep of the Communal Building. In
1933, however, an estimated 25 percent of the Jewish community
still lived on the south side, near the Communal Building, to
which many now turned for activities to fill the long hours of the
day. Since many who participated had little money available to
spend on entertainment, the fact that Communal Building programs were free also made them more attractive. In 1930 a committee representing the Orthodox congregations (there were five on
the south side) requested that the Federation undertake some renovation of the Communal Building to accommodate the increased
activities there. An additional inducement for the renovation was
the fact that, after relocating in a downtown office building in
1929, the Federation was also forced to return its headquarters to
the Communal Building in 1932 as an economy measure.[22]

The increased use of both the Communal Building and the
Kirshbaum Center, coupled with the many free or reduced memberships granted to many families, strained the budget of the

JCCA. The Association began emergency borrowing from the Jewish Federation to cover its deficits. Throughout the decade, however, the JCCA deficit continued to grow, reaching $8,000 in 1936. The Federation's own funds, which still came from the Community Fund, were also greatly reduced. Because of poor Community Fund campaigns, the Federation's appropriations were severely cut. In 1934 the Federation requested $51,000 from the Fund but received only $40,000. Jewish Welfare Fund campaigns also suffered. Campaign workers had a hard time collecting pledges made while times were still good. Some delinquent donors were even threatened with legal action, but in many cases the donor simply did not have the money to pay. Jewish Welfare Fund campaigns reached their low point—$36,000—in 1933, the worst year of the depression. After the economic upturn in 1934, the amounts raised began to increase slightly.[23]

Following the restriction of immigration in the 1920s, few Jewish immigrants had settled in Indianapolis. In the late thirties, this situation began to change. Central European Jews in flight from Nazi oppression began coming to Indianapolis. Unlike their nineteenth-century predecessors, they came not as independent wanderers but as part of an organized relief effort set up in New York to disburse them systematically across the country, in a manner similar to the operation of the Industrial Removal Office. In February 1937 the Jewish Welfare Fund received a communication from the National Coordinating Committee for German Refugees that a "large influx of German Jewish refugees to New York" was creating a German Jewish colony in the city with the potential of increasing anti-Semitism. Communities in the American heartland were "urged to accept some of these families to lighten the burden on New York" and reduce the danger of anti-Semitism. Later that year a committee representing the Jewish Federation, the Jewish Welfare Fund, the Jewish Family Service Society, and the Council of Jewish Women was formed to cooperate in bringing refugees to Indianapolis. Efforts to settle the German refugees in the city proceeded along lines similar to the old Industrial Removal Office operation. The committee received biographies of refugees who had agreed to be settled inland, and several hundred letters with copies of the biographies were sent to industries throughout the city and state. Not surprisingly, the effort was not very successful. In 1937 jobs were still scarce, and there were few employers who would agree to hire an unknown German-speaking refugee at a level equal to the refugee's training or skill. The New York office insisted that the only way to place the refugees was for Indianapolis to take the families and find jobs for them after their arrival. The Indianapolis committee was wary of this proposal, thinking it would entail a great deal of expense at a time when its resources were being strained by distress within its own community. Finally it was agreed to take one family as an experiment. The first couple, a former judge and his wife, arrived in the spring of 1938. After that, more families were taken (at first two at a time, then one or two a week), and a social worker, Sol Blumenthal, was hired by the Indianapolis Committee for Refugees to supplement the work of the volunteers.[24]

By 1941 about 250 refugees were living in Indianapolis. Others had been settled by the Indiana Committee for Refugees, a state committee supported by B'nai B'rith, elsewhere in the state. Finding employment for the refugees was not easy. Unlike the skilled and unskilled workmen who were clients of the IRO, these had been professional people or independent businessmen. Many did not speak English, while their European training as doctors or lawyers often did not qualify them for similar work in America. Employment meant not only finding employers who were sympathetic to one's situation, but adjusting to life at a lower scale. One couple became caretakers of an old-age home in Fort Wayne. Others were hired by the Real Silk Company and other Jewish firms. Some refugees, however, could not find adequate employment. In order to assist them, the Refugees' Handicrafts Exchange was opened in 1939 by the Indianapolis Committee for Refugees, with the support of the Council of Jewish Women. The shop sold homemade baked goods, jams and jellies, and needlework produced by the refugees. In addition, many refugees were forced to sell family silver, jewelry, and other precious heirlooms at the shop. With the declaration of war in December 1941, however, the refugees were classified "enemy aliens." As a consequence, the Refugees' Handicraft Exchange was closed and their Newcomers Club disbanded, as the Federation did not think it "advisable to continue a club of refugees during war."[25]

By the time the last group of Jewish immigrants had settled in

Indianapolis in the late 1930s, the south side was no longer considered the center of the community. In fact, never again would such a large proportion of Indianapolis Jewry live in such a concentrated area. Only the Sephardim still lived exclusively on the south side, according to a 1933 survey, and this may have partially contributed to that group's solidarity. Although four Ashkenazi synagogues still remained on the south side, their membership had been severely reduced by the northern migration, and mergers were periodically discussed. In January 1939 the United Hebrew Congregation proposed a merger with Ezras Achim. The next month, Ezras Achim made a similar proposition to Sharah Tefilla. Neither proposal was taken up, although the Orthodox lay leadership seemed to sense that a unification of all the south side *shuls* was inevitable. Following the natural tendency of institutions to maintain themselves against all odds, the synagogues struggled on alone, averting one financial disaster after another.[26]

While the synagogues maintained their separate identities throughout the thirties and forties, the rancor and animosity which had characterized relationships between the various Jewish groups in the prewar period became muted. To the second generation, born in America, it mattered little that their parents were Hungarian, Russian, or Polish. Instead, many of the second generation had a strong identity as south siders, and they united to defend what they saw as their common interests. South side synagogues cooperated in supervising the work of the *shoḥetim,* the *mikveh,* and *kashrut.* Even the barriers between Sephardim and Ashkenazim began to break down, not only through such formal efforts as the Communal Building's Adult Advisory Council (organized in 1935) but also through more natural processes. Children played together, families lived near each other, and women shopped together. Moreover, all the groups were growing increasingly more acculturated, so the differences between them became more moderate. Gladys Cohen Nisenbaum, the daughter of Sephardic immigrants, recalls that while her mother never learned English and spoke only Ladino, Gladys learned English at an early age from her older siblings and had Ashkenazi playmates. In 1932 the first three marriages between Sephardim and Ashkenazim took place, uniting dozens of Sephardic and Ashkenazi brothers, sisters, parents, and cousins.[27]

Anti-Semitism and the Jewish Response

While American Jews shouldered the crises of the Great Depression like all Americans, they carried an extra burden—an increasing anxiety over the mounting fury of the anti-Jewish campaign in Germany. With shock and disbelief, American Jews watched as German Jews were systematically deprived of their civil rights, their means of livelihood, and their basic freedoms. Even before the horrors of *Kristallnacht* in 1938, when synagogues throughout Germany were pillaged and destroyed, American Jewry was terrified by the Nazi persecution of the Jews. *Fortune* magazine's study of American Jewry in 1936 commented that through witnessing the events in Germany American Jews had lost their air of confidence about the future.[28]

Not only was the Jewish community frightened by the growing support and intensity of the Nazi party's anti-Semitic campaign, but there was also concern over the growth of anti-Semitism in America. Three forms of anti-Semitism plagued America through the thirties and forties: fringe group (Nazi-oriented) anti-Semitism, urban ethnic anti-Semitism, and social and occupational anti-Semitism. Except in a few large cities—in particular Brooklyn and Boston, where a large Irish population was violently anti-Semitic, strongly isolationist and pro-appeasement—the anti-Semitism that affected most Jews was social and occupational. In some cities, Jewish jobseekers in the depression faced the added hardship of employment ads requesting "Christians only" and firms and industries that would not hire Jews. The exclusion of Jews from certain elite social clubs could also damage a business or professional career, since these were often the setting for arranging business deals or making contact with potential clients. Even this form of anti-Semitism was strong in certain regions and cities and relatively weak elsewhere. In 1943 a journalist traveling across America found almost no signs of militant anti-Semitism in the Midwest, the South, and the West. Only in Minneapolis did he find evidence of widespread anti-Semitism. Even here, it was not the rabid, poisonous variety of anti-Semitism but a more subtle social form most apparent in upper middle-class circles.[29]

The difference between anti-Semitism in Minneapolis and in Indianapolis was a matter of degree. In Minneapolis, Jews were excluded from all the business and service clubs; Indianapolis, like most other cities, admitted Jews to most of its clubs. (As in many cities during this period, Jews were excluded from Rotary.) Anti-Semitism in Indianapolis was discreet. Jewish leaders suspected that there was discrimination against Jews in employment but could not prove it. Eli Lilly and Company, the city's largest manufacturer, employed nearly 4,000 people, only two of whom were Jewish, although they sold their products to many Jewish pharmacists. Yet a Jewish chemist who worked there claimed that he sensed no discrimination whatsoever.[30]

In contrast to the anti-Semitism of the Midwest, the kind of anti-Semitism found in eastern urban centers was more vicious and virulent. It was strongest in cities where large Irish Catholic communities lived close to large Jewish settlements. This anti-Semitism was fed by traditional anti-Semitic church doctrine, the competition for jobs in a depression economy, and the influence of priests like Charles Coughlin and Francis Morran who were anti-Semitic, anti-New Deal, and isolationist. In Boston, Jews were accused of draft dodging; anti-Semitic leaflets were left on subway seats; and gangs of Irish youths beat up Jewish youths.[31]

Anti-Semitic fringe groups could be found throughout America in the 1930s. An estimated 121 anti-Semitic groups were established in the decade, many on the assumption that they would receive financial support from the Nazi government. The strength and support for these different groups varied enormously. Many were little more than one man with a post office box and a home printing press. Others were active groups with large memberships. In Chicago the Friends of Democracy, a pro-fascist group, held frequent, noisy meetings. The Christian Front, a primarily Irish Catholic group, held street-corner meetings and advocated boycotts of Jewish merchants. In Detroit, long a hotbed for such groups, the German-American Bund flourished. Many prominent Bundists found jobs in the Ford automobile plant. When the Bund was suppressed, they continued to work through other organizations such as the Ku Klux Klan. There was a chapter, of sorts, of the German-American Bund in Indianapolis, but it was pathetically small. It was oganized by Charles W. Soltau, a third-generation American who issued invitations to German-Americans to attend an organizational meeting at his home in March 1938. Notice of

the meeting aroused such widespread hostility, however—
including a stoning attack on Soltau's home—that it was can-
celled. Soltau, a bachelor, was later convicted for refusing to appear
for military induction.[32]

While groups like the German-American Bund and William Pelley's Silver Shirts were disturbing (Pelley was based in Noblesville,
Indiana, during the period), Jews were equally distressed by the
growth of Nazism in Germany and the fear that Nazism would be
exported to American shores. However, the cautious restraint that
had characterized the Jewish community's response to the rise of
the Klan in the 1920s was not duplicated in the 1930s. Increasing
numbers of the Indianapolis Jewish community were now
American-born. Americanization and acculturation had brought a
greater self-confidence and self-assurance to the community, which
led, in turn, to the community's taking offensive action against
anti-Semitism in the 1930s. As events outside their local communities began to take on greater importance, American Jewry
developed a sense of national unity. This feeling was enhanced by
the Anglo-Jewish press's detailed coverage of anti-Semitic incidents. The record in Indianapolis very much reflected what was
occurring nationally, as the Indianapolis Jewish community responded to the fear of anti-Semitism with a variety of defensive
and offensive measures designed to prevent or retard the growth of
anti-Semitism locally.[33]

The organized Jewish response to anti-Semitism fell into a
number of clearly defined areas. There were efforts to promote
ethical conduct among Jews; to encourage Jewish immigrants to
obtain American citizenship; to disassociate Jews from left-wing
politics; to educate non-Jews about Jews and Judaism and about
Hitler and Nazism; and to promote brotherhood and interfaith activities. The Indianapolis B'nai B'rith lodge—not surprisingly,
given B'nai B'rith's sponsorship of the Anti-Defamation League—
took a leading role in nearly every organized effort to fight anti-
Semitism in the city. In December 1933, disturbed by "the actions
and mannerisms of certain Jews which are aiding the prejudices
against our race and promoting ill feeling toward persons of Jewish
faith," the B'nai B'rith lodge called a meeting of representatives of
most of the city's Jewish organizations (for some reason, the city's
women's groups were not invited to the initial meeting) "to de-

termine what methods and attitudes to pursue to eliminate any unethical practices or conduct ... of those contributing to these prejudices." Once again, as in the reaction to the Klan in the twenties, Jewish responses appeared to blame Jews for anti-Semitism and tacitly acknowledged that the anti-Semites were right.[34]

At about the same time that B'nai B'rith members were worrying that Jewish manners and gestures were promoting prejudice, another group of communal leaders were concerned about the high number of Jewish graduates of the Indiana University Medical School being recommended for internships. While internships were awarded solely on the basis of scholastic achievement, some Jews worried that accusations might be made that Jewish students were being given preferential treatment or, more likely, that Jewish students won the internships because they were pushy and aggressive. So fearful were some Jews about potential anti-Semitic reactions, they are reported to have made the unbelievable suggestion to I.U. Medical School Dean Willis Gatch that *fewer* Jews be recommended for internships. This absurd proposal was vigorously rejected.[35]

It was not only Jewish individuals who were expected to act immaculately, but Jewish institutions as well had to maintain certain standards "for the sake of the impression created in the neighborhood." This was a deciding factor in the Jewish Federation's board of governor's decision to maintain the policy of closing the Communal Building and the Kirshbaum Center on Saturdays and religious holidays despite the fact that in April 1933 the board of the JCCA had voted to *open* the Kirshbaum Center at noon on Saturdays. Since the JCCA was a secular organization controlled by secular-minded Jews, it was not surprising that they wanted to keep the center open. Although it was understandable that the board of the Federation, which theoretically represented all Jews, might have felt that it was improper for a Jewish organization to remain open on these days, particularly since this would be offensive to traditional Jews, it was not Jewish opinion that concerned the board. (Many members of the Federation's board of governors agreed with Rabbi Feuerlicht that it was not "contrary to the spirit of Judaism to engage in recreation on the Sabbath.") What guided the decision was the Jewish "image" in the larger community. Some board members argued that Jews should maintain the *ap-*

pearance of observing the Sabbath, even if they did not, in order to appear more "respectable" in gentile eyes. These concerns, as voiced by the Federation's president, G. A. Efroymson, were overriding:

> As self-respecting Jews who desire to live in peace and harmony with our gentile neighbors and who desire to maintain our self-respect in their eyes, we can not flaunt our activities before them on Sunday and remain open on Saturday as well.

Board members apparently believed that by appearing to be Sabbath observers the level of anti-Semitism would somehow decline. The Federation board vetoed the decision of the JCCA and decided that both centers would remain closed on Saturday. (In 1950, the Kirshbaum Center was finally permitted to remain open on Saturdays, but for Jewish servicemen only.)[36]

Jewish aliens continued to be the subject of an intense Americanization campaign. Jewish leaders, nervous about talk of the "international Jew" and the foreign radical, were anxious to have their community appear as thoroughly American as possible. Throughout the thirties, citizenship rallies and naturalization classes sponsored by B'nai B'rith, the Council of Jewish Women, and the JCCA encouraged Jewish aliens to obtain American citizenship. A survey conducted by the Americanization Committee of B'nai B'rith in 1936 showed that 140 Jews in Indianapolis were not yet naturalized. Americanization workers hoped to reduce this figure to zero.[37]

Causes of even greater concern than the not-yet Americanized Jew were Jewish involvement in radical politics and the use of Jewish communal facilities by radical groups. The anti-Semitic charge linking Jews with Bolshevism troubled Jewish leaders everywhere, but it was especially worrisome in such a politically conservative city as Indianapolis. The city's Jewish leaders made every possible effort to disassociate the Jewish community from radical political activity. In April 1931 a local communist group requested the use of the Kirshbaum Center auditorium. This request was denied, and the Jewish Federation board voted to deny the use of its building to any "group opposed to our government" and to any communist groups. In 1936 after the League Against War and Facism held a meeting at the Kirshbaum Center, the

Jewish Federation board of governors reaffirmed its policy regarding the use of its buildings by political groups. The political leanings of employees of the Federation and its constituent agencies were also scrutinized. Noting that some employees were reported to have "radical leanings" and had attended "meetings of a nature that would reflect discredit upon the Jewish community as a whole," the Federation's board decided that its committee on community relations should investigate the situation, since it was believed that "the general community holds these employees responsible for the opinions of the entire community." The committee interviewed the staff members in question and concluded that "while no prohibitive measures in restraint of thought should be exercised, employees should refrain from radical tendencies during working hours."[38]

It is hard to know the actual extent of Jewish left-wing activity in Indianapolis during this period. While the great majority of Jews did not support left-wing political groups, a small group did. After the communists lost control of the Workmen's Circle to the socialists in the 1920s, the defectors organized a number of Jewish communist groups. The only one of these groups known to have an Indianapolis branch was Icor, the American Association for Jewish Colonization in the Soviet Union. Icor members focused their support for the Soviet Union on the Soviet plan to establish a Jewish settlement, or "Jewish Autonomous Region," in Birobidzhan in the Soviet Far East. The Jewish colonization of Birobidzhan, which began in 1928, was generally supported by the Jewish territorialists and the communists and was opposed by the Zionists, who wanted to see Jewish settlement only in Palestine. The Indianapolis branch of Icor, which had a clubhouse at 914½ South Meridian, sponsored public lectures on life in the Soviet Union. In December 1934, for example, Mrs. Anna Goldberg lectured in Yiddish on the life of women in the Soviet Union. The granting of the status of "Jewish Autonomous Region" to Birobidzhan in May 1934 was cause for celebration in Icor circles. The Indianapolis chapter marked the occasion with a picnic the following month. Picnic-goers were entertained by a dramatic sketch presented by the John Reed Club. Organized radicalism in the early depression days clustered around the John Reed clubs (named for the hero of American communists), which sprang up in many American cities. Apparently, the Jewish members of Icor had established links with non-Jewish radicals in the city.[39]

Perhaps no action of the Jewish community better indicates the general level of anxiety about anti-Semitism than the organization of a campaign to keep news of Jewish communal doings out of the general press. In the 1920s Ernest Cohn, chairman of the Federation's publicity committee, had worked hard to gain publicity for Federation and, in particular, Jewish center activities. In 1926–1927, for example, the *Indianapolis News* ran a weekly column covering Jewish center activities. By 1934, however, the committee had completely reversed its policy. The previous objective—to keep Federation activities before the general public by means of a series of newspaper articles—was replaced by a resolution passed in April 1934 that the Jewish Federation eliminate, as much as possible, publicity items regarding its activities from the public secular press and that it recommend similar action to its constituent agencies. The committee sponsored an open meeting of representatives from all Jewish organizations in the city to discuss the issue, at which a series of recommendations regarding press coverage of Jewish events was approved. The guidelines suggested that only programs of broad general interest or programs which would increase non-Jewish understanding of Jews should be publicized. Notices of fund-raising campaigns and, in particular, amounts of money raised in campaigns were branded as "extremely detrimental to our best interests." The committee clearly wanted to avoid publicity that might create the impression that Indianapolis Jewry was powerful, wealthy, and influential beyond its numbers. Even if Indianapolis Jewry had not directly experienced the violent anti-Semitism of Brooklyn, Boston, or Berlin, they were obviously nervous about doing anything that might draw attention to the Jewish community and raise the degree of anti-Semitism already present in the city to an unpleasant level.[40]

At the same time that communal leaders decided to adopt a low profile in regard to internal Jewish matters, they also decided to promote programs to educate non-Jews about Judaism and to inform them of the events occurring in Nazi Germany. The Open Forum, the annual lecture series of nationally known speakers at the Kirshbaum Center, took on a new significance. In 1940 the JCCA was considering discontinuing the series, which usually included one or two speakers on Jewish themes while the remainder spoke on international or American political affairs from a perspective that was sympathetic to Jewish concerns. The Federation's board of governors viewed the preservation of the Open Forum as a gesture of community goodwill, as well as a means of giving the Jewish perspective on the world crisis a wide hearing. At the urging of the Federation, the Open Forum was continued. In 1940 the Indianapolis Hebrew Congregation established an Institute on Judaism, a daylong seminar for Protestant and Catholic clergy on some aspect of Judaism which eventually became an annual event. The first institute featured Rabbi Samuel S. Cohon, professor of theology at the Hebrew Union College in Cincinnati, who spoke on the Talmud. In more informal ways individual Jews tried to educate the general public about the situation in Germany. In May 1933 Rabbi Milton Steinberg spoke to the Indianapolis Rotary Club on Hitlerism. His speech made such an impact that he received several requests from groups throughout the state to repeat it. Two years later Rabbi Morris Feuerlicht spoke to the Indiana Pastors' Conference, condemning the Nazi government and asking for help in challenging Nazi propaganda.[41]

By the late thirties the national Jewish defense agencies were already quietly working throughout the Midwest, gathering supporters and attempting to establish themselves as the spokesmen for community relations. The Anti-Defamation League—backed by the long-established B'nai B'rith lodge—had a local Indianapolis committee which met primarily on a crisis basis when some incident occurred that required attention. Their constructive or educational work was confined to the placing of appropriate books in local libraries. The American Jewish Congress also had a strong local group. The American Jewish Committee, trying to gain a local toehold, was backing the Federation proposal to establish a local public relations committee. The committee was organized in 1939, but it was relatively weak at first because some local leaders felt it was unnecessary. The Public Relations Committee (the name was changed to the Jewish Community Relations Council in 1947) sought to promote interfaith activities; maintain good relations between Jews and non-Jews; promote high ethical standards among Jews; protect Jewish rights; support civic and community welfare programs; and publicize the Jewish contribution to Ameri-

can life. The committee was governed by a board of elected dele-
gates representing every facet of the community—all the
synagogues, Zionist groups, women's groups, men's groups, Federation agencies, etc. The thoroughly representative character of the
board symbolized the feeling that anti-Semitism was a concern of
all Jews. Moreover, it was the one issue that united all Jews—
Reform and Orthodox, Zionist and anti-Zionist. When faced with a
true enemy, Jews could finally put aside their individual differences and unite—more or less—in common cause. The first
chairman of the committee was Samuel Mueller (ca. 1877–1958),
an executive with the Indianapolis Chamber of Commerce who
served until 1942. Maurice Goldblatt, assistant rabbi at IHC, then
become the committee's first paid executive director on a part-time
basis. The committee co-sponsored, with Catholic and Protestant
groups, an annual series of interfaith services and lectures during
"Brotherhood Week." They also organized a series of radio programs and other educational projects. In addition, they conducted
behind-the-scenes campaigns against economic and social discrimination, such as Rotary's restriction against Jewish members.
In 1941 the committee organized a protest against a proposal by the
state superintendent of public instruction to introduce religious
education into the public schools. (The issue of religious instruction in public schools would become an increasingly important
element of the committee's agenda in the 1950s.)[42]

Goldblatt, who also helped to found the Indianapolis Round
Table of Christians and Jews in 1944, resigned in 1946 partly under
pressure from his congregation, who wanted him to devote all his
time to the synagogue. In 1947 Charles Posner was hired as the
first full-time professional executive director of the Jewish Community Relations Council, which became a full-fledged constituent
agency of the Federation that same year.[43]

The growing interest in community relations work in Indianapolis in the 1940s was part of a national trend. Disturbed by
rising anti-Semitism and fearful of the influence of Nazi doctrine
on potentially sympathetic Americans, many local communities
established community relations councils in the 1940s. The general interest in community relations strengthened the national defense agencies as well—the Anti-Defamation League, the American Jewish Committee, and the American Jewish Congress—as

local federations increased their annual appropriations to these agencies. With growing funds and increased interest in their activities, the national organizations began to establish local or regional offices. The regional office would often be operating in direct competition with a locally-sponsored community relations council, a source of potential conflict. It was the local federations, of course, that had helped contribute to the defense agencies' new wealth. In the early 1940s, the Anti-Defamation League attempted unsuccessfully to set up a regional office in Indianapolis. The American Jewish Committee at first backed the autonomous local Public Relations Committee, but in 1945 the national organization formed its own local chapter and began sponsoring lectures and programs. One of the first programs was a "Clinic on Anti-Semitism" held after Friday night services at IHC in 1946.[44]

Divisions in the Local Community

If Jews could not even completely forget their differences in order to fight anti-Semitism, internal Jewish affairs in the thirties and forties were even more riddled with conflict. Declining funds forced a reconsideration of priorities, and second-generation eastern European Jews challenged the authority of the old German Jewish communal leadership.

While all Federation agencies suffered financially during the thirties, it was the Jewish Community Center Association that ran the largest deficits. The deficit reached a high of $8,000 in 1936, at a time when the Federation's total budget was only $40,000. The Federation structure allowed each agency to design its own budget, which it then presented to the Federation for approval. The Federation in turn submitted the budgets to the Community Fund, which then allocated funds to the Jewish Federation for dispersal to the appropriate agencies. Members of the Federation board of governors, sensing that they had lost control of their constituent agencies, suggested a restructuring of the apparatus so that the Federation could regain budgetary control of its constituent agencies and reduce their deficits. However, no restructuring was accomplished.[45]

With the Federation weakened already by its financial crisis, a second attack was launched on its financial authority by the

Big Eagle Camp in Zionsville, the successor to Camp Ida Wineman, provided an overnight camping program from 1930 until 1957 when the camp was sold to the Union of American Hebrew Congregations. (IHS)

Philip Kraft, a Romanian immigrant, moved to Indianapolis from New York City in 1921 and established Kraft's South Side Baking Company. Here he poses with a race car and driver he sponsored for the Indianapolis 500. (IHS)

Crowded street scene at Washington and Illinois in 1947 shows L. Strauss & Company about to move to the large corner building. The city's major retailers began opening suburban branches in the late 1950s. (ISL)

An English class for refugees from Nazi Germany organized by Jewish Social Services. (IHS)

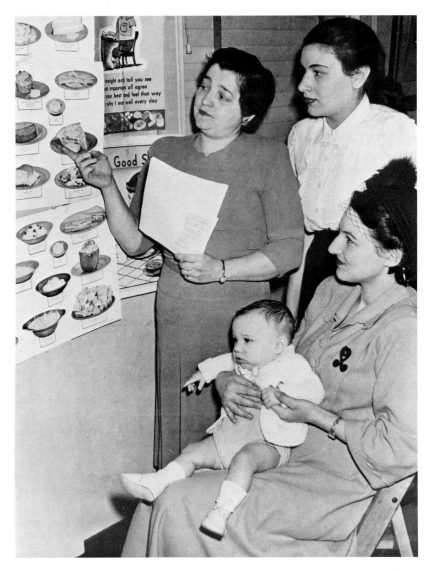

After the war the National Council of Jewish Women organized a home institute to teach refugee mothers American homemaking, including instruction in nutrition and proper diet. (IHS)

A familiar scene in Shapiro's Delicatessen, photographed in the late 1940s. The store, which is still on South Meridian Street, is one of the last remnants of the old Jewish south side. (IHS)

Etz Chaim (Sephardic) Congregation confirmation class, probably from the 1940s. (IHS)

In 1914 the Communal Building sponsored one of the city's first Boy Scout troops, which was also the first Jewish troop organized in the state. This is a troop from the 1940s. (IHS)

A preschool class at the Kirshbaum Center, probably from the 1940s. (IHS)

Members of the Kirshbaum Men's Club promoting an affair, the Matzo Ball, in the 1940s. (IHS)

During the Second World War, the Jewish community provided help and support to Jewish soldiers stationed at nearby military bases. Here members of the Jewish War Veterans Auxiliary wrap Hanukkah gifts for the soldiers. (IHS)

The Kirshbaum Center at 23rd and North Meridian. The building was sold and then razed by its new owners in the 1950s. (IHS)

Morris Strauss (left) and Louis Borinstein examining a copy of the *Indiana Jewish Chronicle* in 1946. Strauss published this, the state's first Jewish newspaper, from 1923 to 1969. (IHS)

A confirmation class at Congregation Beth-El Zedeck in 1949. Rabbi William Greenfeld is fourth from the right in the second row. (IHS)

Nandor Fruchter served as rabbi of Central Hebrew Congregation and Congregation B'nai Torah from 1942 to 1971. (IHS)

Children enjoying a meal in the JEA *sukkah* in 1952. (IHS)

A Hebrew class at the Jewish Educational Association in 1957. Note the preponderance of boys in the classroom. (IHS)

Indianapolis Jewish Community Relations Council display of literature at the CIO State Convention in 1951. New attitudes after the war helped to make racial bigotry and discrimination "unpopular." (IHS)

Dancing at the Golden Age Club meeting in the 1950s. The club was organized by the National Council of Jewish Women in 1950. (IHS)

Cornerstone laying for the new Jewish Community Center in 1957. Amy Cook Lurvey is in the white hat. (IHS)

A Jewish Community Center field trip in the 1960s. (IHS)

A model Passover seder at the Jewish Educational Association in
1961. The community's rabbis often disagreed over whether the JEA
should emphasize the secular curriculum (Hebrew language) or the
religious curriculum (prayers, ceremonies, etc.). (IHS)

National Council of Jewish Women members working at the Council
Thrift Shop in 1960. (IHS)

National Council of Jewish Women volunteers at Central State Hospital, a mental institution, in 1959. (IHS)

Etz Chaim, the Sephardic congregation, left the south side and purchased a former Lutheran church at 64th Street and Hoover Road in 1963. (JWF)

Congregation B'nai Torah, an Orthodox synagogue, constructed this building at 65th Street and Hoover Road in 1967. (JWF)

In 1962 three south side synagogues merged to form United Orthodox Hebrew Congregation and built a synagogue on the north side of Central Avenue. (JWF)

Congregation Beth-El Zedeck, a Conservative synagogue, moved to the far north side in 1958. (JWF)

Indianapolis Hebrew Congregation, a Reform Congregation and the city's first synagogue, constructed a new building at 65th and North Meridian in 1958. (JWF)

Augusta Plaza at 71st Street and Michigan Road in Indianapolis. Completed in 1960, this was one of the first shopping centers built by Melvin Simon and Associates. Simon, a New Yorker, was stationed near Indianapolis during the Second World War. After the war he settled in Indianapolis and became one of the major shopping center developers in the country.

Gerald Kraft, an Indianapolis native, active in state and regional B'nai B'rith activities for many years, was elected International President of B'nai B'rith in 1982.

Community Fund, source of all Federation revenue. For the fiscal year 1939–1940, the Community Fund agreed to increase the Jewish Federation's allocation by $1,200 (to $42,950) but only if the extra money was used for the employment of a boys' worker by the JCCA. The board of governors viewed this earmarking of funds by the Community Fund as a dangerous precedent which could "lead to disharmony in the Jewish community and with the Community Fund" and to a further loss of Federation control over its agencies. In 1943 the Community Fund established a new policy requiring all constituent agencies to send monthly statements and requests for funds directly to the Community Fund. This step further undermined the Federation's management of its agencies. Over Federation objections, the Community fund stood by this new arrangement, which completely circumvented the Federation, denying it any control over its agencies' spending. However, even with this new arrangement, the JCCA continued to run substantial annual deficits.[46]

The high deficits of the JCCA and the inability of the Federation to control its constituent continued for some ten years. Finally in 1945 a Committee of Nine, composed of three representatives each from a Citizens Committee, the Jewish Federation, and the Jewish Welfare Fund, was organized to study the problems of communal organization. The committee apparently felt that the situation had deteriorated to the point that no real change could be effected under the present administrations. H. Joseph Hyman, the Federation's executive director, and Allan Bloom, general secretary of the JCCA, were both asked to resign. The committee also proposed merging the Jewish Federation and the Jewish Welfare Fund (which was vetoed by the Jewish Welfare Fund; the two did not merge until 1948) and expanding the board of governors so that it was more representative of the total Jewish community.[47]

The question of whether the governing board of the Jewish Federation was representative of all groups within the Jewish community was not an issue that would have concerned the founders of the Jewish Federation. At the time of its establishment in 1905, the Federation was perceived as a philanthropic organization established to help the impoverished eastern European immigrants. By the 1920s, with the severe decline in immigration, the aims of the Federation began to change to emphasize providing for the needs of the Jewish middle class, as symbolized by the establishment of the Kirshbaum Center in 1926. Yet while Federation programs tacitly acknowledged the acculturation of the eastern European immigrants and the growth of a middle-class second generation, no attempts were made to bring members of this group into the Federation power structure. Except for the occasional Orthodox rabbi, Federation board members were primarily wealthy Reform Jews, most of whom were anti-Zionist and assimilationist. By the 1930s, however, the self-confident American-born children of the eastern Europeans began to challenge not only the control but also the direction and objectives of the Federation. No longer supplicant and grateful receivers of charity, they considered themselves equal in status to the Federation leadership and wanted a voice in the direction of communal affairs.

The challenge to the Federation leadership was led by Elias Charry, rabbi of Congregation Beth-El Zedeck, the synagogue that seemed to symbolize the rising prosperity of the second generation. Within a few years, Beth-El Zedeck had become a large, influential, wealthy congregation, a close rival to the older Reform congregation, IHC. Charry, Zionist leader Daniel Frisch, and others from Beth-El Zedeck advocated the organization of a community council that would have on its board representatives of every Jewish organization in the city. (Community councils were established in several American cities in the 1930s.) The proposed community council would supervise the selection of representatives to the board of the Jewish Federation, thus ensuring that board members represented a diversity of interests and groups. Longtime members of the Federation board such as Rabbi Morris Feuerlicht, Samuel Mueller, and Ernest Cohn hotly defended the Federation structure against the charge that it was undemocratic. They readily admitted, though, that no board member even "remotely represented the large group of Orthodox Jews." Zionists and Sephardim were also underrepresented. Obviously, those in power liked the status quo and had no desire to change it. Nevertheless, the board appointed a committee to study the situation. The committee suggested establishing a Jewish Federation Council, to be composed of representatives of every adult Jewish organization in the city. The Jewish Federation Council would, in turn, select the Federation's board of governors. The committee also suggested that the Council organize several committees to take responsibility for a number of new functions.[48]

The implicit aim of all the proposed committees was to reduce anti-Semitism whether by "improving" Jewish behavior or educating non-Jews about Jews. These proposals included the establishment of a Jewish board of arbitration to settle civil disputes between Jews, thus keeping certain cases out of the courts (and the press). A committee on community ethics would attempt to eliminate unethical business practices and improper behavior (also a concern of B'nai B'rith). A public relations committee would work to educate non-Jews about Judaism and promote good community relations. Although the plan was never instituted, the Federation organized a public relations committee soon after. However, even in cities that did establish community councils in the thirties, the eastern European challenge to the federation failed. The community council supporters wanted the federation to become the community fund raiser, while the community council would become the communal spokesman and policy maker. However, the federation retained its power because it held on to the all-important purse strings. In most cases, the community council eventually became a constituent agency of the federation responsible for community relations.[49]

Seven years after the failure of the community council proposal, the report of the Committee of Nine, while not proposing the formation of a community council, adopted several recommendations of the earlier community council proposals. The report also stressed the importance of democratizing the Federation board and suggested the representation of all major organizations on an expanded Federation board of governors. Other proposals designed to democratize Federation leadership included a limit of six consecutive years for any elected board member and an easier mechanism for nominating members for election. These modifications were all included in the new constitution of October 1945. The new constitution also prohibited any paid employee of a Jewish organization from serving on the board. The trend to further expand and democratize the Federation board was continued with the recommendations accompanying the final merger of the Jewish Federation and the Jewish Welfare Fund in May 1948.[50]

Not surprisingly, given the scarcity of funds, no new institutions were developed during the thirties and forties. The Jewish Shelter House and Old Home, maintained in inadequate quarters on the south side for many years, was finally able to move when the five Borinstein brothers—Louis J., Abram L., Wilfred R., Philip E., and Leslie C. Borinstein—donated their parents' family home to be used as an old-age home in 1938. A two-story home at 3516 North Central Avenue, it became known as the Joseph and Annie Borinstein Home for the Aged. An addition was built to the home, and slowly professional staff replaced the group of volunteer women who had provided somewhat erratic care and conducted the home's affairs for so many years. The number of residents rose from seven in 1945 to fifteen in 1948. A real program for the patients was developed with nurses, regular medical care, and social services provided by Jewish Social Services. (The name was changed from Jewish Family Service Society in 1946.) Jewish center staff provided recreational activities for the residents. When Nathan Berman became director of Jewish Social Services in 1946, he also became the Borinstein Home's first professional director. The facilities of the Borinstein Home, however, proved to be a chronic and unsolvable problem, because the two-story family house was just not suited to be an old-age home.[51]

Another communal institution that finally found a permanent home on the north side was the Jewish Educational Association (JEA). Since the 1920s, the JEA had held classes in a series of north side institutions—Central Hebrew Congregation, the Kirshbaum Center, and then in Congregation Beth-El Zedeck. In 1945 the Jewish Educational Association finally purchased a building—a two-story house at 3456 North Central Avenue, one door from the Borinstein Home. Never a particularly strong organization, the JEA withstood a serious challenge to its continuing role as the community's Hebrew school in 1945. A proposal to establish an independent Hebrew school, strongly backed by the synagogue's administration, was finally voted down by the membership of Congregation Beth-El Zedeck in June 1945.[52]

One last new development of the period was the successful introduction of a second Jewish newspaper for the statewide Jewish community. (The first, the *Indiana Jewish Chronicle*, was established in 1921.) In March 1933 a small four-page monthly newspaper, the *Jewish Post*, made its first appearance. Founded by two young brothers, Leonard and Arvin Rothschild, who charged fifty cents for a year's subscription, the early *Jewish Post* was militantly Jewish, claiming on its masthead that it was the "only Jewish newspaper in the state of Indiana edited and printed entirely by Jews." In 1934 the *Jewish Post* became a semimonthly. In 1935 the paper, now a weekly, was bought by Gabriel M. Cohen, editor and publisher of the *Spokesman* of Louisville. With these two local newspapers as a nucleus, Cohen hoped to create an independent national Jewish newspaper. Using Indianapolis as his base of operation, he developed a network of local correspondents and then began the publication of a series of regional or state editions of the *Jewish Post* which became the *National Jewish Post* in 1945. In 1957 the paper absorbed *Opinion,* a journal of Jewish life and letters, and the name was changed to the *National Jewish Post and Opinion.* Local communal news appeared on a few pages of each of the *Jewish Post and Opinion*'s regional editions with the rest of the newspaper devoted to wire service news and national columnists. In Indianapolis Cohen became something of a gadfly, campaigning for a community council and further democratization of the Federation, and asking that the press be allowed to attend and report on Federation board meetings.[53]

A third statewide Jewish newspaper, the weekly *Indiana Jewish Tribune,* first appeared on May 19, 1933. Published by Aaron M. Neustadt, a son of Rabbi Isaac E. Neustadt, it had a brief life. Aaron and his brother Ben also published the *Ohio Jewish Chronicle* in Columbus, where they had moved with their widowed mother several years earlier. Perhaps the Neustadt brothers also had dreams of establishing a national Jewish newspaper, but the *Indiana Jewish Tribune* failed to succeed, and Aaron Neustadt returned to Columbus.[54]

Historians have described American Jewry in the 1930s as a community united by the most fragile threads. Deep religious, cultural, and political differences still divided the community. The growth of Zionism and its increasing militancy—by the mid-1930s membership in Zionist organizations was once again climbing—only seemed to make the possibility of unity even more remote. Tragically, the crisis of the Holocaust split the community even further and intensified its insecurity. American Jewry was weak and divided at a time when it should have been united and strong.

The community could not offer national policy makers a single message and request. Instead, a dozen proposals were presented to the administration by a stream of "spokesmen." Jews even disagreed over the proper form in which to protest the anti-Jewish campaign in Germany. Some Jews advocated public displays of protest, such as a boycott of German products and mass rallies. The more established elements in the community found these displays too "emotional" and advocated quiet, behind-the-scenes activity.[55]

Indianapolis was probably never as divided as the larger American Jewish communities. In a relatively small Jewish community the numbers simply could not support the subtle gradations of Orthodox, Zionist, and socialist organizations that existed in a large community. In order to have any organized Jewish life at all, Jews were forced to compromise. Thus, while national leaders throughout the 1930s and 1940s argued over the issue of the refugees and their rescue, the divisions in Indianapolis were relatively slight. Indianapolis Jewry's response to the crisis—particularly after the economic upturn—was to raise increasingly larger sums of money and give more to overseas and refugee causes and to Palestine. Before the full extent of the Nazi plan for the Jews was known, there were disagreements over how much money should go to local causes. In 1939 the JEA put in a request for $500 more than they had received the year before. The money was to help pay the salary of the Sephardic rabbi who also served as the children's teacher. However, some of the "big givers" reportedly objected to even this small increase to the JEA. They were particularly incensed because the Jewish Welfare Fund had passed a resolution that all money raised over the previous year should go to overseas and refugee causes. At the urging of the Jewish Welfare Fund board, the JEA gave up the $500 increase.[56]

With the outbreak of war in Europe, the annual Jewish Welfare Fund campaign increased dramatically, jumping from $73,600 in 1938, to 131,400 in 1939. Allocations to overseas causes began to dominate the budget. In 1939, 60 percent of the budget, or $78,000, went to the United Jewish Appeal, which had been formed in 1939 to jointly raise and dispense funds for the Joint Distribution Committee, the United Palestine appeal, and the National Coordinating Committee Fund (refugee aid). However, this was not enough for some board members who advocated neglecting local institutions in order to give an even higher proportion to UJA. The following year, the same percentage, 60 percent ($80,000), went to UJA. Again, G. A. Efroymson and other board members argued for giving more to UJA—$125,000*—at the expense of the local community.[57]

America's entry into the war late in 1941 brought another jump in funds raised by the campaign from $139,500 in 1941, to $171,000 in 1942. Moreover, with America now participating in the war, American Jews could take a more active role in helping the allies. While many Indianapolis Jews served in the armed forces during the Second World War, those at home also helped. Jewish organizations conducted drives to send warm clothing to civilians in the European war zone. They gave assistance to the city's refugees. They provided recreational activities for Jewish soldiers stationed at nearby bases, Fort Benjamin Harrison and Camp Atterbury. A USO sponsored by the Jewish Welfare Board was established at the Kirshbaum Center in 1942. Services were held on the bases, and the Council of Jewish women provided a day lounge at Camp Atterbury. A newsletter, *Speaking of Home,* was published at the Kirshbaum Center for the Jewish servicemen stationed at nearby bases as well as for all the enlisted members of the Indianapolis community. Families welcomed soldiers to their homes for the Passover *seder* and for *Shabbat* dinners, trying to maintain a façade of normality in abnormal, unsettling times.[58]

---

*In 1940 the Jewish Welfare Fund raised only $132,500, far short of the campaign goal of $151,160, and even further from the board's "secret" goal of $171,000.

⧎ VI

The Postwar Era

1945—1959

"STIRRED BY VIVID DESCRIPTIONS of the plight of the surviving Jews of Europe," the *Jewish Post* reported in April 1945, "leaders of the Indianapolis Jewish Community added $100,000 to the quota of the 1946 drive for the United Jewish Appeal." In the spring of 1946 in city after city across America similar scenes were enacted as communities were urged to triple or quadruple their previous year's goal in order to save the surviving remnant of European Jewry and resettle them in Palestine or other countries. Of the once great European Jewish communities it was estimated that there were only 1.4 million Jews who had survived the war, outside of the Soviet Union. American Jewry, which constituted less than one third of the world Jewish population before the war, now represented about half of world Jewry. Moreover, America contained not only the largest but also the wealthiest community. At the same time that the United States emerged as a world superpower, American Jewry became the leading Jewish community in the world.[1]

The most immediate response of American Jewry to the horrors of the Holocaust (the term was not actually used until the 1950s) was to give unprecedented amounts of money to the United Jewish Appeal. The dramatic appearance of death camp survivors at the

United Jewish Appeal Conference in December 1945, the publication of eyewitness accounts and photographs of the camps, and the
growing awareness of the extent of destruction had the effect of
tripling donations to the UJA from 1945 to 1946. Although in the
face of such evil there was probably little American Jewry could
have done to prevent the mass slaughter, perhaps some of the
enormous increase in donations reflected a form of survivor guilt.
Many American Jews must have realized, at least unconsciously,
that if their grandparents had not left eastern Europe for America,
they too would probably have perished.[2]

The realization that the Jews as a people had been singled out
for extermination was almost too painful for most American Jews
to face. Like a child that has just lost his parents and is too shocked
to cry or react with the appropriate emotions, American Jewry
went about the motions of grieving without any public cries of an-
guish. Instead, they busied themselves in the raising of vast sums
of money to send to Europe and Palestine. It seemed to be the only
way many could respond to events almost too horrible to believe.

Nationally, donations to the United Jewish Appeal tripled from
$35 million in 1945 to $101 million in 1946. Similarly, the amount
raised by the Indianapolis Jewish community tripled from $196,000
in 1945 (through the United War and Community Fund) to
$625,000 in 1946. The campaigns continued at a high level for two
more years, as fund raisers managed to surround the campaigns
with an emotional intensity fed by the vivid pictures of the European destruction and the plight of the refugees. In addition, the
healthy economic climate of postwar America enabled donors to
give away record sums.

The emotions generated by the establishment of the State of
Israel and the opening of its doors to the refugees produced the
high-water mark of fund raising in 1948 when $148 million was
raised for the United Jewish Appeal. Indianapolis raised $1,004,600
in 1948, a figure which would not be matched until 1967 in the
aftermath of the Six-Day War.[3]

Not only were greater sums raised in 1946, 1947, and 1948 than
ever before and than would be equalled for some time to come, but
during these three years the Jewish Federation allocated an unpar-
alleled proportion of its campaign to overseas causes (as represented by its annual appropriation to UJA). In 1946 the Federation

campaign was a special event in which all of the proceeds went to the United Jewish Appeal. In 1947, 80.8 percent went to UJA and in 1948, 73.5 percent. Beginning in 1949 the total amount raised began to decline and so did the proportion allocated to UJA, which received about 51.8 percent of the total raised in Indianapolis throughout the 1950s (see Table 3).

Table 3.
Proceeds Raised by Jewish Welfare Federation Campaigns from End of the Depression to the Present

Campaign Year	Amount Raised	Amount Allocated to UJA	% Allocated to UJA
1939	131,400	78,000	60.0
1940	132,500	80,000	60.0
1941	139,500	—	—
1942	171,000	87,500	51.0
1943[a]	170,000	—	—
1944[a]	170,000	105,000	61.0
1945[a]	196,000	120,000	61.0
1946 supp.	625,000	625,000	100.0
1946	196,000	—	—
1947	780,497	630,497	80.8
1948	1,004,600	738,339	73.5
1949	597,300	378,138	63.3
1950	543,900	317,139	58.3
1951	587,200	347,422	59.1
1952	513,500	275,719	53.7
1953	429,300	202,250	47.1
1954	357,570	160,000	44.7
1955	361,300	162,710	45.0
1956	493,300	266,044	53.9
1957	536,600	281,477	52.4
1958	370,100	172,800	46.6
1959	445,600	210,158	47.2
1960	401,800	177,300	44.1
1961	382,600	166,951	43.6
1962	436,400	196,052	44.9
1963	405,000	182,766	45.1
1964	462,200	210,048	45.4
1965	475,000	212,558	44.7

Campaign Year	Amount Raised	Amount Allocated to UJA	% Allocated to UJA
1966	524,424	238,160	45.4
1967	1,066,712	776,742	72.8
1968	975,143	658,618	67.5
1969	1,025,338	671,749	65.5
1970	1,130,124	752,014	66.5
1971	1,324,577	897,067	67.7
1972	1,517,931	1,024,224	67.5
1973	1,606,993	1,033,199	64.3
1974	2,684,077	1,907,872	71.1
1975	2,343,673	1,551,675	66.2
1976	2,350,000	1,505,010	64.0
1977	2,400,794	1,514,064	63.1
1978	2,603,831	1,593,136	61.2
1979	2,680,790	1,600,000	59.7
1980	3,000,732	1,700,000	56.7
1981	2,900,000	1,651,930	57.0

[a]Funds raised in cooperation with United War and Community Fund

If the record sums given to UJA represented both a way to mourn the death of European Jewry and a way to express survivor guilt, then the creation of the state of Israel in 1948 marked the end of the first period of mourning. Welfare fund contributions declined dramatically in all communities after 1948 although the needs of those who settled in Israel were still very great. But Israel's day-to-day struggle to survive in the late 1940s and early 1950s, a less heartrending and more mundane business than the drama of beginning, attracted less international attention and publicity. As a consequence, fund raising became more difficult. However, the decline in welfare fund campaigns did not signify an absolute drop in Jewish philanthrophy. After years of anxiety about events in Europe and the Middle East, American Jews began to look to their own neglected institutions. Greater interest developed in raising money for synagogues, homes for the elderly, Jewish centers, and hospitals.[4]

American observers have viewed the tranquility of the 1950s as a reflection of the attempt on the part of many Americans to forget fifteen troubled years of depression and war. Just as Americans after the First World War wanted to shut the door to Europe—

source of war, tragedy, and political radicalism—Americans after the Second World War reacted in a similar way. The country turned inward in the 1950s; isolationism, long an American political tradition, flourished. Public displays of patriotism became the hallmarks of civic life. A militant anti-Communist movement matched the Red Scare of 1919–1920 in intensity and fanaticism. American Jews, caught up in the move to new suburban neighborhoods, also seemed almost to want to forget the tragedies of European Jewry. In 1949, in discussing the slow progress of that year's annual fund-raising drive, the executive director of the Jewish Welfare Federation, Sidney Cahn, reported that there was unanimity among the large contributors that local needs should be considered strongly in the 1949 campaign. When the campaign raised only 60 percent of the previous year's total, the board of directors stood by the budget committee's policy that local needs would take precedence over international ones. It was agreed to give UJA the excess revenue only after all other allocations and campaign expenses had been paid. The United Jewish Appeal received 63.3 percent of the 1949 campaign, down from 73.5 percent in the previous year. This paralleled a decrease in funds allocated to UJA nationally—from 69.1 percent in 1948 to 59 percent in 1949. However, because the combined 1949 campaigns raised $28.6 million less than in 1948, this was a drop in revenue for UJA of $30.5 million, the equivalent of a 33 percent decline in funds (see Table 3).[5]

With dozens of urgent demands for money being presented to local leaders, the annual federation campaign began to assume greater prominence in each local community. It became an arena in which advocates of Israel, Jewish hospitals, social and defense agencies, and educational institutions fought for attention and a larger share of the campaign dollar. The annual campaign became ritualized during this era as fund raisers developed a whole series of techniques to squeeze more money out of reluctant donors. Since the control of the campaign and its appropriations were an obvious source of power, the local campaign became the central focus of communal leadership.

With advocates of Israel pitted against supporters of hospitals, schools, and social and defense agencies, even within the ranks of Israel's supporters, the long-range goal was often lost in the short-term struggles for power. Israeli leaders were well aware that their country could not develop a viable economy by relying on the

charitable contributions of Diaspora Jewry, which were subject to
the vagaries of local fund-raising campaigns. The Jewish state also
received loans from local American banks—negotiated for UJA by
federations—as well as loans and grants from the American government, which were widely supported by the public partly because Israel was seen as a defense against Communism. However,
the young state also needed long-term investments to reduce its
dependence on outside contributions. In September 1950 Prime
Minister David Ben-Gurion proposed to a conference of fifty-nine
American Jewish leaders (Julian Freeman represented Indianapolis
at the meeting) that Israel promote the sale of interest-bearing
development bonds. These bonds would give the state the capital it
needed for long-term economic growth. However, American Jewish
leaders were less than enthusiastic about the idea, fearing a bond
drive would undercut United Jewish Appeal and federation campaigns. They also worried that the American government might
oppose the idea. But President Truman embraced the proposal, and
Ben-Gurion appointed Golda Meir to sell the bond idea to the
American community.[6]

The development of the American Financial and Development
Corporation (later called the Israel Bonds Organization)—
grudgingly sanctioned by the federations—posed the first serious
threat to the dominance of the local federation campaign. Even
though the purchase of a bond was not technically a donation but
an actual interest-bearing investment, it was treated like a charitable contribution. Adding to the confusion was the fact that the
annual bond drive was organized along lines similar to the UJA
campaign. (The first executive director of the bond organization
was Henry Montor, formerly executive director of UJA.) Anxious
that the Federation campaign maintain its dominance in Indianapolis, Federation leaders organized a coordinating committee
to regulate all local fund raising for Jewish causes. The committee
insisted that no other fund raising be conducted between March 1
and June 15, the period reserved for the Federation-UJA campaign.
Since local leaders in the bond drive were also Federation officers
and board members, the sanctity of this time period was preserved.
The first bond campaign conducted in Indianapolis in 1951 raised
$600,000, and relations between the two organizations remained
amicable.[7]

The following year, however, the bond organization's leadership

grew restive under Federation-UJA control of local campaign tim-
ing and decided to prove that, as agents of the Israeli government,
they were not subject to federation authority. In order to provoke a
head-on confrontation, the bond leadership scheduled a dinner
featuring Golda Meir as the speaker for March 30, 1952. This night
had already been scheduled for the big gifts banquet that opened
the Indianapolis Federation's campaign, and Golda Meir had previously agreed to speak for the Federation banquet. Presumably because Julian Freeman (1897–1980) was then serving as president of
both the Indianapolis Jewish Welfare Federation and the Council of
Jewish Federations and Welfare Funds, Indianapolis was chosen as
the site to play out this particularly nasty fight. When the Federation refused to reschedule their dinner, the leadership of Israel
Bonds launched a vicious attack on Freeman and Rabbi William
Greenfeld (ca. 1906–1960) of Congregation Beth-El Zedeck. (Ironically, Greenfeld was to be presented the man-of-the-year award by
the Indiana State of Israel Bonds Organization in 1956.) Freeman
was accused of wanting "to rule all of American Jewry with the
same iron fist he uses in Indianapolis. . . . to establish himself as
the dictator over the machinery of every form of fund raising for
Israel." The Federation eventually did postpone its dinner, but the
Federation leadership was conspicuously absent from the bonds
dinner. It took many years for the Israel Bonds Organization to re-
establish itself in Indianapolis.[8]

With the dramatic need for a homeland for the Jewish survivors
of the war and the establishment of the State of Israel, most of the
force went out of the Zionist/anti-Zionist controversy. (Although,
as we have seen, even between supporters of Israel there could be
bitter infighting.) Membership in Zionist organizations rose
dramatically: nationally the Zionist Organization of America grew
from 50,000 in 1940 to 225,000 in 1948, and in the same period the
membership of Hadassah, the women's Zionist organization, more
than tripled. In 1946 a drive to double the membership of the Indianapolis Zionist District from 500 to 1,000 easily met its goal.
Hadassah—whose first Indianapolis chapter, the Henrietta Szold
chapter, was established in 1923—added a Business and Professional Women's chapter in 1942 and Ha'Ima (the mother) chapter
for young women in 1957. Orthodoxy, which had initially remained aloof from political Zionism, over the years came to sup-

port the Zionist movement through Mizrachi, the religious Zionist organization that supported the Zionist movement on the assumption that the Jewish state would be governed by *halakhah* (Jewish law). By the 1940s not only did all of the Orthodox rabbis of Indianapolis urge Indianapolis Jewry to join the Indianapolis Zionist District, but by 1942 there were local chapters of both Mizrachi Men and Mizrachi Women.[9]

Only in the Indianapolis Hebrew Congregation (IHC) did any vestiges of anti-Zionism remain. While some Reform rabbis were Zionists, Rabbi Morris Feuerlicht, who led IHC for over forty years, was a supporter of classical Reform, which rejected political Zionism. In his congregation there remained pockets of support for the American Council for Judaism, a group which not only was violently opposed to the establishment of a Jewish state but held the position that Jews were members of a religious group and nothing more. By 1945 support for the American Council's position was waning, and few Jewish groups would even grant a forum to the group's executive director, Rabbi Elmer W. Berger. In that year, the IHC Brotherhood sponsored a symposium on Zionism featuring Berger. At first the Brotherhood was unable to find a Zionist spokesman even willing to appear on the same platform with Berger, but a representative from the League for Labor Palestine, Rabbi Jacob Weinstein, finally agreed to speak.[10]

Among IHC members support for the American Council for Judaism did not die with the birth of the State of Israel. In 1954 a group of parents who were dissatisfied both with Rabbi Maurice Goldblatt, a supporter of the Zionist movement for many years, and with the religious school curriculum broke away from IHC. The group organized their own Sunday school, using a curriculum furnished by the American Council for Judaism. When the School for Reform Judaism approached the Jewish Educational Association (JEA) for permission to use its facilities, the board voted to defer this potentially explosive issue to the Federation board of directors. The request provoked a long and bitter debate; those opposed were particularly concerned that granting the request might hasten the formation of an American Council for Judaism chapter in Indianapolis. In the end, the Federation decided to grant the request on the grounds that "the JEA was a Jewish community supported institution and should be available to any group wishing to use it for the purpose of Jewish instruction." The School for Reform Judaism lasted for three years and had an enrollment of about sixty-five students. Parents of the students met regularly for discussions of Jewish topics with Hugo Green, then a rabbinical student at the Hebrew Union College in Cincinnati. Some of the school's founders saw it as the potential nucleus for a second Reform congregation. However, following Goldblatt's resignation and certain modifications of the curriculum of the IHC Sunday school, the group voted to disband and return to IHC.[11]

The decline that began in 1949 in federation campaigns and in the sums given to UJA reflected a shifting in contributors' interests from events abroad to their local communities. Following the end of World War II, numerous building projects were undertaken throughout America to renovate or build new Jewish institutions. A backlog of building needs had accumulated during the years of depression and war. By the early 1950s, dozens of campaigns for synagogues, Jewish hospitals, centers, and homes for the aged had been inaugurated.[12]

The great demand for new buildings partly reflected several important changes within the American Jewish community. After World War II Jews were part of a massive migration from dense urban residential districts to small towns and suburbs on the outskirts of major metropolitan areas. This movement to the suburbs, to areas where Jews lived among Christian neighbors of equal or higher status, brought in its wake a whole series of changes to the American Jewish community. The most significant change was the rise of the synagogue to a position of dominance. Synagogue membership increased dramatically in the 1950s. For example, the Conservative movement claimed 75,000 member families in 1937 and 200,000 in 1956. In Indianapolis, membership in Beth-El Zedeck, the city's Conservative congregation, doubled between 1945 and 1958 (to 760 families). Will Herberg in *Protestant, Catholic, Jew* explained the American postwar religious revival as the translation of the desire to maintain an ethnic community into religious terms. To be religious in postwar America was acceptable; in fact it was the only acceptable way to maintain a separate identity from one's neighbors. In a society which celebrated the melting pot, secular ethnic movements seemed unnecessary, foreign, and rather exotic. All kinds of secular Jewish institutions that had been linked to the immigrant experience declined in the 1950s. The Jewish left, for example, nearly disappeared due to the vanishing Jewish working class and the general decline of socialism in America. The membership of the Indianapolis Workmen's Circle, the city's only Jewish socialist organization, fell so precipitously in the 1950s that the branch finally closed. All kinds of Jews who had never belonged to a synagogue and even some who had grown up in antireligious households suddenly found themselves moving to the suburbs and joining a synagogue, often for the "sake of the children." One woman who grew up in a strong Workmen's Circle household and whose family never belonged to a synagogue commented that when she and her husband moved from the south side to the more suburban north side, they joined IHC so their children could attend religious school and meet other Jewish children.[13]

In this atmosphere, the suburban synagogue took on a whole new set of functions. It helped to educate Jewish children so that they could explain what Judaism was to their Christian friends. It served to equalize Jew and Christian ("You have a church, we have a synagogue"). Just as the church was the major institution providing religious education, the synagogue school came to dominate the field of Jewish education in the 1950s. By 1959, 82.7 percent of all children attending weekday Jewish schools in the United States were attending congregational schools. By the mid-1960s, more than 90 percent of the Jewish schools in the United States were sponsored and maintained by congregations.[14]

This is not to say that American Jews became religious in the 1950s. Rabbis still complained of poor attendance, although the percentage of Jews who attended services once a month actually increased from 18 percent in 1947 to 31 percent in 1955. (This was still much lower than Catholic and Protestant attendance.) Rather, the synagogue became an educational and social center comparable to a Protestant church. The synagogues erected in the 1950s were synagogue-centers with prominent classroom facilities, auditoriums, libraries, and facilities for preschoolers, teenagers, young married couples, and the elderly.[15]

The first Indianapolis synagogue to initiate a building campaign was IHC. While other congregations had moved north, IHC was still located at 10th and Delaware streets, far from most of its congregants' residences in a changing neighborhood and in a turn-of-the-century building that was woefully inadequate for a membership of over six hundred families. The congregation had been wanting to move for many years. As early as 1925 the congregation had asked the noted architect Albert Kahn to lay out ambitious plans for what was then called an "institutional synagogue." The IHC project had been planned to include a sanctuary-auditorium, religious school building, and indoor and outdoor recreational facilities including tennis courts, a baseball field, and even a miniature golf course. A site had been selected at 40th and North Meridian streets, and a fund-raising campaign was begun. Under the enthusiastic leadership of Albert M. Rosenthal (ca. 1875–1935), $187,000 was easily pledged, but after Rosenthal himself became ill the campaign slowed down. Not long after the stock market crash of 1929, the fund-raising committee realized that they had little possibility of redeeming the pledges. At a formal meeting of the congregation all the pledges were cancelled and the project abandoned.[16]

In February 1945, the IHC membership voted to build a new temple on the north side "as soon as circumstances permit," presumably after the wartime ban on construction was lifted. It was another ten years, however, before the congregation began its building campaign in earnest, during which time the congregation completely outgrew its religious school facilities. As a result both of the postwar increase in synagogue membership and of the "baby boom," religious school enrollment increased by 112 percent from 1949 to 1959 (from 232 to 498).[17]

IHC's new synagogue was built on a twenty-acre site at 65th and North Meridian streets at what was then just north of the Indianapolis city limits. The fund drive for $750,000 for the new synagogue, officially begun in September 1956, was oversubscribed by $101,137 in early November. The new temple was dedicated on May 9, 1958. (The handsome old building at 10th and Delaware streets was sold in November 1957 for $50,000 to The Peoples' Temple, a Christian cult led by Reverend Jim Jones, who later achieved notoriety in the jungles of Guyana. The building was destroyed by fire in April 1975.)[18]

Congregation Beth-El Zedeck, located about two and one-half miles north of IHC at 34th and Ruckle streets, had also outgrown its building, particularly its school facilities, since the group's membership doubled between 1945 and 1958. The congregation bought about fourteen acres of land at Spring Mill Road that had been purchased originally by the Federation for its own building plans. On October 27, 1957, the cornerstone was laid for the $1.25 million building, which was dedicated on August 31, 1958.[19]

Beth-El Zedeck's old building was sold to Central Hebrew Congregation, then located at Central Avenue and 21st Street, which had merged with United Hebrew Congregation of the south side in August 1957. The 325 families of Central Hebrew and the 60 families of United Hebrew combined to make this the largest Orthodox congregation in Indiana. On September 1, 1958, the congregation, renaming itself Congregation B'nai Torah, moved into its new facilities.[20]

Four congregations remained on the south side, although very few of their members still lived there. After years of struggling to collect a *minyan* in order to hold services, on March 26, 1958, Congregation Ezras Achim (the peddlers' *shul*) voted to "dissolve the shule . . . as a place of Worship" and transfer all cash on hand to the Ezras Achim Cemetery Association. Four years later Rabbi Solomon Silberberg of Congregation Sharah Tefilla addressed a special meeting of the Ezras Achim Cemetery Association and pleaded with "the members of Ezras Achim Congregation [to] . . . join in a common cause to save Judaism in Indianapolis, to combine the three South Side Congregations, Sharah Tefilla, Knesses Israel, and Ezras Achim, and to be able to build a new orthodox congregation on the north side in the near future." The proposal was adopted, and on January 19, 1964, ground-breaking ceremonies were held at 5879 Central Avenue, site of the future synagogue of the United Orthodox Hebrew Congregation. The congregation hoped to complete the synagogue in time for the High Holy Days of that year, but the $250,000 quota for the building campaign was not met in time, and the new building did not open until February 1966.[21]

While synagogues dominated the list of new Jewish institutions built in the 1950s, many other Jewish institutions also initiated building campaigns. Between 1948 and 1960, for example, $41.4 million was spent nationally on new Jewish centers. In addition Jewish homes for the aged increased from 63 in 1945 to 74 in 1960, and their bed capacity rose from 6,000 to 12,428. Moreover, the number of children enrolled in Jewish schools (communal, congregational, and day schools) rose from 239,000 in 1948 to 553,600 in 1958. Spending for Jewish schools increased almost ninefold from $6 million in 1944 to over $51 million in 1959.[22]

By 1945 the Jewish institutions of Indianapolis had suffered from neglect for fifteen years. Many were now located in aging, shabby buildings in deteriorating neighborhoods with relatively few Jewish residents. Moreover, the facilities were not considered suitable for the kind of programming that would appeal to the relatively affluent and now almost entirely American-born Jewish community. For example, the Jewish center staff was anxious to organize outdoor recreational programs, but the Kirshbaum Center was located on a busy city street with no open land. Their day-camp program was held at a city park. The center leadership felt that an outdoor pool would attract more members, but there was no land available on which to build one. Under the direction of Sidney Cahn, who became executive director of the Jewish Federation after the resignation of H. Joseph Hyman in 1945, a series of studies and analyses of the community's Jewish institutions were undertaken. Community members who were board members or active in one of the Federation's constituent agencies helped prepare a self-study of that agency and its program with specific recommendations for improvement. This was the first time the Federation had undertaken a serious self-study, and this technique of formal evaluation would be used several times in the future to help chart a new course. Concurrently, staff members of the National Jewish Welfare Board with the help of lay people—the "Citizens' Committee of 100"—prepared a study of the Jewish Community Center Association (JCCA) and its program. In conjunction with this report, demographer Erich Rosenthal conducted the first scientific population study of the Indianapolis Jewish community.[23]

This series of studies from the late-1940s formed the basis for serious discussions about communal needs, priorities, and future planning. Staff from the National Jewish Welfare Board and the Council of Jewish Federations and Welfare Funds had conducted a study of the south side and the Communal Building (including a population survey) in 1943. In 1944 educator Leo L. Honor of Chicago prepared a report on the Jewish Educational Association (JEA). On the basis of the findings of the 1943 Communal Building survey, the program there was discontinued in 1947. At Honor's recommendation the JEA abandoned the Neustadt building on the south side and moved out of Beth-El Zedeck to its own building in 1946.[24]

Although all the Federation's agencies were studied, it was the program of the JCCA that was found to be most inadequate. The Jewish center movement in the mid-1940s was a movement in search of a purpose. The earliest "Jewish centers" had been literary or cultural and social groups which sprang up in a variety of American cities in the 1840s, often calling themselves Young Men's Hebrew Associations. Beginning in the 1880s with the advent of mass migration, these YMHAs and the newly established "Jewish settlements" became essentially social service agencies concerned with the adjustment and Americanization of the Jewish immigrant. The end of mass immigration in the mid-1920s had meant that the Americanization programs were no longer so important. Moreover, the earlier immigrants and their children were now self-confident American Jews who were as knowledgable about American life as their former benefactors. During the years of depression and war the Jewish centers were occupied first in providing services for the unemployed and later for Jewish servicemen. It was only after the war that many leaders in the movement became aware that the center had outlived its earlier purposes and needed to formulate a new set of objectives. In 1945 the National Jewish Welfare Board initiated a study to determine JWB's relations to the communities of the country, its field of responsibility, and the general effectiveness of its program.[25]

While the report of the survey commission made many suggestions, its major recommendation was that the program of the Jewish center should emphasize Jewish content and stress those "spiritual-cultural factors which constitute the Jewish way of life." The report, published in 1948 as The JWB Survey, was a clear victory for the "sectarians" over the "non-sectarians," those lingering remnants of the Jewish settlement movement who had transferred the nonsectarian ideology of the settlement movement into the Jewish settlements. Instead, The JWB Survey paid homage to Mordecai M. Kaplan as the spiritual father of the modern Jewish center movement. In Kaplan's view, the Jewish center should be a bet am (house of the people) or Jewish neighborhood center: "a fellowship in which every man, woman, and child would be a member and every phase of social life, economic, cultural, and religious, would be an object of collective concern." An institution which had once helped Jewish immigrants to become more American would now help American Jews to become more Jewish, as an agency for Jewish survival.[26]

The local study of the Indianapolis program echoed the recommendations of the national study: the Jewish content of all center programs should be increased. The report also stressed the importance of developing programming for young children and teenagers. A Jewish-sponsored and Jewish-oriented nursery school, for example, would "help [Jewish children] develop a sense of security as Americans and Jews and . . . learn to live democratically with other children."* Programming for adolescents would provide opportunities for Jewish teenagers to meet and socialize. However, the report found serious faults with the Kirshbaum Center as a setting for Jewish group work. The study described the building as shabby and dilapidated. The site allowed for no outdoor activities which were felt to be important. In addition, the building was poorly designed and noisy, so that quiet, small-group discussions were difficult. The facilities for programs for teenagers and pre-school and primary school children were considered totally inadequate, since the center could not offer the privacy thought to be necessary for both groups to have effective programs.[27]

When the Kirshbaum Center opened in 1926 it was located in the center of the north side Jewish community. By the late 1940s it was no longer easily accessible to the majority of the Jewish community. The 1948 population study revealed that only 5.2 percent of the Jewish community lived in the Kirshbaum Center area (between 21st Street and Fall Creek). The south side contained only 11.4 percent of the Jewish community; 4.2 percent lived in the lower north side (10th Street to 21st Street, the location of the Indianapolis Hebrew Congregation); 29.1 percent lived in the central north side (Fall Creek to Maple Road); and 36.7 percent lived on the far north side (Maple Road to city limits). The remaining 13.4 percent were scattered in other neighborhoods. Moreover, the far

---

*Not only did the Jewish center subsequently establish a nursery school, but so did the JEA. Several attempts to merge or at least coordinate the two nursery schools have failed. IHC organized their own nursery school in 1957.

north side appeared to be the one area of the city where the Jewish population would continue to increase. Of those families considering moving either out of or within the city in 1948, 239 or 36.6 percent were considering a move to the far north side. With a view to eventually relocating on the far north side, the 1948 study of the JCCA recommended remodeling the Kirshbaum Center and building a small branch on the north side with facilities for outdoor recreational activities and for programs for children and adolescents. John Sohn, the Indianapolis architect whose firm had designed the Kirshbaum building, was hired to draw up plans for a complete renovation of the building. The plan included additional meeting rooms, nursery school rooms, a teen lounge, an improved health club, and an enlarged auditorium. When it was discovered that the addition would cost at least $450,000, the Jewish Welfare Federation decided instead to sell the Kirshbaum Center and build a new facility on the north side. The Kirshbaum Center was put up for sale in 1951. (It was not, however, sold until 1959.) In 1953 the Federation purchased nearly eighteen acres of land near 69th Street and Spring Mill Road for the site of a new Jewish center. Shortly after, the Federation acquired an additional twenty acres of land adjoining the site as a reserve for future communal expansion and on the assumption that some of the city's synagogues might wish to relocate there.[28]

A. M. Strauss, a Fort Wayne architect, was hired to draw up plans for a multipurpose center (estimated cost, $1 million) with extensive athletic facilities, an auditorium, game rooms, meeting rooms, nurseries, and classrooms. A campaign was inaugurated to raise $500,000, with the hope of beginning construction sometime in 1954. However, pledges came in slowly. Finally the Federation board decided to build the outdoor swimming pool in time for the summer season of 1956, hoping that the attractions of the pool would increase donations. Plans for the building were scaled down; the indoor pool, handball courts, health club, and other facilities were eliminated, although they were added later. Then in 1956 the Lilly Endowment and the Indianapolis Foundation announced that they would give $40,000 and $10,000 respectively for the new center, though both foundations had previously refused requests for funds on the grounds that the center would be used only by persons who were able to pay membership fees. In June 1957 the cornerstone of the new building was dedicated, and on February 2, 1958, the new center officially opened to the public.[29]

When the Jewish Welfare Federation purchased its acreage near 69th Street and Spring Mill Road in 1953, board members hoped that both Beth-El Zedeck and IHC might locate on this land and that the proposed Jewish Center could be designed to house the educational and social facilities of both congregations. In fact, the Federation even drew up a rough description of how the three institutions could share buildings. The Jewish Center, IHC, and Beth-El Zedeck would build adjacent buildings of "a single harmonious architectural design. The congregations would construct only houses of worship; . . . in between would be the Jewish Community Center" with facilities for Sunday school classrooms for both congregations which would be used during the week for the JEA's afternoon Hebrew school, as well as additional meeting rooms and auditoriums. Proponents of this joint building plan argued that this would provide the necessary buildings at a lower cost, including lower maintenance costs. As logical as such a plan might appear, the perceived self-interest and strong desire for separate identity of Jewish institutions often creates obstacles to such cooperation. The plan was never adopted. Beth-El Zedeck did purchase about fourteen acres of land from the Federation, but they constructed upon it their own separate and independent facility. IHC refused even to purchase the land and constructed their own building elsewhere.[30]

As we have noted, Jews were moving to suburban neighborhoods where other respectable families attended church on Sunday while their children were in Sunday school; hence, the synagogue Sunday school, modeled on the church Sunday school, came to dominate the field of Jewish education. During this period, many communal Hebrew schools were absorbed by congregational schools. Indianapolis was one of a small number of cities to continue to maintain its communal Jewish school under Federation auspices. The Jewish Educational Association provided instruction in Hebrew language, prayer, the Bible, and Jewish history on weekday afternoons while the three major synagogues—IHC, Beth-El Zedeck, and B'nai Torah—operated Sunday schools emphasizing the teachings and practices of their own particular group—Reform, Conservative, or Orthodox.[31]

That the JEA was able to overcome challenges from the synagogues and maintain its position as the major institution providing
Hebrew instruction in the city is probably due to three factors: the
longevity of the school (it was founded in 1911); the continuing
core of patrons and workers committed to the institution; and the
widely held feeling that one communally supported school was
more efficient financially than several congregational schools. That
is not to say, however, that the JEA was either well supported or
well attended. In 1959 the administration of Beth-El Zedeck, in
arguing for the expansion of the congregational Sunday school to a
weekday afternoon program,* estimated that only 136 out of 340
school-age children at Beth-El Zedeck were attending the JEA.
From 1955 to 1966 only about 55 percent of the boys and about 11
percent of the girls aged nine to thirteen who were attending congregational Sunday schools also attended the JEA. The breakdown
by congregation for boys was as follows: 21.25 percent of those enrolled at IHC, 68.5 percent of B'nai Torah, and 77 percent at Beth-El
Zedeck; for girls, less than 2 percent at IHC, 14.6 percent at Beth-El
Zedeck, and 22.8 percent at B'nai Torah. In absolute numbers,
elementary school enrollment (nine- to thirteen-year-olds) ranged
from a low of 175 in 1955–1956 to a high of 279 in 1962–1963.[32]

These statistics are interesting for a number of reasons. The enrollment figures were abysmally low from any perspective, but
they were particularly poor for girls. While all the synagogue attendance figures were low, the Reform congregation's were by far
the lowest. Even among children attending congregational Sunday
schools, only a minority also attended the JEA's afternoon school.
Indianapolis Jewish parents apparently still clung to the old idea
that a Jewish education was primarily important for boys and not
as significant for girls. Reform Jews appeared to be the least committed to providing a Jewish education for their children. And most
Jewish parents were only giving lip service to the value of Jewish
education. Of those sending their children to Sunday school, only a
minority were willing to make the necessary arrangements to send
them for Hebrew instruction after school as well.

In 1958 the president of the JEA, Bernard Stroyman, asked the
Jewish Welfare Federation to initiate a campaign to raise $150,000

*The proposal was rejected by 64 percent of the membership in February 1960. In
1945 the same proposal had also been defeated.

for a new building for the JEA. The Federation's budget and policy committee suggested instead that the new JEA be built as an addition to the Jewish Center building with a "buffer" between the two institutions. The JEA board, however, did not like the idea. They argued that the noise from center activities would disrupt quiet classroom work. Moreover, school-bound children entering through the Jewish Center-shared space might be enticed into forgoing Hebrew studies for a quick game of basketball. The board feared that the JEA students might also feel envious at seeing their non-attending friends enjoying recreational activities while they had to attend class. While an architect might have designed a building to overcome these obstacles, the really important problems were more difficult to solve. The JEA board wanted its own building to stand as a clear demonstration from the Federation (and the community) that Jewish education was just as important as group work. In the minds of the JEA board members, a JEA building which was a mere addition to the center building—no matter how efficient and cost effective that might be—would stand as a symbol that the JEA (and Jewish education) was less important than the Jewish Center (and recreational activities). That the two organizations might share common goals and values or even cooperate in programming did not occur to the JEA board. From a perspective all too common in Jewish institutional life, Indianapolis Jewish institutions viewed one another as competitors, rather than as partners, and the size and grandeur of their respective buildings stood as symbols of their status and accomplishments. Indianapolis, like all other American Jewish communities, suffered from an "edifice complex." A luxurious new building, rather than the programs that went on inside, demonstrated the success of an organization. The JEA board stood firm on its request for a separate building. Amidst some concern that raising funds for a JEA building campaign might hurt the Federation's campaign and reduce the amount that would be raised for Israel, the Federation board agreed to support the project.[33]

The JEA building, designed by architect Howard Wolner, was completed in September 1960 at a total cost (including building, furnishings, and equipment) of about $195,000. The Inland Container Foundation, because of the "cultural value of the program and building to the general and Jewish community," gave $25,000 toward the building. In 1966 a language laboratory was added to the building with funds raised by the JEA Auxiliary and a grant from the Lilly Endowment. The building also houses the community's Jewish library.[34]

The social and economic changes that had forced a reexamination of the Jewish Center's goals also affected the agency with the longest tradition of service in the community. Since the establishment of the Hebrew Ladies Benevolent Society in 1859, a communal agency in one form or another had given aid and relief to impoverished immigrant families. By 1947, however, Jewish Social Services was dispensing relief to fewer than 10 percent of the families which it assisted. (The name was changed from Jewish Family Service Society in 1946.)[35]

Increasingly, the issues which faced the agency were problems of middle-class families. While members of the middle class certainly have problems, they tend to differ from those of the poor. When getting food on the table was no longer a concern, all sorts of other tensions in families often came to the surface. Moreover, American families in the 1950s were coming to expect happiness as an ideal. When they were not happy, they often turned to a professional for help. In contrast, their parents (who held much lower expectations) may have suffered silently through miserable marriages. When the older generation needed advice on domestic problems, they often turned to a level-headed aunt for help. But with the growing influence and popularization of psychoanalytic and psychological theories, Americans came to distrust the advice of the well-meaning relative and put their faith in "the expert."

Jewish Social Services moved increasingly into the field of counseling (and away from relief) in the 1950s. Since their clients were no longer poor, some agency staff felt that by instituting a sliding fee scale, the agency would remove the stigma that their services were only for the poor and attract more clients. The sliding fee scale was introduced in 1951.[36]

Services provided by Jewish Social Services in the 1950s included child adoption and foster home placement, vocational counseling, refugee resettlement, help for the elderly (including the provision of social services for the Borinstein Home for the Aged), homemaker services (housekeeping for children with ill parents), and family and individual counseling. By 1955 the largest number of cases served were for emotional problems (marital problems, parent-child relationships, adult personality adjustment, and unmarried mothers). The second largest group of problems were those of health and old age, followed by housing, employment, and financial problems, resettlement and aid for refugees, and child care and adoption services. The trend toward a greater proportion of agency time being devoted to psychotherapeutic counseling continued to increase. In 1956, 25.3 percent of the clients came for help with emotional problems. In 1959, 40 percent of the clients fell into that category, while 50 percent were in that group in 1963. The agency's typical client was no longer an impoverished immigrant family in need of money or groceries but a middle-class family with marital or family problems requiring intensive counseling. By 1964 nearly half (42 percent) of the agency's clients came from the middle-class to upper middle-class area of the city north of 56th Street; only 7 percent lived below Washington Street on the south side.[37]

As Jewish Social Services moved farther away from the simpler tasks of dispensing material comfort and into the more complex realm of caring for the psyche, it became more difficult for volunteers to find a place in the organization. Caring for the helpless—the homeless, the poor, the elderly, and young children—had traditionally been women's tasks. As the number of homeless and poor Jews declined, and the tasks of caring for young children and the elderly became professional fields of their own, the role of women in the Jewish communal structure became more and more circumscribed. In the 1930s members of the socially aware National Council of Jewish Women attempted to gain some professional expertise in order to work as volunteers with unemployed Jews and their families. A group of Council members attended lectures on social services at the Indiana University School of Social Work and then volunteered their services to the Jewish Federation. The assignments they were given, however, were not commensurate with their level of preparation, and the women were angry and disappointed. The message seemed to be that female assistance was welcomed as long as it remained in a subordinate role.[38]

The Council women did, however, take a major role in helping refugee families, who began arriving in the late 1930s. The National Council of Jewish Women worked closely with the Indianapolis Committee for Refugees to assist the families in adjusting to their new home. In 1935 the National Council of Jewish Women opened a thrift shop at 2749 Northwestern Avenue. In 1939 they assisted in the opening and management of the Refugees' Handicraft Exchange. After the war the Council's service to the foreign-born committee worked closely with Jewish Social Services to help resettle refugee families in Indianapolis. While Jewish Social Services provided basic help such as monetary relief and aid in finding jobs, housing, and acquiring necessary papers and immigration documents, the Council worked with the immigrants in facilitating the process of adjustment, helping them to understand American life and culture. Council members organized a Home Institute for married refugee women with sessions on child care, budgeting, cooking, and homemaking. They also tutored the newcomers in English and helped them learn American customs. In 1952 the National Council of Jewish Women began a series of informal Sunday afternoon open houses for newcomers at the Kirshbaum Center to help them make new friends as well as learn about the Jewish community's resources. Resettlement work continued throughout the 1950s, but on a greatly reduced basis with an average of only three families a year coming to Indianapolis. Other activities of the Council in the 1950s included the sponsorship of community-wide institutes on human relations, education, youth services, and community service and a Golden Age program at the Borinstein Home, begun in 1950.[39]

Through Hadassah, Indianapolis women raised money for medical and social service projects in Israel. Hadassah sponsored endless rummage sales, donor luncheons, raffles, and bazaars to raise funds for Hadassah projects in Israel. They organized sewing parties to prepare clothing and bandages, and they shipped emergency supplies to Israel. In 1980 the combined membership of the three Hadassah chapters in Indianapolis was over one thousand.[40]

While most women participated in communal life through Hadassah, the National Council of Jewish Women, and other women's organizations, a handful of women also sat on the more powerful boards of the Federation or the JCCA. Only a few women rose to positions of communal prominence before the 1970s. One or two women have been found on the Federation board since its inception, and some have served as officers. However, in the move to democratize the Federation board in 1945 to include representatives of all Jewish organizations in the city, many women's groups, such as B'nai B'rith Women, were excluded because they were considered "auxiliaries." Thus the number of women who would serve on the Federation board was limited even further. One woman—Sarah Goodman—rose to the presidency of the Federation, serving from 1953 to 1954. She was one of only a few women in the country to have served their communities in that position. The exclusion of women from the real positions of power and authority within the Jewish community does appear to be changing, albeit slowly. In the early 1960s, Lee Barnett, who was serving as first vice-president of the JCCA, was told by the board that she should forget about running for the presidency, since there would never be a woman president of the Jewish Center. Nevertheless, Barbara C. Levy was elected to the presidency in 1978.[41]

While internal Jewish affairs were transformed in the postwar period, Jewish relations with the larger community underwent an even more dramatic change. Every poll of gentile attitudes to Jews recorded a massive decline in anti-Jewish feeling beginning in the late 1940s. For example, the number of respondents who held hostile stereotypes of Jews dropped significantly. In 1940, 63 percent of those polled said Jews as a group had "objectionable traits," while only 22 percent said this in 1962. Furthermore, by the 1960s 43 percent in another poll believed that Jews had no distinctive group traits at all.[42]

Hostile attitudes toward Jews had risen sharply during the war years, reflecting the tensions and dislocations of the final years of World War II. There was widespread hostility to minority groups during the period—the "zoot suit" outbreaks against Mexican-Americans in Los Angeles and race riots in Detroit and New York City. Although in the New York riot, blacks attacked the mainly Jewish-owned shops of Harlem, there were no outbreaks of violence against Jews comparable to those against Latinos and blacks. Still, animus against Jews was present. In a series of surveys conducted between 1940 and 1945, 31 to 48 percent of those polled stated that they would have actively supported a hypothetical anti-Semitic campaign or at least sympathized with it, while 30 percent would have opposed it.[43]

In a twenty-year period following the war, the extent of anti-

Jewish prejudice declined dramatically. By the mid-1960s, Theodore Solotaroff and Marshall Sklare could write, "For most Jews today, bigotry and discrimination are felt to exist, if at all, far from their actual lives." Many reasons have been put forth to explain the erosion of anti-Semitism as an "overt phenomenon." The explanations are numerous and complex, and scholars do not agree on their relative importance. They tend, however, to fall into two categories: changes within the Jewish community itself and changes in American society's attitudes toward minority groups. According to historian John Higham, the decline in anti-Semitism is the natural result of the process of cultural assimilation of white minorities in America. As a result of the restriction of immigration in the 1920s and the relatively few refugees admitted to America in the 1930s and 1940s, the American Jewish population became increasingly native-born. Jews adopted American manners and mores, and the Jewish community lost much of its distinctiveness and visibility. This, in turn, resulted in the recession of prejudice and discrimination. Moreover, Jews, along with other Americans, moved out of the dense ethnic urban neighborhoods into the mixed neighborhoods of suburbia. At the same time they moved out of traditionally Jewish occupations into the salaried professions, corporations, and government service; social integration between Jews and non-Jews increased.[44]

Obviously, social, residential, and economic integration, the movement to suburbia and into corporations, could not have occurred if a hostile environment had prevailed. In fact, overt discrimination gradually became "unfashionable" after the war. With strong governmental support, the National Conference of Christians and Jews, the National Association for the Advancement of Colored People, and other human relations organizations helped create a positive environment for the integration of minority groups. The President's Commission on Civil Rights in 1948 detailed a set of legislative measures and other recommendations to give body and substance to the civil rights outlined in the constitution. Indianapolis's public schools were desegregated in 1949. A few years later, the United States Supreme Court began its pathbreaking series of court decisions that eventually extended civil rights to black Americans. At the same time that the federal government was adding its strength to the civil rights movement, the public was receiving a steady diet of public affairs messages on posters, television, and radio, encouraging tolerance and interfaith goodwill. The messages of these appeals may have been somewhat simplistic—"Americans all"; "The family that prays together, stays together"; "Attend the church or synagogue of your choice"—but the subliminal effect may have been to make it no longer respectable to make casual anti-Semitic (or anti-black) remarks.[45]

The term "transtolerance" has been coined to describe the phenomenon by which prejudice has been made disreputable. Some scholars feel that transtolerance masks deeply held anti-Semitic beliefs which are channeled into more socially acceptable forms and code words. For example, a politician can criticize "Eastern effete intellectuals" and mean Jews without having to say so. Others feel that the institutionalization of safeguards to protect minority rights and opportunities is producing a change in behavior and hence in attitudes toward blacks and Jews.[46]

In an atmosphere openly receptive to the extension and protection of minority rights, Jewish defense agencies began to expand the scope of their activities. These agencies had experienced a tremendous expansion of membership and income in the 1930s and 1940s as a result of fear aroused in American Jews by the German Jewish experience and domestic anti-Semitism. The membership of the American Jewish Committee, for example, increased twentyfold in the 1940s. By the 1940s both the Anti-Defamation League (ADL) and the American Jewish Committee (AJC) were attempting to strengthen their Indiana operations. The ADL wanted to set up a statewide office for investigative work. The AJC field representative was quietly visiting Jewish communities in the state, trying to convince influential community leaders that the state office should be a joint ADL-AJC venture. The two organizations finally compromised and together sponsored the establishment of the Indiana Jewish Community Relations Council in 1947 with offices in Indianapolis. The national agencies financed 80 percent of the state agency's annual budget of $18,000, with the balance shared among the participating communities in the state. (Indianapolis's share of the budget was $1,600.) The first executive director of the agency was Louis B. Greenberg. In 1954 the American Jewish Committee and the Anti-Defamation League withdrew their support of the Indiana Jewish Community Relations Council, and the ADL opened its own Indiana office in downtown Indianapolis. The long-range plans of the ADL had always included opening an Indiana office. When the national office finally had the means to do so, they no longer wanted to divert any funds to "the competition." The Indianapolis Jewish Community Relations Council then assumed greater financial responsiblity for the state office. A merger of the two offices was discussed, but did not immediately occur. To reduce administrative costs, however, in 1955 one executive was assigned to run both agencies, which henceforth shared one office.[47]

While the AJC and the ADL were able to cooperate, at least for a few years, in sponsoring the state agency, the two organizations actually differed in their basic philosophy and approach. Popular opinion considered the ADL "militant" and the AJC committed to quiet, behind-the-scenes work. Publicly the two agencies denied that there was any difference between them. However, in private each agency complained of the ineffectiveness of the other's methods. AJC staff members, for example, were deeply critical of the ADL's "bombastic" techniques. In 1939 *Hardware Journal*, published in Indianapolis, carried an article with an anti-Semitic tinge. Isidore Feibleman, president of the Jewish Federation at the time, called on the editor, whom he knew. The editor was regretful and printed a retraction. This was the kind of quiet approach the AJC preferred. According to AJC's Indiana representative, the American Jewish Congress and ADL national offices then wrote the editor "injudicious letters and smeared things," spoiling Feibleman's good work.[48]

In their early years, defense agencies had emphasized the answering of anti-Semitic accusations. Careful lists of anti-Semitic charges were prepared with each claim patiently and rationally refuted. In the late 1930s, for example, the Woburn Press of London published a series of leaflets, "Anti-Semitic Lies Exposed," with titles such as the *White Slave Trade, International Finance,* etc. Eventually, the agencies realized that such publications actually helped to further disseminate anti-Semitic beliefs. Jewish defense agencies gradually abandoned this essentially negative approach, moving to more positive, social action-oriented methods. Even the term to describe these organizations changed from "defense" and "civic protective" to "community relations." As S. Andhil Fineberg has pointed out, "Like the name 'Anti-Defamation League,' 'defense' and 'protective' suggested combatting enemies; 'community relations' implied cultivating friends."[49]

While some leaders in the community relations field continued to support the educational approach, after the war most professional workers were calling for social action—the use of the "weapons available to the citizens of a democracy, the ballot box, legislation, judicial enforcement and precedent, administrative regulation, petition, powers of municipal and state governments, test cases to establish basic principles, and pressure of political parties." The assumption behind this approach was that an open society with equality for all will naturally help to protect Jewish rights. The logical extension of this principle would be that Jewish community relations agencies should fight for the rights of other beleaguered minorities as well. This, in fact, is the position of the "broad constructionists," a term coined by Sidney Z. Vincent, former director of the Jewish Community Federation of Cleveland. Vincent has noted that Jewish organizational life is divided into broad constructionists and narrow constructionists. The broad constructionists argue that "the well-being of society as a whole . . . is a prime determinant of Jewish status, since times of turmoil produce religious hostility, whereas relatively peaceful times diminish the danger." In contrast, the narrow constructionists argue that "the essential and unique responsibility of the Jewish community [is] to be vigorous in specifically Jewish undertakings, where no one else assumes responsibility."[50]

Since the war, Jewish community relations agencies have engaged in both kinds of activities. Increasingly, however, they were concerned with broader social and political goals: the strengthening of democracy and the preservation of constitutional rights. To this end the Jewish community relations agencies in Indianapolis established ties with local organizations working for similar goals, such as the Catholic Interracial Council, the Indiana Civil Liberties Union, the Church Federation, and the American Friends Job Opportunity Programs. In 1956 the Indianapolis Jewish Community Relations Council (JCRC) joined with these organizations and others to found the Indianapolis Human Relations Council with Max Klezmer as its first president. Together these organizations worked for the extension of full civil rights for all minorities. For example, the JCRC, along with many other organizations, petitioned the Indianapolis school board to desegregate the city schools. The JCRC, the Indiana Anti-Defamation League, and other Jewish community relations agencies supported and lobbied for fair employment and fair housing legislation. They sponsored educational programs as well. Institutes on racism, human relations, and fair housing were organized jointly with the Church Federation, the Catholic Interracial Council, and other community relations groups.[51]

The remainder of the items which filled the agendas of the community relations agencies were of more specifically Jewish interest. The repeal of Sunday closing laws, or at least exemption clauses for Jewish shopkeepers, was a national issue in the 1950s. Most local communities had ordinances banning Sunday sales. Community relations agencies argued that this was discriminatory against individuals whose day of rest was not Sunday and lobbied for a law that would permit either a Saturday or Sunday closing. In Indianapolis the agencies also organized compaigns to abolish discriminatory practices of certain social clubs such as the Elks Club and Rotary. Education programs relating to Israel were a major interest. Community members lobbied Indiana's congressmen and senators and organized letter-writing campaigns to urge their support for loans or grants to the young state. Articles appearing in the *Star* or *News* which were unsympathetic to Israel were systematically answered with letters to the editor. The JCRC also organized a speakers bureau to provide speakers on Israel for civic groups and social clubs.[52]

Local incidents were also handled or monitored by the community relations agencies. When a wooden cross was burned on the lawn of the Jewish Center and IHC's building defaced with anti-Semitic symbols and slogans, the agencies made sure the city newspapers did not report the incident (although the two local Jewish newspapers could not be dissuaded). Those concerned felt that both incidents were the work of teenagers and should not be taken seriously. A newspaper report would only cause panic among the Jewish community as well as possibly give encouragement to other groups to try the same thing. In 1950 a group of Jewish businessmen organized a boycott against 7-Up because the local distributor had made some anti-Semitic remarks to a group dining at the Columbia Club. Louis B. Greenberg, the JCRC executive director, tried to stop the boycott because he feared there might be an adverse reaction and reprisals from other 7-Up distributors, salesmen, and drivers hurt by the boycott. The boycott leaders were finally convinced that continuing the boycott was unwise.[53]

One of the prime concerns of Jewish community relations agencies during the 1950s, the question of religion in the public schools, presents a paradox. The separation of church and state is a cornerstone of the American constitutional system. Yet Christians often disagree over the extension of the doctrine to issues like prayer in school, released time for religious instruction, and nativity scenes in school pageants. Some will argue, for example, that a "nondenominational" prayer that offends no one will give an uplifting, moral tone to the school day. As for Christmas trees and pageants, many Christians fail to regard Christmas as a religious holiday, arguing that it is a part of American culture, like Thanksgiving and the Fourth of July. Thus, an issue which should theoretically be of the widest possible concern has come often to be viewed as a "Jewish issue."

It is indicative of the Jewish community's growing self-confidence and assertiveness in the 1950s that the JCRC decided to take on the sensitive and potentially explosive issue of religious practices in the city schools.

In 1959, as a result of growing concern among Jewish parents about the extent of religious observance in the public schools, the Indianapolis JCRC undertook a detailed school-by-school survey of religious practices in the Indianapolis schools. Members of the National Council of Jewish Women interviewed each principal concerning the extent of prayer recitation, released-time practices, and holiday observances in his school. The results of the survey revealed extensive breaches of the separation of church and state doctrine. For example, in most of the schools children recited the Lord's prayer each morning. Large numbers of children participated in released-time programs, leaving school to receive religious instruction at a nearby church. Christmas observances were quite elaborate, and many included Christmas pageants with specifically religious themes. Some teachers also discussed Easter, and some read bible stories in class.[54]

The results of the JCRC survey and the recommendations for

change submitted to the city school superintendent ruffled many feathers. There were many Jews in the community who would have preferred that the JCRC keep a lower profile. Some believed that the JCRC's emphasis on the removal of religion from the public schools "tend to generate . . . anti-Semitism and encourage discrimination." Others were uncomfortable in general with the JCRC's left-of-center politics and were disturbed by their forays into civil rights activism. Still others had broader philosophical disagreements with the JCRC, maintaining that it claimed to speak and act on behalf of all Jews without being a duly representative body and that, through its support of the JCRC, the Federation had departed from its original purposes as a philanthropic agency in order to enter the political arena—and indeed it had.[55]

The JCRC, however, did not alter its policies or programs. With the coming of the sixties and the growing strength of the civil rights movement, the agency moved increasingly into the political arena. It became a conduit for Jewish participation in the two major political movements of the decade—the civil rights and the antiwar movements. With the rise of these two movements the JCRC grew in stature and prominence. In many ways the JCRC and its programs dominated Jewish life in the first half of the sixties. Specifically Jewish matters were temporarily overshadowed by the broader issues of the decade. It was only a matter of time, however, before political events would once again thrust Jewish concerns to the foreground.

❧ VII

The Six-Day War and Beyond

1960 TO THE PRESENT

IN THE TWENTIETH CENTURY wars abroad have dramatically opened and closed new chapters in American Jewish life. The First World War marked the end of the period of mass migration. The Second World War, having destroyed the European center of world Jewry, left American Jewry as the largest, wealthiest, and most dynamic Jewish community in the world. The events of the Arab-Israeli Six-Day War of June 1967 were not as catastrophic for the Jewish people—after all, Israel emerged the victor—but nevertheless marked a turning point in the course of American Jewish history. It is now clear that a new era for American Jewry was forged in the battles for the Golan Heights, the West Bank, and East Jerusalem.

Beginning on May 15, 1967, when Egypt, Syria, Jordan, and Iraq began mobilizing their forces against Israel, until June 10 when the Six-Day War ended, most Americans were caught up in the Middle East crisis. As the pressure of the mobilized Arab forces mounted Israel almost seemed perched on the edge of destruction. In the tension of the crisis many American Jews experienced an emotional awakening to the strength of their bond to the Jewish state. As Lucy Dawidowicz observed, "The conflict aroused in American

218

Jews unpredictably intense feelings regarding Israel, Jewish survival and their own sense of Jewish identity." The citizens of Israel were no longer "they" but "we." In its hour of danger Israel came to stand for many American Jews as the symbolic redemption of the Holocaust. Suddenly 1967 raised the possibility of genocide once again and offered a second chance to do whatever was necessary to ensure Israel's survival. Israel's destruction would have meant that Hitler had triumphed. Some Jewish intellectuals argued that a second defeat in one lifetime would have brought an end to Jewish faith. When a congregant asked Rabbi Irving Greenberg of Riverdale, New York, "What shall we do if Israel fights and we lose?" Greenberg replied, "You will find a sign outside our synagogue that we are closed." But Israel achieved a lightening quick victory, and the tension and gloom that had previously hovered over American Jewry were replaced by outpourings of joy and pride. With the reunification of the city of Jerusalem and the recapture of the Western Wall, it was as if the heart of the Jewish people had been returned to them.[1]

In describing this response, Rabbi Arthur Hertzberg wrote, "The immediate reaction of American Jewry to the crisis was far more intense and widespread than anyone could have foreseen. Many Jews would never have believed that the grave danger to Israel would dominate their thoughts and emotions to the exclusion of all else." American students by the thousands volunteered for service in Israel. Over the course of the summer of 1967 alone, 7,500 college and high school students went to Israel to work in programs such as the Sherut La'Am volunteer program. Thousands more have gone to Israel since then. The great bulk of American Jews, of course, neither left America to volunteer their services to the state nor decided to make *aliyah* (settle permanently in Israel), although some 2,700 American Jews did so in the ensuing three years. In the days and weeks following the war most American Jews provided help to Israel in the way they were accustomed to doing—by giving and raising enormous sums of money.[2]

Professional fund raisers, who over the years had developed a grab bag of techniques to make reluctant givers donate more than they had initially intended, were overwhelmed by the unsolicited gifts of money that came pouring into United Jewish Appeal (UJA) and federation offices. Large numbers of people personally brought their contributions to the campaign office, as if this physical act would involve them more intimately in the crisis. American contributions to Israel quadrupled between 1966 and 1967, from $64 million to $242 million. Rallies, marches, and prayer meetings followed by fund raising were held everywhere. In Indianapolis a fund-raising meeting was hastily scheduled within a few days after the war's end. Although there had been little advance publicity, some nine hundred people attended, all eager to give money for Israel even though the regular campaign drive had just concluded. Frank Newman, Jewish Welfare Federation (JWF) executive director at the time, described the excited, emotional atmosphere of the meeting:

> We had planned to have ushers with tape-recorders go down the aisles and record the pledges on tape. However, in the excitement of the hour, members of the audience kept running up to the podium, making a brief testimonial into the microphone and throwing money at us. We had to abandon our plan of tape-recording the pledges, and when it was all over we had an awful time trying to match people with gifts.

When the money was finally all counted the Federation had topped the one million dollar mark for the second time in its history, and it had more than doubled the amount raised the previous year. (The first time the Federation raised over one million dollars was in 1948.)[3]

Israel's victory brought Diaspora Jewry pride and a sense of deliverance and release from tension. Many Jews enjoyed the new image of the Jew which emerged from the war, no longer the victim but the victor. More significant, however, were the substantial changes in the outlook and perspective of American Jewry which began to crystallize shortly after the war.

Nathan Glazer has pointed to three factors which he feels account for the tremendous impact the Six-Day War had on the American Jewish community in contrast to the Arab-Jewish War of 1956, which had almost no impact at all: the growing emotional response among American Jews to the Holocaust; the response of black and white radical groups in the United States to the position of Israel; and the role of Russia, home of the second largest Jewish community in the world and chief big-power enemy of Israel. Each of these emphasized the aloneness and distinctiveness of Jews.

Each seemed to justify to Jews the right to see themselves as specially threatened and specially worthy of survival.[4]

Long-suppressed guilt that American Jews felt as survivors who had stood helplessly by while millions were slaughtered by the Nazis began to emerge in the early 1960s. The trial of Adolf Eichmann in Israel in 1961 helped to push these feelings to the surface. The trial raised questions of morality and politics, obedience to unjust laws, the cooperation of Jewish leadership with the Germans, and the alleged passivity of Jewish victims. Hannah Arendt's 1963 book on the trial, *Eichmann in Jerusalem*, probed these issues even more painfully. With the Jewish people now facing annihilation once again, many American Jews experienced a reliving of the Holocaust. Once again they were being put to the test, but this time there would be no passivity. Publicly and vocally American Jews demonstrated their solidarity with Israel and the unity of the Jewish people.[5]

The events of the Six-Day War, triggering as they did memories of the Holocaust, tended to emphasize the uniqueness and solidarity of the Jewish people. Developments in the civil rights movement and left-wing politics, which had occurred even before 1967, only added to this sense of Jewish isolation. The hostile reaction of many black groups and radical political groups to the Israeli victory caused a final severing of many old political alliances. Jewish groups and Jews had been heavily involved in the civil rights movement. In the 1950s many Jewish groups devoted time and money to projects designed to help impoverished blacks. One of the organizations of this period, the American Jewish Society for Service, took Jewish students into city slums not only to provide help to urban slum dwellers, but also to allow the students to investigate the effects of poverty first-hand. The society, which was founded by a group of Reform rabbis, organized summer work camps for Jewish college students modeled after the work camps of the American Friends Service Committee. The society's first summer work camp was in Indianapolis where the students spent the summer working with a black self-help housing project, Flanner House Homes, building homes for black families in the Indianapolis slums. The work camp's contacts with the Indianapolis Jewish community were minimal. The campers attended services weekly, swam at the Kirshbaum Center, and invited various Jews to attend their discussion sessions, but they were much more interested in involving themselves in the black community.[6]

For the first half of the 1960s, Jews remained deeply involved in the civil rights movement. In the summer of 1964, for example, hundreds of white students, many of them Jewish, worked in Mississippi and other southern states, advancing the cause of civil rights. Relations between blacks and whites in the movement began to deteriorate, however, as more militant blacks took over the control of the movement and began to emphasize black solidarity. In 1965 the cry of "black power" was heard, symbolizing the growing militancy of the movement. Militant blacks began removing whites from their organizations and making exclusivist and separatist demands for separate university housing, all-black classes, etc. Some vicious, verbal condemnations of all whites deeply wounded many former white allies. Moreover, some Jewish shopkeepers were badly hurt by the summer riots which began in 1964 and continued through 1968. This strained Jewish sympathies for the black struggle even further while it raised concern for the small Jewish shopkeepers hurt by the riots.[7]

As the nonviolent civil rights movement was rapidly overshadowed by the militant black power movement, white radicals formed parallel political movements. Fueled by the growing anti-war movement, Students for a Democratic Society began gaining prominence. Jewish students, who were heavily represented in SDS and similar organizations, seemed hardly aware of their Jewishness. In 1967, however, many experienced a dramatic awakening of their Jewish identity. That the great powers once again stood silent while Arab spokesmen promised Jewish genocide was bad enough, but even their own allies, black militants and New Leftists, turned on Israel. Some black leaders began to call the Arabs their blood brothers and Israel an outpost of western imperialism. The New Left, combining domestic anti-Semitism with an attack on Zionism, denounced Israel, equating the Zionist "oppressors" of the Palestinian Arabs with American Jews "comfortably ensconced in bourgeois America . . . oppressing and exploiting the black masses." The final rupture in the movement came at the National Conference of New Politics held early in September 1967. A "Black Caucus" which had been granted 50 percent of the conference votes insisted on a resolution condemning the "imperialistic Zionistic war." Efforts to soften the resolution by recognizing Israel's right to survival failed. This was the breaking point for many Jewish leftists who walked out, severing their connections with the New Left.[8]

Further reinforcing the Jewish community's feelings of isolation was the reaction of the Christian community to Israel's victory. Most official church bodies initially remained silent or issued ambivalent statements. Long established missions and schools in the Middle East made Protestant missionaries sympathetic to the Arab cause. Many church groups took up the cause of the Palestinian refugees. Meeting after the war, the influential National Council of Churches issued a resolution criticizing Israel's "territorial expansion by armed force" and suggesting that Jerusalem be made into an international city. Many Jewish leaders were bitterly disappointed by the Christian world's seeming lack of understanding of the importance of Israel and the centrality of Jerusalem to the Jewish people. Years of interfaith dialogue had given Jews the impression that Christians had become more sensitive to the Jewish position.[9]

Gradually American Jews abandoned the social action programs of the 1950s and 1960s and began to pay increasing attention to specifically Jewish problems: in Bernard Martin's words, "the maintenance and enhancement of a sense of Jewish identity, the strengthening of Jewish education, the promotion of the security and interests of Israel, the alleviation of the situation of the Jews of the Soviet Union, and other related issues." In a broad sense the Jewish community had moved from universalism to particularism.[10]

It was not only attack from without that challenged Jewish survival and heightened concern for the preservation of Jewish identity. Two major threats to Jewish existence were growing in strength before the sealing of the Straits of Tiran: an extremely low birthrate and a rising incidence of intermarriage. Since the end of the period of mass immigration, average Jewish family size had been decreasing as Jewish economic and social status had risen. This trend was accelerated in the 1960s and 1970s by the tendency of Jews to delay marriage and postpone childbearing and by the increasing number of Jewish women entering the professions. By 1978 Jews had the lowest birthrate of any ethnic group in the United States.[11]

While the Jewish population was shrinking because of the low birthrate, rising intermarriage further challenged Jewish survival. Widespread intermarriage between Jews and non-Jews is certainly the ultimate test of Jewish acceptance and acculturation, yet a high proportion of intermarriages within a Jewish community creates the fear that Jewish life will be diluted to the point that it barely exists. Two studies of intermarriage in Indiana in 1967 revealed very high intermarriage rates for Jews. Erich Rosenthal studied all marriages in Indiana involving at least one Jewish partner for the years 1960 to 1963. He found a rate of intermarriage for Marion County (i.e., Indianapolis) of 34.5 percent. The rate for the rest of the state, where there is a much lower proportion of Jews (excluding the counties surrounding Chicago and Lake Michigan), was 63.5 percent.[12]

Even before the June war Jewish leaders in Indianapolis were expressing concern over the need to strengthen Jewish identity and commitment. In 1965, in an attempt to redefine its educational goals, the Jewish Educational Association (JEA) commissioned Samuel Grand, a well-known Jewish educator, to study the JEA and recommend improvements. This was followed, a year later, by a JEA self-study. The 1966 study concluded that "to terminate Jewish education at Bar Mitzvah time" was "to freeze . . . Jewish awareness at an immature period." The study recommended the institution of a summer school, the strengthening of the high school program, and the possible establishment of a communal day school. Philip Pecar, who served as Federation president from 1978 to 1981, attended the General Assembly of the Council of Jewish Federations and Welfare Funds as the first winner of the L. L. Goodman Young Leadership Award in 1966. Pecar reported to the board of directors that there was a "budding awareness that communities were failing to provide facilities for creating a commitment to identify with things Jewish, for perpetuating Jewish culture through education. Only Federation," commented Pecar, "which cuts across all denominational lines, could exercise the degree of planning and coordination needed to round Jewish education into the deeper program needed."[13]

Other groups in America, particularly Roman Catholics, had organized their own systems of schools to intensify the commitment and religious education of their children. Except for the ultra-religious, however, most American Jews shied away from the idea of separate Jewish schools. American Jews embraced the free public school system, eagerly applying themselves to economic advancement through education. Jewish education, which, after all, would not help one's child get into a good university or professional school, was relegated to Sunday morning and perhaps one or two afternoons after school. There it had to compete for attention with after-school sports, clubs, and music lessons. Even most Jewish educators admitted that Jewish education in America was a rather poor affair. But the proportion of parents who were genuinely concerned about their children's Jewish education was small. Following the Second World War, however, enrollment in Jewish day schools began to grow. The great majority of the students still came from Orthodox homes, but they were no longer just from the most religious families. In the early 1950s the Conservative movement established its first day schools, known as the Solomon Schechter schools. (The first Reform-sponsored schools opened in the 1970s.) Increasingly, the parents who sent their children to day schools were not "religious fanatics" but committed Jews who were disturbed by the low level of knowledge of Judaism demonstrated by graduates of afternoon and Sunday schools. The day school, combining a half-day of Jewish and Hebrew education with a half-day of conventional school studies, aimed to provide both a good Jewish and a good secular education.[14]

Social factors also led increasing numbers of parents to choose a Jewish day school for their children. Jewish survival had been challenged by the Holocaust and then the Six-Day War, as well as by the more benign forces of low fertility and high intermarriage. Many parents hoped that by educating their children in a Jewish school their children would develop a strong Jewish identity as well as make lasting Jewish friends. Ultimately, many hoped the day school experience would convince their children of the importance of choosing Jewish marriage mates and maintaining a Jewish home. Other, more negative factors also increased Jewish day school enrollment. By the 1970s the drug culture spawned by the "hippies" of the late 1960s had entered the public schools. In many schools drugs were readily available and widely used. In addition, some Jews, like other white parents, took their children out of public schools to avoid the busing of school children—designed to achieve racial integration—which began in the 1970s. In choosing a private school for their children, some parents chose a Jewish school, even though their own involvement in Jewish life may have been slight. While the first Jewish day schools were in New York City and other large Jewish communities, by the early 1970s nearly every Jewish community of any size had at least one Jewish day school. The number of day schools in North America increased from 33 in 1940 to 437 in 1972. By 1978 21 percent of all children who attended any kind of Jewish school were enrolled in a day school. (In 1958 the figure was 8 percent.)[15]

Indianapolis was one of the last American Jewish communities to establish a day school because, for the most part, those in positions of communal leadership were strongly opposed to the idea. The JEA *Self-Study* of 1966 had proposed the establishment of a day school. As a consequence the JEA board prepared another study to determine how many children might attend such a school. The JEA board itself was divided on the issue but nevertheless presented the proposal to the Federation leadership, who unhesitatingly opposed the idea both on practical and ideological grounds. The Federation leaders were individuals from Reform or Liberal-Conservative backgrounds, perhaps the children of immigrants, most of whom had only a modest Jewish education themselves. To them the day school was "parochial"; it smacked of the ghetto and the world they or their parents had abandoned. To them America was the golden land of opportunity and the public school the road to success. They could not understand how Jewish parents could abandon the free public school system. Some could not even understand how parents could place such a high value on Jewish education, seemingly placing it above secular education in importance. To many Federation board members the idea of a Jewish day school was extremely distasteful. How could Jews give up the privilege of attending public schools like all other Americans and instead willingly segregate themselves in their own schools? Although many board members reacted to the issue emotionally, the major reasons they gave for rejecting the proposal were that there would not be enough students for the school and that it would be too great a financial burden from which only a minority within the community would benefit.[16]

At this point the ranks of the proponents of the day school were strengthened by the arrival of Congregation B'nai Torah's new rabbi, twenty-six-year-old Ronald Gray. Gray was shocked at the poor Jewish and Hebrew knowledge of his Orthodox congregants' children and he joined the group campaigning for the day school. Gray was also motivated by the desire to provide his own children with a day school education. Spurned by both the JEA board and the Federation, the day school group decided to proceed on their own. In September 1971 the Hebrew Academy of Indianapolis opened. Twenty-two children were enrolled in four grades, kindergarten through third. The school was housed at B'nai Torah for its first five and one-half years, and in March 1977 moved to its own building at 6602 Hoover Road. The school was also the beneficiary of an $80,000 grant from the Lilly Endowment in 1972. The school, which offers a dual program of Jewish and secular studies for preschool through seventh grade, enrolled 186 students in 1981. An additional ten students attended the Midrasha, an after-school Hebrew and Judaica program for junior high and high school students. Although traditional in outlook the school is "modern" Orthodox and thus could appeal to some non-Orthodox families. From the beginning it did attract children from a variety of backgrounds: Reform, Conservative, and Orthodox, in addition to children from families with no synagogue affiliation. Many of the non-Orthodox families liked the fact that their children could learn about traditional observances. Others may have chosen the school because of concern over the declining quality of public school education and busing; still others may have liked the idea of their children learning in a Jewish setting with Jewish classmates.[17]

The creation of the Hebrew Academy was significant in that it was the first major Jewish institution (apart from synagogues) to be established outside the bounds of the Federation and without its help. For the most part the Hebrew Academy's supporters were not active in Federation affairs. Many of them were Orthodox and members of B'nai Torah, while Federation affairs were led primarily by members of IHC and Congregation Beth-El Zedeck. Many of them were relative newcomers to Indianapolis. Some of the Academy's largest contributors were survivors of the Holocaust who had settled in Indianapolis and had become quite wealthy, such as the brothers Mark and Hart Hasten. However, while many of its strongest supporters are Orthodox, it has not come to be seen as solely an Orthodox institution. The rabbis of both the Conservative and Reform congregations currently send their children to the school, and the wife of the senior Reform rabbi is on the Academy faculty.

Although the Hebrew Academy has attracted children from a variety of backgrounds and has the support of all the city's rabbis, it has not been a community unifier. Rather, it has split the community into two camps—those who are for the Hebrew Academy and those who are against it. In 1983 the Bureau of Jewish Education requested permission from the Jewish Welfare Federation to operate their own day school. In order to determine whether Indianapolis could support a second day school, decide whether the Hebrew Academy should receive a regular allocation, as well as review the question of Federation involvement in day school education in general, the Federation formed a Day School Committee, chaired by Philip Pecar, in the summer of 1983. The original issue, which was whether the Hebrew Academy should receive a regular Federation allocation (it currently receives $12,500 from the Federation for scholarships), has become an emotional one, confused by personalities, personal attitudes toward Jewishness and Jewish identity, and differing opinions on the appropriate balance one should strike between being Jewish and being American. The Hebrew Academy opponents view the Hebrew Academy supporters as "too Jewish" and sectarian, while the Hebrew Academy proponents call their critics "assimilationists." In part, the split is a generational one. The Federation leaders, those Reform and Conservative Jews who came to maturity in the 1920s, 1930s, or 1940s and have memories of the Klan, university quota systems, and other discriminatory acts against Jews are generally opposed to the segregation of Jewish children into a day school. In contrast, those young adults who grew up in the late 1940s, 1950s, or 1960s, have enjoyed the benefits of an open society, and have no memories or fears of anti-Jewish discrimination are generally receptive to the day school idea. Influenced as well by the national movement toward positive reinforcement of ethnicity which began in the late 1960s, these Jewish parents find that attendance at a Jewish day school does not conflict with their concept of being a good American. While the Federation leadership is generally "anti-day school," many of the younger Federation and agency executives currently send their children to the Hebrew Academy. An institution like the Hebrew

Academy demonstrates the extent to which Jewishness has come to assume a more central position in the lives of a younger generation of American Jews. In this way it symbolizes the changes that have affected all branches of Judaism since 1967.

The establishment of the Hebrew Academy is significant for another reason as well. Jewish communal priorities have always tended to rest with the needy—the poor, the sick, the aged, and the helpless; yet the Hebrew Academy was created to help ordinary Jews provide a stronger Jewish education for their children. In contrast, Hooverwood, which was established at about the same time, reflects the Jewish community's long-standing commitment to provide for the needs of its elderly. Since 1920 when the South Side Hebrew Ladies Charity Organization began to care for elderly boarders, the Jewish community had supported a home for the elderly. In 1938 the home for the elderly moved to the old Borinstein family home at 3516 North Central Avenue. The facilities, however, were never adequate. In 1945 Sidney Cahn, the newly appointed executive director of the Jewish Federation, characterized the Borinstein Home as "one of the community's most neglected services and . . . probably one of the most backward Jewish institutions in America." Although within the next few years the situation improved, the Borinstein Home, even with an addition, was never able to provide an adequate physical setting for the elderly. The construction was not fireproof; there were open stairways and too many stairs; corridors and doorways were too narrow for wheelchairs; and bathroom facilities, dining space, and parking were inadequate. The building's problems appeared even more serious when the institution gradually changed from a home for the well but poor elderly to an institution for the chronically ill.[18]

As the life expectancy of Americans and the number of elderly persons in the population grew, the demand for nursing home beds became increasingly acute. Moreover, the aging of the American Jewish population has been even more dramatic than the trend in the general population. While the American elderly population has more than doubled in the last thirty years, in the Jewish population, because of the low Jewish birthrate, the proportion over sixty-five is even greater than within the general population. In 1976, 12.4 percent of the American Jewish population was over sixty-five. A survey conducted in 1978 by the JWF Committee on

Aging identified 1,650 individuals age sixty and over—15 percent of the Jewish population of Indianapolis. By contrast, the 1970 federal census found that 10.7 percent of the Indianapolis metropolitan area population was sixty-two and over. Medical advances that prolonged the lives of individuals suffering from chronic illnesses created a further demand for nursing home beds. In 1952 with the help of the United Fund, the Borinstein Home added an eight-bed infirmary as well as nine new bedrooms. The new facilities, however, soon became as overcrowded as the old. In 1956 an anonymous donor purchased the Binford house located next door to the Borinstein Home. This building was remodeled and attached to the Borinstein Home, bringing the Home's capacity up to forty-two beds. Further pressure for beds came from the expansion of the service area to include the entire state of Indiana. By the mid-1960s the waiting list for applicants ranged between ten and fifteen at all times.[19]

By 1964 the Federation had decided to build a new home for the elderly. Much of the new institution's design would be based on the results of a questionnaire distributed to all those who attended the JWF annual meeting in July 1964. The nonsectarian home was to have a kosher kitchen and 155 beds. Designed by the architectural firm of C. Wilbur Foster and Associates of Indianapolis, the structure has two floors—the upper floor being for those who are very senile and those with very limited physical capabilities. The 8,000-square-foot facility is located on seven acres of wooded land just north of the Bureau of Jewish Education (formerly the Jewish Educational Association) and was originally to be named Shalom Woods. However, some JWF board members registered disapproval of the association of the word *Shalom* with a home for the aged, commenting that it might as well be called "Goodbye Woods." (This was a tacit acknowledgement that homes for the aged had become places to die.) The name was changed to the more tactful Hooverwood. The $2.4 million home was financed by a $786,000 Hill-Burton grant (federal hospital funds which required that the institution be nonsectarian), $60,000 from the Lilly Endowment, a grant from the Indianapolis Foundation, $100,000 from the sale of the Borinstein Home to the Tabernacle Presbyterian Church, and from private contributions. Hooverwood was formally dedicated on March 22, 1970, and in a little over a year the home had 136 residents. It is now considered one of the finest nursing homes in the city and state.[20]

A variety of social services for the well elderly had developed over the years. One of the oldest of these was the Golden Age Club, organized by the National Council of Jewish Women in 1950. Because of the concern that many elderly persons did not eat nutritious meals the Jewish Center applied for Title VII federal funds to provide a kosher hot lunch twice a week. The lunch was followed by an afternoon of card playing at the Jewish Center. For those who needed help or companionship during the day, Hooverwood organized a day care program. IHC sponsored New Horizons, a monthly program of lunch and entertainment. The education subcommittee of the JWF committee on aged care presented educational programs for the elderly and their children.[21]

When the plans for Hooverwood were being drawn up the consensus was that the needs of the sick aged should take precedence. However, there were many who thought the Jewish community should also construct apartments for the well aged. In 1965 the long-range planning committee of IHC had recommended that the synagogue build a facility for the well aged, but the idea was dropped. Once Hooverwood was established and filled, however, it became apparent that it was not for everyone. Initially the population at Hooverwood was a balance of well and sick aged, but over time the balance shifted very heavily to the sick aged. (By 1980 only five residents could be characterized as well.) As the Hooverwood population became almost entirely sick aged, greater awareness developed of the need for housing for the well aged. The 1978 Jewish Older Adult Oral Survey showed a fairly large interest in community-sponsored well aged housing. (47.3 percent expressed an interest in moving to well aged housing—25 percent at the present time, and 19.7 percent at a future time.) After many years of discussion and a few false starts, the groundbreaking for the Park Regency Apartments at 8851 Colby Road took place in October 1980.[22]

The 111-unit facility was completely funded by a grant from the Department of Housing and Urban Development, which provides federal funds for subsidized housing for the elderly. To receive funds for such a project, only 10 percent of the tenants may be over a certain income level, and they must be at least sixty-two years of age. Like Hooverwood the facility is nonsectarian, although in both the home and the apartment complex the majority of the residents are Jewish. The unit was completed in the spring of 1981. At the same time the JWF Housing Corporation, formed to supervise Park Regency, became the newest constituent agency of the Federation.[23]

The Jewish Federation had been organized "to establish and provide an efficient and practical mode of collecting voluntary contributions," but the Federation's founders would certainly have been awed by the extensive commitments of the JWF by the 1950s. In the postwar period, the Federation and its constituent agencies greatly expanded their services. But while the community was receptive to the expansion they were not always as willing to donate the funds to support these services. From a peak in 1948, the year of Israel's independence when $1,004,600 was collected, the campaign fell to a low of $357,570 in 1954. This decline may have been partly due to the fact that the city's two largest congregations, IHC and Beth-El Zedeck, were then raising funds for new buildings. But, whatever the cause, in the face of the poor results every local agency budget had to be reduced and many national agencies threatened to withdraw from the Federation and conduct their own local campaigns. The funds raised by the campaign increased slowly after that, but the results were very uneven, with wide swings from one year to the next. For example, from 1955 to 1957, when the combined total of funds raised by local federations increased by 33 percent, the amount raised in Indianapolis jumped by 48.5 percent. When the national total dropped by 10 percent from 1957 to 1958, the amount raised in Indianapolis declined by 31 percent.[24]

Oscar (Art) Mintzer,* who served as JWF executive director from 1953 to 1959, attributed the wide swings in campaign results to the fact that an unusually small percentage of contributors accounted for a large proportion of the funds. According to Mintzer, two-thirds of the funds raised came from 3 percent of the givers. Mintzer felt that this pattern left the community dependent on a

---

*He replaced Sidney Cahn, who resigned to go into business in Lafayette, Indiana. Mintzer had previously served as federation executive in Peoria, Illinois, and Waterbury, Connecticut. Mintzer left to become the executive of the Jewish Welfare Federation of Alameda and Contra Costa Counties in California.

handful of people who, if displeased, could withhold their gifts and seriously damage the campaign. There were reports of instances of large donors either withholding their gifts or sending them directly to UJA because of their dissatisfaction with the local allocation of funds. However, this structural pattern was fairly typical of most communities in the mid-1950s and still remains so. Jewish fund raising is aimed primarily at the large donor, and campaigns are structured around that fact. In 1958 Henry L. Zucker, executive director of the Jewish Community Federation of Cleveland, noted that "The strategy of a welfare fund campaign must take into account the fact that a relatively small number of gifts produces the bulk of the money. Two thirds of the money is contributed by three percent of the givers. . . ." Mintzer presented various proposals that he felt would improve the campaign, but no real change occurred.[25]

Frank Newman, who replaced Mintzer as the Federation executive late in 1959, came to Indianapolis from Newark, New Jersey, where he had been affiliated with the Jewish Community Council of Essex County. A native of Chicago, Newman had previously held positions with the Jewish Community Center in Yonkers, New York, with federations in St. Louis and Gary, Indiana (where he was the first federation executive), and as a field representative for the Council of Jewish Federations and Welfare Funds.[26]

Newman focused his attention on improving and professionalizing the Federation's annual fund-raising drive. He brought in a group of professionals from radio, television, and advertising (including radio announcer Sid Collins, "the Voice of the Indy 500") to analyze the weaknesses of the campaign and work with the campaign leadership to implement changes. The business and professional divisions, long the basis for the campaign's structure, were eliminated. Instead, the campaign was restructured into categories of giving. In 1964 the categories were "copper" (under $10), "bronze" ($10–$24), "silver" ($25–$49), "gold" ($50–$99), "platinum" ($100–$299), "diamond" ($300–$499), and special gifts ($500 and over). Competition among the division teams was encouraged to stimulate workers. That same year the Indianapolis Jewish Welfare Foundation was established to receive monies from grants, wills, and bequests and to provide a permanent endowment fund for the Federation. All kinds of promotional techniques were tried, including door-to-door solicitation on one Sunday a year. One year each donor was given a yardstick with the slogan, "We Measured Up. We Gave to our Jewish Welfare Federation." When the returns from the door-to-door canvass diminished it was dropped and a one-day telethon, now called "Super Sunday," was substituted.[27]

A yearbook, *The Roll of Honor,* was published beginning in 1962, listing all contributors, and a campaign newsletter, *JWF Report,* was introduced. This became a year-round publication in 1972. *The Roll of Honor,* whose aim was to encourage a "higher level of giving," was not a particularly popular publication. It was discontinued in 1965. Slowly the campaign results began to climb. By 1966 the campaign was back up to $524,424. The 1967 campaign had raised $531,000, only a modest increase over the previous year, when the Six-Day War erupted. In the supplementary campaign conducted following the Israeli victory an additional $535,712 was raised, all of which went to the Israel Emergency Fund.* Whether the various promotional techniques actually had a significant effect on donors is a moot point. It was finally the threat to Israel and the fear of another genocide that truly raised the level of donations.[28]

The campaign declined by 8.9 percent the following year, but it has never fallen to anywhere near the pre-1967 figure. The next big jump—from $1,606,993 to $2,684,077 (a 67 percent increase)—was registered in 1974, the first campaign conducted after the Yom Kippur War in 1973. Campaign figures remained high, partly fueled by high inflation and partly by the continuing Arab threat to Israel. The campaign passed the $3 million mark in 1980.

As long as Israel appears threatened the funds raised annually by local communities will probably remain high. People give to federation campaigns for a variety of reasons. For some it represents their only contact with organized Jewish life. For others the size of their gift provides them with a certain status in the Jewish community. (All Federation officers are expected to give "generously" to the campaign.) For many the memory of the Holocaust

---

*As in many cities, since the mid-1950s almost every Indianapolis campaign has had two lines on its pledge card, one for the regular campaign and one for a special fund which goes entirely to UJA. However, in order not to hurt the regular campaign, the JWF would not accept a pledge to the special fund unless the donor had pledged at least as much to the regular campaign as the year before. This special fund is now called the Israel Emergency Fund.

and the fragility of Israel's existence spurs them to give partly as a way of expressing their solidarity with the Jewish people. S. P. Goldberg, a Jewish communal researcher, has pointed out that Jewish giving rises as Jewish *tzooris* (problems) increase. If Israel ever signs a peace treaty with the Arab nations Jewish fund raising will almost certainly decline.[29]

Newman not only wanted to professionalize the Federation's annual fund-raising drive, but he also wanted the Federation to regain its position of dominance within the community. He felt that the Federation had become weak. It had lost control of its constituent agencies, some of which were almost hostile to the Federation. Agency directors resented the JWF executive director's attempts to supervise them. Some agency heads believed that Mintzer had wanted to restructure the Federation to reduce the agencies' autonomy by returning them to the status of committees and taking over many of their functions. When the JWF formulated a policy statement on its own budgetary practice, specifying the Federation's role in supervising agency finances and reviewing their budgets, the Jewish Center retaliated with an alternative statement. Entitled "Federation-Agency Relationship," it emphasized the mutual cooperation of Federation and agency:

> [The] Federation reaffirms its beliefs in a non-functional Federation with agency boards having full responsibility and authority for the operation of the agencies and the Federation board having responsibility for fundraising, allocation of funds after review of agency budgets, and coordination of constituent activities.[30]

This atmosphere of hostility and suspicion created difficulties for the Federation. From the mid-1940s through the mid-1960s the turnover of agency executives was high. Undoubtedly the fluctuation in operating funds from one year to the next contributed to this, but a weak central structure and the lack of communication and cooperation between agencies were factors as well. Shortly after he came to Indianapolis Newman organized "Rabbis and Pros," regular meetings of all the community's rabbis and agency professionals to discuss issues of mutual concern. "Federation Sabbath," which began in 1969, was another means of emphasizing the Federation's potential role as a community unifier. Once a year the Federation began to sponsor a communal Friday night worship

service at one of the three major congregations on a rotating basis
with a sermon by a prominent national Jewish figure. No other
synagogues hold services that night. Increasingly the Federation
also began to perform a more central role in administration. In
1969 the Federation computerized all of its records. It then took
over the responsibility for all agency payrolls, printing, and other
services. Centralized purchasing of supplies is also being con-
templated. Over the years the community has become less
polarized, and antagonism between agencies and between the
agencies and the Federation has been reduced. The Jewish Center
board, which had developed a somewhat hostile attitude to the
Federation, eventually became a major source of new Federation
leadership. Two former presidents of the JCCA, Martin L. Larner
(1904–1978) and Irwin Katz, served as JWF presidents in 1970–
1972 and 1972–1975 respectively.[31]

Indianapolis Jewry today is a more unified and uniform community than it has been since the original German Jewish settlement of the mid-nineteenth century. The lines that divided
groups—German versus eastern European, native versus immigrant, south side versus north side, peddler versus department store
magnate—have blurred almost to the point of disappearing, as have
the antagonistic positions of Zionist/anti-Zionist, atheist/Or-
thodox, etc. This has resulted in less conflict in communal affairs.
Except for a small number of refugees who came after the Second
World War (whose children were born in this country) and an even
smaller number of recent Soviet immigrants, the community is
almost entirely second- and third-generation American. In a 1978
survey of Indianapolis Jews, 85.9 percent of the respondents described themselves as American born. College attendance, once the
privilege of a wealthy few, is now expected for all Jewish sons and
daughters. In 1948 only 15.6 percent of Indianapolis Jews between
the ages of 20 and 49 had completed college (19.2 percent of the
men, 11.8 percent of the women). For those fifty and older the
figures were 7.6 percent of men, 2.5 percent of women. By 1971 the
National Jewish Population Study found that 58.3 percent of all
Jews between the ages of 25 and 29 had completed college (72.3
percent of men and 45.4 percent of women); 34.5 percent had
completed course work beyond the undergraduate degree (47.6 percent of men and 22.5 percent of women).[32]

Not only have Jews been graduating from universities at about double the national rate, but increasing numbers of Jews have been entering the professions, which had once attempted to limit the number of Jewish practitioners. As a consequence the occupational structure of the Jewish community has been dramatically altered. In the 1948 Indianapolis Jewish population survey, 43.1 percent of all employed Jews over fifteen were described as "proprietors" (i.e., self-employed businessmen), while only 11.2 percent were classified as professionals. Nationally by 1971, 24.6 percent of Jewish men between the ages of 25 and 29 (but only 1.3 percent of Jewish women) had a professional degree. Thirty percent of the employed respondents surveyed by the National Jewish Population Study in 1971 were classified as "professional, technical, and kindred workers," compared to 20 percent in 1957. Whereas the typical Jewish male resident of Indianapolis of the first half of the century would have been a small businessman, today he is more likely to be a doctor, a dentist, a lawyer, or an accountant. Many more women than in earlier years are also pursuing professions.[33]

For decades the wealthiest Jews in Indianapolis were all affiliated with the Reform congregation, IHC. Wealth clearly correlated with synagogue affiliation. In 1932 all of the city's seventeen Jewish department-store executives and all but one of the city's fourteen Jewish doctors belonged to IHC. (The sole exception belonged to Beth-El Zedeck.) The Conservative Beth-El Zedeck had a few wealthy congregants and a large number of comfortable, middle-class ones. Central Hebrew Congregation, a "modern" Orthodox synagogue, claimed a few professionals as members (three lawyers and two dentists in 1932) and a large number of small businessmen. Following in approximately descending order after Central Hebrew Congregation were all the south side congregations—Sharah Tefilla, United Hebrew Congregation, Knesses Israel, Ezras Achim, and Etz Chaim.[34]

Since wealth and communal influence usually go hand in hand, communal leadership was dominated until the 1940s by persons who were members of IHC. In 1946 Jacob A. Goodman, a member of Beth-El Zedeck, became the first president of the Federation who was not a member of IHC. Since that time, however, only a few members of Beth-El Zedeck have been elected to the post. To date, no Federation president has been a member of any of the three Orthodox synagogues.

Along with social changes in the composition of Indianapolis

Jewry there have been important philosophic ones as well. Historian Melvin Urofsky commented on this phenomenon in a national context in a speech to the General Assembly of the Council of Jewish Federations and Welfare Funds in 1980: "All of the old conflicts have faded away—downtown versus uptown, Zionism versus socialism, American Jewish Committee versus American Jewish Congress—to be replaced with complexities rather than divisions." While there are issues and conflicts which are still unresolved, there is more mutual respect between groups, and there are trends and changes which have affected all groups and brought them closer together.[35]

One of the most noticeable transformations is the revival of interest in Jewish tradition. The return to tradition or at least a reversal of the steadily declining interest in tradition appeared most prominently in those young adults who were born in the late 1940s and early 1950s. The causes for this revival are many. The youth rebellion of the 1960s awakened interest in esoteric (primarily Eastern) religious rituals, some of which was translated by some Jews into an interest in reviving Jewish rituals. The "black is beautiful" movement and the rise of ethnic awareness in the 1970s increased Jewish interest and awareness. For some young Jews, becoming an observant Jew was a simple act of rebellion against the "bland" religion of their parents. For others, entering a *yeshivah* was but one step of many in a search for personal satisfaction. However, while the revival of Jewish tradition might have seemed like an act of adolescent rebellion to some, its effects have been durable. The interest in Jewish tradition has spread up the age scale, and it has not been confined to one group. Each of the three major synagogues in Indianapolis has readopted traditions which they had previously abandoned. Their rabbis report an increasing interest in Jewish ritual, particularly among their younger members.

At IHC, a stronghold of classical Reform for decades, the transformation has probably been the most dramatic. In 1971 the congregation hired its first cantor. Previously their choir, which sang from a loft above the pulpit, had been led by a music director. Traditionally it is the cantor, not the rabbi, who leads the service, which is chanted, not read. A choir, providing performances of specific songs, is an adaptation from the Christian service. Their second cantor, Janice Lowenstein Roger, who joined the congregation in 1979, is the first cantor to sing from the pulpit rather than from the choir loft, and she has introduced some of the more traditional chanting into the service. In 1977 Jonathan Stein, who was then associate rabbi under Murray Saltzman, proposed to the worship committee that the rabbis be permitted either to add a Jewish symbol, a *tallit* or *atarah,* to the black robe which they wore on *Shabbat,* or to dispense with the robe completely. As Stein remarked, "the plain black robe contains no redeeming Jewish feature, and is . . . a plain and simple imitation of our Christian neighbors." According to Stein, who became senior rabbi in 1978, the wearing of the *atarah* symbolized the transfer of political power from the old generation of Indianapolis-born classical Reform Jews to a new generation of leaders who were not necessarily the children of IHC members. Since 1976 the congregation's presidents have either been people who did not grow up in Indianapolis and/or were not previously members of Reform synagogues. The first woman president, June Herman, was elected in 1979. The congregation has adopted several new programs to fulfill the congregants' growing interest in acquiring traditional Jewish knowledge, such as a session before the Saturday morning service to discuss the week's Torah portion and adult *bar* and *bat mitzvah.* For many years IHC did not even hold traditional *bar* or *bat mitzvah* ceremonies; thus, this represents quite a change of direction for the congregation.[36]

Since the 1920s Beth-El Zedeck has been a relatively liberal congregation. It is affiliated with both the Conservative and Reconstructionist movements. (The latter movement was founded by Mordecai M. Kaplan and is a liberal offshoot of the Conservative movement.) Since 1977 the husband-and-wife team of Dennis C. and Sandy Eisenberg Sasso, both graduates of the Reconstructionist Rabbinical College, have been the congregation's rabbis. (The Jewish Theological Seminary in New York City, the Conservative movement's seminary, only began to admit women to its rabbinical program in 1984.)

A number of elements in the Beth-El Zedeck service distinguished it as a liberal congregation. For example, an organ to accompany the musical portions of the service was introduced during the term of Rabbi William Greenfield. Its introduction generated controversy, as it usually does because of the organ's strong association with the Christian church service. An electric ark equipped with a mechanism to open and close automatically was installed at the time the new building was completed. Although the use of such an automatic device violates the prohibition against "making a fire" on the Sabbath and Holy Days, no congregants objected to its use. Unlike most Reform congregations, however, Beth-El Zedeck has always maintained a kosher kitchen. Like IHC, Beth-El Zedeck has revived a number of traditional practices. Although the organ is still used, the electric ark has been disconnected, in part because it never worked well and in part because the rabbis Sasso preferred not to use it. The rules of *kashrut* are more strictly observed in the synagogue's kitchen, and a *mashgi'ah* is now employed to supervise the *kashrut* of the food preparation. Beth-El Zedeck has also developed an adult *bar* and *bat mitzvah* program (known as *ben* and *bat torah*), as well as a Hebrew literacy program for adults. The Saturday morning service at Beth-El Zedeck is almost entirely in Hebrew, although the Friday night service is a mixture of Hebrew and English prayers.[37]

Beth-El Zedeck recently abandoned the observance of the second day of the festivals (excluding *Rosh Hashanah*), an innovation which had the effect of bringing congregational practice much closer to that of the Reform movement. This change was proposed by the rabbis Sasso, who suggested to the religious practices committee that the "congregation conform to a one-day observance of the Holy Day of Festivals (except for *Rosh Hashanah*) in keeping with the Biblical Calendar and in conformity with practices in the land of Israel." From a more practical perspective, the Sassos also argued that attendance at festival services was poor with by far the greatest number participating on the second or "less holy" day because of the *yizkor* (memorial) service on that day. The change was implemented in 1980. Beth-El Zedeck is one of only a few Conservative congregations to institute such a change, although there is a precedent for it. Changes in Conservative practice emanate from the committee on Jewish law and standards of the Rabbinical Assembly, which issues responsa argued in the traditional manner and based on *halakhah* as well as on the contemporary social situation. Thus, in the 1950s when most Conservative synagogues moved to the suburbs the committee issued a responsum making it acceptable for Conservative Jews to ride to synagogue. The 1969 responsum regarding the elimination of the second day of festivals other than *Rosh Hashanah* has not been taken up as widely as the decision to permit riding to synagogue.[38]

At Congregation B'nai Torah, an Orthodox synagogue from its founding, the traditional revival appears more dramatically in the changing makeup of the congregation than in the readoption of traditional rituals. In 1967 the congregation moved from its building at 34th and Ruckle streets to a new synagogue at 65th Street and Hoover Road, near most of the city's Jewish institutions. Until about ten years ago B'nai Torah was primarily a congregation of aging eastern European immigrants. Ronald Gray, who became rabbi of the congregation in 1970, recalls that he performed a lot of funerals in the early years. In recent years, however, the congregation has attracted many young families who desire a more traditional kind of Judaism. As a result, there are now more young children among its members than there have been in many years. The level of observance within the congregation has also increased. While many Conservative and some Reform congregations have one special *Selihot* service, either before *Rosh Hashanah* or between *Rosh Hashanah* and *Yom Kippur,* for the past two years B'nai Torah has held a *Selihot* service every night between *Rosh Hashanah* and *Yom Kippur.* The traditional practice actually was for the special *Selihot* or penitential prayers to be said at dawn (and in Sephardic communities also after midnight) before the *Shaharit* (morning) prayers. For the past three years, the congregation has also sponsored a Talmud class. More families erect their own *sukkah* for the festival of *Sukkot.* More women use the *mikveh* for ritual purification. (A new *mikveh* adjoining the synagogue was completed in 1969. The *mikveh* and an apartment for the *mikveh*'s custodians were both financed by the Federation.) However, nearly all congregants drive to synagogue (the synagogue's adjacent parking lot is filled with cars on *Shabbat*), and only a very few adhere strictly to the laws of *kashrut.* While the synagogue maintains separate seating for men and women, the women's section is neither in the back of the sanctuary nor in a balcony. Instead, the men's and women's sections are merely separate sections or different sides of the sanctuary divided by an aisle.[39]

IHC continues to retain its long-standing primacy as the

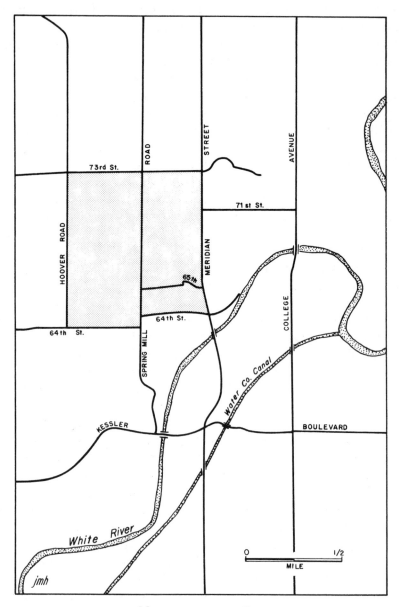

Map 3:   1970s–1980s

synagogue with the largest membership in the city. In 1981, 1,100 families belonged to IHC, 900 to Beth-El Zedeck, and 275 to B'nai Torah. In terms of sheer size, IHC and Beth-El Zedeck are clearly dominant, although B'nai Torah demonstrates the resurgence of modern Orthodoxy in Indianapolis.[40]

IHC and Beth-El Zedeck both operate religious schools on Sunday mornings. Their children attend either the Bureau of Jewish Education (BJE) or the Hebrew Academy for Hebrew instruction. In 1980 the enrollment of the Beth-El Zedeck school included 350 students from kindergarten through twelfth grade. The enrollment of the IHC Sunday school was 465. An important part of the Sunday school curriculum is to teach children the basic beliefs and practices of either Reform or Conservative-Reconstructionist Judaism. B'nai Torah recently discontinued its Sunday school primarily because so many of the congregation's children now attend the Hebrew Academy.[41]

In addition to the three major synagogues there are two smaller synagogues whose existence reflects the common bonds shared by the members—the United Orthodox Hebrew Congregation (UOHC) and Etz Chaim. In the case of the former, which came into being in 1962 as a result of the merger of three south side synagogues (Sharah Tefilla, Knesses Israel, and Ezras Achim), the members are bound together by ties of family and nostalgia for the old south side Jewish community. In 1981, 135 families belonged; many, however, also belonged to one of the city's major synagogues. Membership in UOHC served for them as a link to the old south side, to the *shuls* in which they had worshipped as children or in less prosperous days and to the cemeteries where their parents are buried. Not surprisingly United Orthodox Hebrew Congregation has no religious school. In 1981 the rabbi of UOHC was David Korb.[42]

Although Sephardim can be found among the members of all three major synagogues, and there have been many marriages between Sephardim and Ashkenazim, the Sephardim in Indianapolis also continue to maintain their own congregation. In 1963 the congregation purchased the Pleasant View Lutheran Church at 64th Street and Hoover Road, near the Jewish Center and JEA. Membership in Etz Chaim functions not only as a link to the past but as a means of maintaining their distinctive ethnic identity within the larger Jewish community. Like the members of UOHC, many of Etz Chaim's seventy-five members maintain membership in a major synagogue as well. The Indianapolis Sephardic community retains a very strong sense of identity and of separateness from the Ashkenazim. The insults they (or their parents) suffered as new-comers are not easily forgotten. However, Ashkenazi attitudes to Sephardim have changed dramatically in recent years, in part be-cause of Sephardic economic success and in part because of the rising interest in ethnicity among the American middle class as a whole. Symbolic of this change, in 1978 IHC sponsored a special Sephardic *Shabbat* service and *oneg shabbat* featuring Sephardic music and food, as well as Ladino musical parodies written and performed by Judge William Levy. In 1981 the rabbi of Etz Chaim was Yigal Tsaidi, a native Israeli, who also served on the faculty of the Hebrew Academy.[43]

The revival of the idea of cultural pluralism in America in the 1970s and the celebration of America's multicultural heritage dur-ing the American Bicentennial lent support to those Jewish leaders pressing for a greater emphasis on Jewish culture and tradition in communal institutions. To the question "What's Jewish about the Jewish Center?" the answer in the 1950s would have been that the Jews there make it Jewish. The Jewish Center's programs at the time were almost entirely social and recreational, and there was little to distinguish it, aside from the membership, from any other middle-class communal center. Since the late-1960s, however, the Jewish Center has very deliberately shifted its orientation and added programs of Jewish content to its schedule in addition to adding a Jewish emphasis to existing programs. Under Julius Dorfman, who served as executive director from 1967 to 1981, the Jewish Center became quite self-consciously Jewish. A Yiddish class was organized, the day-care center introduced Jewish pro-gramming, and the BJE began teaching adult education courses at the center. In 1980–1981 Jewish programs included a *Tu bi-Shevat* "*seder*" for families to celebrate the New Year of the Trees. In con-junction with the BJE, the center sponsored a lecture series on var-ious Jewish subjects. The center also presented a series of films on Jewish themes. To help families who wanted to celebrate Passover and put on a *seder* but needed help in preparing the many tradi-tional elements of the meal the center sponsored a course on pre-paring for Passover. Not only has the programming embraced

Jewish materials, but the whole tone of the center has become more Jewish than at any time since the 1940s. For example, the summer day camp operated by the old Kirshbaum Center was called "Ki-Wa-Ca," an Indian-sounding acronym which stood for Kirshbaum-Washington-Camp. Now the day camps all have Hebrew, not "Indian," names—Gan Yeladim, Masada, Tikvah, and Maccabiah. Dorfman, who was personally more observant than his predecessors, also insisted on the stricter observance of Jewish laws at the center. During his term the Jewish Community Center swim team was not permitted to participate in swimming meets on Friday afternoons or Saturdays, times when most meets are held.[44]

Ironically, while the Jewish Center has become more "Jewish," the percentage of non-Jewish members is probably higher than ever before. In 1975–1976 the center was extensively renovated, expanding in size from 40,000 to 60,000 square feet. A health club was added, and the athletic facilities were greatly improved, attracting many new non-Jewish members. (Since the center receives funds from United Way, it is nonsectarian in its membership policy.) Moreover, many of the center's offerings are not intrinsically Jewish, such as its cardiac rehabilitation program, its seminars on financial planning, stress management, parenting, assertiveness training, and winetasting, and many of its children's programs.[45]

By its very nature the Bureau of Jewish Education (BJE) has always sponsored essentially Jewish programs. The revival of Jewish particularism in the community, however, has manifested itself at the BJE as well. As more adolescents and adults have expressed an interest in expanding their Jewish knowledge, the high school and adult education programs have grown. The BJE has also developed a role as an advocate of Jewish education beyond the confines of its own institution. In 1973, largely because of the efforts of the BJE and some of its board members, Hebrew became a part of the foreign language curriculum at North Central High School, where the great bulk of the Jewish high school population was enrolled. The organization, which changed its name to the Bureau of Jewish Education in 1980, sponsors a media center, an Educational Directors' Council, teacher education workshops, and other services. A computer center of Jewish education is currently being planned. It will replace a language laboratory that was never effectively integrated into the curriculum and was closed several years ago.[46]

The heart of the BJE program, however, is still its afternoon

Hebrew school. Here too change for the better is evident as a higher proportion of children attend the Hebrew school than in the 1950s and 1960s. In 1981 there were 360 children enrolled in grades kindergarten through eight, and an additional 50 attended the Hebrew high school. School enrollment is no longer primarily composed of boys and of children from Beth-El Zedeck, as it was in the mid-1960s. Almost all of Beth-El Zedeck's children and over half of the children from IHC now attend. A few come from B'nai Torah (although most of them attend the Hebrew Academy) and from Etz Chaim as well as from families with no synagogue affiliation. Since 1979 the executive director has been Uri Korin, an Israeli with a doctorate in educational administration and curriculum development from Kent State University in Ohio.[47]

In many communities in recent years concern for strengthening Jewish education has reached beyond the local community to the university. The establishment of university courses in Jewish studies, many of them funded by private donors, began to multiply in the late 1960s. Many leaders saw Jewish studies as a way of providing a stronger Jewish background for Jewish college students and of extending Jewish knowledge beyond the unsophisticated "Sunday school" level. To some individuals the presence of Jewish studies in the university curriculum somehow helped to legitimize the Jewish experience. Jewish studies could also deepen interfaith understanding in that Judaica courses could be used to explain Jews and Judaism to non-Jewish students. Moreover, Jewish studies courses could provide an important meeting ground for Jewish students, many of whom avoided the campus Hillel House. Since most Jews meet their prospective spouses at college, courses in Jewish studies might help to lower the rate of intermarriage as well as to strengthen Jewish identity. In the late 1950s, Dr. Jacob K. Berman of Indianapolis organized the Indiana University Committee for the Chair of Hebrew Language and Literature to collect funds to hire a professor of Hebrew for the Bloomington campus. In 1961 Henry A. Fischel, a German Jew with a doctorate in semitics from the University of Edinburgh, came to fill the position. As the course offerings in Judaica grew, a Jewish Studies program was established at Indiana University in 1971 under the directorship of Professor Alvin Rosenfeld. Since 1979 the Indianapolis Jewish Welfare Federation, along with the federations in Fort Wayne and South

Bend, have helped to support the program. In the late 1970s funds were raised for a position in Jewish history. In 1979 Todd M. Endelman, who previously taught modern Jewish history in the Bernard Revel Graduate School of Yeshiva University, joined the Jewish Studies faculty.[48]

The desire to strengthen Jewish identity and intensify Jewish experience, whatever the ultimate objective, has united Jews who would have had little to say to one another a generation ago. The bitter divisions between Zionist and anti-Zionist, atheist and observant dissolved some time ago. The trend toward unity has continued to the point that even the two extremes of Orthodoxy and Reform Judaism, while they might not readily admit it, have influenced one another. A generation ago an Orthodox and Reform rabbi stood far apart on most issues. While the Orthodox rabbi stressed the relative importance of *halakhah* and traditional observance, the Reform rabbi emphasized Jewish social activism as an affirmation of prophetic Judaism and the importance of interfaith understanding. Today these differences, while they certainly still exist, are not so dramatic. Moreover, since 1977 the rabbis of the major synagogues of Indianapolis have all been men and women in their thirties. Ronald Gray, who assumed the pulpit of B'nai Torah in 1970, is the first American-born Orthodox rabbi to serve in an Indianapolis pulpit. A native of Atlanta, Georgia, he was trained at the Rabbi Isaac Elchanan Theological Seminary of Yeshiva University in New York City. An activist in a way that sets him apart from former generations of Orthodox rabbis, in 1978 Gray organized the Indianapolis Board of Rabbis as a forum to discuss issues of mutual concern. The Orthodox rabbinate has generally been the most wary and suspicious of organizations such as the Synagogue Council of America or city rabbinical boards. It is thus quite unusual for an Orthodox rabbi to set out to establish such an institution. Moreover, the board has generally supported Gray on positions that would normally be associated with Orthodoxy. For example, the Board of Rabbis has adopted the position that all Federation-sponsored meals (i.e., fund-raising banquets, etc.) should observe the laws of *kashrut.* This is yet another example of the return to particularism which has transformed American Judaism in the past fifteen years.[49]

It is not only the rabbinical leadership in Indianapolis that is relatively new and youthful. Because of resignations and retirements all of the Federation agencies, except for the Jewish Community Relations Council (JCRC), appointed new directors in 1980 and 1981. The current executive director of the JCRC was appointed in 1977. Moreover, the factionalism and competition which previously engendered hostility between agencies and prevented cooperation have largely dissipated. The "Rabbis and Pros" group brought the city's Jewish professionals together for the first time. They and their agencies are now attempting to coordinate services more than they have in the past. One of the first products of the new agency-synagogue cooperation was a course for potential converts to Judaism, "Information on Judaism," which began in 1968. Both rabbis and agency professionals participated in the course, which met at the JEA.[50]

In 1981 the Federation established a New Americans Committee to coordinate interagency Russian resettlement programs and supervise services to Soviet immigrants. The committee has produced a community policy statement delineating each agency's responsibility for the Soviet immigrants. The BJE is responsible for English and Judaic instruction, the Jewish Center for providing social activities through its Russian Club, the Jewish Family and Children's Services (JF&CS) for help with employment, housing, medical care, etc., and the National Council of Jewish Women for the "family circle" volunteers, etc. Resettlement of the Soviet Jews has been a major priority of the JF&CS, second only to counseling services, since the first family arrived in 1974 with the assistance of the Hebrew Immigrant Aid Society. Between 1974 and 1981, 177 Soviet Jews settled in Indianapolis.[51]

By their very nature Jewish community relations agencies are concerned with the larger community. However, here too 1967 marked a turning point in directing these agencies to issues that more directly concerned Jews. Until 1979 there were two major community relations agencies in Indianapolis: the Federation-sponsored JCRC and the Indiana Anti-Defamation League. The Indiana ADL was created in 1955 when the national ADL withdrew its support of the Indiana JCRC shortly after that organization had consolidated its office and directorship with the Indianapolis JCRC. Robert Gordon (1924–1976), a native of Milwaukee, came from the ADL's Wisconsin office to take over the work of the new agency.

Gordon remained the director of the Indiana ADL until 1976 when he was forced to retire because of poor health. He died a few months later. Morris Casuto replaced him, but in 1979 Casuto was transferred to a newly opened office in San Diego and the Indiana office was closed. Since that time the state's affairs have been handled by the ADL office in Columbus, Ohio.[52]

During the twenty-four years that the ADL maintained its Indiana office, cooperation between the JCRC and the ADL was slight. Each agency more or less went its own way, although there was general agreement on what the issues were. In the 1950s and 1960s these were religion and the public schools, social discrimination, Sunday closing laws, support for Israel, and most importantly, the civil rights movement. In the summer of 1958 Robert Gordon participated in a special ADL program which sent northern ADL professionals to the South for special training. Each participant was then assigned to a state and given a car with local license plates. (Robert Gordon was assigned to Mississippi.) He then traveled the state visiting local communities and advocating the extension of full civil rights to blacks. During the early 1960s, when northern whites were going South to work in the civil rights movement and were often arrested, the JCRC offered to post bond for any young Jews from Indianapolis who were imprisoned in the South. David H. Goldstein, executive director of the JCRC from 1961 to 1965, went to Selma, Alabama, twice to participate in civil rights marches, once with Rabbi Maurice Davis of IHC.[53]

The involvement of Jewish community relations agencies in the civil rights movement lessened dramatically as more militant blacks took control of the movement in the late 1960s and expelled the white leadership. Moreover, the emergence of black anti-Semitism, coupled with the strong condemnation of Israel in 1967 by militant blacks, new left groups, and many Protestant churches, convinced the community relations agencies of the need to return to the defense of purely Jewish interests. Soon after 1967 defense of and support for Israel headed the agenda of community relations agencies, followed closely by support for Soviet Jewry. The general awakening of Jewish consciousness to the events of the Holocaust inspired a whole new range of programming to increase public awareness of the destruction of European Jewry. The JCRC sponsored educational programming in this area, such as an exhibit on the Holocaust at a large shopping mall in 1973. Members of the JCRC's Holocaust Committee also worked with the Indianapolis Public Schools' Social Studies Curriculum Department to develop a proposal for the creation of a Holocaust curriculum within the Indianapolis Public Schools. An annual Holocaust Memorial Day became a part of the communal calendar.[54]

In 1971 the JCRC began to sponsor a half-hour television program, "A Jewish Perspective," which appeared on alternate Sunday mornings. The program, whose implied purpose was to educate non-Jews about Jews and Judaism, provided a forum for the presentation of a wide variety of Jewish concerns. Topics discussed included Reconstructionism, Jewish involvement in religious cults, Jewish holidays, history of the Indianapolis Jewish community, and many other subjects.[55]

The violation of the doctrine of the separation of church and state, a major issue for the JCRC in the 1950s, became a less important question after the Supreme Court declared prayer in school to be unconstitutional. In 1976, however, the Indiana Civil Liberties Union and the JCRC decided to confront jointly a sensitive issue: the use of public property for religious displays. Their major objective was to prevent the construction of the traditional nativity scene in University Park, a municipal park. Unfortunately, the attempt backfired, revealing a high level of latent anti-Semitism among many citizens of Indianapolis. In November 1976, Barbara Williamson, executive director of the ICLU, and Emily Fink, executive director of the JCRC, reached a verbal agreement with the superintendent of Parks and Recreation and Mayor William Hudnut III, himself a Presbyterian minister, that there would be no nativity scene in University Park that year. A week before Christmas word of the agreement was leaked to the *Indianapolis Star*, which gave the item a banner headline "Protest Ends University Square Nativity Scene." Within the next few days the paper proceeded to exploit and sensationalize the issue to the fullest. Not only did the emotional issue help to sell papers, but the *Star*, an extremely conservative newspaper, supported those who wanted the nativity scene to stay. Not only was the nativity scene put up in the park, but in the end it appeared that many citizens subscribed to the doctrine of church-state separation only to a degree. The letters written to the *Star* overwhelmingly supported the retention of the nativity scene. Jewish agencies and individuals received many hate letters and phone calls. Moreover, even many members of the Jewish community seemed to feel that the JCRC should leave well enough alone and focus on more urgent issues. These Jews felt their position in America was less threatened by a park manger scene than by other more potent forces.[56]

With the rise in prominence of the Moral Majority and other religiously fundamentalist and politically right wing groups in the late 1970s, Jewish community relations agencies began to increase their interest in domestic issues. Marcia Goldstone, the current executive director of the JCRC, believes that domestic rather than international issues are becoming more important as many basic civil liberties come under increasing attack. Goldstone believes the changing perspective of the JCRC was symbolized by the agency's recent move from the JWF office in the English Foundation to the Interchurch Center. Since the ADL closed its office in the interchurch building, there had been no Jewish presence there. From its new office in the Interchurch Center, the JCRC can join with like-minded groups to fight such issues as the proposed ban on abortions or the proposed constitutional amendment to permit prayer in school.[57]

Some critics of the Jewish establishment contend that it is too crisis oriented and overly focused on fund raising for Israel to be able to respond to social change or to the needs of the ordinary American Jewish family. However, there are signs that this is changing as communal agencies have begun to try to meet the needs of all kinds of families and all kinds of Jews, rather than just the elderly and the infirm. In Indianapolis, for example, programs for Jewish singles—those with children, without children, the young, and the middle-aged—are now offered by a variety of agencies and synagogues. Two newly established divisions of the Federation emphasize the growing importance of two groups—young singles and working women. The Young Professionals Division is for young singles as opposed to the older Young Leadership Division, which includes primarily married people. The Career Women's Division was organized in 1979 for working women who felt out of place at meetings of the Young Women's Division, which mainly attracted young mothers who were staying home to raise their children. The Women's Conference runs programming for women year-round as opposed to the Women's Division which does fund raising. A recent one-day symposium of the Women's Conference at Indiana University with speakers from the Jewish Studies program focused on the changing role of the American Jewish woman.

In 1964 an article in *Look Magazine* with the dramatic title "The Vanishing American Jew" highlighted what many American Jews already knew: the Jewish birthrate was falling, and Jews were failing to reproduce themselves. Moreover, the rising number of intermarriages was further reducing the size of the Jewish community. Would the day come when there would be no Jewish community in America? asked *Look.* Was this the price of living in an open society? The National Jewish Population Study of 1970–1971 confirmed that the rate of intermarriage was indeed high. The demographers found an overall Jewish intermarriage rate of 17 percent. Since the rate has risen sharply in recent years this percentage will continue to increase as the older, more endogamous generations die. Moreover, it was only in a majority of marriages that the non-Jew converted to Judaism or the children were raised as Jews. In addition, the fertility rate of American Jews—the average number of children born to a Jewish woman—had dropped from 3.2 in 1957–1961, to 2.1 in 1962–1966, to 1.4 in 1967–1971. (A rate of 2.1 is considered necessary to maintain a population.)[58]

A pessimist has been defined as one who sees the glass as half-empty rather than half-full. After years of worrying over the half-empty glass the Jewish community has finally turned its focus to the half-full glass, undertaking programs to strengthen the Jewish identity and commitment of the existing Jewish population. The concern over "Jewish survival" has been translated into a growing interest in Jewish education, in day schools, and in family-oriented Jewish activities. The *havurah* movement—small Jewish fellowships (often affiliated with a synagogue) which meet regularly for prayer, study, meals, social activities, and, often, cooperation on political or social action projects—and the development of family life education are both products of the concern for increasing commitment and group loyalty as well as the desire to promote the Jewish knowledge of American Jewry. Many Jewish communities today try to provide "something for everyone"—programs for Jews of all ages and interests that will help to maintain the bond to the

Jewish community. Demographer Erich Rosenthal sees a direct correlation between this sort of active Jewish community and a relatively low rate of intermarriage. According to Rosenthal it is a misconception to blame a high level of exogamy solely on the small size or low density of a local Jewish population. He argues that community organization has a direct effect on the level of inter-marriage. A well-organized, active Jewish community helps to create an atmosphere that encourages Jewish endogamy. While no one program could be singled out as directly influencing the inter-marriage rate, the combination of programs may help to strengthen group loyalty which, in turn, results in a rate of intermarriage lower than it would be if these programs did not exist.[59]

Communal leaders have also come to realize that a Jew marry-ing a non-Jew no longer means an automatic loss to the Jewish community. Many non-Jews are personally attracted to Jewish family life, Jewish customs, and traditions even though they may not choose formal conversion. While demographers agree that these constitute a minority of cases, many children of mixed mar-riages are being raised as Jews even when the non-Jewish parent did not actually convert. Those non-Jews who do choose formal con-version are being greeted by a much more positive attitude within the Jewish community. They have even been given a new, more positive appellation—"Jews by choice." Jewish institutions are now more welcoming to converts and have begun to consider the special needs of these Jews, which continue long after the conver-sion lessons have been completed. Congregation Beth-El Zedeck, for example, recently inaugurated a series of informal discussions for converted Jews and their Jewish partners to share the problems they face living with their new identity. Just as the arrival of each new wave of immigrants ultimately changed the composition of the American Jewish community, the integration of these new Jews, who were not raised as Jews, into the community is certain to produce changes for American Jewry.

Viewed from a perspective of twenty years, *Look Magazine*'s prediction that the American Jew is destined to disappear appears not to be coming true. In the end most American Jews want to remain Jewish. Moreover, there seems to be less discomfort today with some of the negatively perceived aspects of Jewishness than there was in earlier decades. Certainly the triumph of ethnicity in

America has helped many Jews to feel more positive about their Jewishness. There appear to be fewer Jews trying to "pass" as non-Jews and less of a need to do so, either for economic or social reasons. One observes fewer Jews changing their names. (One could argue, however, that this is because the father or grandfather had already changed it.) There are even instances in which children have changed their surname back to the original family name. Fewer Jews today seem to have "nose jobs," that is, the surgical alteration of a large "Jewish" nose into a more demure "non-Jewish" one. Even today's levels of intermarriage, although they seem high, actually signify a marked persistence on the part of most Jews to remain Jewish. U. O. Schmelz, a demographer, points out that, since Jews are a small minority throughout America (with the exception of New York City), if Jews were to contract marriages randomly—that is without Jewishness being a factor in marriage choice—hardly any endogamous marriages would occur. Erich Rosenthal takes this construct back one step further by considering that self-segregated residential patterns create Jewish neighborhoods which, in turn, tend to promote Jewish marriages. According to Rosenthal, if residences of American Jews were evenly distributed over the United States and if mate selection occurred at random—that is, without considering religious background—the intermarriage status rate of Jewish men and women would be 98 percent. In an open society where there are few restrictions to social movement the elaborate apparatus developed by the local Jewish community helps to maintain social and cultural boundaries and to stem the loss of Jews into the larger community.[60]

"We are One!"—the current slogan of the United Jewish Appeal—can be dismissed as an empty slogan created merely to produce more funds for UJA or it can be seen as a phrase which captures the essence of Jewishness. When reduced to the bare bones most Jews will say that what is most important is Jewish survival: the Jewish people—not just Zionists or Reform Jews or Jewish vegetarians—should endure. Most Jews want to remain as Jews, and they want to know that the Jewish community will continue. Underneath all the building campaigns, the self-studies, the surveys, and reports, that is the simple message.

Appendix A.

OFFICERS OF MAJOR ORGANIZATIONS

Jewish Federation Superintendents

Samuel D. Wolf	1905–1906	Samuel B. Kaufman	1908–1921
Samuel J. Levinson	1906–1908	George W. Rabinoff	1921–1927

Jewish Federation and Jewish Welfare Fund Executive Directors

George W. Rabinoff	1927–1928	Sidney Cahn	1945–1948
H. Joseph Hyman	1928–1945		

Jewish Welfare Federation Executive Directors (title changed to executive vice-president in 1969)

Sidney Cahn	1948–1953	Louis B. Solomon	1982–1984
Oscar A. Mintzer	1953–1959	Harry Nadler	1984–
Frank H. Newman	1959–1982		

Jewish Federation Presidents

Sol S. Kiser (chairman of organizing committee and first president)	1904–1905	Edward A. Kahn	1914–1916
		Joseph Wineman	1916–1919
		Gustave A. Efroymson	1919–1934
Gustave A. Efroymson	1905–1913	Dr. Harry A. Jacobs	1934–1937

255

Isidore Feibleman	1937–1940	Ernest Cohn	1944–1946
Samuel Mueller	1940–1944	Jacob A. Goodman	1946–1948

Jewish Welfare Federation Presidents

Jacob A. Goodman	1948–1949	Ben Domont	1965–1967
Julian Freeman	1949–1953	Liebert I. Mossler	1967–1970
Sarah Wolf Goodman	1953–1954	Martin L. Larner	1970–1972
Maurel Rothbaum	1955	Irwin Katz	1972–1975
Samuel Kroot	1956–1958	Walter E. Wolf, Jr.	1975–1978
Manuel I. Leve	1958	Philip D. Pecar	1978–1981
David M. Cook	1959–1962	David H. Kleiman	1981–1984
William L. Schloss	1962–1965	Dr. Edward Gabovitch	1984–

Jewish Welfare Fund and Federation Campaign Chairmen

Louis J. Borinstein	1940	Sigmund J. Beck	1965
William L. Schloss	1941	Marvin Lasky	1966
Lazure L. Goodman	1942	Edgar Joseph	1967
UNITED WAR FUND	1943–1945	Martin L. Larner	1968
Julian Freeman	1946	Sidney Tuchman	1969
Morris Goodman		Joseph A. Rothbard	1970
Samuel J. Mantel	1947	Ben Kroot	1971
Jacob Solotken		Joseph A. Rothbard	1972
Lazure L. Goodman	1948	Herbert J. Backer	1973
Samuel Ziffrin		Jack H. Larman	1974
Abe J. Miller	1949	Ben Paller	1975
Liebert I. Mossler		Herbert Simon	1976
Morris Goodman	1950	Melvin Simon	
Lazure L. Goodman	1951	Irwin Katz	1977
Edward M. Dayan	1952	Martin L. Larner	
Lazure L. Goodman	1953	Liebert Mossler	
David M. Cook	1954	David H. Kleiman	1978
Lazure L. Goodman	1955	Philip D. Pecar	1979
Samuel S. Schahet	1956–1957	Walter Wolf	
Wilfred R. Borinstein	1958	Irwin Rose	1980
Samuel S. Schahet	1959	Sigmund Beck	
Milton J. Fineberg	1960–1961	Irwin Rose	1981
Bernard Stroyman	1962	Leonard Berkowitz	
David M. Cook	1963	Gerald Kraft	1982
Ben Domont	1964	Robert A. Rose	1983–1984

Communal Building Educational Directors

Alan Pleve	1923–1925	Allan Bloom	1925–1926

Jewish Community Center Association General Secretaries
(title changed to executive director ca. 1945)

Allan Bloom	1926–1945	Seymour Kline	1962–1964
Irvin Larner	1945–1947	Morris Cohen	1964–1966
William Steinberg	1947–1950	Julius Dorfman	1967–1981
Alfred Dobrof	1950–1959	Harry Nadler	1981–1984
Harold Robbins	1959–1962		

Jewish Community Center Association Presidents

Leonard Strauss	1926–1934	Martin L. Larner	1963–1966
Sidney J. Sternberger	1934–1936	Gerald Kraft	1966–1969
Jacob L. Mueller	1936–1939	Dr. Edward R.	
Theodore Dann	1939–1948	Gabovitch	1969–1972
Carl Lyman	1948–1950	David H. Kleiman	1972–1975
Irwin Katz	1950–1952	Herbert C. Brodsky	1975–1978
Samuel Kroot	1952–1955	Barbara C. Levy	1978–1980
Martin L. Larner	1955–1958	Charles Cohen	1980–1982
Irwin Katz	1958–1961	Bruce Frank	1982–1984
Sherman Weinstein	1961–1963	Claudette Einhorn	1984–

Public Relations Committee of the Jewish Federation Executive Dirctor
(became the Jewish Community Relations Council in 1947)

Rabbi Maurice Goldblatt	1942–1946

Jewish Community Relations Council Executive Directors

Charles Posner	1947–1951	David Goldstein	1961–1965
David A. Sawyer	1951–1954	Theodore Walden	1965–1968
Maurice Mezoff	1954–1955	Norman Sider	1968–1974
Albert Chernin	1955–1958	Emily Fink	1974–1977
Marshall Cohen	1958–1959	Dr. Marcia Goldstone	1977–
Irving Levine	1959–1961		

Public Relations Committee of the Jewish Federation Chairman

Samuel Mueller	1939–1942

Jewish Community Relations Council Presidents

Julian Kiser	1948–1951	Max Klezmer	1955–1958
David M. Cook	1951–1954	Bertha Lichtenstein	1958–1960
Norman Abrams	1954–1955	Sigmund J. Beck	1960–1963

Rabbi Sidney Steiman	1963–1965	Ezra Friedlander	1977–1979
Philip D. Pecar	1965–1969	Gladys Nisenbaum	1979–1980
Joseph Greenberg	1969–1971	Alan Goldstein	1980–1983
Irving L. Fink	1971–1973	Dr. M. E. Hodes	1983–
Max Nelson	1974–1977		

United Hebrew Schools Principals

Louis Hurwich	1911–1916	J. Grossman	1919–1920
Bernard Isaacs	1916–1919	W. Alkow	1920–1924

Bureau of Jewish Education* Executive Directors

Hyman Perez	1924–1926	Max Furer	1961–1971
S. Kasdan	1926–1928	Akiva Gerstein	1972–1975
Meyer Gallin	1928–1947	Gideon Goren	1975–1979
Gershon Gelbart	1947–1948	Uri Korin	1979–
Aaron Intrater	1949–1960		

United Hebrew Schools Presidents

Solomon Finkelstein	1911–1912	Wolf Davis	1919–1920
Charles Medias	1912–1915	Charles Medias	1920–1923
Samuel Grenwald	1915–1918	Moses A. Rabinowitz	1923–1924
Charles Medias	1918–1919		

Bureau of Jewish Education* Presidents

Louis Sakowitz	1924–1925	Jacob Nelson	1966–1968
Isaac Marks	1925–1926	Gus Domont	1968–1970
Jacob Solotken	1934–1936	Ralph Segall	1970–1972
Max Plesser	1936–1937	N. William Weinstein	1972–1973
Louis Grossman	1938–1939	Dr. M. E. Hodes	1973–1976
Aaron Unger	1939–1941	Marilyn Roger	1976–1978
Edward M. Dayan	1941–1950	Gary Schahet	1978–1980
David Hollander	1951–1956	Lawrence Greenwald	1980–1982
Bernard Stroyman	1958–1964	Don Katz	1982–1984
Isadore Katz	1964–1966	Lawrence Reuben	1984–

Jewish Family Service Society Caseworker

Sara Weinberg	1928–1935

*Name changed in 1980 from Jewish Educational Association

Jewish Family and Children's Services * *Executive Directors*

Nathan Berman	1946–1955	Conrad Nathan	1964–1968
Jacob Guthartz	1956–1963	Julius Markfield	1968–1980
Juanita K. Graham	1963–1964	Martin Percher	1980–
(acting executive director)			

Jewish Family and Children's Services * *Presidents*

Jeckiel W. Joseph	1929–1934	Jerome Leviton	1969–1970
Dr. A. S. Jaeger	1934–1948	Nathan Nisenbaum	1971–1972
Mrs. Harry Joseph	1949–1952	Ivan Chalfie	1972–1975
Dr. Bennett Kraft	1952–1955	Reuben Shevitz	1975–1977
Mrs. David Cook	1955–1957	Mrs. Sigmund Brenner	1977–1979
Morris Jacobs	1957–1960	Robert A. Garelick	1979–1981
Max Reifer	1960–1962	Dr. Daniel H. Spitzberg	1981–1982
Bernard Landman	1962–1966	David E. Regenstrief	1982–1984
Robert Finn	1967–1968	Jack Thompson	1984–

Joseph and Annie Borinstein Home for the Aged *Executive Directors*

Nathan Berman	1946–1952	M. Bill Newman	1962–1970
Morton Leeds	1953–1962		

Hooverwood Executive Directors

Lazar B. Brener	1970–1980	Jeffrey Stern	1981–

South Side Hebrew Ladies Charity Organization *Presidents*

Celia Schwartz	1902–	Mathilda Newman	1910–1922
Gussie Hoffman			

Jewish Shelter House and Old Home Presidents

Mathilda Newman	1922–1923	Hannah Frankfort	ca. 1928

Joseph and Annie Borinstein Home for the Aged *Presidents*

Mrs. Sam Dorfman	ca. 1939	David Hollander	1959–1961
Sarah Messing Stern		Bertha Falender	1961–1963
Sidney Mahalowitz	1944–1955	Joseph Borinstein	1963–1968
Norton Fishbein	1956–1957	Leo Selig	1968–1970
A. A. Borts	1957–1959		

*Name changed in 1969 from Jewish Social Services

Hooverwood Presidents

Walter E. Wolf, Jr.	1970–1972	Dorothy Klineman	1978–1980
Lewis Lurie	1972–1974	Dr. Harold Stadler	1980–1982
Arnold Marks	1974–1976	Eugene Step	1982–1984
Marvin Sablosky	1976–1978	Lyle Rosensweig	1984–

Hebrew Academy Directors

| Cantor Edwin Epstein | 1971–1978 | Raymond Stern | 1981– |
| Rabbi Joel Green | 1978–1981 | | |

Hebrew Academy Presidents

| Hart Hasten | 1971–1977 | Mark Hasten | 1977– |

Appendix B.

A NOTE ON SOURCES

When I began work on this project, much of the primary material bearing on the history of Indianapolis Jewry was in private hands. Most of it has now been deposited at the Indiana Historical Society, where it will be available for future researchers. The single largest collection is that containing the records of the Jewish Welfare Federation, the earliest of which begin in 1905. This collection includes an extraordinary range of documents, from the earliest communal relief records to the reports and studies of the 1970s and 1980s.

While the Federation was the central organization in the community, the records of other organizations were important for understanding other viewpoints and attitudes. The minute books of the Indianapolis B'nai B'rith lodge (1923–1944), for example, were helpful in discovering Jewish reactions to anti-Semitism and the development of programs to fight anti-Semitism. The Workmen's Circle minute book (1918–1926) illuminated the concerns of the nonreligious south side Jewish immigrant, the minute books of Congregation Ezras Achim (1936–1962) those of the south side Orthodox community. These records are now at the Indiana Historical Society. In addition, the library of the society has a large collection of photographs, synagogue anniversary books, histories, studies, and organizational reports, as well as the tapes of interviews that were conducted for this book. Thus, the Indiana Historical Society is now the major depository for the historical records of the Indianapolis Jewish community.

The Indiana Historical Society, however, has very little material for the

study of the early German Jewish community. For the history of this
community from the 1850s through the early twentieth century, one must
consult the archives of the Indianapolis Hebrew Congregation. The
synagogue has retained its own minute books from 1856 to the present,
and these were critical in understanding the formative years of the community, as were the minute book of the Tree of Life Mutual Benefit Association (1870–1882), and the minute books and records of the Montefiore
Society (1893–1898). The Indianapolis Hebrew Congregation Archives also
possesses copies of several extremely rare Indianapolis Jewish publications: *Jewish Youth* (1894), *Menorah* (1910–1914), and *Schmooz Gazette*
(1906). (The latter two were published by the Indianapolis B'nai B'rith
lodge.)

For the period from 1900 through the 1920s, three collections at the
American Jewish Historical Society, Waltham, Massachusetts, were very
important. The records of the Baron De Hirsch Fund and the Industrial
Removal Office contain an extraordinary amount of correspondence between Indianapolis Jewish communal leaders and the New York offices of
these organizations that were sending immigrants to Indianapolis. Many
subjects relevant to the history of Indianapolis are touched on in these
letters—industrial conditions, employment, residential patterns, Jewish-
Christian relations, intracommunal conflict, and immigrant adjustment,
to name a few. Lastly, George Rabinoff's papers were critical for understanding the transformation of the community in the 1920s. Rabinoff, director of the Jewish Federation in the 1920s, helped to guide the Federation
through a period of change. Mention should also be made of Milton Steinberg's papers at the American Jewish Historical Society, although they
were not available at the time this history was written. Steinberg was
rabbi of Congregation Beth-El Zedeck from 1928 to 1933.

Newspapers were another important source for this history. The best
collection of Indiana Jewish newspapers is at the Indiana State Library.
They have complete runs of the *Indiana Jewish Chronicle, Indiana Jewish
Post and Opinion,* and *Indiana Jewish Tribune.*

Notes

Introduction

1. Alvin Chenkin and Maynard Miran, "Jewish Population in the United States," *American Jewish Year Book* 81 (1981): 170.
2. John Higham, "Social Discrimination Against Jews in America, 1830–1930," *Publications of the American Jewish Historical Society* 47 (1957): 26.
3. *Indianapolis News*, December 6, 1894.
4. *Indianapolis News*, Oct. 28, 1950.
5. James H. Madison, *Indiana Through Tradition and Change* (Indianapolis, 1982), pp. 3–6.

I. Point of Arrival

1. *Indianapolis Daily Citizen*, Oct. 26, 1858.
2. *Ibid.*
3. The three most populous Indiana cities in 1850 were New Albany, 8,181; Indianapolis, 8,091; Madison, 8,012; by 1860 the three most populous were Indianapolis, 18,611; New Albany, 12,647; Evansville, 11,484. John D. Barnhart and Donald F. Carmony, *Indiana; From Frontier to Industrial Commonwealth*, 4 vols. (New York, 1954), 1: 419; Emma Lou Thornbrough, *Indiana in the Civil War Era, 1850–1880* (Indianapolis, 1965), pp. 557–59.
4. Henry Feingold, *Zion in America* (New York, 1974), pp. 63–65; Louis Berg, "Founders and Fur Traders," *Commentary* 51 (May 1971): 80–81.

5. Joseph Levine, *John Jacob Hays, The First Known Jewish Resident of Fort Wayne* (Fort Wayne, 1973), pp. 1, 3, 6; Ira Rosenswaike, "The Jewish Population of the U.S. as Estimated from the Census of 1820," in *The Jewish Experience in America*, ed. Abraham J. Karp, 5 vols. (Waltham, 1969), 2: 15; Malcolm Stern, *First American Jewish Families* (Cincinnati, 1978), p. 106.

6. Barnhart and Carmony, *Indiana*, 1: 164–65; Rosenswaike, "Jewish Population of 1820," p. 15. While the 1820 census did not ask religious affiliation, the Jewish names in the census have been identified through other sources.

7. *Dictionary of American Biography*, s.v. "Judah, Samuel"; *Encyclopaedia Judaica*, s.v. "Judah"; Stern, *First American*, p. 141. Collections of Judah family papers, 1787–1927, are in the Lilly Library of Indiana University, Bloomington, and in the Indiana Historical Society Library, Indianapolis.

8. Rosenswaike, "Jewish Population of 1820," p. 15; David Philipson, "The Jewish Pioneers of the Ohio Valley," *Publications of the American Jewish Historical Society* 8 (1900): 43–46; I. Harold Sharfman, *Jews on the Frontier* (Chicago, 1977), p. 170.

9. Feingold, *Zion in America*, pp. 68–69.

10. Selma Stern-Taeubler, "The Motivation of the German Jewish Emigration to America in the Post-Mendelssohnian Era," in *Essays in American Jewish History* (Cincinnati, 1958), pp. 249–55; *Allgemeine Zeitung des Judentums*, Sept. 28, 1839, quoted in Joseph L. Blau and Salo W. Baron, eds., *The Jews of the United States, 1790–1840, A Documentary History*, 3 vols. (New York, 1963), 3: 804.

11. Eric E. Hirshler, ed., *Jews from Germany in the United States* (New York, 1955), pp. 36–37; Bernard Baum, "Recollection," typescript (1902–1903), p. 8, Indiana Historical Society Library.

12. Jacob P. Dunn, *Indiana and Indianans*, 5 vols. (Chicago, 1919), 3: 1544; *Indianapolis Star*, Aug. 15, 1934; Edward and Louis Frohman Day Book, Rushville, Ind., and interview with Harold Wolf, Wabash, Ind., quoted in William W. Wimberly II, *The Jewish Experience in Indiana Before the Civil War: An Introduction* (Fort Wayne, 1976), pp. 8–9; *Encyclopaedia Judaica*, s.v. "Gimbel," "Indiana"; Elizabeth Weinberg, Madison, Ind., November, 1980, personal communication.

13. Frederick D. Kershner, Jr., "A Social and Cultural History of Indianapolis" (Ph.D. diss., University of Wisconsin, 1950), pp. 1–9; Edward A. Leary, *Indianapolis: The Story of a City* (Indianapolis, 1971), pp. 61-68; Thornbrough, *Indiana in the Civil War*, pp. 322–40, 557–59.

14. Myra M. Auerbach, "A Study of the Jewish Settlement in Indianapolis" (M.A. thesis, Indiana University, 1933), pp. 3–4; Jacob P. Dunn, *Greater Indianapolis*, 2 vols. (Chicago, 1910), 1: 628. Dunn and Auerbach each give slightly different versions of the story of the first arrivals. According to Dunn, the first Jewish settlers were Moses Woolf and Alexander and Daniel Franco of Plymouth, England, who came in 1849. However, the name of Daniel Franco does not appear in the city directory until 1857. Auerbach records Woolf and Alexander Franco as the first Jewish residents of the city, having sailed from Plymouth, England, in 1849. However, she describes Woolf as a married man. Neither account mentions Sarah Franco.

U.S. Federal Census 1850, Indiana, Marion County, p. 222. The names of all the signers of the IHC bylaws and constitution of 1856 were checked in the index to the 1850 federal census for Indiana. No other known Jews appeared in the census index for Marion County. Nothing more is known about Abraham Joseph. *Indianapolis Journal*, June 15, 1901. Frederick Knefler (1833–1901), the younger son of the family, enlisted as a private in Company H, 11th Indiana Volunteers, during the Civil War and retired with the rank of brigadier general, the highest rank held by a Jew in the Union Army. Knefler, who did not personally identify himself as a Jew, served as chairman of the board charged with the supervision of the construction of the Soldiers' and Sailors' Monument at the Circle. He did not live to see it completed.

15. *Occident* 10 (April 1852): 50; Isaac M. Wise, *Reminiscences*, trans. and ed. David Philipson (Cincinatti, 1901), pp. 292, 294.

16. Dunn, *Greater Indianapolis*, 1: 628; Ethel and David Rosenberg, *To 120 Years! A Social History of the Indianapolis Hebrew Congregation* (Indianapolis, 1979), pp. 11–13. The fourteen founders were Moses Woolf, Herman Semmons, Adolph Dessar, Max Glaser, Julius Glaser, Dr. Nathan Knefler, Adolph Rosenthal, Dr. Isaac M. Rosenthal, Alexander Franco, Daniel Franco, Jacob Goldman, Herman Bamberger, Henry Rosenthal (then of Kokomo; he later moved to Indianapolis), and Moses Heller (of Knightstown). The first officers were Moses Woolf, president; Dr. Isaac M. Rosenthal, vice-president; Max Glaser, treasurer; Adolph Dessar, secretary; Max Dernham, Adolph Rosenthal, and Julius Glaser, trustees.

17. Indianapolis City Directories, 1855–1870.

18. *Ibid.*; *Indianapolis Journal*, Mar. 2, June 15, 1901; R. G. Dun and Company Credit Reports, Indiana, v. 67 (1861–1884), Dun & Bradstreet Collection, Baker Library, Graduate School of Business Administration, Harvard University, Cambridge, Mass.; *American Israelite*, Nov. 6, 1868.

19. *American Israelite*, Nov. 6, 1868; IHC Minute Book, 1856–1875, Nov. 2, 1856, IHC Archives, Indianapolis.

20. IHC Minute Book, 1856–1875, Aug., Sept. 13, Sept. 22, Oct. 18, 1857.

21. *Ibid.*, July 4, Aug. 8, Aug. 22, 1858; *Occident* 17 (Apr. 28, 1859): 30.

22. Marc L. Raphael, *Jews and Judaism in a Midwestern Community: Columbus, Ohio, 1840–1975* (Columbus, 1979), p. 62; *Encyclopaedia Judaica*, s.v. "Bamberger, Seligmann Baer"; IHC Minute Book, 1856–1875, Oct. 3, Oct. 31, 1858.

23. IHC Minute Book, 1856–1875, Dec. 6, 1856; Dunn, *Greater Indianapolis*, 1: 628; Morris M. Feuerlicht, "A Hoosier Rabbinate," in *Lives and Voices*, ed. Stanley F. Chyet (Philadelphia, 1972), p. 176.

24. Leary, *Indianapolis*, p. 72; IHC Minute Book, 1856–1875, Oct. 3, 1858.

25. Kershner, "History of Indianapolis," pp. 13–18; Leary, *Indianapolis*, pp. 75–76; IHC Minute Book, 1856–1875, Oct. 3, 1858.

26. IHC Minute Book, 1856–1875, Oct. 2, Mar. 6, 1859, Oct. 7, Dec. 2, 1860.

27. Dunn, *Greater Indianapolis*, 1: 628; Indianapolis City Directories, 1864, p. 299; 1865–1866, p. 121; 1867, p. 321; 1878; *Die Deborah* 4 (April 15, 1859): 278; IHC Minute Book, 1856–1875, Sept. 8, 1861. The first

officers of the Tree of Life Mutual Benefit Association were Maurice
Solomon, president; John W. Lyons, vice-president; C. B. Feibleman, secretary; A. Garratt, treasurer. The first officers of the Hebrew Ladies Benevolent Society were Mrs. Alexander Franco, president; Mrs. M. Myer, vice-president; Mrs. Adolph Dessar, secretary; Mrs. Julius Glaser, treasurer; Mrs. Max Glaser, Mrs. Rosenthal, and Mrs. Riedenberg, trustees.

28. Tree of Life Mutual Benefit Association Minute Book, 1870–1882, IHC Archives.

29. IHC Minute Book, 1856–1875, Oct. 2, Mar. 6, 1859, Oct. 7, Dec. 2, 1860.

30. *Ibid.*, Sept. 8, 1861.

31. *Ibid.*, Apr. 18, 1858; Herman Bamberger, "The Indianapolis Hebrew Congregation," in *Temple Fair Journal*, ed. Ralph Bamberger (Indianapolis, 1899), n.p.

32. IHC Minute Book, 1856–1875, Sept. 28, May 4, June 3, 1862, Oct. 4, 1863; Rosenberg, *To 120 Years!*, pp. 27–28.

33. Lloyd P. Gartner, *History of the Jews of Cleveland* (Cleveland, 1978), p. 33; Louis J. Swichkow and Lloyd P. Gartner, *The History of the Jews of Milwaukee* (Philadelphia, 1963), pp. 42, 50, 370.

34. Rosenberg, *To 120 Years!*, pp. 27–28; Thornbrough, *Indiana in the Civil War*, pp. 470–79; IHC Minute Book, 1856–1875, Oct. 4, 1863.

35. Rosenberg, *To 120 Years!*, p. 28; Bertram W. Korn, *American Jewry and the Civil War* (Philadelphia, 1951), p. 26.

36. Rosenberg, *To 120 Years!*, pp. 28, 32. The members of the fundraising committee were Moses Myer, Moses Woolf, A. Hays, Leon Kahn, Herman Bamberger, E. M. Hays, and Joseph Solomon. The members of the schoolhouse committee were Joseph Mitchel, Felix Deitsch, and E. Marcus.

37. Rosenberg, *To 120 Years!*, p. 32.

38. Kershner, "History of Indianapolis," pp. 52–54; Robert G. Barrows, "A Demographic Analysis of Indianapolis, 1870–1920" (Ph.D. diss., Indiana University, 1977), pp. 17–18.

39. Dun Credit Reports, Indiana, pp. 120/107, 106/119, 78/ 65; Indianapolis City Directory, 1864, pp. 80, 116. Herman Bamberger served in the 107th Infantry during the war, as did David Dessar of the clothing firm of Dessar Bros., who was a lieutenant. Simon Wolf, *The American Jew as Patriot, Soldier and Citizen* (New York, 1895), pp. 173–74.

40. Auerbach, "Jewish Settlement in Indianapolis," p. 39.

41. Dun Credit Ledgers, Indiana, pp. 120/107, 226/229, 217/220, 128/131.

42. Wolf, *The American Jew*, pp. 172–79; *Daily Evening Gazette*, May 1, 1865; Rosenberg, *To 120 Years!*, p. 30.

43. *Temple Fair Journal*, n.p.; *General Ordinances of the City of Indianapolis* (Indianapolis, 1904), p. xviii; *Indiana Daily State Sentinel*, May 2, 1865.

44. *Indiana Daily State Sentinel*, Jan. 28, 1860.

45. Charles Kettleborough, *Constitution Making in Indiana*, 3 vols. (Indianapolis, 1916), 2: 62.

46. George Theodore Probst, "The Germans in Indianapolis, 1850–1914" (M.A. thesis, Indiana University, 1951), pp. 64, 65, 69.

47. Thornbrough, *Indiana in the Civil War*, p. 554; Kershner, "History of Indianapolis," p. 51; Barrows, "Demographic Analysis of Indianapolis," pp. 57, 61; Robert L. Lafollette, "Foreigners and their Influence on Indiana," *Indiana Magazine of History* 25 (1929): 21.

48. Rosenberg, *To 120 Years!*, pp. 34–38; *Indianapolis Star*, Jan. 31, 1930; Dunn, *Greater Indianapolis*, 1: 629; Mayer Messing, List of circumcisions performed, 1871–1910, recorded in a copy of *Sod Haschem* (Vienna, 1837), IHC Archives.

49. Rosenberg, *To 120 Years!*, pp. 38–39.

50. W. R. Holloway, *Indianapolis: A Historical and Statistical Sketch of the Railroad City* (Indianapolis, 1870), p. 242; Barrows, "Demographic Analysis of Indianapolis," pp. 22–24; Kershner, "History of Indianapolis," p. 67.

51. Auerbach, "Jewish Settlement in Indianapolis," pp. 42–43.

II. Achievement and Acceptance

1. Charlotte Cathcart, *Indianapolis From Our Old Corner* (Indianapolis, 1965), pp. 9, 12; Claude Bowers, *My Life* (New York, 1962), p. 14; Meredith Nicholson, "Indianapolis: A City of Homes," *Atlantic Monthly*, June 1904, p. 839.

2. Nicholson, "City of Homes," p. 836.

3. Frederick D. Kershner, Jr., "A Social and Cultural History of Indianapolis" (Ph.D. diss., University of Wisconsin, 1950), p. 159.

4. Indianapolis City Directories, 1874–1899.

5. *Ibid.*, 1900–1935.

6. *Indianapolis Star*, Mar. 12, 1914, Dec. 31, 1947.

7. *Ibid.*, Oct. 25, 1950, July 21, 1936.

8. *Ibid.*, Mar. 12, 1914; Anna McKenzie, *Red Book of Indianapolis* (Indianapolis, 1895), pp. 67–68. In February 1969, Genesco, Inc., a Nashville, Tennessee conglomerate, purchased L. Strauss and Company, then the oldest retail establishment in the city. In August 1979, Thad Larson, the firm's president, purchased L. Strauss from Genesco, making it the only major store in Indianapolis today that is locally owned. *Indianapolis News*, Feb. 20, 1969, Aug. 1, 1979.

9. *Indianapolis Star*, Dec. 12, 1928, Oct. 25, 1950, Dec. 31, 1947.

10. John D. Barnhart and Donald F. Carmony, *Indiana: From Frontier to Industrial Commonwealth*, 4 vols. (New York, 1954), 4: 587–88.

11. *Indianapolis Star*, Dec. 12, 1928; *Indianapolis Star Magazine* (sesquicentennial edition), Apr. 17, 1966; *Indianapolis Times*, July 1, 1962.

12. *Indianapolis News*, Nov. 5, 1946; *Indianapolis Star*, Feb. 15, 1955, Oct. 25, 1950; *Indianapolis Times*, Apr. 16, 1941; *Indianapolis Star*, Dec. 31, 1947, Oct. 25, 1950; C. W. Efroymson, Indianapolis, Ind., December 1981, personal communication. During Walter Wolf's presidency, Wasson's became the city's first major department store to move into a regional shopping center—Eastgate—in 1957. Under the guidance of Wolf and then his son Louis C. (1927–1967), who became president in 1963, additional branches were established in and beyond Marion County. In August 1967 Louis Wolf and his sixteen-year-old son William were killed when their single-engine plane crashed in a swampy area near Nabesna, Alaska. Wolf,

who piloted the plane, and his son were on a bear-hunting trip. Two months later Wasson's was sold to Goldblatt Brothers of Chicago, but under their management quality declined and eventually the stores became unprofitable. In 1979, the main store at Meridian and Washington streets was closed; in 1980, Goldblatt's closed the remaining Wasson's stores as well. *Indianapolis Times*, Oct. 25, 1959, Jan. 6, 1963; *Indianapolis Star*, Aug. 28, Sept. 8, Oct. 30, 1967, Apr. 8, 1980; interview with C. W. Efroymson, Dec. 21, 1979.

13. Ethel and David Rosenberg, *To 120 Years! A Social History of the Indianapolis Hebrew Congregation* (Indianapolis, 1979), pp. 189, 183; *Indianapolis News*, Nov. 5, 1946.

14. Jacob P. Dunn, *Indiana and Indianans*, 5 vols. (Chicago, 1919), 4: 1678; *Indianapolis Star*, Aug. 15, 1934.

15. Dunn, *Indiana and Indianans*, 4: 1678; *Indianapolis Star*, Aug. 15, 1934.

16. Job Offers Accepted, Job Offers Declined, Indianapolis, Industrial Removal Office Records (IRO), American Jewish Historical Society, Waltham, Mass.; Maude Louvenbruck, *The Near-Southside Community, As It Was—And As It Is* (Indianapolis, 1974), pp. 6, 15.

17. Dunn, *Indiana and Indianans*, 4: 1678; Jewish Federation of Indianapolis, *Annual Report*, 1906, 1907; *Indianapolis Star*, Dec. 31, 1948, Nov. 2, 1954; Martha Bellinger, "Music in Indianapolis, 1900–1944, *Indiana Magazine of History* 42 (Mar. 1946): 61–62.

18. "Sol S. Kiser," *Indianapolis Men of Affairs, 1923* (Indianapolis, 1923), p. 347.

19. *Ibid.*; "Sol Meyer," *Indianapolis Men of Affairs*, p. 435; *Indianapolis News*, Nov. 17, 1939; *Indianapolis Star*, Nov. 13, 1935, May 12, 1931.

20. Jewish Federation of Indianapolis, Board of Governors, Minute Book, 1905–1908, Sept.–Oct., 1905, JWF Records, Indiana Historical Society Library, Indianapolis.

21. Morris M. Feuerlicht, "A Hoosier Rabbinate," in *Lives and Voices*, ed. Stanley F. Chyet (Philadelphia, 1972), pp. 166–67; "Sol S. Kiser," *Indianapolis Men of Affairs*, p. 347; Indianapolis Jewish Federation, IRO Records; Samuel Joseph, *History of the Baron de Hirsch Fund* (n.p., 1935), pp. 184–204; *Indianapolis Star*, Nov. 13, 1935; McKenzie, *Red Book of Indianapolis*, pp. 67–68; Rosenberg, *To 120 Years!*, p. 189; *Temple Fair Journal*, ed. Ralph Bamberger (Indianapolis, 1899), n.p.

22. "Sol S. Kiser," *Indianapolis Men of Affairs*, p. 347.

23. *Indianapolis Star*, Dec. 17, 1917; "Sol S. Kiser," *Indianapolis Men of Affairs*, p. 347.

24. *Indianapolis News*, Nov. 17, 1939.

25. Jacob P. Dunn, *Greater Indianapolis*, (Chicago, 1910), 2: 814; *Indianapolis News*, Sept. 21, 1922.

26. *Indianapolis Star*, Feb. 2, 1935; *Indianapolis News*, Sept. 21, 1922.

27. *Indianapolis Star*, Feb. 2, 1935; Dunn, *Greater Indianapolis*, 2: 814; "Samuel Elias Rauh," *Indianapolis Men of Affairs*, p. 521.

28. *Indianapolis Star*, Dec. 31, 1947.

29. *Indianapolis Star*, Dec. 21, 1928; Kershner, "History of Indianapolis," p. 126; *General Ordinances of the City of Indianapolis* (Indianapolis, 1904), p. xxviii.

30. *Indianapolis Star*, Dec. 21, 1928.

31. *Temple Fair Journal*, n.p.; *Indianapolis Star*, Aug. 27, 1939, Oct. 17, 1934; Jewish Federation of Indianapolis, Board of Governors, Minute Book, 1905–1908, Oct. 17, 1905; *Indianapolis Star*, Feb. 2, 1935; Rosenberg, *To 120 Years!*, p. 48.

32. Jewish Federation of Indianapolis, Board of Governors, Minute Book, 1905–1908; Jewish Federation of Indianapolis, *Annual Report*, 1905–1926; *Indianapolis Star*, Feb. 4, 1959; *Woman's Who's Who of America, 1914–1915*, s.v. "Rauh, Flora Mayer"; Feuerlicht, "A Hoosier Rabbinate," pp. 166–67; Jewish Federation of Indianapolis, Board of Governors and Executive Committee, Minute Books, 1914–1916, 1916–1919, 1919–1928.

33. "Louis Newberger," *Indiana State Bar Association Report* (Indianapolis, 1916), p. 369–70; "Louis Newberger," *Courts and Lawyers of Indiana*, 3 vols., ed. Leander J. Monks (Indianapolis, 1916), 3: 1352–53; "Prominent Indiana Lawyers," *Temple Fair Journal*, n.p.

34. "Nathan Morris," *Indiana State Bar Association Report* (Indianapolis, 1903), pp. 144–46; "Nathan Morris," *Courts and Lawyers of Indiana*, 3: 1378.

35. "Louis Newberger," *Indiana Bar Report*, p. 372; Jewish Federation of Indianapolis, *Annual Report*, 1906–1914; Jewish Federation of Indianapolis, Board of Governors and Executive Committee, Minute Book, 1914–1916; Feuerlicht, "A Hoosier Rabbinate," pp. 166–67.

36. *Indianapolis Journal*, Apr. 13, 1903.

37. *Ibid.*, Apr. 15, 1903.

38. Reform Advocate, *History of the Jews of Indianapolis* (Chicago, 1909), p. 15; Jewish Federation of Indianapolis, *Annual Report*, 1906; *Indianapolis Star Magazine*, Apr. 5, 1908; Woodburn Masson and George Shirts, comp., *Municipal Code of the City of Indianapolis* (Indianapolis, 1917), p. 521.

39. *Indianapolis News*, Apr. 28, 1947; *Indianapolis Star*, Feb. 4, 1954; Rosenberg, *To 120 Years!*, pp. 182–84.

40. *Indianapolis News*, June 5, 1965; *Indianapolis Star*, Jan. 24, 1949.

41. *Indianapolis Star*, Jan. 24, 1958.

42. *Indianapolis News*, Apr. 28, 1927.

43. McKenzie, *Red Book of Indianapolis*, pp. 74–120.

44. Stephen Birmingham, *"Our Crowd"; The Great Jewish Families of New York* (New York, 1967), pp. 257–58; E. Digby Baltzell, *Philadelphia Gentlemen; The Making of a National Upper Class* (Glencoe, 1958), pp. 19–21; E. Digby Baltzell, *The Protestant Establishment; Aristocracy and Caste in America* (New York, 1964), p. 27.

45. For a more extensive discussion of Jewish political and civic activism see William Toll, *The Making of an Ethnic Middle Class; Portland Jewry Over Four Generations* (Albany, N.Y., 1982), pp. 77–80. Rosenberg, *To 120 Years!*, pp. 47, 59; *Universal Jewish Encyclopedia*, s.v. "Indianapolis"; *Indianapolis Star*, Aug. 30, 1943; *Indianapolis News*, June 10, 1941.

46. *General Ordinances of Indianapolis*, pp. xviii, xxviii; *Indianapolis News*, Apr. 28, 1947, Apr. 18, 1924; John Braeman, *Albert J. Beveridge, American Nationalist* (Chicago, 1971), pp. 74, 142; *Indiana Jewish Chronicle*, Aug. 29, 1924; *Indianapolis Star*, Aug. 28, 1924, Apr. 9, 1905.

47. Cleaver to Judah, May 5, 1887, Box 2, Judah-Brandon Papers, Indiana Historical Society Library.

48. Claude G. Bowers, *Indianapolis in the "Gay Nineties,"* ed. Holman Hamilton and Gayle Thornbrough (Indianapolis, 1964), pp. 85, 92–96, 100–101, 115, 118–19, 147, 149, 186.

49. Rosenberg, *To 120 Years!*, p. 46.

50. *Ibid.*, pp. 46–47.

51. *Ibid.*, pp. 49–52; *Temple Fair Journal*, n.p.; Feuerlicht, "A Hoosier Rabbinate," p. 177. The Moses window was later moved, minus the magnificent purple flowing robes, to the congregation's building at 6501 North Meridian Street. C. W. Efroymson, Indianapolis, Ind., Dec., 1981, personal communication.

52. Rosenberg, *To 120 Years!*, pp. 52–53.

53. Feuerlicht, "A Hoosier Rabbinate," pp. 154–62.

54. Feuerlicht, "A Hoosier Rabbinate," pp. 183–225. Before debating Feuerlicht, Darrow had debated Rabbi Jacob Tarshish in Columbus and Rabbi Barnett R. Brickner in Cleveland on the same topic. For the Columbus debate see Marc L. Raphael, *Jews and Judaism in a Midwestern Community: Columbus, Ohio, 1840–1975* (Columbus, 1979), p. 270.

55. Feuerlicht, "A Hoosier Rabbinate," pp. 158–59; *Indianapolis Times*, Apr. 15, 1955; National Council of Jewish Women, Indianapolis, Scrapbook No. 1, 1896–1933, in possession of Mrs. Mary Fink, Indianapolis; National Council of Jewish Women, *Proceedings of the First Convention, Held at N.Y., Nov. 15–19, 1896* (Philadelphia, 1897), pp. 77–78.

56. Reform Advocate, *History*, p. 23; *Schmooz Gazette*, Dec. 3, 1906, IHC Archives, Indianapolis; *Menorah*, 1 (Aug. 1910).

57. *Schmooz Gazette*, Dec. 3, 1906.

58. Isidore Feibleman, "The Old Youths' Social," *Jewish Youth* 1 (Mar. 15, 1894): 26–28.

59. Feibleman, "Youths' Social," p. 28.

60. *The First Year of the Montefiore Society, 1893–1894* (Indianapolis, 1894); Montefiore Society Minute Book, 1897–1898, IHC Archives; *Montefiore Magazine* 2 (Oct. 1894); "A Show of Minstrelsy," Oct. 29, 1896, IHC Archives.

61. *Jewish Youth* 1 (Feb.–July 1894); Montefiore Society Minute Book, 1897–1898.

III. Immigrants and Natives

1. "Indianapolis," *Ha-Meliz*, no. 77, 1884, p. 1237.

2. Nathan Glazer, *American Judaism*, 2d. ed., rev. (Chicago, 1972), p. 60; Henry Feingold, *Zion in America* (New York, 1974), p. 120.

3. W. R. Holloway, *Indianapolis: A Historical and Statistical Sketch of the Railroad City* (Indianapolis, 1870), p. 242; George Rabinoff, "The Jewish Federation of Indianapolis," typescript (1928), p. 2, JWF Records, Indiana Historical Society Library, Indianapolis; *Indianapolis News*, Dec. 6, 1894, May 14, 1904; *American Jewish Year Book* 10 (1907): 173; 13 (1911): 267–68; 16 (1914): 354; 17 (1915): 191; 22 (1920): 373; 30 (1928): 107; 52 (1951): 18; 57 (1956): 127; 62 (1960): 58; 73 (1972): 389; 74 (1973):

311; 75 (1974–1975): 308; 79 (1979): 183. In 1915 the Jewish Federation reported to the *American Jewish Year Book* that the Jewish population was 8,000. From 1918 until 1947 the Federation estimated that the population remained at about 10,000. This was revised down to 7,000 after the population survey of 1948. In the 1950s the Jewish population was estimated at between 8,000 and 8,500. In the 1970s it was estimated at 10,000. Since 1978 the Jewish Welfare Federation has estimated it at between 10,000 and 11,000. Jewish Welfare Federation, *Population Survey Tables* (Indianapolis, 1948); *Jewish Encyclopedia*, s.v. "Indianapolis," "United States"; Myra M. Auerbach, "A Study of the Jewish Settlement in Indianapolis" (M. A. thesis, Indiana University, 1933), p. 45; *Universal Jewish Encyclopedia*, s.v. "Indianapolis"; *Encyclopaedia Judaica*, s.v. "Indianapolis." National estimates of Jewish population were made in 1926 and 1936 by the Jewish Statistical Bureau in conjunction with the Decennial Census of Religious Bodies of the United States Census Bureau. In 1948 the *American Jewish Year Book* asked local federations and field reporters of fund-raising organizations to estimate local population. They found that the new figures were considerably lower than the 1937 figures in a majority of the cities. The *Year Book* staff concluded that the 1937 figures were too high. *American Jewish Year Book* 50 (1948): 650–82.

4. *American Jewish Year Book* 16 (1914–1915): 354; Samuel B. Kaufman to H. L. Sabsovich, June 10, 1910, Baron De Hirsch Fund Records, American Jewish Historical Society, Waltham, Mass.; Crystal Brenton Fall, "The Foreigner in Indianapois" (M.A. thesis, Indiana University, 1916), n.p.

5. Holloway, *Indianapolis*, p. 242; Maude Louvenbruck, *The Near-Southside Community, As It Was—And As It Is* (Indianapolis, 1974), pp. 3–10; Congregation Sharah Tefilla, *Golden Jubilee* (Indianapolis, 1932), p. 2; Indianapolis City Directories, 1873–1879.

6. Charles Feibleman, "Highlights of the History of the Indianapolis Jewish Community" (Speech given at the Indianapolis celebration of the American Jewish Tercentenary, November 25, 1954), pp. 7–8, JWF Records; Indianapolis City Directories, 1880–1890.

7. Congregation Sharah Tefilla, *Golden Jubilee*, p. 2; conversation with Leigh Darbee, May 6, 1981.

8. Aryeh Lev [Louis] Hurwich, *Zikhronot meḥannekh ivri* (Boston, 1960), p. 12. The citations are to an English manuscript translation of Hurwich's chapter on Indianapolis by M. E. Hodes. Another translation of the chapter appears in a privately printed volume by Ben Z. Neustadt, *A Tree of Life* (Columbus, Ohio, 1975); Kaufman to David M. Bressler, Sept. 18, 1910, Indianapolis Jewish Federation, Industrial Removal Office Records (IRO), American Jewish Historical Society, Waltham, Mass.; interview with William B. Miller, June 29, 1981.

9. Indianapolis City Directories, 1884–1900.

10. *Ibid.*, 1893–1900; "Indianapolis Jewish Bruder Verein," *Menorah* 3 (Jan. 1913): 4.

11. Congregation Knesses Israel, *Golden Anniversary* (Indianapolis, 1944), n.p.

12. Indianapolis City Directories, 1884–1904; Congregation Knesses Israel, *Golden Anniversary*, n.p.; Hurwich, *Zikhronot*, pp. 11–12; *Indianapolis News*, May 14, 1904; *Indianapolis Star*, Jan. 31, 1930.

13. Benjamin Fishbein to Charles I. Hoffman, July 1904?, Charles I. Hoffman Papers, Jewish Theological Seminary Archives, New York City.

14. Hoffman Papers; *Encyclopaedia Judaica*, s.v. "Hoffman, Charles"; Mrs. Nandor [Ruth] Fruchter, *Congregation B'nai Torah: The First 50 Years* (Indianapolis, 1973), p. 17.

15. Diary, Hoffman Papers.

16. Diary, Hoffman Papers; *Encyclopaedia Judaica*, s.v. "Hoffman, Charles."

17. Fruchter, *Congregation B'nai Torah*, pp. 17–19.

18. Auerbach, "The Jewish Settlement," p. 13. A directory of local organizations in the *American Jewish Year Book* of 1907 listed one additional synagogue for Indianapolis, Beth Hamedrosh Hagodol. According to the directory, the congregation was established in 1902; it was located at S. Illinois and McCarty streets; and its rabbi was Isaac E. Neustadt, who was also listed as the rabbi of both Sharah Tefilla and Knesses Israel. Nothing more is known about this congregation. *American Jewish Year Book*, 10 (1907): 173.

19. Sylvia Nahmias Cohen, "The History of the Etz Chaim Sephardic Congregation and Community of Indianapolis," typescript (Indianapolis, 1978), p. 1; Abraham D. Lavender, "The Sephardic Revival in the U.S.: A Case of Ethnic Revival in a Minority-within-a-Minority," in *A Coat of Many Colors: Jewish Subcommunities in the U.S.*, ed. Abraham D. Lavender (Westport, Conn., 1977), p. 307; David de Sola Pool, "The Levantine Jews in the U.S.," *American Jewish Year Book* 15 (1913–1914): 212.

20. Conversation with Ann Ofengender, June 14, 1983; Jack Glazier, "Ashkenazic-Sephardic Relations in an American Jewish Community" (Paper delivered at the Central States Anthropological Society Meetings, Cleveland, Ohio, April 8, 1983), pp. 4, 7; Cohen, "Etz Chaim," p. 1; Jewish Federation, Executive Committee Minute Book, 1907–1908, July 3, Aug. 14, 1907, JWF Records.

21. Cohen, "Etz Chaim," pp. 1–4; "Turkish Double Wedding," *Menorah* 4 (Nov. 1914): 6–7; Rabinoff, "The Jewish Federation," p. 56.

22. Auerbach, "The Jewish Settlement," p. 31.

23. Rabinoff, "The Jewish Federation," pp. 60–64; Auerbach, "The Jewish Settlement," p. 14; Cohen, "Etz Chaim," p. 4; *Indiana Jewish Chronicle*, Nov. 30, 1928; interview with William B. Miller, June 29, 1981. In 1982 the Rochessim and Rochessot were still active.

24. In 1900 the officers of Mebaashereth Zion were L. M. Horinstein, president; Moses A. Rabinowitz, secretary; and A. Bryan, treasurer. Federation of American Zionists, *Proceedings of the 3d Annual Convention*, Aug., 1900 (New York, 1900), p. 79; Moses Rabinowitz to Stephen S. Wise, Dec. 1, 1898, Stephen S. Wise Papers, American Jewish Historical Society; Jewish Federation of Indianapolis, *Annual Report*, 1906, p. 11; Hurwich, *Zikhronot*, p. 110.

25. "Indianapolis Jewish Bruder Verein," *Menorah* 3 (Jan. 1913): 4; Arthur Liebman, *Jews and the Left* (New York, 1979), p. 290.

26. Jewish Federation of Indianapolis, *Annual Report*, 1909, p. 14, 1914, p. 16; Rabinoff, "The Jewish Federation," p. 65. There is also a record in 1910 of a Workmen's Circle Hall at 921 South Meridian Street. *Indianapolis Star*, Jan. 25, 1910.

27. Workmen's Circle Minute Book, 1918–1926, Apr. 28, 1918, July 3, 1919, July 21, Sept. 25, Oct. 23, 1921, Indiana Historical Society Library. The library collection was initiated in 1918. The origins of the afternoon school are obscure, but it was still in existence in the 1930s.

28. *Ibid.*

29. Conversation with Lee Barnett, Apr. 22, 1980; Liebman, *Jews and the Left*, pp. 302–305. There was at least one organization of Jewish Communists and Communist sympathizers in Indianapolis—Icor (the American Association for Jewish Colonization in the Soviet Union). Icor actively supported the Jewish colonization of Birobidzhan in the Soviet Far East (see chapter 5).

30. *Indiana Jewish Chronicle*, Apr. 13, 1923; Cohen, "Etz Chaim," p. 5; Rabinoff, "The Jewish Federation," p. 58.

31. Stanley R. Brav, "The Jewish Woman, 1861–1865," *American Jewish Archives* 17 (Apr. 1965): 49–50; *Indiana Jewish Chronicle*, Apr. 13, 1923; interview with William B. Miller, June 29, 1981.

32. The first officers of the South Side Hebrew Ladies Charity Organization were Mrs. Martin C. Schwartz, president; Mrs. L. Kaminsky Block, secretary; Mrs. H. Mazur, treasurer. "Report of the Committee on the Study of the Aged Home Situation for the Jewish Federation," typescript (Indianapolis, 1930?), p. 1; Jewish Federation Minute Book, 1905–1908, Report of the Superintendent, Oct., 1907, Sept., 1908; Jewish Federation Executive Committee Minute Book, 1908, July 28, 1908; Baron De Hirsch Fund Records, Box 55; Genevieve C. Weeks, *Oscar Carleton McCulloch, 1843–1891* (Indianapolis, 1976), p. 177.

33. Jewish Federation of Indianapolis, *Annual Report*, 1906, p. 4; Rabinoff, "The Jewish Federation," pp. 41–42.

34. "Report of the Aged Home," pp. 1–2.

35. Jewish Federation Minute Book, 1919–1928, Board of Governors, Jan. 6, Mar. 10, May 5, 1921; "Report of the Aged Home," p. 2.

36. Cohen, "Etz Chaim," pp. 7–8; Glazier, "Ashkenazic-Sephardic Relations," p. 6.

37. Officers of the Hebrew Co-operative Society were Jacob Sattinger, president; L. Horinstein, treasurer; and Louis Abramson, secretary. All three were members of Workmen's Circle. *Indianapolis Star*, Jan. 21, 22, 25, 1910; "A List of Events in 5670," *American Jewish Year Book* 12 (1910–1911): 109.

38. Paula E. Hyman, "Immigrant Women and Consumer Protest: The New York City Meat Boycott of 1902," *American Jewish History* 70 (Sept. 1980): 91, 94, 95; conversation with Lee Barnett, Apr. 22, 1980; "Arrivals thro' the Industrial Removal Office, 1911–1914," JWF Records.

39. The precise dates of these boycotts are not known. Conversation with Lee Barnett, Apr. 22, 1980; Hyman, "Immigrant Women," p. 95.

40. Ethel and David Rosenberg, *To 120 Years! A Social History of the Indianapolis Hebrew Congregation* (Indianapolis, 1979), pp. 27, 34; Indianapolis City Directories, 1894–1896; *Menorah* 2 (Nov. 1896): 362; Diary, Hoffman Papers.

41. The first officers of the United Hebrew Schools were Solomon Finkelstein, president; Charles Medias, vice-president; Moses A. Rabinowtiz, secretary; and Isaac Ciener, treasurer. Hurwich, *Zikhronot*, pp. 11–12;

Diary, Hoffman Papers; *Indianapolis Sunday Star,* Dec. 18, 1910; United Hebrew Schools Minute Book, 1911–1920, in possession of Mrs. Hilda Ettinger, Indianapolis.

42. Hurwich, *Zikhronot,* p. 12; *Encyclopaedia Judaica,* s.v. "Hurwich, Louis."

43. United Hebrew Schools Minute Book, 1911–1920, Oct. 25, Nov. 27, 1911; Hurwich, *Zikhronot,* p. 101.

44. Hurwich, *Zikhronot,* pp. 60, 73, 78, 86, 87, 91; United Hebrew Schools Minute Book, 1911–1920, July 30, 1913.

45. Hurwich, *Zikhronot,* pp. 78, 86, 96.

46. United Hebrew Schools Minute Book, 1911–1920, Mar. 20, 1912, Sept. 9, Apr. 1, 1914, Nov. 24, Feb. 3, 1915, Dec. 9, 1918; Hurwich, *Zikhronot,* pp. 99, 100, 112, 114.

47. United Hebrew Schools Minute Book, 1911–1920, July 20, Oct. 6, Nov. 10, 1915, May 3, July 12, 19, Sept. 9, Oct. 4, 1916, Apr. 7, 1919.

48. United Hebrew Schools Minute Book, 1911–1920, June 13, July 11, 1917, Mar. 10, 1919, Feb. 11, 1920.

49. Louvenbruck, *The Near-Southside,* pp. 6–7; Boxes 73, 81, IRO Records; conversation with Jack Glazier, May 6, 1981; Rabinoff, "The Jewish Federation," p. 59, "Arrivals thro' the I.R.O."

50. "Arrivals thro' the I.R.O."; Jewish Federation of Indianapolis, 1905–1909, Sol S. Kiser, 1905–1915, Boxes 73, 81, IRO Records.

51. "Arrivals thro' the I.R.O."; Jewish Federation Minute Books, 1905–1908, 1914–1916; Kaufman to Bressler, Feb. 16, 1910, IRO Records; Abraham Cronbach, "Autobiography," *American Jewish Archives* 11 (Apr. 1959): 15.

52. Conversation with Phyllis Gorfain, June 29, 1981.

53. Cohen, "Etz Chaim," pp. 2–3; conversation with Jack Glazier, May 6, June 29, 1981.

54. Although Jewish physicians such as Edgar Kiser tried to discourage women from using her, "Tia" (aunt) Rackel Camhi was the Sephardic community's midwife for many years. Cohen, "Etz Chaim," p. 7; conversation with Jack Glazier, June 29, 1981.

55. Cohen, "Etz Chaim," p. 8; Jewish Federation Minute Book, 1914–1916; *Indianapolis Star,* July 23, 1976.

56. Frederick D. Kershner, Jr., "A Social and Cultural History of Indianapolis" (Ph.D. diss., University of Wisconsin, 1950), p. 165; *Indianapolis Star,* July 23, 1976; *Indianapolis Times,* Feb. 6, 1957; conversation with Hilda Ettinger, June 17, 1980; *Indianapolis Star,* May 24, 1957.

57. Interview with Jules Medias, July 17, 1981; *Indianapolis News,* Nov. 1, 1938, Apr. 18, 1940.

58. Interview with Jules Medias, July 17, 1981.

59. Interview with William B. Miller, June 29, 1981; *Indianapolis News,* Dec. 17, 1928; Hurwich, *Zikhronot,* p. 97; *Indianapolis News,* May 9, 1959; *Indianapolis Star,* Feb. 2, 1959.

60. *Indianapolis Star,* Nov. 7, 1955; *Indiana Jewish Chronicle,* Aug. 4, 1922; *Indianapolis News,* July 28, 1922.

61. Jewish Federation of Indianapolis, *Annual Report,* 1906, p. 9; Rabinoff, "The Jewish Federation," p. 3.

62. Kershner, "History of Indianapolis," p. 306; Jewish Federation of Indianapolis, *Annual Report,* 1907, p. 22, 1908, p. 31, 1910, p. 31.

63. *Indianapolis Star Magazine*, Apr. 5, 1908.

64. *Ibid.*; Jewish Federation of Indianapolis, *Annual Report*, 1908, p. 31.

65. Jewish Federation of Indianapolis, Board of Governors, Minute Book, 1905–1908, Sept. 8, 1908; Jewish Federation of Indianapolis, *Annual Report*, 1909–1911.

66. *American Jewish Year Book* 7 (1904): 52; *Indianapolis Star*, Sept. 21, 1941.

67. *Indianapolis Star*, Jan. 13, 1965; National Council of Jewish Women, Indianapolis, Scrapbook, no. 1 1896–1933, in possession of Mrs. Mary Fink, Indianapolis; Jewish Federation of Indianapolis, *Annual Report*, 1906–1914, 1923, 1928; *Indianapolis Star Magazine*, Apr. 5, 1908.

68. *Reform Advocate*, *History of the Jews of Indianapolis* (Chicago, 1909), p. 15.

69. The first officers of the Nathan Morris House were Flora Rauh, president; Caroline Kahn, secretary; and Della Krauss, financial secretary. Jewish Federation of Indianapolis, *Annual Report*, 1906; *Indianapolis Star Magazine*, Apr. 5, 1908.

70. Ralph Bamberger, "The B'nai B'rith Free Milk Station," *Menorah* 1 (Aug. 1910): 26–27; Rabinoff, "The Jewish Federation," p. 65; *Schmooz Gazette*, Dec. 3, 1906, p. 2; *Menorah* 1–4 (1910–1914).

71. Peter Romanofsky, ". . . 'To Rid Ourselves of the Burden . . .': New York Jewish Charities and the Origins of the Industrial Removal Office, 1890–1901," *American Jewish Historical Quarterly* 64 (June 1975): 332, 336–37.

72. *Ibid.*, pp. 338–40.

73. *Ibid.*, pp. 334, 338–40.

74. Morris M. Feuerlicht to Bressler, Mar. 29, 1905, Baron De Hirsch Fund Records.

75. Daniel J. Elazar, *Community and Polity* (Philadelphia, 1976), pp. 160, 163.

76. Diary, Hoffman Papers; Jewish Federation of Indianapolis, *Annual Report*, 1906, pp. 3–6.

77. Jewish Federation of Indianapolis, *Annual Report*, 1906, p. 3. According to a letter from Morris M. Feuerlicht to David M. Bressler, Mar. 29, 1905, the IRO committee consisted of: Sol S. Kiser, Chairman; Rabbi Morris M. Feuerlicht, Secretary; Jos. Borinstein, Treasurer; S. F. Helstein, Chairman, Employment Committee; B. Fishbein, Louis Borinstein, Jacob Neerenberg, A. Marer, J. W. Jackson, Martin Schwartz, Julius Fallender, E. L. Segar, Dr. H. Ostroff, Rabbi I. E. Neustadt, Rabbi A. Kantrowitz, Rabbi M. Messing, Rabbi C. I. Hoffman, Rabbi Jacob Hartman, Jos. Wineman, Louis Wolf, Henry Hamberger, A. Kirschbaum, G. Kiser, A. Weiler, S. E. Rauh, and M. Bamberger. Box 55, Baron De Hirsch Fund Records.

78. Jewish Federation of Indianapolis, *Annual Report*, 1906, pp. 15, 16, 19.

79. *Ibid.*, p. 15. The orphanage, a B'nai B'rith project, and the old-age home served cities, such as Indianapolis, that were too small to support their own institutions. The Denver hospital, another B'nai B'rith-supported institution, cared for tuberculosis patients from the entire country who were sent there for care.

80. Jewish Federation Minute Book, 1905–1908, Board of Governors, May 28, 1908.

81. Jewish Federation of Indianapolis, *Annual Report*, 1906, p. 4; Samuel J. Levinson to Bressler, June 18, 1907, Kaufman to Bresslr, Nov. 30, 1908, Local Agent: Indiana, 1905–1909, IRO Records.

82. Jewish Federation Minute Book, 1905–1908, Report of the Superintendent, Oct., 1907.

83. *Ibid.*, Report of the Superintendent, Apr., 1908.

84. Jewish Federation of Indianapolis, *Annual Report*, 1906, p. 12, 1908, pp. 4, 6, 16, 1911, p. 14; Jewish Federation Minute Book, 1905–1908, "Rules and By-Laws of the Jewish Foster Home," Aug. 19, 1907.

85. Hurwich, *Zikhronot*, p. 115; conversation with Hilda Ettinger, June 17, 1980.

86. Conversation with Jack Glazier, May 6, 1981; Glazier, "Ashkenazic-Sephardic Relations," p.6.

87. Jewish Federation Minute Book, 1919–1928, Report on Newsboy Problem, Oct. 27, 1919, Board of Governors, Dec. 4, 1919, Feb. 5, 1920. For a similar incident in Portland, Oregon see William Toll, *The Making of an Ethnic Middle Class; Portland Jewry Over Four Generations* (Albany, N.Y., 1982), pp. 62–64.

88. Jewish Federation of Indianapolis, *Annual Report*, 1906, pp. 10–12, 1914, pp. 15–16; "Communal Building Purchased," *Menorah* 3 (Jan. 1913): 4; *Indianapolis Star*, Feb. 2, 1913, Oct. 22, 1922; Dorothy Anne Forman, "A Study of the Jewish Communal Building of Indianapolis" (M.A. thesis, Indiana University, 1940), p. 16.

89. "The B'nai B'rith Free Milk Station," *Menorah* 1 (Aug. 1910): 26–27; Jewish Federation Minute Book, 1919–1928, Executive Committee, June 12, 1919, Board of Governors, Sept. 18, Oct. 30, 1919, Feb. 5, Apr. 1, May 6, July 1, Sept. 2, 1920; *Indianapolis Star*, Jan. 2, 1961.

90. Jewish Federation of Indianapolis, *Annual Report*, 1910, pp. 7, 22, 1911, p. 9, 1923, n.p.; Jewish Federation Minute Book, 1918–1919, Executive Committee, June 20, 1918, Rabinoff, "The Jewish Federation," pp. 24–26.

91. Jewish Federation Minute Book, 1919–1928, Board of Governors, Apr. 1, 1920, Aug. 5, 1926, Executive Committee, Mar. 22, 1923; Rabinoff, "The Jewish Federation," pp. 24–27; Auerbach, "The Jewish Settlement," pp. 75–76.

92. B'nai B'rith Esther Lodge No. 323 to IRO, Feb. 1, May 8, 1905, Box 23, Mayer Messing to Bressler, Nov. 25, 1903, IRO Records; Feuerlicht to Bressler, Mar. 14, 1905, Baron De Hirsch Fund Records; Kaufman to Bressler, Jan. 19, 1910, Indianapolis Jewish Federation, IRO Records.

93. Kaufman to Bressler, Jan. 13, Jan. 4, 1910, IRO Records.

94. Bressler to Edward A. Kahn, Oct. 23, 1908, *ibid.*

95. Kaufman to Bressler, Feb. 14, 1910, *ibid.*

96. Kaufman to Bressler, Jan. 5, 1910, Aug. 5, 1909, Feb. 14, Aug. 14, 1910, *ibid.*

97. Kaufman to Bressler, Feb. 14, 1910, *ibid.*

98. Charles Brodsky to IRO, Sept. 1912, miscellaneous correspondence, Kaufman to Bressler, Apr. 8, 26, 1910, *ibid.*

99. Levinson to Bressler, Nov. 13, Dec. 13, 28, 1907, G. A. Efroymson to IRO, June 3, 1908, *ibid.*

100. Jewish Federation of Indianapolis, *Annual Report*, 1906, p. 10,

1907, p. 19, 1908, p. 26, 1909, p. 15, 1910, p. 24, 1911, p. 13; "Arrivals thro' the I.R.O."; Bressler to Kaufman, Oct. 9, 1914, IRO Records.

IV. On Native Ground

1. Nathan Glazer, *American Judaism*, 2d. ed., rev. (Chicago, 1979), p. 79.

2. Jewish Federation Minute Book, 1919–1928, Board of Governors, Nov. 9, 1922, JWF Records, Indiana Historical Society Library, Indianapolis; *Jewish Post*, Dec. 14, 1934; *American Jewish Year Book* 22 (1920): 373; 30 (1928): 107; 50 (1948): 650–82; 79 (1979): 183; 81 (1981): 176.

3. Glazer, *American Judaism*, pp. 82–83.

4. *Ibid.*, p. 83.

5. Samuel B. Kaufman to David M. Bressler, Aug. 15, 1910, Indianapolis Jewish Federation, 1910–1918, Industrial Removal Office Records, American Jewish Historical Society, Waltham, Mass.; Jewish Federaton Minute Book, 1919–1928, Rabinoff to Efroymson, Feb. 15, 1925; Myra M. Auerbach, "A Study of the Jewish Settlement in Indianapolis" (M.A. thesis, Indiana University, 1933), p. 49.

6. Glazer, *American Judaism*, pp. 81–82; Auerbach, "The Jewish Settlement," p. 49.

7. Interview with C. W. Efroymson, Dec. 21, 1979.

8. John A. Davis, "The Ku Klux Klan in Indiana, 1920–1930: An Historical Study" (Ph.D. thesis, Northwestern University, 1966), pp. 9, 27, 34, 61; Kenneth T. Jackson, *The Ku Klux Klan in the City 1915–1930* (New York, 1967), p. 237.

9. Robert L. LaFollette, "Foreigners and their Influence on Indiana," *Indiana Magazine of History* 25 (1929): 27; Davis, "The Klan in Indiana," pp. 9, 34; Jackson, *Klan in the City*, pp. 243–44; James H. Madison, *Indiana Through Tradition and Change* (Indianapolis, 1982), p. 8.

10. LaFollette, "Foreigners and their Influence," p. 21; Davis, "The Klan in Indiana," p. 9.

11. Madison, *Indiana*, p. 48.

12. *Ibid.*, pp. 55, 56, 58, 66–74.

13. *Indiana Jewish Chronicle (IJC)*, Dec. 8, Oct. 27, 1922.

14. B'nai B'rith Indianapolis Lodge No. 58 Minute Book, May 11, 1923, Indiana Historical Society Library.

15. Davis, "The Klan in Indiana," p. 51; Madison, *Indiana*, p. 51; *IJC*, June 29, 15, 22, 1923; Jackson, *Klan in the City*, p. 151–52. During the term of anti-Klan mayor Samuel Lewis Shank (1921–1925), such an ordinance was almost unnecessary. Shank prohibited masked parades, ordered the arrest of news dealers handling *The Fiery Cross*, and was determined to enforce a ruling against the burning of crosses. In this Shank had the complete support of Police Chief Herman F. Rikhoff.

16. Jewish Federation of Indianapolis, *Annual Report*, 1926, p. 19; *IJC*, March 26, 1926, Oct. 12, 1923.

17. "Real Freedom" (editorial), *IJC*, Mar. 30, 1923.

18. "The Enemy Within" (editorial), *ibid.*, Mar. 7, 1924, Sept. 14, 1923.

19. Morris M. Feuerlicht, "A Hoosier Rabbinate," in *Lives and Voices,*

ed. Stanley F. Chyet (Philadelphia, 1972), p. 200; *Indianapolis Times*, Jan. 15, 1954.

20. *Indianapolis Star*, Dec. 16, 1925.

21. *IJC*, Oct. 31, 1924; conversation with Albert S. Goldstein, Jr., Mar. 18, 1980; Albert S. Goldstein, Sr., to Dorothy Schlessinger, Sept. 8, 1961, JWF Records.

22. *IJC*, Jan. 25, Mar. 21, Apr. 18, 1924; *Indianapolis Star*, Feb. 8, 1934, Nov. 1, 1973; *IJC*, Apr. 30, Oct. 29, 1926, May 18, 1928; *Indianapolis News*, May 4, 1961.

23. *IJC*, June 5, 1925, Mar. 5, 1926, Dec. 5, 1924, June 8, 1928.

24. Davis, "The Klan in Indiana," p. 318; *Indianapolis Star*, Feb. 26, 1940; *IJC*, Aug. 16, 1929, July 27, 1923; conversation with Phyllis Gorfain, June 29, 1981; *IJC*, July 13, 1923.

25. *Jewish Post*, Feb. 9, 1940.

26. Jewish Federation Minute Book, 1919–1928, Board of Governors, Sept. 17, Dec. 3, 1925.

27 *Indianapolis Times*, Jan. 29, 1953; "Leo Kaminsky," Citizens Historical Association, Marion County, Indiana State Library; Jewish Federation of Indianapolis, *Annual Report*, 1926, p. 19; Jewish Federation Minute Book, 1919–1928, Executive Committee, Jan. 28, 1926.

28. Jewish Federation of Indianapolis, *Community Life* [annual report], 1923, n.p.

29. Jewish Federation Minute Book, Executive Committee, 1914–1918.

30. Jewish Federation of Indianapolis, *Annual Report*, 1906–1927.

31. *Indianapolis Star*, Dec. 16, 1916; Jewish Federation Minute Book, 1919–1928, Executive Committee, Mar. 13, 1919, Board of Governors, Jan. 23, 1919.

32. Jewish Federation Minute Book, 1919–1928, Board of Governors, Jan. 8, 1920, Oct. 6, 1921, July 6, 1922.

33. *Ibid.*, Rabinoff to Efroymson, Feb. 15, 1925, Board of Governors, June 4, 1925, A. M. Rosenthal to Raphael Kirshbaum heirs, June 19, 1925, Board of Governors, Oct. 15, 1925, Jan. 6, 1926; *Indianapolis Star*, June 10, 1935; *IJC*, Nov. 14, 1924, June 26, 1925.

34. During the Second World War, George Rabinoff was associate director of Chicago's Jewish Charities and Jewish Welfare Fund and served the United Nations Relief and Rehabilitation Agency as deputy director of the Division of Welfare and Displaced Persons in Europe. From 1947 to 1951, he was director of the Training Bureau for Jewish Communal Service, reflecting a lifelong concern with the professional training of Jewish communal workers. For ten years, 1951–1961, he was director of the National Social Welfare Assembly. His last professional activity was to spend a year aiding the development of social work in Australia. *Encyclopaedia Judaica*, s.v. "Rabinoff, George W."; correspondence, 1921–1928, Box 5, George Rabinoff Papers, American Jewish Historical Society.

35. Jewish Federation Minute Book, 1919–1928, Board of Governors, June 10, July 8, Aug. 5, 1926, Sept. 17, 1925; *Indianapolis News*, Jan. 17, 1972; *Indianapolis Star*, Jan. 31, 1954.

36. *First Annual Report of the Jewish Community Center Association of Indianapolis* (JCCA), 1927; Jewish Federation Minute Book, 1919–1928,

Board of Governors, July 12, 1928, Jewish Welfare Fund, Executive Committee, Jan. 21, 1929.

37. *First Annual Report of the JCCA,* 1927; "The Open Forum of Indianapolis," [1926], JCCA program, 1927, JWF Records.

38. *First Annual Report of the JCCA,* 1927; JCCA program, 1927, "Dedication of the Completed Kirshbaum Community Center," [1928], JWF Records; *Second Annual Report of the JCCA,* 1928; conversation with Pearl Levi, Feb. 11, 1980; Martha Bellinger, "Music in Indianapolis, 1900–1944," *Indiana Magazine of History* 42 (Mar. 1946): 61–63; *Indianapolis Times,* Nov. 16, 1938; *Indianapolis Star,* Jan. 31, 1954, Sept. 28, 1930; *Indianapolis News,* Apr. 20, 1953.

39. Jewish Federation Minute Book, 1919–1928, Board of Governors, Oct. 6, 1921.

40. Jewish Federation of Indianapolis, *Community Life,* n.p.; George Rabinoff, "The Jewish Federation of Indianapolis," pp. 12–13, JWF Records.

41. Jewish Federation Minute Book, 1919–1928, Board of Governors, Nov. 3, 1921, Sept. 17, 1925, Executive Committee, Apr. 15, 1926, Oct. 26, 1928, Board of Governors, Dec. 9, 1926, Jan. 6, Feb. 10, 1927, Oct. 4, Dec. 6, 1928; Rabinoff, "The Jewish Federation," p. 13.

42. *IJC,* Mar. 1, 1929; "Jackiel W. Joseph," Citizens Historical Association, Marion County, Indiana State Library.

43. *Indianapolis Sunday Star,* May 5, 1918; John R. Seeley et al., *Community Chest* (Toronto, 1957), p. 89.

44. Indianapolis Community Fund, *Constitution and By-Laws* (Indianapolis, 1924), n.p.; Jewish Federation Minute Book, 1919–1928, Board of Governors, July 12, 1923.

45. Jewish Federation Minute Book, 1918–1919, Myron R. Green to Jewish Federation officers, June 29, 1918, Board of Governors, Dec., 1918, Green to Efroymson, Nov. 9, 1918, Board of Governors, Jan. 8, May 6, 1920, Dec. 8, 1927, July 7, Oct. 6, 1921.

46. *Ibid.,* 1919–1928, Executive Committee, Nov. 20, 1924, May 14, 1925; Jewish Federation of Indianapolis, *Annual Report,* 1926, p. 12.

47. Jewish Federation Minute Book, 1919–1928, Executive Committee, Dec. 1, 1921, Board of Governors, Dec. 8, 1921.

48. *Ibid.,* Board of Governors, Dec. 8, 1921, Executive Committee, Nov. 25, 1927, May 14, 1925, Feb. 4, 1926.

49. *Ibid.,* Organization Committee of the Jewish Council, Jan. 5, Feb. 16, 1927, Jewish Welfare Fund, Board of Directors, Sept. 6, 1927.

50. *Ibid.,* Jewish Welfare Fund, Board of Directors, Sept. 6, 1927.

51. *Ibid.,* Jewish Welfare Fund, Budget Committee, Apr. 12, May 2, 1927, Board of Directors, May 4, June 16, Sept. 6, 1927, Meeting of Captains of 1928 Fund Campaign, Apr. 10, 1928; *Indianapolis News,* June 10, 1941; Jewish Federation Minute Book, Jewish Welfare Fund, Board of Directors, June 16, 1927, June 18, 1928, Jewish Federation, Board of Governors, July 12, 1928.

52. For a general discussion of the development of Conservative Judaism see Marshall Sklare, *Conservative Judaism; an American Religious Movement,* New augm. ed. (New York, 1972).

53. *IJC,* Dec. 11, 1925.

54. *Ibid., IJC,* June 23, 1922; *New York Times,* July 27, 1934.

55. *IJC,* Dec. 11, 1925, Aug. 17, 1923, Mar. 28, 1924, Mar. 20, 1925.

56. *IJC,* July 18, 1924.

57. *Program, the Dedication of Beth El Synagog and Installation of Its Rabbi* (Indianapolis, 1925); *IJC,* Dec. 11, 1925; *Indianapolis News,* Dec. 14, 1925.

58. *New York Times,* Jan. 29, 1962; *IJC,* Feb. 11, 1927.

59. Congregation Beth-El Zedeck, *50th Anniversary* (Indianapolis, 1978), n.p.

60. *IJC,* Mar. 25, 1927; interview with William B. Miller, June 29, 1981.

61. Cong. Beth-El Zedeck, *50th Anniversary;* Simon Noveck, *Milton Steinberg: Portrait of a Rabbi* (New York, 1978), pp. 42–43.

62. *Ibid.,* pp. 42–45.

63. *IJC,* May 8, Nov. 13, 1925, Dec. 14, 1928, Nov. 8, 1929; *Jewish Post,* Sept. 21, 1934.

64. *Indianapolis News,* Nov. 4, 1975, Aug. 3, 1976; Thomas H. Lovelace to Sarah Wolf, May 1, 1924, in possession of Mrs. Daniel B. Wolf, Carmel, Indiana; conversation with Mrs. Daniel B. Wolf, Nov., 1981.

65. Noveck, *Steinberg,* pp. 42–43; Cong. Beth-El Zedeck, *50th Anniversary.*

66. Noveck, *Steinberg,* pp. 47–52, 288; interview with William B. Miller, June 29, 1981; interview with Julian Freeman, Jan. 9, 1980; interview with Rabbi Dennis C. Sasso, Oct. 30, 1981. Steinberg remained at Park Avenue Synagogue until his death in 1950 at the age of forty-six. He became one of the country's leading rabbis with a national reputation as a serious writer and lecturer. He wrote four books—*The Making of the Modern Jew* (1934); a novel, *As a Driven Leaf* (1939); *A Partisan Guide to the Jewish Problem* (1945); and *Basic Judaism* (1947)—as well as articles for a variety of national magazines.

67. *Indianapolis News,* July 4, 1942, Nov. 6, 1945.

68. The men who filed the incorporation papers in March, 1923, for an Orthodox synagogue and Hebrew school and served on the first board of directors were Hyman Escol, president; Herman Lipschitz, vice-president; M. E. Abrams, secretary; Samuel Thon, treasurer; Abraham Solomon, Harry Efroymson, Jacob Dorman, and Julius Dorfman. One of the early presidents was Benjamin Fishbein, who had served as the first president of the United Hebrew Congregation. *IJC,* Mar. 16, 1923; Mrs. Nandor [Ruth] Fruchter, *Congregation B'nai Torah: The First 50 Years* (Indianapolis, 1973), pp. 1–2; Central Hebrew Congregation, *20th Anniversary Celebration* (Indianapolis, 1943), n.p.

69. An enthusiastic organizer, Rabbi Fruchter labored tirelessly on behalf of Orthodox Judaism. One of his first efforts was the organization of a daily *minyan,* which cynics had believed was not possible to maintain on the north side. Fruchter buttonholed passersby into attending and often rounded up *minyan* members in his car. Under his personal care, the *minyan* succeeded and became a means of attracting new members to the congregation, which eventually became the largest Orthodox congregation in the state. With his wife, Ruth, who served as a volunteer principal until 1970, he also set up a successful Sunday school program for the congregation. Rabbi Fruchter took an active role in civic life, appearing at war bond

rallies and serving as a civilian chaplain at Billings Hospital at Fort Harrison during the Second World War. A committed Zionist, he served as president of the Mizrachi of Indianapolis (religious Zionists) and vice-president of the Indianapolis Zionist District. *IJC*, May 31, 1929; Fruchter, *Cong. B'nai Torah*, pp. 4–6; Central Hebrew Congregation, *20th Anniversary; Indianapolis Star*, Oct. 7, 1971.

70. *IJC*, Feb. 22, 1924, Jan. 15, 1926; *Indianapolis Times*, Aug. 2, 1949.

71. *IJC*, Jan. 15, 1926; Rabinoff, "The Jewish Federation," pp. 61–62; Jewish Federation Minute Book, 1919–1928, Board of Governors, Jan. 6, 1926.

72. *IJC*, Jan. 15, 1926; Rabinoff, "The Jewish Federation," p. 62; *IJC*, Mar. 29, May 3, 1929.

73. Rabinoff, "The Jewish Federation," p. 63; *IJC*, Mar. 1, 1929.

74. Jewish Federation Minute Book, 1919–1928, Board of Governors, Mar. 5, 1925; *IJC*, Apr. 3, 1925; "Distribution of Sacramental Wine," (editorial), *IJC*, Mar. 26, 1926; Rabinoff, "The Jewish Federation," p. 64.

75. *IJC*, Mar. 14, 1924.

76. *IJC*, Oct. 31, 1924, Apr. 3, 1927, Mar. 5, 1926; Leo L. Honor, *The Jewish Educational Association of Indianapolis, A Survey* (Indianapolis, 1944), pp. 2–4.

77. The first officers were Sol Trotcky, president; Max Sacks, vice-president; L. Galerman, secretary; H. Simpson, treasurer; and Rabbi Samuel A. Katz, education committee chairman. Jewish Federation Minute Book, 1919–1928, Board of Governors, Aug. 3, Nov. 9, 1922; *IJC*, Nov. 4, 1927, Nov. 2, 9, 1928, July 26, 1929.

78. The first officers of the Ivriah were A. Rosenthal, chairman; S. Friedman, treasurer; and J. Pilch, secretary. The first officers of the Yahudi Halevi Club were Joseph Calderon, president; and Hannah Calderon, secretary. The first officers of the Jewish Cultural Association were H. E. Pfeffer, general secretary; Abe Cogan, financial secretary and treasurer; Jacob Cohen, literary director; Miss B. Drucker, music director; and J. Pilch, dramatic director. *IJC*, Oct. 10, 1924, Mar. 27, 1925, Mar. 1, 1929, Jan. 23, July 31, 1925; interview with William B. Miller, June 29, 1981.

79. The first officers of the Cosmo were Lena Lee Cohen, president; Miriam Forman, treasurer; and Myra Auerbach, publicity director. The first officers of Alpha Omega were Dr. Leon W. Berger, adviser and chairman; Harry Baillie, secretary; and Ralph Kroot, treasurer. The first president of the Jewish Student Union was Theodore Dann. *IJC*, Dec. 7, Nov. 30, Dec. 14, 1928; *Jewish Post*, Mar. 30, 1934.

80. The first officers of the Yiddish Dramatic Club were J. Kaeseff, president; S. Pasken, treasurer; Irving Tamler, production committee chairman; and A. Abramoff, stage director. *IJC*, Mar. 4, Feb. 11, 1927, Nov. 13, 1925, Feb. 29, 1926, Oct. 26, 1928.

81. *IJC*, May 12, June 23, 1922, June 1, 1923; *Indianapolis Star*, Sept. 25, 1959, July 21, 1973.

V. Years of Crisis

1. *Jewish Post*, Feb. 9, 1940; Morris M. Feuerlicht, "A Hoosier Rabbinate" in *Lives and Voices*, ed. Stanley F. Chyet (Philadelphia, 1972), pp. 173–75.

2. Dixon Wecter, *The Age of the Great Depression, 1928–1941* (New York, 1952), p. 1. Hoover spoke these words upon accepting the nomination of the Republican party in August 1928 and again in his Madison Square Garden speech of October 31, 1932.

3. Jewish Federation Minute Book, Annual Meeting, Apr. 25, 1934, JWF Records, Indiana Historical Society Library, Indianapolis (IHS).

4. Myra M. Auerbach, "A Study of the Jewish Settlement in Indianapolis" (M.A. thesis, Indiana University, 1933), p. 49; Dorothy A. Forman, "A Study of the Jewish Communal Building of Indianapolis" (M.A. thesis, Indiana University, 1940), p. 1; *Indianapolis South Side Communal Building Survey* (Indianapolis, 1943), p. 5.

5. Jewish Federation Minute Book, Executive Committee, Aug. 26, 1932; Murray N. Rothbard, *America's Great Depression* (Princeton, N.J., 1963), p. 290; Margaret H. Hogg, *The Incidence of Work Shortage* (New York, 1932), pp. 82, 34.

6. Hogg, *Work Shortage*, pp. 31, 81, 74.

7. *Jewish Post*, Dec. 14, 1934; Jewish Welfare Federation, *Population Survey Tables* (Indianapolis, 1948), p. 6.

8. Robert S. Lynd and Helen M. Lynd, *Middletown in Transition* (New York, 1937), pp. 9–12, 463.

9. Robert S. Lynd, "The People as Consumers" in *Recent Social Trends in the United States*, 2 vols. (New York, 1933), 2: 864, 908; *Indianapolis Star*, Jan. 22, 1958; *Indianapolis News*, Aug. 14, 1933.

10. Lynd, *Middletown in Transition*, pp. 10, 463; Lynd, "Consumers," p. 908; *Jewish Post*, July 12, August 9, 1935; *Indianapolis News*, June 10, 1941, April 18, 1940, Nov. 19, 1932, July 7, 1952.

11. *Indianapolis Star*, Mar. 13, 1960; *Indianapolis News*, Apr. 17, 1961; *Indianapolis Times*, Aug. 20, 1962; *Indianapolis Star*, May 13, 1931.

12. Auerbach, "Jewish Settlement," p. 113; Lynd, "Consumers," pp. 897–98, 906; Sylvia Nahmias Cohen, "The History of the Etz Chaim Sephardic Congregation and Community of Indianapolis," typescript (Indianapolis, 1978), p. 7.

13. "Jews in America," *Fortune* 13 (Feb. 1936): 133. The *Fortune* study estimated that in 1929, 90 percent of the scrap iron and steel business was Jewish and "practically the whole waste-products industry, including nonferrous scrap metal . . . , paper, cotton rag, wool rag and rubber is Jewish." Some of the Jewish firms in the scrap and waste materials business in Indianapolis included J. E. Budd Co., J. Solotken and Co., A. Borinstein, Inc., Falender Iron and Metal Corp., and Epstein Bros.

14. Jewish Federation Minute Book, Executive Committee, Jan. 29, 1932, Board of Governors, Feb. 11, 1932.

15. *Ibid.*, Executive Committee, Oct. 31, Nov. 28, 1930, Jan. 30, Sept. 28, 1931, Board of Governors, Nov. 6, 1930, Nov. 5, 1931, Mar. 3, 1932.

16. *Ibid.*, Board of Governors, Mar. 13, 1932, Nov. 5, 1931, Nov. 2, 1933; Forman, "Study of the Communal Building," pp. 18–19.

17. Auerbach, "Jewish Settlement," p. 112; Jewish Federation Minute Book, Board of Governors, Nov. 3, 1932.

18. Sydnor H. Walker, "Privately Supported Social Work" in *Recent Social Trends*, 2: 1183–84; Jewish Federation Minute Book, Board of Governors, Dec. 7, 1933, Jan. 4, Apr. 4, Dec. 6, 1934, Executive Committee,

Jan. 26, 1934, Budget Committee, Jan. 29, 1934, Annual Meeting, Apr. 25, 1934.

19. Jewish Federation Minute Book, Board of Governors, Mar. 7, 1935, Executive Committee, Sept. 27, 1935.

20. *Ibid.*, Board of Governors, Dec. 7, 1933; Forman, "Study of the Communal Building," pp. 37–42; *South Side Survey*, p. 17.

21. Jewish Federation Minute Book, Board of Governors, Oct. 10, 1929, Executive Committee, Dec. 28, 1930; *Indiana Jewish Chronicle*, Nov. 1, 1929; *Indianapolis News*, Sept. 19, 1952. The first officers of the Jewish Community Credit Union were Leo Kaminsky, president; Jacob Solotken, vice-president; Philip Kraft, treasurer; and H. Joseph Hyman, secretary. Kaminsky, an attorney, was organizer and leader of the Credit Union League and helped bring about legislation in 1923 enabling the formation of credit unions in Indiana.

22. Wecter, *The Great Depression*, p. 244; Auerbach, "Jewish Settlement," pp. 82, 93; Jewish Federation Minute Book, Executive Committee, July 25, 1930, Jewish Welfare Fund Executive Committee, Jan. 21, 1929, Jewish Federation Board of Governors, Sept. 10, 1931; Forman, "Study of the Communal Building," p. 2.

23. Jewish Federation Minute Book, Board of Governors, Feb. 6, 1930, Jan. 21, 1936, Nov. 2, 1933, Executive Committee, Feb. 11, 1930, Annual Meeting, Apr. 25, 1934; *Jewish Post*, Feb. 9, 1940.

24. Jewish Welfare Fund Minute Book, Committee on National Institutions, Feb. 12, 1937; Jewish Federation Minute Book, Board of Governors, Nov. 4, 1937, Nov. 3, 1938, Feb. 9, 1939, Executive Committee, Feb., Mar. 18, July 8, 1938; *Indianapolis Times*, Apr. 17, 1938.

25. Jewish Federation Minute Book, Board of Governors, Sept. 4, 1941, Nov. 3, 1938, Feb. 19, Mar. 2, 1939, Dec. 29, 1941, Jan. 8, 1942, Executive Committee, Dec. 12, 1941; *Indianapolis Sunday Star*, Feb. 19, 1939; *Indianapolis Times*, July 8, 1939.

26. Auerbach, "Jewish Settlement," p. 49; Ezras Achim Minute Book, 1936–1952, Jan. 3, Feb. 7, 1939, Minute Book, 1952–1962, Nov. 18, 1962, IHS; Mrs. Nandor [Ruth] Fruchter, *Congregation B'nai Torah; The First 50 Years* (Indianapolis, 1973), pp. 16, 23–24.

27. Ezras Achim Minute Book, 1936–1952, Dec. 6, 1938; Forman, "Study of the Communal Building," p. 24; Cohen, "Etz Chaim," p. 3; conversation with Gladys Cohen Nisenbaum, June 14, 1983.

28. "Jews in America," p. 79.

29. Selden Menefee, *Assignment: U.S.A.* (London, 1944), p. 96.

30. Lynd, *Middletown in Transition*, p. 462; Menefee, *Assignment*, p. 97; visit of Solomon A. Fineberg, June 6, 1940, Indianapolis, Indiana-Reports, American Jewish Committee (AJC) Archives, New York City.

31. Menefee, *Assignment*, pp. 16–18. For intergroup conflict in New York see Ronald H. Bayor, *Neighbors in Conflict* (Baltimore, 1978).

32. Nathan C. Belth, *A Promise to Keep* (New York, 1979), pp. 115–19; Menefee, *Assignment*, pp. 107, 137–38; *Indianapolis News*, Mar. 10, 11, 12, 15, 1938; *Indianapolis Star*, Aug. 23, Nov. 12, 1942; *Indianapolis News*, Mar. 11, 1938. Earlier several large land purchases by the Soltau family had caused concern among the residents of Nashville, Indiana, that they might be considering establishing a Bund camp there similar to the infamous Camp Nordland in New Jersey.

33. Belth, *A Promise to Keep*, pp. 120–32.

34. B'nai B'rith Minute Book, 1928–1935, Dec. 4, 8, 1933, IHS.

35. C. W. Efroymson, Indianapolis, Indiana, December, 1981, personal communication.

36. Jewish Federation Minute Book, Executive Committee, Apr. 1933, Board of Governors, May 5, 1933, Oct. 19, 1950.

37. B'nai B'rith Minute Book, Jan. 27, 1936, Jan. 4, 1937.

38. Jewish Federation Minute Book, Annual Meeting, Apr. 23, 1931, Board of Governors, June 4, 1936, Executive Committee, Aug. 28, 1936.

39. *Jewish Post*, Dec. 14, June 22, 1934; Wecter, *The Great Depression*, p. 254; *Encyclopaedia Judaica*, s.v. "Birobidzhan."

40. Jewish Federation of Indianapolis, *Annual Report*, 1925, p. 21, 1926, p. 23, 1927, p. 10; Jewish Federation Minute Book, Board of Governors, Dec. 7, 1933, Apr. 4, 1934; B'nai B'rith Minute Book, 1928–1935, Dec. 3, 1934.

41. Jewish Federation Minute Book, Board of Governors, June 6, 1940; *Jewish Post*, Feb. 16, 1940, Feb. 2, 1945; Ethel and David Rosenberg, *To 120 Years! A Social History of the Indianapolis Hebrew Congregation* (Indianapolis, 1979), p. 75; Simon Noveck, *Milton Steinberg: Portrait of a Rabbi* (New York, 1978), p. 45; *Jewish Post*, Feb. 8, 1935, Mar. 9, 1945.

42. Visit of Solomon A. Fineberg, Nov. 1, 1939, Nov. 6–7, 1941, Indianapolis, Indiana-Reports, AJC; *Purposes and Plan of Operation of the Public Relations Committee*, (Indianapolis, n.d.); *Constitution and By-Laws of the Indianapolis Jewish Community Relations Council*; Jewish Federation Minute Book, Executive Committee, July 7, 1939, Feb. 24, 1942, Board of Governors, Dec. 7, 1939, Jan. 18, 1940, Feb. 20, 1942, Board of Governors, Dec. 7, 1939, Jan. 18, 1940, Feb. 20, May 15, Oct. 7, Dec. 4, 1941, Jan. 8, 1942; *Indianapolis Star*, Jan. 22, 1958. The first officers of the Public Relations Committee were Samuel Mueller, chairman; J. J. Kiser, first vice-chairman; Rabbi Elias Charry, second vice-chairman; Walter E. Wolf, treasurer; and H. Joseph Hyman, secretary.

43. Jewish Federation Minute Book, Executive Committee, Sept. 14, 1944, Board of Governors, Oct. 22, 1946, Nov. 20, 1947, Dec. 5, 1946, Special Board Meeting, July 14, 1947; Rosenberg, *To 120 Years!*, pp. 75–78.

44. Reports of field representatives, Nov. 1, 1939–Mar. 5, 1947, Indianapolis, Indiana-Reports, AJC. The first officers of the Indianapolis chapter of the American Jewish Committee were Maurice Block, Jr. and Roger Kahn, co-chairmen; Philip Adler, Jr., program chairman; and Samuel Mueller, secretary-treasurer.

45. Jewish Federation Minute Book, Board of Governors, Jan. 21, 1936.

46. *Ibid.*, Board of Governors, Dec. 7, 1939, Sept. 9, 1943, June 8, 1944, Executive Committee, Jan. 29, 1943, Jan. 11, June 27, 1944, Jan. 30, Feb. 27, 1945.

47. *Jewish Post*, Feb. 23, Mar. 2, 9, 16, 1945; Jewish Federation Minute Book, Board of Governors, Jan. 16, Mar. 8, Apr. 12, 1945, Joint Meeting of Executive Committees of Jewish Federation and Jewish Welfare Fund, Mar. 12, 1945. The Committee of Nine included Jackiel W. Joseph, Philip Adler, Jr., and Louis D. Young from the Citizens Committee; Ernest Cohn, Samuel Mueller, and Max Klezmer from the Jewish Federation; and William Schloss, J. J. Kiser, and David Sablosky from the Jewish Welfare Fund.

48. Jewish Federation Minute Book, Annual Meeting, Apr. 15, 1937, Board of Governors, June 3, Nov. 4, 1937; *Report of the Committee on the Study of the Community Council to the Board of Governors of the Jewish Federation* (Indianapolis, n.d. [1938?]). The members of the committee were Leonard A. Strauss (chairman), Rabbi Elias Charry, Ernest Cohn, Rabbi Morris Feuerlicht, Meyer Gallin, Dr. A. S. Jaeger, Frances Mazur, and H. Joseph Hyman. With the exception of Charry, all the committee members were "Federation people."

49. *Report of Committee of Community Council;* Daniel J. Elazar, *Community and Polity* (Philadelphia, 1976), p. 181.

50. *Jewish Post,* Feb. 23, Mar. 2, 9, 16, 1945; Jewish Federation Minute Book, Board of Governors, Jan. 16, Mar. 8, April 12, 1945, Joint Meeting of Executive Committees of Jewish Federation and Jewish Welfare Fund, Mar. 12, 1945; *Constitution and By-Laws of the Jewish Federation,* Oct., 1945.

51. Jewish Federation Minute Book, Board of Governors, Mar. 5, 1936, Executive Committee, July 8, 1938; *Report to the Budget and Policy Committee on the Joseph and Annie Borinstein Home* (Indianapolis, 1948).

52. Jewish Federation Minute Book, Board of Governors, June 8, 1944; *Jewish Post,* June 8, 1945.

53. *Jewish Post,* Mar., 1933, Feb. 9, 1934, May 24, Oct. 4, 1935, May 15, 1936, May 3, 10, June 7, 1940, Aug. 20, 1948.

54. *Indiana Jewish Tribune,* May 19, 1933 (only seven issues of the *Tribune* are known to have appeared); Marc L. Raphael, *Jews and Judaism in a Midwestern Community: Columbus, Ohio, 1840–1975* (Columbus, 1979), pp. 321–22.

55. Henry Feingold, *Zion in America* (New York, 1974), pp. 277–84.

56. Jewish Welfare Fund Minute Book, Board of Directors, June 13, Sept. 12, 1939.

57. *Jewish Post,* Feb. 9, 1940; Jewish Welfare Fund Minute Book, Budget Committee, May 25, 1939, Board of Directors, Feb. 12, Apr. 2, 1940.

58. *Indianapolis News,* Jan. 29, 1942; *Jewish Post,* Apr. 6, 13, 1945; Jewish Federation Minute Book, Board of Governors, Jan. 7, 1943.

VI. The Postwar Era

1. *Jewish Post,* April 12, 1946; Harry L. Lurie, *A Heritage Affirmed* (Philadelphia, 1961), pp. 166, 173.

2. Abraham J. Karp, *To Give Life* (New York, 1981), p. 87.

3. Lurie, *Heritage,* pp. 171, 183.

4. *Ibid.,* pp. 171, 183; Sidney Z. Vincent, "Jewish Communal Organizations and Philanthropy" in *Movements and Issues in American Judaism,* ed. Bernard Martin (Westport, Conn., 1978), p. 66.

5. Jewish Welfare Federation (JWF) Minute Book, Board of Directors, June 21, Sept. 7, Dec. 14, 1949; JWF Records; Indiana Historical Society Library, Indianapolis (IHS); Lurie, *Heritage,* p. 185.

6. Karp, *To Give Life,* pp. 96–107; Melvin I. Urofsky, *We Are One!* (New York, 1978), pp. 200–203.

7. Urofsky, *We Are One!,* pp. 202–203; Karp, *To Give Life,* p. 97; Golda Meir/Israel Bonds controversy, 1952, JWF Records.

8. "The Eyes of World Jewry Are on Indianapolis—Is It Free or Is It Throttled?" Golda Meir/Israel Bonds Controversy; *Indianapolis News*, Oct. 21, 1960; Julian Freeman, *Organizing the American Jewish Community* (n.p., 1977?), pp. 27–29.

9. Bernard Martin, "American Jewry Since 1945: An Historical Overview" in *Movements and Issues*, p. 6; Julian Freeman, "History of the Jews of Indianapolis," typescript (Indianapolis, 1978), pp. 138, 139, 197.

10. *Jewish Post*, Mar. 9, 1945.

11. Ethel and David Rosenberg, *To 120 Years! A Social History of the Indianpolis Hebrew Congregation* (Indianapolis, 1979), pp. 77, 80–82, 88; JWF Minute Book, Board of Directors, Jan. 11, 1954.

12. Arnold Gurin, "Financing of Jewish Communal Programs," *American Jewish Year Book* 54 (1953): 182.

13. Nathan Glazer, *American Judaism*, 2d. ed. rev. (Chicago, 1972), pp. 106–108, 125–28; Will Herberg, *Protestant, Catholic, Jew* (New York, 1955), pp. 27–28; interview with Lee Barnett, Apr. 22, 1980.

14. Walter I. Ackerman, "Jewish Education" in *Movements and Issues*, p. 185.

15. Glazer, *American Judaism*, p. 114.

16. Morris Feuerlicht, "A Hoosier Rabbinate" in *Lives and Voices*, ed. Stanley F. Chyet (Philadelphia, 1972), pp. 173–75.

17. *Jewish Post*, Feb. 16, 1945.

18. Rosenberg, *To 120 Years!*, pp. 90–95.

19. JWF Minute Book, Board of Directors, June 11, 1953; *Dedication of the Temple of Congregation Beth-El Zedeck* (Indianapolis, 1958), pp. 1, 33, 34; Freeman, "History of the Jews," pp. 115–16.

20. Mrs. Nandor [Ruth] Fruchter, *Congregation B'nai Torah; The First 50 Years* (Indianapolis, 1973), pp. 16, 19, 22–23.

21. Congregation Ezras Achim, Minute Book, 1952–1962, Mar. 26, 1958, Nov. 18, 1962, IHS; *Indiana Jewish Chronicle*, Jan. 24, 1964; Freeman, "History of the Jews," p. 97.

22. Lurie, *Heritage*, pp. 191–95.

23. Sidney Cahn, *An Evaluation of the Program of the Jewish Federation and its Constituents with Some Suggestions for the Future* (Indianapolis, 1946); Sidney Cahn, *A Supplementary Evaluation and Future Projection of the Federation's Plans* (Indianapolis, 1947); *A Proposed Program for Aged and Chronically Ill for the Jewish Community of Indianapolis* (Indianapolis, 1945); *Report to the Budget and Policy Committee on the Joseph and Annie Borinstein Home* (Indianapolis, 1948); *Special Discussion of Specific Problems in the J.E.A. and Some Recommendations* (Indianapolis, n.d.); *Report of the Community Relations Council Organization Committee* (Indianapolis, 1947?); National Jewish Welfare Board [NJWB], *Survey Report on Informal Educational and Recreational Activities of the Jewish Community of Indianapolis* (Indianapolis, 1948): JWF, *Population Survey Tables* (Indianapolis, 1948). Among Erich Rosenthal's findings was that the community was smaller by about 2,000 to 3,000 people than had been previously estimated. Rosenthal found 6,700 Jews; the Federation's estimate was 8,000 to 10,000.

24. *Indianapolis South Side Communal Building Survey* (Indianapolis, 1943); Leo L. Honor, *The Jewish Educational Association of Indianapolis,*

A Survey (Indianapolis, 1944); JEA of Indianapolis, *Self-Study Report* (Indianapolis, 1966), p. 4; JWF Minute Book, Board of Governors, Feb. 13, June 26, 1947. In 1947 the Communal Building was leased to the Communal Center Association under the Council of Social Agencies. The renamed Concord Center Association purchased the building from the Federation in 1958.

25. Oscar I. Janowsky, *The JWB Survey* (New York, 1948), pp. v, 5, 237–44.

26. *Ibid.*, pp. 8–13, 244–54.

27. NJWB, *Survey Report*, pp. 9, 12–17.

28. JWF, *Population*, p. 7; NJWB, *Survey Report*, pp. 16–17; JWF Minute Book, Board of Directors, July 23, 1951, June 11, 1953; JWF, *Our Community's Future* (Indianapolis, 1951), n.p.

29. JWF Minute Book, Board of Directors, Aug. 16, 1954; *The Center, Yes* (Indianapolis, n.d.); JWF Community Center Building Fund Campaign, "Names that Live Forever" [fund-raising brochure]; JWF Minute Book, Board of Directors, Oct. 20, 1953, June 1, Nov. 14, 1955, Feb. 8, June 25, 1956, Feb. 23, 1957, Feb. 7, 1958, Annual Meeting, Jan. 7, 1957, Budget and Policy Committee, Oct. 5, 1955, Building Committee, Mar. 29, 1956. Apparently both foundations became convinced that the Jewish Center would offer enough programming that would be open to the entire community to meet the guidelines of projects they would support, i.e., projects that enhanced the whole community. Conversation with Frank Newman, August 1982.

30. JWF Minute Book, Board of Directors, June 11, 1953; JWF, JCCA Memorandum, 1951.

31. *Beth-El Speaks*, Nov. 3, 1959, Feb. 9, 1960.

32. *Ibid.*, Nov. 3, 1959; JEA, *Self-Study*, pp. 31–33.

33. JWF Minute Book, Board of Directors, Nov. 24, 1958.

34. *Ibid.*, Aug. 4, 1959, Oct. 26, 1960, Mar. 31, 1966; *Indianapolis Sunday Star Magazine*, Mar. 12, 1967. Bernard Stroyman personally persuaded the directors of the Inland Container Foundation to grant the money to the JEA building fund. Conversation with Frank Newman, August, 1982.

35. Indianapolis Jewish Family and Children's Service (JFCS), "History," typescript (Indianapolis, 1970?), p. 2; Jewish Federation Minute Book, Board of Governors, Apr. 17, 1947.

36. JWF Minute Book, Board of Directors, Feb. 7, 1951.

37. *Indianapolis News*, Jan. 20, 1956; *Jewish Social Services Self-Study* (Indianapolis, 1965); Morris Zelditch, *Survey Report on the Jewish Social Services of Indianapolis* (New York, 1955).

38. Jewish Federation Minute Book, Board of Governors, Dec. 7, 1933.

39. Mrs. Robert [Anita] Schwab, *A Record of Service* (Fort Wayne, 1974); Jewish Federation Minute Book, Board of Governors, Nov. 4, 1937, Nov. 3, 1938, Feb. 9, 1939, Executive Committee, Feb., Mar. 18, July 8, 1938; *Indianapolis Sunday Star*, Feb. 19, 1939; *Indianapolis News*, Feb. 8, 1952.

40. Freeman, "History of the Jews," p. 136.

41. JWF Minute Book, Board of Directors, Jan. 19, Mar. 27, 1953; Conversation with Lee Barnett, Nov. 23, 1981.

42. Charles H. Stember, *Jews in the Mind of America* (New York, 1966), pp. 7–8.

43. *Ibid.*, pp. 8, 265–66.

44. *Ibid.*, pp. 3, 13, 14, 17.

45. Nathan Reich, "The Year in Retrospect," *American Jewish Year Book* 50 (1948–1949):115; Stember, *Jews in Mind*, p. 20.

46. Stember, *Jews in Mind*, p. 21.

47. S. Andhil Fineberg, "Jewish-Christian Relations" in *Movements and Issues*, pp. 244–45; *Jewish Post*, Jan. 26, Aug. 10, 1945; Freeman, "History of the Jews," pp. 165, 169, 179, 199; Reports of field representatives, Nov. 1, 1943-Mar. 5, 1947, Indianapolis, Indiana-Reports, American Jewish Committee (AJC) Archives, New York City.

48. Visit of Solomon A. Fineberg, Nov. 1, 1939, Indianapolis, Indiana-Reports, AJC.

49. Fineberg, "Jewish-Christian Relations," p. 244.

50. David Petegorsky, quoted in Fineberg, "Jewish-Christian Relations," p. 251; Vincent, "Jewish Communal Organizations," pp. 278–79.

51. Freeman, "History of the Jews," pp. 168–72; Richard A. Hurwitz, "A History of the Anti-Defamation League of B'nai B'rith in Indianapolis," typescript (Indianapolis, 1978?), pp. 6–9; Raymond T. Bosler and John G. Ackelmire, "Human Relations" in *Indiana: A Self-Appraisal*, ed. Donald F. Carmony (Bloomington, 1966), p. 276.

52. Hurwitz, "History of ADL," pp. 6–8; Freeman, "History of the Jews," pp. 165–72.

53. Reports of field representatives, June, 1950–Dec., 1959, Indianapolis, Indiana-Reports, AJC.

54. Indianapolis Jewish Community Relations Council (JCRC), *Survey of Religious Practices in Indianapolis Public Schools, March and April, 1959.*

55. Indianapolis JCRC, *Statement on Religion in the Public Schools, Sept. 19, 1960*; JWF Minute Book, Annual Meeting, July 12, 1964, Special Board Meeting, Jan. 22, 1950.

VII. The Six-Day War and Beyond

1. Melvin I. Urofsky, *We Are One!* (New York, 1978), p. 351; Lucy S. Dawidowicz, "American Public Opinion," *American Jewish Year Book* 69 (1968):198.

2. Arthur Hertzberg, "Israel and American Jewry," *Commentary* 44 (August 1967):69; Urofsky, *We Are One!*, pp. 352–53.

3. Dawidowicz, "American Public Opinion," p. 206; interview with Frank Newman, August 12, 1981.

4. Nathan Glazer, *American Judaism*, 2d. ed., rev. (Chicago, 1972), p. 171.

5. Dawidowicz, "American Public Opinion," pp. 203–4; Glazer, *American Judaism*, pp. 172–73.

6. Irwin Stark, "Jewish Work-Camp in Indianapolis," *Commentary* 13 (January 1952): 7–13.

7. Glazer, *American Judaism*, pp. 167–69.

8. *Ibid.*, pp. 168–75; Dawidowicz, "American Public Opinion," pp. 228–29; Urofsky, *We Are One!*, p. 371.

9. Dawidowicz, "American Public Opinion," p. 218–21; Urofsky, *We Are One!* pp. 382–83.

10. Bernard Martin, "American Jewry Since 1945: An Historical Overview" in *Movements and Issues in American Judaism*, ed. Bernard Martin (Westport, Conn., 1978), p. 19.

11. *Ibid.*

12. Harold T. Chrisdensen and Kenneth E. Barber, "Interfaith vs. Intrafaith Marriage in Indiana," *Journal of Marriage and the Family* 29 (August 1967): 461–74; Erich Rosenthal, "Jewish Intermarriage in Indiana," *American Jewish Year Book* 68 (1967): 243–64. Only two states—Indiana and Iowa—collect information regarding religion on marriage license applications.

13. Samuel Grand, *Report of Survey of J.E.A. of Indianapolis* (Indianapolis, 1965); Jewish Educational Association of Indianapolis, *Self-Study Report* (Indianapolis, 1966), p. 50; Jewish Welfare Federation (JWF) Minute Book, Board of Directors, Feb. 16, 1967, JWF Records, Indiana Historical Society Library, Indianapolis.

14. Walter I. Ackerman, "Jewish Education" in *Movements and Issues*, p. 197; David Singer, "The Growth of the Day-School Movement," *Commentary* 56 (August 1973): 54.

15. Singer, "Growth of the Day-School," p. 55; Hebrew Academy of Indianapolis, *Souvenir Journal . . .* (Indianapolis, 1972), pp. 1, 3, 5, 9; Ackerman, "Jewish Education," p. 195.

16. Interview with Uri Korin and Marilyn Roger, November 11, 1981; interview with Rabbi Ronald Gray, November 11, 1981.

17. The first officers of the Hebrew Academy were Hart N. Hasten, president; Irwin Prince, vice-president; Gilbert G. Cohen, treasurer; and Mrs. Joseph Epstein, secretary. The first director was Edwin Epstein. Hebrew Academy, *Souvenir Journal*, pp. 1, 3, 5, 9; interview with Korin and Roger, November 11, 1981; interview with Gray, November 11, 1981; conversation with Sylvia Blain, December 2, 1981.

18. *Report to the Budget and Policy Committee on the Joseph and Annie Borinstein Home* (Indianapolis, 1948), p. 1; Liebert I. Mossler to Jack Killen, Indianapolis Foundation, November 20, 1967, JWF Records.

19. Sidney Mahalowitz, *Planning for Care of the Aged* (Cleveland, 1954), p. 2; Mossler to Killen, November 20, 1967; Jack J. Diamond, "A Reader in the Demography of American Jews," *American Jewish Year Book* 77 (1977): 298; *Jewish Older Adult Oral Survey* [Indianapolis, 1978], n.p.

20. JWF Minute Book, Annual Meeting, July 12, 1964, Executive Committee, July 31, 1967; Mossler to Killen, Nov. 20, 1967; Board of Directors, Nov. 7, 1966, Executive Committee, July 31, 1967, Dec. 30, 1969, Apr. 30, June 28, 1971.

21. Conversation with Julius Dorfman, March 20, 1980.

22. Philip Adler to Ben Domont, May 18, 1965, JWF Records; interview with Carolyn Leeds, November 18, 1981; *Jewish Older Adult Survey*, n.p.

23. Interview with Leeds, November 18, 1981; *JWF Report*, Sept., 1981, p. 1. Dr. Maurice Kaufman was the first president of the JWF Housing Corporation.

24. JWF Minute Book, Board of Directors, April 25, 1955, Budget and Policy Committee, June 9, 1959.

25. *Ibid.*, Budget and Policy Committee, June 9, 1959, *Building the Successful Campaign* (New York, 1958), p. 14. Quoted in Marc Lee Raphael, "Federated Jewish Philanthropy and Communal Democracy: In Pursuit of a Phantom" in *Understanding American Jewish Philanthropy*, ed. Marc Lee Raphael (New York, 1979), p. 158.

26. Interview with Newman, July 30, 1981.

27. JWF Minute Book, Board of Directors, Dec. 19, 1962, Apr. 22, 1963, Oct. 27, 1964, Feb. 15, 1965; interview with Newman, August 12, 1981.

28. JWF Minute Book, Board of Directors, Sept. 30, 1963, Executive Committee, July 31, 1967.

29. Sidney Z. Vincent, "Jewish Communal Organizations and Philanthropy" in *Movements and Issues*, p. 66.

30. Interview with Newman, August 12, 1981; JWF Minute Book, Board of Directors, August 4, 1959.

31. JWF Minute Book, Board of Directors, Oct. 26, 1960, Feb. 16, 1967, June 27, 1968; *Joint Worship Service*, Jan. 10, 1969; interview with Newman, August 12, 1981.

32. Conversation with Frances Feldman, November 18, 1981; Betty Carroll Levine, "Religious Commitment and Integration into the Jewish Community" (Ph.D. dissertation, Purdue University, 1979), pp. viii, 131. Levine mailed a questionnaire to a random sample of persons whose names appeared on the JWF list. She received 376 responses. JWF, *Population Survey Tables* (Indianapolis, 1948), p. 1; Erich Rosenthal, "The Jewish Population of the United States: A Demographic and Sociological Analysis," in *Movements and Issues*, p. 38.

33. JWF, *Population*, p. 6; Rosenthal, "Jewish Population," pp. 41–42.

34. Myra M. Auerbach, "A Study of the Jewish Settlement in Indianapolis" (M.A. thesis, Indiana University, 1933), pp. 51–56.

35. Melvin I. Urofsky, "American Jewish Leadership," *American Jewish History* 70 (June 1981): 408.

36. Interview with Rabbi Peter Schweitzer and Rabbi Jonathan Stein, November 11, 1981; Ethel and David Rosenberg, *To 120 Years! A Social History of the Indianapolis Hebrew Congregation* (Indianapolis, 1979), p. 144; *The Temple Bulletin*, Oct. 7, 1977, Feb. 10, 1978.

37. Interview with Rabbi Dennis C. Sasso, Oct. 30, 1981.

38. *Ibid.*; "Congregation Beth-El Zedeck to Abide by Biblical-Israeli Observance of Festivals" (press release, n.d.); Phillip Sigal and Abraham J. Ehrlich, *A Reponsum on Yom Tov Sheni Shel Galuyot*, January 1969.

39. Interview with Gray, November 11, 1981.

40. Interview with Schweitzer and Stein, November 11, 1981; interview with Sasso, October 30, 1981; interview with Gray, November 11, 1981.

41. *Ibid.*

42. Conversation with Abe Rambatz, November 1981.

43. Conversation with Jack Glazier, May 6, 1981; Sylvia Nahmias Cohen, "The History of the Etz Chaim Sephardic Congregation and Community of Indianapolis," typescript (Indianapolis, 1978), pp. 12–14; *The Temple Bulletin*, Feb. 10, 1978.

44. European Jewry developed a number of customs for *Tu Bi-Shevat* (15th of Shevat), the Festival of the New Year of the Trees. Ashkenazim ate

fifteen different kinds of fruit and recited psalms in accompaniment. Sephardic Jews gave *Tu Bi-Shevat* a greater significance and called it the Feast of Fruits. An actual *seder* service modeled on the Passover *seder* and with additional poems and readings was published in 1753. Conversation with Dorfman, March 20, 1980; interview with Leeds, Nov. 18, 1981; Jewish Community Center *Bulletin*, March, 1980; Jewish Community "Summer Camps" (brochure); Jewish Community Center *Program Guide*, January–May, 1980.

45. Conversation with Dorfman, March 20, 1980; JCC *Program Guide*, January–May, 1980.

46. Interview with Korin and Roger, Nov. 11, 1981; "Bureau of Jewish Education" (brochure).

47. *Ibid.*

48. Conversation with Alvin Rosenfeld, December 8, 1981; conversation with Cheryl B. Cohen, August 27, 1982.

49. Interview with Gray, Nov. 11, 1981.

50. JWF Minute Book, Executive Committee, June 27, Sept. 25, 1968.

51. Robert Rose was the first chairman of the New Americans Committee of the JWF. *JWF Report*, February, 1981, p. 1; *Community Policy Statement of the New Americans Committee of the JWF of Indianapolis, Inc.* (Indianapolis, 1981); interview with Bernard Cohen, November 18, 1981; conversation with Feldman, Nov. 18, 1981.

52. JWF Minute Book, Board of Directors, 1955, June 25, 1956; *Indianapolis Star*, Dec. 6, 1976; Richard A. Hurwitz, "A History of the ADL of B'nai B'rith in Indianapolis," typescript (Indianapolis, 1978?).

53. Reports of field representatives, June 11, 1958, Indianapolis, Indiana—Reports, American Jewish Committee Archives, New York City; JWF Minute Book, Board of Directors, April 20, 1965; David H. Goldstein, "A Tourist View of Selma," May 19, 1965, JWF Records; conversation with Marcia Goldstone, Nov. 18, 1981; Julian Freeman, "History of the Jews of Indianapolis," typescript (Indianapolis, 1978), pp. 172–74.

54. Freeman, "History of the Jews," pp. 180–85; *JWF Report*, April, 1980, p. 3.

55. *JWF Report*, May, 1980, p. 3.

56. Gerald L. Houseman, "Antisemitism in City Politics: The Separation Clause and the Indianapolis Nativity Scene Controversy, 1976–1977" *Jewish Social Studies* 42 (Winter 1980): 21–36.

57. Conversation with Goldstone, Nov. 18, 1981.

58. Thomas B. Morgan, "The Vanishing American Jew," *Look Magazine*, 5 May 1964, pp. 42–46; U. O. Schmelz, "Jewish Survival: The Demographic Factors," *American Jewish Year Book* 81 (1981): 79, 85.

59. Erich Rosenthal, "Intermarriage among Jewry: A Function of Acculturation, Community Organization, and Family Structure" in *Movements and Issues*, p. 263.

60. Schmelz, "Jewish Survival," p. 85; Rosenthal, "Intermarriage among Jewry," p. 262.

Glossary

Aliyah. Hebrew, "ascent," "going up": term used for emigration to Israel.

Ashkenazim. Originally the name *Ashkenaz* was identified with Germany. Eventually it was applied to all Jews of central, northern, and eastern European origins and customs, i.e., to all Jews of western tradition as opposed to the *Sephardim* of the oriental tradition.

Atarah. Special rabbinical headdress.

Bar Mitzvah. An adult male Jew obligated to perform the commandments; hence, the ceremony at which a thirteen-year-old boy becomes an adult member of the community for ceremonial purposes.

Bat Mitzvah. Feminine of *bar mitzvah.*

Daven. Yiddish: common word among *Ashkenazim* meaning "to pray."

Galitzianer. Someone from Galicia.

Goldene Medinah. Yiddish, "golden land": used by eastern European Jewry as a name for America.

Halakhah. Jewish law.

Hazzan. Cantor.

Heder, Hadarim (plural). Hebrew, "room": popularly applied to an elementary religious school of the type prevalent in eastern Europe, often situated in a single room in the teacher's house.

Heimish. Homey, comfortable.

Ivrit-be-Ivrit. Hebrew, "Hebrew by Hebrew": Hebrew teaching method.

Kashrut. Jewish dietary laws.

Landsleit. Group of people from the same town or region in Europe.

Landsman. Fellow countryman.

Landsmanshaftn. Fraternal societies of Jews from the same town or region in Europe.

Litvak. Lithuanian.

Mashgi'ah. Religious supervisor, particularly in the observance of *kashrut.*

Melammed, Melammdim (plural). A teacher, usually of younger children. The term had a derogatory connotation, being applied to the lowest category of the teaching profession.

Meshullah(im). Emissary sent by rabbinical academies to distant lands to collect funds for the institutions.

Mikveh. Ritual bath.

Minyan. Quorum of ten adults required for liturgical purposes. In Orthodox Judaism only men are counted to make up a *minyan.*

Mohel(im). Ritual circumciser.

Polische. Polish.

Rahmanot. A mixture of pity, mercy, and sympathy.

Rosh Hashanah. Jewish New Year.

Russische. Russian.

Selihot. Special penitential prayers.

Sephardim. Originally applied to Jews of the Iberian peninsula and their descendants. After the expulsion of Jews from Spain in 1492 the word *Sephardi* was given wider usage as the Jews from Spain imposed their culture and traditions upon the Jewish communities of North Africa and the Middle East.

Shammash. Sexton in the synagogue.

Shehitah. Ritual slaughter which renders an animal or bird fit for consumption according to Jewish law.

Shnorrer. Beggar.

Shohet. Ritual slaughterer.

Shtetl. Yiddish, eastern European market town.

Shul. Yiddish, synagogue.

Sukkah. Booth or tabernacle erectd during the harvest festival of *Sukkot.*

Tallit. Prayer shawl.

Talmud Torah. Hebrew, "study of the torah": developed as a term for the place where education, particularly of an elementary nature, was provided. The Talmud Torah was often a community-supported school.

Treife. Not kosher.

Tu Bi-Shevat. Fifteenth of Shevat, the festival of the New Year of the Trees.

Yarmulke. Yiddish word for the skull cap worn as a headcovering in accordance with Orthodox Jewish custom.

Yeshivah, Yeshivot (plural). Rabbinical seminary.

Yizkor. Memorial service.

Yom Kippur. Day of Atonement.

Zedakah. Charity.

Zooris. Yiddish: problems.

INDEX